BL
2181-

A SHORT DICTIONARY OF
BRITISH ARCHITECTS

by the same author

A SHORT DICTIONARY OF ARCHITECTURE
including some Common Building Terms
(with Betty Beatty, ARIBA)

A SHORT DICTIONARY
OF
BRITISH ARCHITECTS

BY

DORA WARE

WITH AN INTRODUCTION ON
The Character of the Architect

BY

JOHN GLOAG
FSA, Hon. ARIBA, Hon. FSIA

ILLUSTRATED

London
GEORGE ALLEN AND UNWIN LTD
RUSKIN HOUSE   MUSEUM STREET

FIRST PUBLISHED IN 1967

*This book is copyright under the Berne Convention.
Apart from any fair dealing for the purposes of private
study, research, criticism or review, as permitted under
the Copyright Act, 1956, no portion may be reproduced
by any process without written permission. Inquiries
should be made to the publishers.*

PRINTED IN GREAT BRITAIN
in 10 *point Baskerville type*
BY UNWIN BROTHERS LTD
WOKING AND LONDON

THE CHARACTER OF THE ARCHITECT

BY JOHN GLOAG

Large-scale architecture existed in pre-Roman Britain, and the builders of Stonehenge, and the much bigger architectural concept at Avebury, were clearly men with creative vision who understood planning and post-and-lintel structural technique. John Aubrey saw and described Avebury in the seventeenth century, before it was despoiled. 'This old monument', he wrote, 'does as much exceed in greatness the so renowned Stonehenge, as a cathedral doeth a parish church. . . .' Smaller monuments are dotted about the island; but buildings by professional architects, using a formalized system of design, did not appear until after the Claudian conquest in the first century, when Britain became the most westerly province of the Roman Empire. Roads came first to establish communications. Then cities were planned; amphitheatres, aqueducts, drains, and other amenities demanded by the Roman way of life, were introduced; temples, baths, forums, palaces for officials, and great country houses were erected; some, like the temple of Claudius at Colchester, impressively stately;[1] and for four centuries, a period as long as that separating the reigns of Henry VIII and Elizabeth II, the standardized architecture of Rome persisted, with such variation as the Doric, Tuscan, Ionic, Corinthian and Composite orders allowed, but otherwise changeless, dull, and sometimes intimidating. Generations of competent but nameless architects stamped the official character of the Empire on the face of the land; their activities continued far into the fourth century; and such remains as the Lydney settlement in the Forest of Dean, adjacent to the temple of the god Nodens, built *c.* 364–7, are evidence of a continued ability to create a large architectural complex.[2] No evidence of outstanding individual character emerges from the fragmentary excavated ruins of Romano–British buildings; native sculptors might occasionally inject an un-Roman, barbaric vitality into their work, like the Medusa mask on the central shield of the pediment of the Temple of Sulis-Minerva,

---

[1] *Temples in Roman Britain*, by Dr M. J. T. Lewis (Cambridge University Press, 1966). Se. II, pages 61–4, and plate 2a.
[2] *Report on the Excavation of the Prehistoric, Roman, and Post-Roman Site in Lydney Park, Gloucestershire*, made for The Society of Antiquaries of London, by R. E. M. Wheeler, D.Lit, FSA, and T. V. Wheeler, FSA (Oxford University Press, 1932).

7

at Bath, or the third century capitals from Cirencester, with Celtic gods glowering above the acanthus foliations; but the buildings and those who designed them conformed to a monotonous pattern that remained unbroken until the fall of the Empire.

Architecture and architects were in eclipse during the dark centuries between the end of Roman Britain and the establishment of the Anglo-Saxon kingdoms; a few names have come down to us, such as Bishop Eadbert, who used lead plates to cover the walls and roof of the timber-framed church at Lindisfarne, built in 652, as recorded by Bede; but churchmen who repaired or sponsored buildings were the patrons and employers of craftsmen; they were not designers. The Saxon abbots, Ealdred and Ealmer, who collected materials from the ruined Roman city of Verulamium late in the tenth century for building the Abbey Church of St Albans, were not architects; nor were the mediaeval ecclesiastics whose blend of piety, ambition, and financial acumen enriched the country with splendid churches and religious houses. As that eminent architectural historian Bruce Allsopp has said: 'It is now proved beyond possibility of doubt that the design of the great Gothic churches and castles was the work of professional designers, whom we should now call architects. The fantastic suggestion, once widely believed to be true, that they were the work of abbots and bishops in their spare time, is now quite discredited. The even more crazy belief that the cathedrals were the spontaneous expression of popular religious fervour is also disposed of.'[1]

Architects in mediaeval England were professional designers, who directed and organized the work of building craftsmen, and were probably master masons as well, executant craftsmen in their own right. Miss Ware rightly names the earliest of these as William the Englishman, who succeeded William of Sens in the work of repairing and rebuilding Canterbury Cathedral in the last quarter of the twelfth century, and the recorded dates of his professional activity, 1174–84, are the earliest in her biographical dictionary. Thereafter a few names may be identified with the successive phases of English Gothic. In the Graeco–Roman civilization architectural design had influenced in terms of ornament the character of nearly everything in use, from chairs to chariots. By the fourteenth century Gothic architecture exerted a comparable influence not only on such

[1] *A General History of Architecture*, by Bruce Allsopp, B.Arch, Dip.CD, FRIBA, AMTPI (London: Sir Isaac Pitman & Sons Ltd., 1962 edition).

ancillary crafts as joinery, but on the work of goldsmiths and silver-
smiths; and by the fifteenth century, a native style in building and
furnishing was clearly recognizable; different from French, German
and Spanish Gothic, and wholly English in character. A capacity for
assimilating and anglicizing foreign ideas was apparent until the
national style was challenged in the first half of the sixteenth century
by the Renaissance style, which reached England long after it was
mastered and practised in European countries.

Hitherto *style*, as we now understand that term, had been unknown in England. Designers and craftsmen had worked in a living
tradition; developing their creative powers within the limits of the
Gothic idiom, but unfettered by the stylistic conventions that had
petrified Roman architecture. The revival of the classic orders by
Renaissance architects might have restored that servitude had they
worked for patrons as mentally inflexible as Roman patricians and
bureaucrats; but the Renaissance occurred in Italy, and the Italian
city states of the fifteenth century had regenerated the intellectual
and artistic life of Europe. The resistance of English designers and
craftsmen to this foreign style, which they thought of as 'Italianate',
was an instinctive aversion not only to change, but to an art that
was exclusive and aristocratic, as opposed to Gothic art, which was
inclusive and popular. To master the rules and proportions of the
Renaissance style demanded far more than changes in the appear-
ance of buildings; the whole approach to life and art had to be re-
shaped; the comfortable, homely rhythms of Gothic tradition dis-
carded; and an unfamiliar terminology acquired. Few, if any,
English designers appeared to have changed their thinking; and the
buildings of the early Renaissance in England suggest that a resistance movement by traditionalists at first defeated the wishes of the
patrons, who paid the piper but were unable to call the tune; a
situation that was resolved by the patrons composing the tune
themselves. This was to have a profound effect on English architecture, for it originated the tradition of the architectural amateur,
who cultivated a sensitive and critical appreciation of the proportions and details of the classic orders, so that the architects of the
seventeenth and eighteenth centuries enjoyed the incomparable
advantage of working for educated patrons.

In Italy and France the architect, as he had been known and
established in the Roman Empire, was reinstated as a professional
man; but with a far more adventurous outlook than his Roman

9

predecessor; all the accumulated structural knowledge of the mediaeval builders at his command, and patrons who stimulated and encouraged his imagination. He fulfilled at least some of the requirements set forth by Vitruvius in the opening chapter of the first of his ten books on architecture, who had said that the architect 'should be a good writer, a skilful draughtsman, versed in geometry and optics, expert at figures, acquainted with history, informed on the principles of natural and moral philosophy, somewhat of a musician, not ignorant of the sciences both of law and physic, nor of the motions, laws, and relations to each other, of the heavenly bodies'.[1]

In sixteenth-century England the names of a few architects are known, some identified from records only; but the English architect does not emerge as a professional man, of comparable stature with his European contemporaries, until the following century, after Inigo Jones had revealed through his work the significance of the orders as a system of design. That great progenitor of English classic architecture is also the first architectural personality we meet: vain, socially accomplished, ambitious, and able to rouse other great men to fury. 'When I want a word to express the greatest villain in the world, I call him an Inigo', said Ben Jonson to the Prince of Wales, who became Charles I. A concise and admirable portrait of the architect is given by Eric Linklater in his book, *Ben Jonson and King James*.[2] The surviving examples of work that may be attributed to him are as unmistakably English as early Tudor native Gothic. The capacity for absorbing and reshaping foreign, antique or exotic ideas and fashions was characteristic of the work of English architects from the mid-seventeenth to the early nineteenth century. During the great period of architecture that begins with the restoration of Charles II and ends with the accession of Queen Victoria, the professional architect was usually an educated gentleman, on terms of social equality with his noble and wealthy patrons; an urbane and productive relationship that declined only when a new, artistically insensitive rich class changed the nature of patronage in the Victorian period.

The character of the architect has always reflected something of the emotions, desires, and weaknesses of his patrons. At various times he has met the wishes of patrons as different as a mediaeval

---

[1] Gwilt's translation (London: Priestley and Weale, 1826).
[2] London: Jonathan Cape, 1931. Chap. XXII.

bishop with an urge to build towers and spires higher and higher, ostensibly for the glory of God, but often to gratify inflated pride; a Georgian nobleman indulging a taste for magnificence or whimsicality; a Victorian manufacturer tricking out his factory as a Venetian palace and his home as a Gothic castle; or an *avant-garde* intellectual of the 1930s, disclosing much of his private life to the world in an open-planned, almost transparent fantasy of glass, steel and concrete. Such demands could have been satisfied only by men who to some extent shared the beliefs and taste of their patrons; but the character of the architect is far from passive. In the present century his sense of social and civic responsibility is as strongly developed as his sense of responsibility to his client, and he is easily the most highly civilized member of the community. Century by century his works have revealed the character of the age he has lived in, and something of his own character too, though the personal taste of an architect is perhaps easier to discern from the buildings he designed in the eighteenth and nineteenth centuries than it is today, when so much patronage is under the direct or indirect control of accountants, men of great integrity but small imagination; or the collective patronage of committees and councils – bodies that ostensibly mean well but often do ill by stealth – or, worst of all, the large-scale developer, who often lacks not only a sense of social and civic responsibility but sense of any kind.

After the mid-seventeenth century the biographical record of architects is amplified; more and more names appear, and the list of buildings that may be attributed would have become unmanageable in a single volume, had not Miss Ware wisely decided to confine them to the principal, and existing, works of each architect; for her admirable dictionary covers a total period of nearly nine hundred years.

© JOHN GLOAG
1966

AUTHOR'S NOTE

It has been easy to include some architects in this book, and difficult to exclude others: the intention is to provide summarized biographies of a representative selection in terms of period, style, fame and achievements. The examples given of their work are limited, as far as possible, to buildings that can still be seen, and are spread over a wide area. No dictionary of this character could have been compiled without reference to the extensive and invaluable research work of Mr H. M. Colvin, for the period 1660 to 1840, embodied in his *Biographical Dictionary of English Architects*; and to Professor Nikolaus Pevsner's *Buildings of England* series, which cover the whole period, from Anglo-Saxon times to the present century. Apart from those authorities, the principal sources of reference consulted include the many published biographies and autobiographies of, and works by, well-known architects : obituary notices in such journals as the *Builder* (now *Building*), *Building News*, *Journal of the Royal Institute of British Architects*, *The Times*: articles in *Architectural History*, the *Architectural Review*, *Country Life*: as well as the following standard works of reference:

Anecdotes of Painting, by Horace Walpole.
Architect in History, The, by M. S. Briggs.
Architecture in Britain, 1530–1830, by Sir John Summerson.
Church Builders of the Nineteenth Century, by Basil Clarke.
Collins Guide to English Parish Churches, edited by John Betjeman.
Dictionary of Architecture, The, published by the Architectural Publication Society.
Dictionary of National Biography, The.
Dublin: 1660–1860, by Maurice Craig.
Early Victorian Architecture in Britain, by Henry-Russell Hitchcock.
English Architecture since the Regency, by H. S. Goodhart-Rendel.
Georgian Buildings of Bath, by Walter Ison.
Georgian Edinburgh, by Ian G. Lindsay.
Georgian London, by Sir John Summerson.
Georgian Norwich and its Builders, by Stanley J. Wearing.
Glasgow at a Glance, edited by Andrew McLaren and A. M. Doak.
Gothic England, by John Harvey.
Gothic Revival, The, by Sir Kenneth Clark.
Introduction to Elizabethan and Jacobean Architecture, An, by Marcus Whiffen.
Introduction to Tudor Architecture, An, by John Harvey.
Lives of the Painters, Sculptors and Architects, by A. Cunningham.
Seaport: Architecture and Townscape in Liverpool, by Quentin Hughes.
Stones of Manchester, The, by Cecil Stewart.
Tyneside Classical, by Lyall Wilkes and Gordon Dodds.
Victorian Architecture, edited by Peter Ferriday.

ABBREVIATIONS

AA   Architectural Association

FIBA   Fellow of the Institute of British Architects

FRIBA   Fellow of the Royal Institute of British Architects

FRS   Fellow of the Royal Society

FSA   Fellow of the Society of Antiquaries of London

IBA   Institute of British Architects (founded 1834, and granted a Royal Charter in 1866)

RA   Royal Academician

RDI   Royal Designer for Industry (Royal Society of Arts)

RIBA   Royal Institute of British Architects

CONTENTS

INTRODUCTION BY JOHN GLOAG   7

AUTHOR'S NOTE   13

ABBREVIATIONS   14

BIOGRAPHIES A TO Y   19

INDEX OF PERSONS   269

INDEX OF PLACES   273

PLATES

I. Sir Henry Wotton, 1568–1639
Inigo Jones, 1573–1652   *facing page* 32

II. Sir Christopher Wren, 1632–1723
Sir John Vanbrugh, 1664–1726   33

III. James Gibbs, 1682–1754
William Kent, *c.* 1685–1748   64

IV. Richard Boyle, 3rd Earl of Burlington,
1694–1753
Lancelot Brown, 1716–1783   65

V. James Paine, *c.* 1716–89: and his son
Sir William Chambers, 1726–96   96

VI. Robert Adam, 1728–92
Henry Holland, 1745–1806   97

VII. John Nash, 1752–1835
Sir John Soane, 1753–1837   128

VIII. Sir Robert Smirke, 1781–1867
John Claudius Loudon, 1783–1843   129

IX. Sir Charles Barry, 1795–1860
Lewis Cubitt, b. 1799   224

X. Sir Joseph Paxton, 1801–65
Augustus Welby Northmore Pugin, 1811–52   225

XI. Sir George Gilbert Scott, 1811–78
George Godwin, 1815–88   256

XII. Sir Matthew Digby Wyatt, 1820–77
Sir Edwin Lutyens, 1869–1944   257

BIOGRAPHIES

ABEL, John: 1577–1674
A West Country architect and carpenter, to whom Charles I granted the title of King's Carpenter in 1645 for constructing grain mills during the Siege of Hereford. His work was chiefly in Herefordshire, and included the roof of St Bartholomew, Vowchurch (*c.* 1613), Lady Margaret Hawkins Grammar School, Kington (1625), the Old Town Hall, Leominster (1633), and ceilings and screen at St Mary (Dore Abbey), Abbey Dore (1633).

ABERCROMBIE, Sir Patrick, FSA, FRIBA: 1879–1957
The son of a Manchester stockbroker: educated Uppingham: apprenticed to a Manchester architect: spent some time in the Liverpool office of Sir Arnold Thornely: Junior Lecturer at Liverpool University School of Architecture: Lecturer and Research Fellow to the Liverpool Chair of Civic Design 1910, succeeding to the Chair 1915: Professor of Town Planning at London University 1935–46: Consultant Architect to the Department of Health for Scotland 1936. First editor of the *Town Planning Review*: co-founder of the Council for the Preservation of Rural England: first President of the International Union of Architects: President of the Town Planning Institute: member of the Royal Fine Art Commission and of the Royal Commission on the Location of Industry: knighted 1945: RIBA Royal Gold Medallist 1946: Gold Medal of the American Institute of Architects 1949: Author of *The Preservation of Rural England* (1926), and *Town and Country Planning* (1933). Reputation as a town-planner was world wide, and activities as such on an international scale: consulted by the Colonial Office: reported on preservation and town planning schemes for Bath, Bournemouth, Bristol, Clydeside, Cumberland, Cyprus, Doncaster, East Kent, Edinburgh, Hong Kong, Hull, Plymouth, Sheffield, Stratford-upon-Avon, the Thames Valley, Warwick, the West Midland Region, the siting and building of the University of Ceylon, the replanning of Addis Ababa for the Emperor of Ethiopia. Produced the County of London Plan, in collaboration with J. H. Forshaw, in 1943, and the Greater London Plan in 1945.

ABRAHAM, Robert: 1774–1850
A builder's son: articled to James Bowen, surveyor. Gained a reputation as an arbitrator early in his career, which helped him to secure the patronage of many influential families: established an extensive practice as an architect in London. His work, much of which has now disappeared, included the County Fire Office, Regent Street, London (1819: dem.), Nos. 176–186 Regent Street, London (1820: dem.), the School at Mildenhall, Wilts. (1823), conservatories and garden buildings at Alton Towers, Staffs. (1824: with his son, H. R. Abraham), and additions to the College of Heralds, Queen Victoria Street, London (1844).

ADAM, James: 1730–94
Third son of William Adam the elder, and younger brother of Robert Adam: educated Edinburgh University: travelled in Europe 1760–3: joined the family practice. Architect of the King's Works 1769–82: author of *Practical Essays on Agriculture, etc., together with Observations on Inclosures, Fences, Farms and Farmhouses* (1789): co-author with Robert Adam of *The Works in Architecture of Robert and James Adam* (published between 1773 and 1822). His work was largely confined to assisting and collaborating with Robert Adam: independently he designed the Shire Hall, Hertford (1768–9).

ADAM, John: c. 1721–92
Eldest son of William Adam the elder, and elder brother of Robert Adam: educated Edinburgh University: entered his father's office: collaborated in and completed many of his father's designs including Pollok House, Pollokshaws, Glasgow (1752), and succeeded to his architectural practice. May have been associated, in a business capacity, with his brothers' architectural practice in London. Designed the Lion Bridge and Denwick Bridge, Alnwick Park, Northumb. (1773).

ADAM, Robert, FRS, FSA: 1728–92 (Portrait: see Plate VI)
Second son of William Adam the elder, a successful Scottish architect. Born at Kirkcaldy: educated at the High School, Edinburgh, and Edinburgh University: spent the years 1754–8 on the Continent, where he was admitted a member of St Luke's Academy, Rome: explored and measured the remains of Diocletian's Palace at Split. On his return set up in practice with his brothers James and

William, becoming extremely busy and prosperous. He was Architect of the King's Works jointly with Sir William Chambers 1761–9: Surveyor of Chelsea Hospital 1765 until his death in 1792: elected M.P. for Kinross 1769: one of the original members of the Architects' Club formed in 1791. The author of *Ruins of the Palace of the Emperor Diocletian at Spalatro in Dalmatia* (1764), and, with his brother James, of *The Works in Architecture of Robert and James Adam* (the 1st volume published 1773, the 2nd 1779, the 3rd posthumously 1822). In 1768 the brothers attempted a large planning project at the Adelphi, but it proved a financial disaster from which they saved themselves by selling the property by lottery. In 1773 they undertook a similar town-planning development at Marylebone, which, though it did not fail financially, proved impossible to complete as they had intended. The wide use, in this scheme, of a stucco for which the brothers had acquired the patent, involved them in court proceedings, where they won the case, though pamphlets were published afterwards which attempted to damage their reputations and practice. Robert Adam's work included the screen wall at the Admiralty, London (1760): interiors, gateway, garden buildings, tower, and conservatory at Croome Court, Worcs. (1760 and at intervals till 1791): Market Hall, High Wycombe, Bucks. (1761): three-arched bridge and circular temple in grounds of Audley End, Essex (1763–4): interiors, south portico, offices and mausoleum at Bowood, Wilts. (1762–70): Adelphi, London (1768–72: dem.): Luton Hoo, Beds. (1768–75: altered since): No. 8 Queen Street, Edinburgh (1770): Chandos House, Chandos Street, London (1771): south front of Stowe House, Bucks. (1771–9): Royal Society of Arts, No. 8 John Adam Street, London (1772–4): Nos. 46 and 48 Portland Place, London (1774): Town Hall, Bury St Edmunds, Suffolk (1774–80): south and east sides of Fitzroy Square, London (1790 onwards): Trades House, Glassford Street, Glasgow (1791).

ADAM, William, the elder: 1689–1748
A Scotsman, of Kirkcaldy, the father of John, Robert, James and William Adam. He owned property; was interested in speculation; was Master Mason in North Britain to the Board of Ordnance, and became the most important and successful Scottish architect of his time. Engravings of his works (with some of other Scottish architects) were published early in the nineteenth century under the

title of *Vitruvius Scoticus*. He worked on the Highland forts built after the 1745 Rebellion: enlarged and reconstructed many large Scottish houses: his work included the Royal Infirmary, Edinburgh (1738: dem.), and the wings and east front of Hopetoun House, nr. Edinburgh.

ADAM, William, the younger: *c.* 1738–1822
The youngest son of William Adam of Kirkcaldy, and youngest brother of John, Robert and James Adam. A member of the brothers' architectural practice in London, though largely in a business capacity, and no independent architectural work can be attributed to him.

AIKIN, Edmund: 1780–1820
The son of Dr John Aikin of Warrington, Lancs.: articled to a surveyor: entered Royal Academy Schools 1801: assistant to General Sir Samuel Bentham with whom he collaborated on the design of a bridge over the River Swale, 1812. After some years in London, established a practice in Liverpool 1814, his work consisting chiefly of shops and villas, and where he designed the Wellington Assembly Rooms, 1815. Contributed articles on architecture to *Rees' Cyclopaedia*, and published *Designs for Villas and other Rural Buildings with Remarks on the Prevailing Defects of Modern Architecture, and an Investigation of the Style best adapted for the Dwellings of the Present Times* (1808): *An Essay on Modern Architecture* (1808): *An Essay on the Doric Order* (1810): *An Account of the Cathedral Church of St Paul* (1813): and *Remarks upon the Architecture of the Reign of Queen Elizabeth* (appended to Lucy Aikin's *Memoirs of the Court of Elizabeth*, published 1818).

AITCHISON, George, the elder: d. 1861
Entered Royal Academy Schools 1815: studied under H. H. Seward 1815–21. Was architect to the London and Birmingham Railway Company, surveyor to the St Katharine's Dock Company and to the Commissioners of Sewers for the Precinct of St Katharine, and the designer of Tring railway station, Herts. (1838).

AITCHISON, George, the younger, RA, FRIBA: 1825–1910
The son of George Aitchison the elder: educated Merchant Taylors' School: articled to his father: entered Royal Academy Schools: after a period of European travel became his father's partner in

1859. Began independent practice in 1861 after the death of his
father, whom he succeeded as architect to the St Katharine's Dock
Company: was District Surveyor for East Wandsworth and Tooting
Graveney. President of the Architects' Benevolent Society 1897–8:
Professor of Architecture at the Royal Academy 1887–1905: at the
RIBA Vice-President 1889–93, President 1896–9, Royal Gold
Medallist 1898. A member of many foreign architectural bodies, he
won a number of medals for overseas architectural exhibitions, took
an active part in architectural education, acted as assessor in many
important competitions, lectured, wrote articles on architecture, and
edited Ward's *Principles of Ornament* (1892). His large and flourishing
practice included a great deal of furniture design and decorative
schemes for interiors, and he had many wealthy and influential
clients in London for whom he undertook such commissions. His
work included warehouses and wharves on the Thames: Nos. 59–61
Mark Lane, London (1864): Leighton House, Holland Park Road,
London (1865): redecoration at Goldsmiths' Hall, Foster Lane,
London (1871): and Founders' Hall, St Swithin's Lane, London
(1877–8).

ALAN of WALSINGHAM: d. *c.* 1364
A monk at Ely, Cambs., in 1314, where he designed work in gold and
silver: became Sacrist to the Cathedral and Monastery 1321, and
later held the office of Prior, which he retained till *c.* 1363. As
Sacrist he was responsible for the Cathedral and Monastery buildings, and there is little doubt that he designed the octagonal crossing
tower at Ely Cathedral (1322–30) after the collapse of the Norman
tower in 1322. He may also have designed the church of St Mary-
the-Less, Cambridge (built *c.* 1340–52).

ALDRICH, Henry: 1648–1710
Educated Westminster School and Christ Church, Oxford: entered
the Church: became Dean of Christ Church 1689: he was a man of
cultivated taste and learning, author, musician, the owner of a
considerable library, and with a wide knowledge of architecture.
His *Elementa Architecturae* was unfinished at his death, but the
completed parts were published in 1750 under the title of *Elementa
Architecturae Civilis*. His work included the church of All Saints,
Oxford (1706–10), and the Peckwater Quadrangle at Christ Church,
Oxford (1706–14).

ALEXANDER, Daniel Asher: 1768–1846

Educated St Paul's School: entered Royal Academy Schools: won the Silver Medal 1782: was a pupil of Samuel Robinson. Appointed Surveyor to Trinity House, and to the London Dock Company 1796: he had a large practice both as an architect and as an engineer. His work included The Mote, nr. Maidstone, Kent (1793–1801): London Docks buildings and warehouses, Wapping, London (1802–31): Dartmoor Prison, Princetown, Devonshire (1805–9: built for French prisoners of war, it became a convict prison later and has since been much altered): the Baptist College, Bristol (1806–12): the County Prison, Maidstone, Kent (1810–17): St Michael, Princetown, Devonshire (1811–15): the Lighthouse at Harwich, Essex (1818): and at Yarmouth, I.O.W., where he is buried, he designed the church tower in 1831 as a navigational aid. His son Daniel (1795–1843) assisted his father until 1820, when he took Holy Orders. In 1818 he designed the library at Beddington House, nr. Croydon, Surrey, and rebuilt the tower and nave of the church of St Peter, Walton-on-the-Hill, Surrey.

ALLASON, Thomas: 1790–1852

Born in London: a pupil of William Atkinson: won the Royal Academy Silver Medal 1809, and the Society of Arts Gold and Silver Medals 1810 and 1816 respectively. Toured the Continent 1814, making a special study of Greek architecture, and travelling in the capacity of draughtsman for *Topography illustrative of the Battle of Platoea* (1817), and *The Actual State of the Plain of Olympia and of the ruins of the City of Elis* (1824): on his return published *Picturesque Views of the Antiquities of Pola in Istria* (1817). Held the appointments of commissioner of sewers for Westminster and part of Middlesex, surveyor to the Stock Exchange, surveyor to the Alliance Fire Company, and surveyor to the Pollen, Ladbroke and Pitt Estates in London, and the d'Este Estate in Ramsgate: designed furniture, interior decoration, many villas and mansions, schemes of landscape gardening. His work included the Alliance Fire Company's office, Bartholomew Lane, London (dem.); Sulhamstead Park, Berks.: and extensions to the house and garden buildings at Alton Towers, Staffs. His son, Thomas (d. 1868), succeeded to his practice and many of his appointments, and rebuilt the western part of the Stock Exchange, London, in 1853–4.

ALLEN, George, FIBA: 1798–1847
A pupil of James Elmes: won the Royal Academy Silver Medal
1820. Surveyor to the Haberdashers' Company, the Deptford Creek
Bridge Company, the district of Rotherhithe and Hatcham, and the
parishes of St Olave and St Nicholas, Deptford: widely employed on
valuation work in south-east London. The publication of his *Plans
and Designs for the future Approaches to the New London Bridge* in 1827
and 1828 resulted in many of his ideas being used in this project.
His work included schools, a workhouse, and many wharves and
warehouses in Southwark, and Christ Church, Bermondsey,
London (1847: with W. B. Hays).

ALLOM, Thomas: 1804–72
Born in London: articled to Francis Goodwin: travelled extensively
in Europe and Asia: was a talented artist, illustrated a number of
topographical works, and executed the drawings for the Houses of
Parliament designed by Sir Charles Barry. He is believed to have
succeeded Thomas Allason as surveyor to the Ladbroke Estate in
London, and from *c.* 1852 onwards was responsible for laying out
many of the streets and squares around Ladbroke Grove. His work
included St Peter, Kensington Park Road, Paddington, London
(1852): the Town Hall, Harwich, Essex (1864: built as the Great
Eastern Hotel): and the hotel at Lord's Cricket Ground, St John's
Wood, London (1867).

ANDERSON, Sir Robert Rowand, LL.D, FRIBA: 1834–1921
Born at Forres, the son of Robert Anderson, a solicitor: had four
years' legal training; studied construction and design while serving
with the Royal Engineers: entered the Architectural Section of the
School of the Board of Manufactures: spent a year in continental
travel. Set up in practice in Edinburgh *c.* 1875: became very
successful: his output was large and included a number of memorials
in Edinburgh. Knighted 1902: first President of the Scottish
Institute of Architects: Royal Gold Medallist 1916: was largely
responsible for the foundation of the Edinburgh School of Applied
Art, and for commissioning the drawings which formed a major
part of the National Art Survey of Scotland. His work included the
Medical Schools, Edinburgh (1875): Central Station Hotel,
Glasgow (1884): Govan Old Parish Church, Glasgow (1884):
the Pearce Institute, Glasgow (1903 and 1905): the Scottish

National Portrait Gallery and Museum of Antiquities, Edinburgh: and the Montrose Memorial, St Giles' Cathedral, Edinburgh.

ANDREWS, George Townsend: 1805–55
Awarded a Society of Arts premium 1824: entered the Royal Academy Schools 1825: was assistant to P. F. Robinson on York County Gaol, from 1826–36. Practised in Yorkshire, where his work included the railway stations at Scarborough (1845: enlarged later): Hull and Whitby (1847) and Richmond (1848): All Saints, Newton-upon-Ouse (1849): Richmond School (1849: additions later): and St Lawrence, Flaxton-on-the-Moor (1853–4).

ANGELL, Samuel, FIBA: 1800–66
Entered the Royal Academy Schools 1816: a pupil of Thomas Hardwick: Surveyor to the Saddlers' Company: the author (in collaboration with W. Harris) of *Metopes of the Temple at Selinus* (1826). His work included Lamb's Chapel and Almshouses, Monkwell Street, London (1825: dem.): and the General Hospital, King's Lynn, Norfolk (1834: additions later).

ARCHER, Thomas: *c.* 1668–1743
The son of Thomas Archer of Umberslade, Warwicks.: educated Trinity College, Oxford: travelled abroad. He held the appointment of Groom Porter at Court, under Anne, George I and George II: the sinecure post of Comptroller of Customs at Newcastle: and was one of the Commissioners for Building Fifty New Churches, in 1711. He owned the estate of Hale in Hampshire, and probably designed his own monument in the church there, where he is buried. His work included the north front of Chatsworth House, Derbys. (1704–5) and the Cascade House in the grounds (1702): stables, offices and some work on the House, at Aynhoe Park, Northants (1707–14): Roehampton House, Wandsworth, London (1710–12: enlarged since): St Philip, Birmingham (1710–15: now the Cathedral): St Paul, Deptford, London (1712–30): St John, Smith Square, London (1714–28): Hale House, Hants (*c.* 1715: altered since).

ASHPITEL, William Hurst: 1776–1852
A pupil of D. A. Alexander to whom he was also assistant, notably on the survey and designs for the London Docks; later assisted John Rennie on the Kennet and Avon Canal, and was for a time a partner

of James Savage. Subsequently he practised independently; his work included early buildings for the Horticultural Society: additions and alterations at North Mimms Park, Herts.: Chart Park, Dorking, Surrey (dem.): and Shenley Rectory, Herts.

ASHPITEL, Arthur: 1807–69

Born at Hackney, London, the son of William Hurst Ashpitel: trained in his father's office: started independent practice in London 1842: was in partnership with John Whichcord the younger 1850–4: then spent some time in Rome, and subsequently retired from practice, devoting himself to literary work. He contributed articles to the *Encyclopaedia Britannica*, the *Dictionary of Architecture*, and to professional journals: was the author of satirical political pamphlets: edited an edition of Nicholson's *Carpentry*, and *A Treatise on Architecture*: collaborated with Whichcord in the publication of *Observations on Baths and Wash-houses*, and *Erection of Fireproof Houses in Flats*. He was Vice-President of the Institute in 1862, and one of its examiners: he had a large practice: built many private houses and mansions, some blocks of artisans' dwellings, public baths and washhouses: his work included St Barnabas, Homerton High Street, Hackney, London (1843–52) and the Vicarage (*c.* 1850): St Peter, Ilford, Essex (1862): and St John, Blackheath, London.

ATKINSON, Peter, the elder: 1725–1805

Born near Ripon, Yorks., he worked first as a carpenter: later, as assistant to John Carr, he was engaged in work at Buxton, Chatsworth and Harewood. When Carr retired, he took over much of his work, and established a good practice of his own in Yorkshire, where he designed Hackness Hall (1791).

ATKINSON, Peter, the younger: *c.* 1776–1842

The son of Peter Atkinson: trained in his father's office, became his partner 1801. Among his patrons were the Duke of Devonshire and the Earl of Harewood: he was Surveyor and Steward to York Corporation: from 1819–28 was in partnership with R. H. Sharp, a former pupil: between 1821 and 1831 he built a number of churches in Lancashire and Yorkshire for the Commissioners for Building New Churches: his sons, John (d. 1875) and William (retired 1878), practised as architects in Manchester. His work included rebuilding and facing at Hainton Hall, Lincs. (1807): the City Gaol (1802–7), the Library (1812) and House of Correction (1814), all in York: Christ Church, Scarborough, Yorks. (1826–8): St Paul, Birkenshaw, Yorks. (1829–30).

ATKINSON, Robert, OBE, FRIBA: 1883–1953

Born at Wigton, Cumberland: trained at Nottingham School of Art and University College, Nottingham: travelled on the Continent and in the USA. Worked as assistant to a Newcastle architect, and then to John Belcher, before setting up in practice in London. Principal of the AA School 1912–24, and its director 1924–30. He was a pioneer of cinema design: his work included the Gresham Hotel, Dublin: the Regent Cinema, Brighton, Sussex: the Town Hall, Wallington, Surrey (1935): The White House, Albany Street, London (1936): the Technical College and College of Art, Croydon, Surrey (1953–9: with A. F. B. Anderson).

ATKINSON, Thomas Witlam: *c.* 1799–1861

Born in Yorkshire, he worked as a bricklayer, stone-carver, and drawing instructor before becoming Clerk of the Works to George Basevi, and then to H. E. Kendall: from 1827 to 1834 practised as an architect in London: then for some years was in partnership with A. B. Clayton in Manchester, returning to London about 1840: does not appear to have practised on any scale after that, but travelled widely in Europe, notably in Russia. His *Gothic Ornaments selected from the different Cathedrals and Churches in England* was published in 1829: *Oriental and Western Siberia* in 1858, and *Travels in Upper and Lower Amoor* in 1860. His work included St Nicholas, Tooting, London (1833): St Luke, Cheetham, Manchester (1836–9).

ATKINSON, William: *c.* 1773–1839

Born at Bishop Auckland, Co. Durham. He began as a carpenter, but through the patronage of the Bishop of Durham became a pupil of James Wyatt, entered the Royal Academy Schools, and won the Gold Medal in 1797. He enjoyed the patronage of many influential people: built up a large and flourishing practice: was a talented chemist, geologist and botanist: introduced 'Atkinson's Cement' (or Roman Cement) to London, where it appeared in use for the first time about 1816. Architect to the Ordnance Office 1813–29, and designed the Ordnance Office in Pall Mall: in 1805 published *Picturesque Views of Cottages*. His work included extensive remodelling

28

of Panshanger House, Herts. (1808–22): Ditton Park, Bucks. (1813–17): Garnons, Herefs. (1815: additions since): additions to Hylands, nr. Chelmsford, Essex (1819–25): alterations to Deepdene House, Surrey (1819–26): Silvermere, nr. Cobham, Surrey (*c.* 1820): No. 100 Park Lane, London (1824–7).

ATWOOD, Thomas Warr: d. 1775
A member of the Common Council of Bath. Through family influence was appointed City Architect to the Estates and Waterworks in Bath, in the latter half of the eighteenth century, though by trade he was a prosperous plumber and glazier. Acquired property leases in the city, where he built the Paragon Crescent (1769–71), and Oxford Row (1773): in his capacity of City Architect he designed Grove Street Prison (1772), and the Guildhall, though the latter was subsequently built to the designs of Thomas Baldwin, after Atwood's death.

BAILEY, George, FIBA: 1792–1860
Entered the Royal Academy Schools in 1813: a pupil of Sir John
Soane in 1806, and his assistant till 1837. He was the first Curator
of the Soane Museum; Hon. Secretary of the IBA, and assisted the
Architectural Publication Society, formed in 1848, with much
material for the *Dictionary of Architecture*.

BAKER, Sir Herbert, KCIE, RA, FRIBA: 1862–1946
Born near Cobham, Kent, the son of T. H. Baker: educated Ton-
bridge School: trained at the Royal Academy School of Design
and the Architectural Association: articled to his uncle, Arthur
Baker, 1879: assistant to Sir Ernest George 1882: won the Ashpitel
Prize of the RIBA 1889: in 1892 began to practise in South Africa,
where he met and became a close friend of Cecil Rhodes. Knighted
1926: Royal Gold Medallist 1927: HON. DCL Oxford 1937. In
1913 he started to practise in London, and in 1914 at Delhi, where
he was associated with Sir Edwin Lutyens in the design of the
Secretariats, Legislative Buildings, and circular Council Chamber.
Entered into partnership with A. T. Scott 1931: became architect
to the Governments of South Africa, India and Kenya, and was one
of the principal consultants of the War Graves Commission after
the 1914–18 War. He was the author of *Cecil Rhodes by his architect*
(1934), and *Architecture and Personalities* (1945). His work included the
Cathedral of St George, Cape Town (1897–8: with F. Masey):
Rhodes Memorial, Cape Town (1905–8): Union Buildings,
Pretoria: Delville Wood Memorial: War Memorial Building at
Harrow School, Middlesex (1921): design of Cubley Garden Estate,
Penistone, Yorks. (1921–2): reconstruction of the Bank of England,
London (1921–37): St Andrew, Ilford, Essex (1924): the Grand-
stand, Lord's Cricket Ground, St John's Wood, London (1926): re-
modelling interior of Howick Hall, Northumb. (1928: with A. T.
Scott): India House, Aldwych, London (1928–30: with A. T.
Scott): Electra House, Victoria Embankment, London (1931–3):
Scott Polar Research Institute, Cambridge (1933–4): the Chapel
at the Royal Merchant Navy School, Bear Wood, Berks. (1934–5):
South Africa House, Trafalgar Square, London (1935): Church
House, Dean's Yard, Westminster, London (1935–9): Royal
Empire Society, Northumberland Avenue, London (1938).

BAKER, William: 1705–71
Born in London, the son of Richard Baker of London and Leo-minster. In 1736 he married an heiress and settled at her family home, Highfields, Audlem, Cheshire, where he administered the estate and practised as an architect and surveyor in the neighbour-hood and in Shropshire. Much of his work consisted in making surveys and inspections, and supervising alterations and repairs to churches and country houses: it included the Butter Cross, Ludlow, Salop (1743–4): the Infirmary, Shrewsbury (1747): the Market Hall, Montgomery (1748): St John, Wolverhampton, Staffs. (1755): St Michael, Stone, Staffs. (1753). His son Richard (b. 1743) also became an architect.

BALDWIN, Thomas: 1750–1820
A speculative builder in Bath: became City Surveyor 1775, Deputy Chamberlain and Surveyor 1785, and Inspector of the Baths 1787. In addition to planning Bathwick, and extensive building in the city, he produced plans for the development of the Baths in 1789. His dismissal from his civic posts in 1791 was followed by bank-ruptcy in 1793 through the failure of the Bath City Bank, though he continued to practise privately as an architect. He designed Pont Blean, Cards. (1783), Devizes Town Hall, Wilts. (1806–8), and his work at Bath included the Guildhall (1775): Somersetshire Build-ings, Milsom Street (1781–3): Northumberland Buildings (1780): and the Pump Room, Abbey Churchyard (1789–90: completed by John Palmer).

BALFOUR, Colonel Eustace James Anthony, FSA, FRIBA:
    1854–1911
The youngest son of James Maitland Balfour, and brother of Lord Balfour: educated Harrow, and Trinity College, Cambridge: trained under Basil Champneys: set up in practice 1879. In 1890 was appointed Surveyor to the Grosvenor Estate of the Duke of Westminster, and much of his work was connected with rebuilding on the Grosvenor Estates in Mayfair and Belgravia. Was in partner-ship with Thackeray Turner 1885–1911. Commanded the London Scottish Corps of Volunteers 1892–1904, and on his retirement was made an A.D.C. to the King. His work included No. 28 Grosvenor Gardens, London (c. 1880): the north side of Wilton Crescent, London (with Turner): the National Scottish Church, Crown Court, Russell Street, London (1909: with Turner).

BANCKES, Matthew: d. 1706
Surveyor of the Mews at Hampton Court, under William and
Mary: Master Carpenter in the Office of Works 1683–1706:
Master of the Carpenters' Company 1698. Apart from his official
duties he carried out surveys on many important buildings, in-
cluding Wren's Trinity College Library at Cambridge (1676 and
1685–6): he carried out extensive rebuilding of Upper School, Eton
College, Bucks. (1690–4): was responsible for the woodwork at
Winslow Hall, Bucks. (1700): and designed Petersham Lodge,
Petersham, Surrey (destroyed by fire 1721). His son Henry (c. 1679–
1716) was a master mason, who worked at Blenheim Palace, Oxon.
(from 1706): at Marlborough House, London (1709–11): and at
Canons House, Middlesex (1714–15: dem.).

BARRY, Sir Charles, RA, FRS: 1795–1860 (Portrait: see Plate IX)
The son of a London stationer: articled to Middleton and Bailey,
Lambeth surveyors, from 1810–16: from 1817–20 travelled on the
Continent, also visiting Asia Minor, Egypt, and various Mediter-
ranean towns and islands. Set up practice in 1820 in London, and
in 1836 won the competition for the new Houses of Parliament: he
was knighted 1852, and was a Vice-President of the Institute 1859.
His work included St Peter, Victoria Gardens, Brighton, Sussex
(1824–8): Royal Institution of Fine Arts, Manchester (1824–35:
now the City Art Gallery): St John, Holloway Road, Islington,
London (1826), and St John's National Schools there: Sussex
County Hospital, Brighton, Sussex (1826–8: additions since): the
layout of Queen's Park, Brighton, Sussex (1829): Travellers' Club,
Pall Mall, London (1829–32): the Athenaeum, Manchester (1837–9:
now Art Gallery Annexe): remodelling of Mount Felix, Walton-on-
Thames, Surrey (1837–40): Palace of Westminster and Houses of
Parliament, London (1840–60: assisted by A. W. N. Pugin, and
completed by E. M. Barry): Helmsley Lodge, Yorks. (1843): Holy
Trinity, Hurstpierpoint, Sussex (1843–5): Treasury Buildings,
Whitehall, London (1844–5).

BARRY, Charles, FSA, FRIBA: 1823–1900
The eldest son of Sir Charles Barry: educated Sevenoaks Grammar
School: trained in his father's office: set up in independent practice,
and undertook much work as referee and arbitrator in competitions:
from 1847–72 was in partnership with Robert Richardson Banks

I

SIR HENRY WOTTON
1568–1639

[*National Portrait
Gallery, London*

INIGO JONES
1573–1652

*National Portrait
Gallery, London*]

II

SIR CHRISTOPHER
WREN
1632–1723

[*National Portrait
Gallery, London*

SIR JOHN VANBRUGH
1664–1726

*National Portrait Gallery,
London*]

(1813–72), who had worked in the office of Sir Charles Barry from 1838–47. Barry was Architect to Dulwich College Estates; President of the Institute 1876–9: Royal Gold Medallist 1877: he was one of the Royal Commissioners at the Paris Exhibition of 1878, and the only British member of the jury which made the architectural awards: for this he received the French Cross of the Legion of Honour: he was an honorary member of the Imperial and Royal Academy of Arts in Vienna. His work included Dulwich College, Dulwich, London (1866–70): St Stephen, College Road, Dulwich, London (1868–82: with R. R. Banks): the Piccadilly entrance range and courtyard to Burlington House, London (1869–73: with R. R. Banks): Tilmouth Park Hotel, Tilmouth, Northumb. (1882).

BARRY, Edward Middleton, RA, FRIBA: 1830–80
The third son of Sir Charles Barry: studied at King's College, London: entered the office of T. H. Wyatt before joining his father, whose work he took over in 1860, and for whom he completed the Houses of Parliament in 1866–8: from 1873–80 he was Professor of Architecture at King's College, London. His work included St Saviour, Eton Road, Hampstead, London (1856): Grammar School, Moorland Road, Leeds (1858–9): Floral Market, and Opera House, Covent Garden, London (1859): Charing Cross Station Hotel, London (1863–4): Star and Garter Hotel, Richmond, Surrey (1864): Cobham Park, Surrey (1870): Hospital for Sick Children, Gt. Ormond Street, London (1871–6): Temple Gardens Building, Middle Temple Lane, London (1878).

BARRY, T. Denville: 1815–1905
An Irishman, the son of Dr Barry of Cork: came to England 1845 and began independent practice. He was City Surveyor of Norwich for some years: in 1872 resumed his practice at Liverpool, in partnership with his sons. He was President of the Liverpool Architectural Society, and did much arbitration and survey work, engineering projects, and many local cemeteries. His work included Holy Trinity, Trinity Rise, Lambeth, London (1857): the south front of the Guildhall, Norwich (1861): the old Corn Exchange, Norwich (1863).

BARTHOLOMEW, Alfred: 1801–45
Born in London: articled to J. H. Good of London: was a linguist and mathematician of some ability, and gave lessons in perspective:

c

one of the founders of a Society called 'Freemasons of the Church', whose aims were 'the recovery, maintenance and furtherance of the true principles and practice of architecture'. He designed the Finsbury Savings Bank, Sekforde Street, Finsbury, London, in 1840, but his architectural practice was small, and he is better known for his literary work: his post as District Surveyor of Hornsey was terminated by his death a few weeks after the appointment was made. In 1831 he published a new version of the Psalms: and was the author of *Hints relative to the Construction of Fire-proof Buildings* (1839): *Specifications for Practical Architecture* (1840): and *Cyclopaedia of the New Metropolitan Building Act.* Editor of the *Builder* in 1844.

BASEVI, George, FRS, FSA: 1794–1845
The son of George Basevi, and distantly related to the family of Disraeli: educated at Greenwich: articled to Sir John Soane 1810: entered the Royal Academy Schools 1813: travelled on the Continent 1816–19, then set up in practice in London. In 1821 was appointed Surveyor to the Guardian Assurance Company: in 1829 Surveyor to the Trustees of Smith's Charity Estate in Chelsea, and to Mr Alexander's Estate in the vicinity: a founder member and Vice-President of the Institute. His work included Belgrave Square, London (1825–40: except the corner mansions): the Stables, Bretton Park, Yorks. (*c.* 1830): Fryer's Callis, Kettering Road, and Truesdale's Hospital, Scotgate, both in Stamford, Lincs. (1832): St Mary's Hall, Eastern Road, Brighton, Sussex (1836): the Fitzwilliam Museum, Cambridge (1837–41): Holy Trinity, Twickenham, Middlesex (1839–41: additions by Dollman): St Saviour, Walton Place, Chelsea, London (1840): Pelham Crescent, Pelham Place, and Thurloe Square, London (1843): the Conservative Club, No. 74 St James's Street, London (1843–5: with Sydney Smirke): St Matthew, Eye, Northants (1846: steeple added by Dollman).

BASILL, Simon: d. 1615
Surveyor of the King's Works 1606–15. He was employed on the building of Cecil House, Strand, London, and also probably at Hatfield House, Herts. His son, Simon (1612–63), was Clerk of the Works at Greenwich and Eltham under Charles I, and at Hampton Court under Charles II.

THE BASTARD FAMILY

The name of a family of builders and architects who flourished at Blandford, Dorset, during the eighteenth century. Thomas (d. 1720), a joiner, is believed to have carried out reconstruction work at the churches of Winterborne Stickland and Almer, Dorset, and the woodwork at Charlton Marshall church, Dorset. His sons John (c. 1688–1770) and William (c. 1689–1766) carried on their father's business, and were responsible for much of the rebuilding of Blandford after the fire there in 1731, notably the Town Hall (1734), and the Church of SS Peter and Paul (1735–9). The Red Lion Inn, Coupar House, and the Greyhound Inn (now the National Provincial Bank) are also believed to be their work. Benjamin (c. 1698–1772), a mason of Sherborne, Dorset, and Joseph (d. 1783), a builder of Basingstoke, Hants, were also sons of Thomas Bastard, and his grandson John (1722–78), a mason, lived in London, designed the Dashwood Mausoleum at West Wycombe, Bucks. (1763–4), and worked at Greenwich Hospital (1770).

BEAZLEY, Samuel: 1786–1851

The son of a military accoutrements maker of Westminster, and the nephew of Charles Beazley (c. 1756–1829), an architect who had been a pupil of Sir Robert Taylor, was later Architect to the Goldsmith's Company, and built the Goldsmiths' Almshouses, Acton, Middlesex (1811). Samuel Beazley was educated at Acton: trained by his uncle: fought in the Peninsular War: was the author of two novels: a prolific playwright and producer of plays. His theatrical interests were reflected in the many theatres he designed. His work included a number of railway stations in Kent, and part of the original London Bridge Station: the colonnade at Drury Lane Theatre, London (c. 1831): Studley Castle, Warwicks. (1834: later the Agricultural College): St James's Theatre, King Street, London (1836: dem.): Hillersdon House, nr. Butterleigh, Devonshire (1848): the Pilot House (1848) and Lord Warden Hotel, Dover, Kent (1850).

BECKETT, Sir Edmund, QC: 1816–1905

Born at Carlton Hill, nr. Newark, Notts., the eldest son of Sir Edmund Beckett, Chairman of the Great Northern Railway: educated Doncaster Grammar School, Eton, and Trinity College, Cambridge: called to the Bar 1841: built up a large and lucrative legal practice: until he succeeded to his father's baronetcy in 1874 Beckett used the additional surname of Denison: he was created Baron Grimthorpe of Grimthorpe, Yorks., in 1886. He joined the RIBA in 1877, but resigned in 1884. As an amateur architect he financed the rehabilitation of St Alban's Abbey, Herts. (1877–85), designing much of the work himself: he attempted collaborations with such well-known architects as Sir George Gilbert Scott and G. E. Street, but co-operation was alien to his temperament, and such arrangements often ended in violent quarrels. He was a skilful designer of clocks and watches: was responsible for the specification of the bell of 'Big Ben' and designed the clock itself. His published works included *Lectures on Gothic Architecture chiefly in relation to St George's Church at Doncaster* (1855): *A Book on Building, Civil and Ecclesiastical, with the Theory of Domes and of the Great Pyramid* (1876): *St Alban's Abbey and its Restoration* (1885). The architectural work he designed, independently and with professional assistance, included St James, Doncaster, Yorks. (1858): St Chad, Far Headingley, Leeds, Yorks. (1868): extensions to Lincoln's Inn Library, London (1871–3): the restoration of Lincoln's Inn Chapel, London (1882): St Mary, Doncaster, Yorks. (1885).

BEDFORD, Francis: 1784–1858
In 1812 he was commissioned by the Society of Dilettanti to make drawings of the Temple of Diana at Magnesia in Greece: he exhibited at the Royal Academy 1814–32, and a collection of his designs is in the Soane Museum. His work included St George, Wells Way, Camberwell, London (1822–4): Holy Trinity, Trinity Church Square, Southwark, London (1823–4): St Mary-the-Less, Black Prince Road, Lambeth, London (1827–8).

BELCHER, John, RA, FRIBA: 1841–1913
Born in Southwark, the eldest son of John Belcher, a successful London architect and surveyor: educated at private schools and in Luxemburg: trained by his father and in other architects' offices: visited Paris 1862–3: then assisted his father, and became his partner 1865: was in partnership with J. J. Joass 1905–13. He was a musician of some ability, sang, composed and conducted: published a paper on 'Musical Arrangements in Churches' (1888), and a 'Report on the Position of Organs in Churches' (1892): was the

author of *Essentials in Architecture* (1893), and, with Mervyn Macart-ney, *Later Renaissance Architecture in England* (1897–9): a Royal Gold Medallist, and President of the RIBA 1904–6, in which capacity he presided over the International Congress of Architects held in London in 1906: awarded many foreign architectural honours. His work included the Institute of Chartered Accountants, Gt Swan Alley, Moorgate, London (1889): the Convent of the Good Shep-herd, nr. Wargrave, Berks. (1894): Pangbourne Tower, Pangbourne, Berks. (1897–8): the Town Hall, Colchester, Essex (1898–1902): Whiteley's Store, Westbourne Grove, London (1908–12: with J. J. Joass): Holy Trinity, Kingsway, London (1910: with J. J. Joass): Royal Society of Medicine, Henrietta Place, Marylebone, London (1910–12).

BELL, Henry: 1647–1717

Born at King's Lynn, Norfolk, the son of Alderman Henry Bell, a mercer, and twice Mayor of Lynn: educated Lynn Grammar School and Caius College, Cambridge: travelled on the Continent. By 1678 he had settled at Lynn, where he was a Common Councillor 1680, Alderman 1690, and Mayor in 1692 and 1703. He carried on his father's business after his death, and practised as an architect in Norfolk and the neighbourhood: was the author of *An Historical Essay on the original of Painting* (published 1728). Factual evidence of his work is scanty, but he is believed to have assisted in rebuilding at Northampton after a disastrous fire of 1675, where the church of All Saints (1676–80) has been attributed to him. Work in King's Lynn included the Customs House (1683): the Market Cross in Tuesday Market (1707–10: dem.): and probably the Duke's Head Inn (1683–9): All Saints, North Runcton, Norfolk (1703–13), may have been his work.

BENSON, William: 1682–1754

The son of Sir William Benson, Sheriff of London. He toured the Continent, became High Sheriff of Wiltshire in 1710, and M.P. for Shaftesbury in 1715. He built Wilbury House, Wilts., in 1710, the design based on one by Inigo Jones. Was appointed Surveyor-General in 1718, supplanting Wren, but resigned in 1719 following an adverse report on his work by a Committee of the House of Lords.

37

BENTLEY, John Francis: 1839–1902

Born at Doncaster, and educated at a private school there: worked for a short time with a firm of mechanical engineers in Manchester: then for Winsland & Holland, a London firm of builders: became a pupil of Henry Clutton in 1858. His practice was much concerned with Roman Catholic religious buildings, and he is best known as the architect of Westminster Cathedral: before starting work there he toured Italy with Cardinal Vaughan, who had appointed him. His work included No. 235 Lancaster Road, Paddington, London (1863): the Presbytery of SS Peter and Edward, No. 43 Palace Street, Westminster, London (*c.* 1865): Convent of the Sacred Heart, Hammersmith, London (1868): interiors at Carlton Towers, Yorks. (1875–9): St John's Preparatory School, Windsor, Berks. (1884): Westminster Cathedral, the Archbishop's House, Clergy House, Choir School and Diocesan Hall, Westminster, London (1895–1903): St Luke, Chiddingstone Causeway, Kent (1897–8): St Francis, Convent Lane, Bocking, Essex (1898).

BENTLEY, Richard: 1708–82

The son of Dr Richard Bentley, the philologist: educated at Trinity College, Cambridge: he received no training as an architect, but was a skilled draughtsman. His friendship with Horace Walpole (which ended in 1761) led to his designing much of the Gothic architecture and furniture at Strawberry Hill, Twickenham, Middlesex. In the 1750s he 'Gothicized' Richard Bateman's villa at Old Windsor, Berks.: in 1756, with Horace Walpole, designed an Umbrello in the grounds of Wentworth Castle, Yorks.: in 1760 designed the Gothic stables at Chalfont House, Chalfont St Peter, Bucks. He illustrated the first edition of Gray's *Poems*, and was the author of a number of plays, among them *Philodamus*.

BIDLAKE, William Henry, FRIBA: 1862–1938

Educated Tettenhall College, Wolverhampton, and Christ's College, Cambridge: articled to Sir R. W. Edis: worked in the office of Bodley and Garner: set up his own practice in Birmingham 1888. His work was mainly ecclesiastical, and he took great interest in architectural education. Appointed Special Lecturer in the History of Architecture at Birmingham School of Art 1893: played a large part in establishing a proper course of training at the Birmingham School of Architecture, of which he became Director.

38

His work at Birmingham included St Oswald, Bordesley (1892–3): St Agatha, Sparkbrook (1899–1901): Bishop Latimer Church, Handsworth (1904): and for himself he built Lorien (formerly Vespers), Best Beech, Wadhurst, Sussex (1924).

THE BILLING FAMILY

The name of a family of builders and architects who practised in Reading, Berks., during the late eighteenth and first half of the nineteenth century. The founder, Richard, was Corporation Surveyor, and engaged in speculative enterprises in the town, which included Southampton Place and Albion Place, and designed the Church of St Mary, Castle Street (1798–9). Richard Billing the younger was associated with him: either together or independently Nos. 45–65 Eldon Square, Reading (1825–35), have been attributed to them, also a Chapel of Ease at Bledlow Ridge, nr. High Wycombe, Bucks. (1834). The work of John Billing included rebuilding at Holy Trinity, Reading (1846): the school at Weston, Lincs. (1852): alterations at St Leonard, Seaford, Sussex (1861–2): he may have designed the Town Hall, Chertsey, Surrey (1851).

BILLINGS, Robert William: 1813–74

Born in London: a pupil of John Britton: and later became an accomplished topographical draughtsman: assisted Sir Jeffry Wyatville on drawings of Windsor Castle, and contributed illustrations to George Godwin's *History and Description of St Paul's Cathedral*, and le Keux's *Churches of London*. He published many collections of illustrations of ecclesiastical and architectural subjects, notably *Illustrations of the Architectural Antiquities of the County of Durham* (1846), and *Baronial and Ecclesiastical Antiquities of Scotland* (1845–52). His architectural practice, which followed his career as an author, consisted largely of restoration work at churches and large country mansions.

BLACKBURN, William: 1750–90

The son of a Southwark tradesman, where he was born: apprenticed to a surveyor: entered the Royal Academy Schools 1772, and won the Silver Medal 1773. He was Surveyor to St Thomas's and Guy's Hospitals: to the County of Surrey: and to the Watermen's Company: Watermen's Hall, St Mary-at-Hill, London (1778–80), is attributed to him. He was a friend and supporter of John Howard,

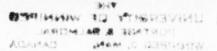

the prison reformer, and built a number of county gaols, including Gloucester (1788–91): Ipswich (1790): Dorchester (1789–95: completed by an architect named Fentiman): and Exeter (completed by Fentiman 1792).

BLASHILL, Thomas, FRIBA: 1831–1905
The son of Henry Blashill of Sutton-on-Hull: educated at Hull, Scarborough, and University College, London. He was President of the AA 1862–3: served on the Council of the Institute: a Fellow of the Surveyors' Institute: Vice-President of the British Archaeological Association: Superintending Architect of the Metropolitan Board of Works, and then under the London County Council 1887–99. He served on a number of government committees connected with building, and contributed many articles and papers to technical journals, on such subjects as fire prevention, sanitation and working-class housing: he was the author of *Sutton-in-Holdernesse, the Manor, the Berewic, and the Village Community*. Much of his work consisted of blocks of working-class dwellings, fire stations and similar LCC requirements: it included Christ Church, Beckenham, Kent (1875–6: with C. F. Hayward): gatehouse to the Blackwall Tunnel, London (1892–7): Westminster Technical Institute, Vincent Square, London (1893: extensions since): Fire Station, Carmelite Street, London (1896–7).

BLOMFIELD, Sir Arthur William, FRIBA: 1829–99
Born at Fulham Palace, London, the fourth son of Charles James Blomfield, Bishop of London. Educated at Rugby and Trinity College, Cambridge: articled to P. C. Hardwick 1852–5: then travelled in Europe with F. P. Cockerell: set up in practice in London 1856. He was President of the AA 1861: a Vice-President of the RIBA 1886: knighted 1889: Royal Gold Medallist 1891. Was Diocesan Architect to the See of Winchester, a Trustee of the Soane Museum; and in 1883 Architect to the Bank of England. His large practice included the building and restoration of many churches, and he had the care of Salisbury, Canterbury, Lincoln, and Chichester Cathedrals at different times. His work included No. 14 Garrick Street, London (1860): St Paul, Shoreditch, London (1860): St John, Colchester, Essex (1862–4): Trinity School of John Whitgift, North End, Croydon, Surrey (1869–71): Christ Church, London Road, St Leonards-on-Sea, Sussex (1875): All Saints,

Fulham, London (1880–1): Royal College of Music, Kensington, London (1883–4): Sion College, Victoria Embankment, London (1886): Law Courts Branch of the Bank of England, London (1886–8): Bancroft's School, Woodford, Essex (1887–9).

BLOMFIELD, Sir Reginald, RA, FRIBA: 1856–1942

The son of the Reverend G. J. Blomfield, and nephew of Sir Arthur Blomfield. Educated Haileybury, and Exeter College, Oxford: trained by his uncle, and at the Royal Academy Schools: set up in practice 1884. He was President of the RIBA 1912–14: Royal Gold Medallist 1913: knighted 1919: Principal Architect of the Imperial War Graves Commission: an original member of the Royal Fine Art Commission, and a member of the Board of Ancient Monuments, and of the Advisory Council of the V & A Museum: was awarded many continental and American academic honours. He was a prolific author of books on architectural history, among them *A History of Renaissance Architecture in England* (1897): *The Mistress Art* (1908): *A History of French Architecture 1494–1661* (1911): and *1661–1774* (1920): *The Touchstone of Architecture* (1925): *Memoirs of an Architect* (1932): *Six Architects* (1935): and *Richard Norman Shaw* (1940). His very large and prosperous practice included All Saints, Carshalton, Surrey (1893: with Sir A. Blomfield): No. 20 Buckingham Gate, London (1895): Saltcote Place, Rye, Sussex (1900–2): Elwyns, Felsted School, Essex (1901): Barclays Bank, Tindal Square, Chelmsford, Essex (1905): the Public Library, Lincoln (1906): houses in North Avenue, Whiteley Village Homes, Surrey (1914–21): the Quadrant, Regent Street, London, and part of Piccadilly Circus, London (1920–3): the Menin Gate, Ypres (1923–6): Lambeth Bridge, London (1932: with G. Topham Forrest).

BLORE, Edward, FRS, FSA: 1787–1879

The son of Thomas Blore, FSA. His early work was largely concerned with drawings for publications on antiquities, topography and architecture. He was attached to William IV and Queen Victoria as 'special architect': was Surveyor to Westminster Abbey (1827–49): a founder of the Royal Archaeological Institute: a founder member of the Institute of British Architects: HON.DCL Oxford 1834. His immense output of drawings form collections at the British Museum, the RIBA, and the Society of Antiquaries. He contributed architectural drawings to Surtees' *History of Durham*,

Baker's *Northamptonshire*, Clutterbuck's *Hertfordshire*, Britton's *English Cathedrals* and *Architectural Antiquities*, Sir James Hall's *Essay on the Origin, History and Principles of Gothic Architecture*, and *The Provincial Antiquities and Picturesque Scenery of Scotland*, sponsored by Sir Walter Scott. His own book, *The Monumental Remains of Noble and Eminent Persons*, was published in 1824. His work included Abbotsford, Roxburghshire (1816 onwards: completed by W. Atkinson): St George, Battersea, London (1828): the Pitt Press, Cambridge (1831–2: additions later): the completion of Buckingham Palace, London, after the dismissal of Nash (1831–7): the Town Hall, Warminster, Wilts. (1832): the Royal Mews, Windsor Castle, Berks. (1839–42).

BLOW, Detmar Jellings, FRIBA: 1867–1939
Educated Hawtreys: a Pugin Student of the RIBA 1892: in partnership with F. Billerey: a member of the Society for the Preservation of Ancient Buildings. Worked in London, South Africa and Japan: his practice included garden architecture and layout: as a draughtsman he was outstanding: he carried out the mason's work on two cottages designed by Ernest Gimson at Ulverscroft, Leics. (Stoneywell Cottage, 1899: and Lea Cottage, 1900). His work included additions to Heale House, Woodford, Wilts. (*c.* 1894): the restoration of Lake House, Wilsford, Wilts. (1898: with assistance from Philip Webb): Fonthill House, in the grounds of Fonthill Abbey, Wilts. (1904): Happisburgh Manor, Happisburgh, Norfolk (1900): the Playhouse, Craven Street, London (1906: with Billerey): Horwood House, Little Horwood, Bucks. (1912: with Billerey): addition to No. 34 Queen Anne's Gate, London (1912): Nos. 103–109 Wardour Street, London (1912).

BODLEY, George Frederick, RA, FSA, FRIBA: 1827–1907
Born at Hull, the youngest son of Dr William Bodley. The family moved to Brighton, where Bodley met George Gilbert Scott, whose pupil he was from 1845–50. Started independent practice 1860, and was in partnership with Thomas Garner 1869–97: they worked closely together, and much of their work cannot be definitely attributed to one or the other. The practice was concerned chiefly with the building of churches, parsonages and other ecclesiastical buildings, and with church decoration and furnishings. Bodley was

Royal Gold Medallist 1899: served on the Council of the Institute for two years: in 1907, he became an HON. DCL of Oxford. He was Diocesan Architect for Leicestershire, and held advisory appointments to the Cathedral Chapters of York, Peterborough, Exeter and Manchester: he was in the process of designing the Cathedral of SS Peter and Paul, Washington, USA, when he died. His work included (with Garner) St Augustine, Pendlebury, Lancs. (1874): the Rectory (1869): the Lodge and School (1894–5): the Master's Lodge, University College, Oxford (1876–9): No. 3 Chelsea Embankment, London (1879): the Chapel, Marlborough College, Wilts. (1883–6): St John the Baptist, Epping, Essex (1890–1): All Saints, Danehill, Sussex (1892): and independently, St Wilfrid, Haywards Heath, Sussex (1863–5): All Saints, Cambridge (1864): Holy Trinity, Prince Consort Road, London (1902).

BOLTON, Arthur Thomas, FSA, FRIBA: 1865–1945
The son of Thomas Bolton, a London solicitor: educated Haileybury, and University College: articled to Sir R. W. Edis 1884: acted as Clerk of Works to Ewan Christian: travelled in Europe: set up in practice 1890. He won the Soane Medal 1893: was Master of the AA Day School 1901–3: and Curator of the Soane Museum 1917–45. He published *The Architecture of Robert and James Adam* (1922): *The Works of Sir John Soane* (1924): *The Portrait of Sir John Soane* (1928): and (with H. D. Hendry) *The Transactions of the Wren Society* (in 20 volumes, begun 1923 and completed 1945): he was the author of an illustrated guide to the Soane Museum, *Description of the House and Museum*. He carried out restoration at many Adam houses, and his work included Nos. 87–102 Mount Street, London (1893): P. & O. Line offices, Cockspur Street, London (1907): Hurtwood, Ewhurst, Surrey (1910): the Adam Room at the British Empire Exhibition, Wembley, London (1923).

BONOMI, Joseph: 1739–1808
An Italian, born in Rome: educated there at the Collegio Romano, and as a pupil of the Marchese Teodili: at the invitation of the brothers Adam he came to England in 1767 and, apart from a visit to Italy, remained here until his death. He was assistant to Thomas Leverton: established an independent practice as a fashionable

architect, and designed and restored many country houses and mansions. He became an Associate of the Clementine Academy at Bologna in 1784: and was appointed honorary architect to St Peter's, Rome, in 1804. His elder son, Ignatius (d. 1870), became an architect, and County Surveyor of Durham, where he practised in partnership with Cory, and built Durham County Gaol (1809–11) and Burn Hall (1821–34): in Leeds, he built the Marshall Mills, Marshall Street (1838–40). Joseph Bonomi's younger son, Joseph (1796–1878), studied sculpture under Nollekens, became an Egyptologist of repute, collaborated with Owen Jones in the design of the Egyptian Court at the Crystal Palace; and from 1861 until his death was Curator of Sir John Soane's Museum. The work of Joseph Bonomi the elder included St James, Gt Packington, Warwicks. (1789–90): the exterior of Uxbridge House, No. 7 Burlington Gardens, London (1790–2: with John Vardy the younger): the Mausoleum, Blickling Park, Norfolk (1793): Eastwell Park, nr. Wye, Kent (1793–1800): Longford Hall, nr. Newport, Salop. (1794–7): Lambton Hall, Co. Durham (1797: rebuilt by John Dobson): Roseneath, Dunbartonshire (1803–6).

BOYLE, Richard, KCG, 3rd Earl of Burlington and 4th Earl of
    Cork: 1694–1753 (Portrait: see Plate IV)
Succeeded to his father's titles in 1704: visited Italy in 1714–15, and in 1719. His enthusiasm for the works of Palladio and Inigo Jones, together with his wealth and influence, made him the most important architectural patron of his time. He introduced the Palladian style of architecture to England, purchased and formed collections of valuable drawings and documents, sponsored the publication of important works on architecture, and helped such gifted men as Flitcroft, Kent, Gibbs and Colen Campbell. He was also a talented practising architect, designer and draughtsman: a member of the Privy Council: Lord High Treasurer of Ireland: Lord Lieutenant of the East Riding of Yorkshire, and a director of the Royal Academy of Music. His work included the remodelling of Burlington House, Piccadilly, London (1716: with James Gibbs and Colen Campbell): the Dormitory ('College') of Westminster School, London (1722: restored after war damage): the rebuilding of Chiswick House, Middlesex (c. 1725: with William Kent): General Wade's house in Gt. Burlington Street, London (1723: dem.): Sevenoaks School, and almshouses, Kent.

BRANDON, David, FSA, FRIBA: 1813–97
Though a contemporary of J. A. and J. R. Brandon (q.v.) he was
not related to them. Articled to George Smith 1828: entered the
Royal Academy Schools: won the Silver Medal 1832: in 1838
became a partner of T. H. Wyatt, and won the Bronze Medal at the
1st International Exhibition in 1851. He was a member of the
Council of the Institute, and its Vice-President in 1866–7 and 1882–5.
His work was mostly concerned with clubs and country houses, and
included entrance lodges and Nos. 18–19 Kensington Palace
Gardens, London (1845: with T. H. Wyatt): St Mary, Wallingford,
Berks. (1854): Taverham Hall, Norfolk (1858–9): St Andrew,
Wraysbury, Bucks. (1862): the Junior Carlton Club, Pall Mall,
London (1866–9): Bayham Abbey, nr. Wadhurst, Kent and Sussex
border (1870–2): Oakburn, Goldhawk Road, London (1878).

BRANDON, John Raphael: 1817–77
Articled to W. Parkinson in 1836, he and his brother Joshua Arthur
(1821–47) collaborated in practice, and in the authorship of *The
Analysis of Gothic Architecture* (1847): *Parish Churches* (1848): and *Open
Timber Roofs of the Middle Ages* (1860), before the younger brother's
early death. Together, the brothers designed the Croydon and
Epsom Atmospheric Railway Station, Epsom, Surrey (1844–5): and
the work of J. R. Brandon included the Catholic Apostolic Church,
Gordon Square, London (1853): St Peter, Gt. Windmill Street,
London (1861: dem.): Holy Trinity, Townshend Road, Richmond,
Surrey (1870).

THE BRETTINGHAM FAMILY
The name of a Norwich family of masons and architects. Robert
(1696–1768) and Matthew (1699–1769) were the sons of Launcelot
Brettingham, a bricklayer and mason: both were apprenticed to
their father. Robert followed his father's trade until 1753, when he
was appointed architect to the Committee for building the Octagon
Chapel at Norwich, but Thomas Ivory superseded him in this post.
His brother, after visiting Europe, built up a prosperous architectural practice, mainly in Norfolk, where he had numerous influential patrons. In Norwich he built the Shirehouse (1749: dem.
and rebuilt by William Wilkins): No. 11 Surrey Street, and Nos.
15–17 Cow Street. Between 1734 and 1759 he was employed by the
Earl of Leicester to superintend the work at Holkham Hall, Norfolk,

designed by William Kent, and in 1761 he published *The Plans and Elevations of the late Earl of Leicester's House at Holkham*. His work included Langley Park, Norfolk (*c.* 1740): No. 5 St James's Square, London (1748): the Naval and Military Club, No. 94 Piccadilly, London (1756–60): Benacre Hall, Suffolk (1763–4). His son Matthew (1725–1803) toured Italy and Greece in 1747 with Revett and Stuart, where he studied architecture and painting. He assisted his father at Holkham Hall: *c.* 1761 was employed by the Earl of Egremont to collect statues for Petworth House: and carried out rebuilding and alterations at Charlton Park, Wilts. (1772–6): Lord North became his patron. Robert Furze Brettingham (*c.* 1750–*c.* 1806), who was the son of a sister of Matthew Brettingham the younger, adopted the family surname in place of his legal one of Furze. He exhibited at the Royal Academy in 1783: was a founder member of the Architects' Club; was Resident Clerk in the Board of Works from 1794 till 1805: built the Temple of Concord in the grounds of Audley End, Essex (1791).

BRITTON, John, FSA: 1771–1857
Born at Kington St Michael, Wilts., the son of a small shopkeeper: his education was scanty: he became in turn a cellarman, clerk, and writer of songs and criticisms of plays and actors. His first topographical work, *The Beauties of Wiltshire*, was published in 1801, in collaboration with Edward Brayley, and his career as an antiquarian and topographical writer and editor began. He was a member of the Art Union: founder of the Wiltshire Topographical Society, and an honorary member of the Institute of Architects. He published *The Beauties of England and Wales* (1801–14): *Architectural Antiquities of Great Britain* (1805–14) and *Supplement* (1818–26): *Cathedral Antiquities of England* (1814–35): *Specimens of the Architectural Antiquities of Normandy* (1826–8: with the elder Pugin): *Dictionary of the Architecture and Archaeology of the Middle Ages* (1832–38): *Autobiography of John Britton* (1850).

BROCK, Edgar Philip Loftus, FRIBA: 1833–95
The son of James Brock, an Army officer: studied at the Royal Academy Schools, gaining a Silver Medal. In 1851, was articled to W. and E. Habershon; later, became E. Habershon's partner, and in 1879 took over the practice on his retirement. Brock was

Honorary Secretary, and later Treasurer, of the British Archaeolo-
gical Association: he built and remodelled many schools, churches
and institutions, and his work included St Andrew, Hastings,
Sussex (1869: with Habershon): the Old Rectory, West Deeping,
Lincs. (1869): St Stephen, Hammerwood, Sussex (1879–80):
Christ Church, Newhaven, Sussex (1881).

BRODRICK, Cuthbert, FRIBA: 1822–1905
Born in Hull, the son of a shipowner: educated privately, and at
Kingston College, Hull: became a pupil of Henry Lockwood in
1837, and remained as his assistant till 1844. Travelled on the
Continent till 1845, when he set up independent practice in Hull:
served on the Council of the Institute in 1874. After his retirement,
he lived in France, painting, and exhibiting his work, and died in
Jersey. His work in Yorkshire included the Royal Institution, Hull
(1852–4): the Town Hall, Leeds (1853–8): the College of Housecraft (formerly an hotel), Ilkley (c. 1860): the Grand Hotel, Scarborough (1863–7): the Congregational Church, Headingley Lane,
Leeds (1864–6): the Institute of Science, Art and Literature, Leeds
(1865–8): the City Baths, Leeds (1882).

BROOKS, James, FRIBA: 1825–1901
Born at Hatford, nr. Faringdon, Berks., the son of a farmer:
educated Abingdon Grammar School: came to London 1847,
entered the office of Lewis Stride: was admitted to the Royal
Academy Schools 1849: set up independent practice in London in
1852. Much of his work was ecclesiastical: from 1881 until his death
he served on a committee of the Incorporated Church Building
Society, and in 1888 became Diocesan Architect for Canterbury:
was a Vice-President of the Institute 1892–6; and Royal Gold
Medallist 1895. His work included St Columba, Kingsland Road,
Shoreditch, London (1867–71): St Chad, Nichols Square, Shore-
ditch, London, and the Vicarage (1868): Ascension Church,
Lavender Hill, Battersea, London (1873: completed by J. T.
Micklethwaite): St Peter, Boham's Road, Hastings, Sussex (1885):
All Saints, Southend, Essex (1889: west bays later). His son, James
Martin (1859–1903), was educated at Wantage Grammar School
and Merchant Taylors' School: studied at the Royal Academy;
entered his father's office 1878, and became his partner in 1892.

47

BROWN, John: nineteenth century
Exhibited at the Royal Academy 1820–44: appointed County
Surveyor of Norfolk 1835: conducted a large architectural practice,
mainly in East Anglia. He restored the central tower of Norwich
Cathedral (c. 1830), and his work included St Peter, Lowestoft,
Suffolk (1833): Jarrolds' Works, Cowgate, Norwich (1834):
Northgate Hospital (formerly the Workhouse), Gt. Yarmouth,
Norfolk (1838): St Margaret, Lee Terrace, Lewisham, London
(1839–41): All Saints, Witham, Essex (1842): the Corn Hall,
Fakenham, Norfolk (1855).

BROWN, Lancelot: 1716–83 (Portrait: see Plate IV)
Widely known as 'Capability' Brown. Born at Kirkharle, Northumb.: went to the village school at Cambo. Began his career as a
gardener, first at Kirkharle, then at Wotton, near Aylesbury, and in
1740 at Stowe, Bucks., where he met William Kent, with whom he
worked closely. In 1749 became a landscape gardening consultant,
later collaborating with Robert Adam and Henry Holland: and was
himself a capable practising architect: appointed Surveyor to H.M.
Gardens and Waters at Hampton Court 1764. His work, examples
of which exist all over the country, included the design and layout
of Croome Court and grounds (1751–2) and St Mary Magdalene,
Croome, Worcs. (1758–63), in collaboration with Robert Adam:
Claremont House and grounds, Surrey (1770–2: with Henry
Holland): he landscaped the parks and grounds of Petworth House,
Sussex (late 1750s): Audley End, Essex (1763): Hainton Hall,
Lincs. (c. 1763): Alnwick Castle, Northumb. (c. 1765): Grims-
thorpe Castle, Lincs. (1772).

BROWNING, Edward: nineteenth century
Believed to have been the son of Bryan Browning, a Lincolnshire
architect, who practised in London at first, but was established in
Stamford in 1842: he built the Town House, Bourne, Lincs. (1821),
and the House of Correction, Folkingham, Lincs. (1825). Edward
Browning practised in Stamford, where his work included the
Stamford Institution, or Camera Obscura House (1842): the Town
Bridge and adjoining former Toll House (1849: with Bryan Brown-
ing): and the High School for Girls (1876): he also designed Clare
Lodge, Wothorpe, nr. Stamford (1850): the Rectory, Creeton,
Lincs. (1851): and All Saints, Fosdyke, Lincs. (1871–2).

BRUCE, Sir William: *c.* 1630–*c.* 1710

The younger son of Robert Bruce of Blairhall, Fife: he played some part in the restoration of Charles II to the Throne: enjoyed many years of royal patronage: held a number of government posts: and was M.P. for Kinross-shire: created a baronet 1668: a member of the Scottish Privy Council 1685–6. He was appointed Surveyor of Royal Palaces and Works in Scotland 1671, and built up a large private practice before he fell from favour after the Revolution of 1688. He worked at Holyrood Palace (1672–9): and designed Kinross House, Kinross-shire (begun 1685): Hopetoun House, nr. Edinburgh (begun 1698: completed by William Adam the elder), and Mertoun, Berwicks. (1703–7), have also been attributed to him.

BRYCE, David, FRIBA: 1803–76

The son of an Edinburgh builder: educated at Edinburgh High School: trained in his father's office and under William Burn, whose partner he became and remained until 1844. In that year Burn moved to London, and Bryce took over the whole of the Edinburgh practice, which was extremely large and prosperous, and in which his commissions included the building and reconstruction of many Scottish mansions. He was a Royal Scottish Academician: a Fellow of the Architectural Institute of Scotland: a Fellow of the Royal Society of Edinburgh. His work included the British Linen Bank, Edinburgh (1850–2): extensive rebuilding at Ford Castle, Northumb. (1861–5): the Union Bank of Scotland, Edinburgh (1872).

BRYDON, John McKean, FRIBA: 1840–1901

Born at Dunfermline, the son of John Brydon, tailor and draper: educated at the Commercial Academy, Dunfermline: received his training from a Liverpool firm, and in the offices of David Bryce in Edinburgh, and Campbell Douglas in Glasgow: was an assistant to Shaw and Nesfield in London: travelled in Italy. For a time he designed furniture and interior decoration; began architectural practice *c.* 1880: was the author of a number of professional papers. Served on the Council of the Institute, and was a Vice-President 1899–1901. His work included Pickhurst, nr. Chiddingfold, Surrey (1883): the Town Hall, Chelsea, London (1885–7): the Chelsea Polytechnic, London (1891–5): the Village Hall, Forest Row, Sussex (1892): government offices in Whitehall, London (1898–

D

1912: completed by Tanner: Ministry of Housing and Local Government, Treasury, Ministry of Defence, Cabinet Office).

BUCKLER, John, FSA: 1770–1851
Born at Calbourne, I.O.W., he was for many years Clerk to the Steward of Magdalen College, Oxford, till his retirement in 1849. He became well known as an architectural and antiquarian draughtsman: had many patrons among the nobility, who commissioned from him drawings and engravings of cathedrals, churches, castles, church furniture and antiquities: collections of his work may be found in the British Museum and in many county libraries and private collections. He designed the tower of Holy Trinity, Theale, Berks. (1827–8).

BUCKLER, John Chessell, FSA: 1793–1894
The eldest son of John Buckler, whose interest in sketching and architectural draughtsmanship he shared. He published *Views of Cathedral Churches in England* (1822: much of it copied from his father's work): *Sixty Views of Endowed Grammar Schools* (1827): *An Historical and Descriptive Account of the Royal Palace at Eltham* (1828): *Remarks upon Wayside Chapels* (1843): *History of the Architecture of the Abbey Church at St Albans* (1847): *Description of Lincoln Cathedral* (1866). He carried out church restorations for Oxford University, and his work included Butleigh Court, Som. (1845): the Museum, Wisbech, Cambs. (1847): Choristers Hall, Magdalen College, Oxford (1849–51: now the Library): the Turl Street front of Jesus College, Oxford (1854–6): the private Chapel of Lilystone Hall, Stock, Essex (1879). His son, Charles Alban (1824–1905), with whom he built Long Ridge Tower, nr. Horncliffe, Northumb. (1878), was a member of the Order of Malta, a distinguished ecclesiologist, and the architect of the Church of the Immaculate Heart of Mary, Hackney, London (1873): St Dominic, St Pancras, London (1874–83): and St Thomas of Canterbury, Hastings, Sussex (1889).

BUNNING, James Bunstone, FSA, FRIBA: 1802–63
The son of a London surveyor: trained in his father's office: articled to George Smith: set up independent practice in the early 1820s. Became District Surveyor for Bethnal Green: Surveyor to the Foundling Hospital Estates; the London Cemetery Company; the Haberdashers' Company: the London & County Bank: the Thames

Tunnel: and the Victoria Life Office: was Architect to the Chelsea Waterworks, and Clerk of the City's Works (City Architect) 1843–63. His practice was large; he worked extensively for humane and welfare organizations, and carried out much street planning and improvement, notably in the City of London, and New Cross. His work included the chapels and lodges at the South London Cemetery, Nunhead, London (1844): the planning of Cannon Street, London (1846 onwards): the Coal Exchange, Lower Thames Street, London (1847–9: dem.): Holloway Prison, Islington, London (1849–51): the Caledonian Market, Islington, London (1855).

BURGES, William, FRIBA: 1827–81
The son of a civil engineer: educated King's College School; articled to Edward Blore 1844: assistant to Matthew Digby Wyatt 1849: from 1849–54 he spent much time travelling on the Continent, and studying MSS at the British Museum. Contributed articles on architecture to professional and other journals, and published *Art Applied to Industry* (1865): was a designer of jewellery and furniture as well as a practising architect. In 1856 he and Henry Clutton won the international competition for Lille Cathedral, but their design was not used. His work included Trinity College, Hartford, Conn., USA (1857–82): St Finbar's Cathedral, Cork (1865–76): St Michael, Lowfield Heath, Surrey (1867): St Mary, Studley Royal, Yorks. (1871–8): All Saints, Murston, Kent (1874): No. 9 Melbury Road, Kensington, London (1875–80): Castell Coch, Glam. (1875–81): St Anne's Court (working-class dwellings), Wardour Street, London.

BURGH, Colonel Thomas: 1670–1730
An Irishman, the son of Ulysses Burgh, Bishop of Ardagh. He was a landowner in Kildare, and served in the Army before succeeding Sir William Robinson as Surveyor-General of H.M. Fortifications in Ireland, in 1700. He was the author of a treatise on surveying entitled *Right-lined Figures* (1724): his work in Dublin included the Royal Barracks (1701–4: enlarged and altered since; now Collins Barracks): the Library of Trinity College (1712–32): Dr Steevens's Hospital (1720–33).

BURLINGTON, Earl of: see BOYLE

BURN, William: 1789–1870
Born in Edinburgh, the son of Robert Burn, a Scottish architect: received his training and work in the office of Sir Robert Smirke in London: succeeded to his father's Scottish practice *c.* 1820, and practised in Edinburgh in partnership with David Bryce till 1844. For some years he held the government appointment of Consulting Architect to Scotland: was a member of the Institute of British Architects. In 1844 he moved to London, where he established a successful private practice, with a reputation for building country houses. Towards the end of his career his nephew, J. Macvicar Anderson, became his partner. His work included St John's Episcopal Chapel, Edinburgh (1816–18): the Edinburgh Academy (1823–36): interiors and outworks at Harlaxaton Manor, Lincs. (1830s): planning and layout of the village of South Stoke, Lincs. (1840–5): Stoke Rochford Hall, South Stoke, Lincs. (1841): Boughton Park, Northants (1844): the Deanery, Lincoln (1847: now Cathedral School): Lynford Hall, Norfolk (1856–61): the Chapel at Boltby, Yorks. (1859): additions and alterations to Leys, Ganarew, Herefs. (1861–2): Spye Park, Bowden Hill, Wilts. (1865–8).

BURNET, Sir John James, RA, FRIBA: 1857–1938
Born in Glasgow, the son of John Burnet, an architect who practised there, where he designed the Clydesdale Bank, St Vincent Place (1870–3): the Stock Exchange (1875–7): Cleveden Crescent (*c.* 1876). The younger Burnet was educated at Western Academy, Glasgow: studied architecture at the École des Beaux Arts, in Paris, 1874–7: in 1878 entered into partnership with his father: in 1905 moved to London where the great success of his Glasgow practice was repeated, and where he founded the partnership with Thomas Tait and Francis Lorne. He was a Fellow of the Royal Society of Edinburgh, and of the Society of Antiquaries of Scotland: a Royal Scottish Academician: knighted 1914: Royal Gold Medallist 1923. He was the architect for much of Glasgow University: planned the War Cemetery at Jerusalem: and his work included the Royal Institute of Fine Arts, Glasgow (1879–80): the Clyde Trust Building, Glasgow (1883–6): the International Exhibition, Edinburgh (1886): King Edward VII Galleries, British Museum, London (1905–14): Kodak House, Kingsway, London (1911): Royal Institute of Chemistry, Russell Square, London (1915): Second Church of Christ Scientist,

Palace Gardens, Kensington, London (1921): Adelaide House, London Bridge, London (1924–5: with Tait): Royal Masonic Hospital, Ravenscourt Park, London (1931: with Tait and Lorne): Burlington School for Girls, Hammersmith, London (1936: with Tait and Lorne).

BURROUGH, Sir James, FSA: 1691–1764

The son of Dr James Burrough of Bury St Edmunds. Educated at the Grammar School there, and at Caius College, Cambridge, of which he was elected Master in 1754: knighted 1759. A talented amateur architect, he was consulted and advised upon a number of Cambridge buildings, including the Senate House, Caius College, Queen's College, Emmanuel College and Trinity Hall. He designed the New Building, Peterhouse (1738–43), and the Chapel at Clare (1763–9: completed by James Essex).

BURTON, Decimus, FRS, FSA, FRIBA: 1800–81

The son of James Burton (or Haliburton): educated privately: trained by his father and George Maddox: entered the Royal Academy Schools 1817: set up in practice 1821. He was commissioned by the Government in 1825 to design arches, lodges and architectural features in Hyde Park. Was one of the earliest members of the Institute of British Architects, and a Vice-President. In his later years he visited the Mediterranean, Canada, and the USA. He carried out many schemes of town planning and landscaping; laid out the Zoological Gardens in Regent's Park, London (1827): and was responsible for many buildings in Kew Gardens, Surrey, where, in collaboration with the engineer, Richard Turner, he designed the Palm House (1844–8): and for the structural details of the Great Conservatory at Chatsworth, the idea of which was originated by Paxton (1836–40: dem. 1920). Burton's work included The Holme (c. 1818) and Grove House, Regent's Park, London (1822–4): Ionic screen, and Constitution Arch, Hyde Park Corner, London, and Lodges at Cumberland, Grosvenor and Stanhope Gates (1825–6): Lodge at Prince of Wales Gate (1847): the Athenaeum Club, London (1828–30: attic storey added since): layout and building of St Leonards-on-Sea, Sussex (1828 onwards: with James Burton): layout and building of the Calverley Estate, Tunbridge Wells, Kent (1828–52): Holy Trinity, Tunbridge Wells,

Kent (1829): Charing Cross Hospital, London (1831-4: additions since): Grimston Park, Yorks. (1840).

BURTON (or HALIBURTON), James: 1761-1837

A Scottish builder who established a highly successful practice in London, largely in the development of the Bloomsbury, Regent's Park and Regent Street schemes, where he worked closely with John Nash: also at Tunbridge Wells and St Leonards-on-Sea, where his son, Decimus Burton, assisted him in the planning and design of buildings for his speculative schemes. From 1800 onwards, he built Russell Square, Montague Street, Bedford Place, the east side of Tavistock Square, and the streets adjoining Cartwright Gardens, in London: also many of Nash's Regent's Park Terraces, much of Regent Street, and Waterloo Place.

BURY, Thomas Talbot, FSA, FRIBA: 1811-77

A pupil of Augustus Pugin in 1824: assisted A. W. N. Pugin and Owen Jones in engraving for their books. Began practice in 1830, and was in partnership with Charles Lee 1845-9: contributed to the *Builder*, and was the author of *Remains of Ecclesiastical Woodwork* (1847), and *History and Description of the Styles of Architecture of Various Countries, from the Earliest to the Present Period* (1849). Assisted A. W. N. Pugin in his work for Sir Charles Barry on the Houses of Parliament: assisted Lewis Vulliamy for a time. He built a large number of churches, chiefly in the southern counties and suburbs and environs of London, and his work included St Paul, Chipperfield, Herts. (1837): St Lawrence, Bovingdon, Herts. (1845): almshouses at Lambourn, Berks. (1852): St Gregory, Welford, Berks. (1852-5): New Lodge, Winkfield, Berks. (1858): St John, Burgess Hill, Sussex (1861-3): St Mary, East Molesey, Surrey (1864-7).

BUSBY, Charles Augustus: 1788-1834

The son of Dr Thomas Busby, musician: studied under D. A. Alexander: and at the Royal Academy Schools where he won the Gold Medal 1807: during a visit to America (*c.* 1815-20) he published 'An Essay on the Propulsion of Navigable Bodies' (1818), the result of a study of New York ferry boats. On his return to England he became involved in a professional dispute with Smirke and Nash, and published a pamphlet vindicating the design in question, in 1822. In the same year he set up in partnership with

Amon Wilds and his son, A. H. Wilds, at Brighton, and with them was responsible for much of the development which took place there between 1820 and 1830 under the control of Thomas Read Kemp. In 1832 he became Surveyor in charge of Brunswick Town at Brighton. Busby was the author of *A Series of Designs for Villas and Country Houses adapted with Economy to the Comforts and Elegancies of Modern Life, with Plans and Explanations to Each* (1808): and *A Collection of Designs for Modern Embellishments, suitable to Parlours and Dining Rooms, Folding Doors, Chimney Pieces, Verandas, Frizes, etc. on 25 Plates* (1810). In collaboration with the Wildses his work at Brighton included the Gothic House, Western Road (*c.* 1822–5): the design and layout of Kemp Town and Brunswick Town (1823–*c.* 1850): St George's Chapel, St George's Road (1824–5): and Portland Place (1824–*c.* 1830). Independently, Busby built the Commercial Rooms, Bristol (1810–11): and SS Andrew and Mary Magdalene, Maidenhead, Berks. (1822–5: dem.).

BUTTERFIELD, William, FSA: 1814–1900
The son of a London chemist: articled to a London builder and to an architect in Worcester, where his architectural career began: by 1844 he had an established London practice, and had become an active member of the Cambridge Camden Society. He contributed articles to the *Ecclesiologist*, and illustrations to 'Instrumenta Ecclesiastica', both published by the Society, and in 1886 published a small book on church seats and kneeling boards: he was Royal Gold Medallist in 1884. He had an enormous practice: built numbers of churches, parsonages, and schools, and carried out many church restorations. His work included Highbury Chapel, St Michael's Hill, Bristol (1842–3): St Cuthbert, Sessay, Yorks. (1847–8): St Augustine's College, Canterbury, Kent (1848): All Saints, Margaret Street, London (1849–59): St Mary Magdalen, West Lavington, Sussex, and the Rectory (1850): All Saints, Wykeham, Yorks., the Parsonage and School (1853): the School, Hutton Buscel, Yorks. (1854): St James, Baldersby, Yorks., the School, Vicarage, and cottages in the village (1856–8): the School at Aldbourne, Wilts. (1857–8): St Nicholas School, Newbury, Berks. (1859): St Cross, New Road, Manchester (1863): Holy Saviour, Hitchen, Herts. (1865): St Augustine, Queen's Gate, London (1868): All Saints, Babbacombe, Devonshire (1868–74): St Mary, Beech Hill, Berks., and the Parsonage (1873): Keble

College, Oxford (1875): Gordon Boys' Home, Chobham, Surrey (1885): the Chapel at the Guards' Depot, Caterham, Surrey (1886).

BYFIELD, George: *c.* 1756–1813
Believed to have been a pupil of Sir Robert Taylor: exhibited at the Royal Academy 1780–1812. Was Surveyor to the Estates of the Dean and Chapter of Westminster: much of his practice was in Worcestershire and Herefordshire: was in partnership with H. H. Seward 1810–13. His work included Perdiswell Hall, nr. Worcester (1787–8: dem.), and the Chapel in the grounds of Brockhampton Park, nr. Bromyard, Herefs. (*c.* 1798). He specialized in prison building and built the old Gaol at Bury St Edmunds, Suffolk (1803: to the designs of the prison governor): the County Gaol at Canterbury, Kent (1803): and Papworth House and Lodge, Cambs. (1809–11).

CAMELFORD, 1st Baron: see PITT

CAMERON, Charles: c. 1740–1812
A Scottish architect, whose book *The Baths of the Romans Explained and Illustrated, with the Restorations of Palladio corrected and Improved* (1772) brought him to the notice of the Empress Catherine of Russia. He was her chief architect till her death in 1796; after a few years of private practice in Russia he became architect to the Russian Admiralty in 1805. His work in Russia included the Great Palace, Pavolvsk (1781–96): the Cathedral of St Sophia (1782–87): extensive alterations at the Palace of Tsarskoe Seloe, nr. St Petersburg (1783–5): the Agate Pavilion (1783–5): the Batourin Palace, Ukraine (1790–1800): the Naval Hospital and Barracks, Kronstadt (c. 1805).

CAMPBELL, Colen, or Colin: d. 1729
Nothing is known of his early life: he was Chief Clerk of the King's Works and Deputy Surveyor, in 1718, under William Benson, but lost his posts, as did Benson, in 1719. The Earl of Burlington became his patron, and is believed to have first become interested in Palladian architecture when Campbell's *Vitruvius Britannicus* was published (in 3 volumes, 1715, 1717, 1725). He was Surveyor to Greenwich Hospital, 1726: in 1729 his edition of Palladio's *Five Orders of Architecture* was published. His work included remodelling at Burlington House, Piccadilly, London (1716: with the Earl of Burlington and James Gibbs): Wanstead House, Essex (1715: dem.): Ebberston Hall, Yorks. (1718): Baldersby Park, Yorks. (1720–1): Stourhead, Wilts. (1721–4: wings by Thomas Atkinson): Houghton Hall, Norfolk (1721–35: executed by Thomas Ripley: corner domes by James Gibbs): Mereworth Castle, Kent (c. 1722–5): the Great Room at Hall Barn, nr. Beaconsfield, Bucks. (1724): remodelling of Compton Place, nr. Eastbourne, Sussex (1726–31: much altered since).

CARLINE, John: eighteenth–nineteenth century
In partnership with John Tilley, a stonemason of Shrewsbury, he designed and built the Welsh Bridge (1791–5): St Alkmund (1793–5): and Claremont Buildings (pre-1815), all in Shrewsbury.

CAROË, WILLIAM

Carline himself designed and built St Michael, Shrewsbury (1829–30), and his son John was the architect of All Saints, Grinshill, Salop (1839–40). With his other son, Thomas, the Carline family carried on a considerable practice in Shropshire as sculptors and architects.

CAROË, William Douglas, FSA, FRIBA: 1857–1938
Born in Liverpool, where his father, A. K. Caroë, was Danish Consul: educated Trinity College, Cambridge: articled to J. L. Pearson: was in partnership with Herbert Passmore for many years. President of the AA 1895, and served on the Council of the Institute. His practice was very large and mainly ecclesiastical: he built and restored many churches: was Consulting Architect to a number of Cathedrals, including Canterbury, Durham, and Southwell, and to the Charity Commissioners: and was Architect to Malvern Priory and Romsey and Tewkesbury Abbeys. His work included St Stephen, Nottingham (1897): St David, Exeter (1897–1900): Houses for Wycombe Abbey School on Marlow Hill, High Wycombe, Bucks. (1898–1902), and the School Chapel (1926): Coleherne Court, Redcliffe Gardens, London (1901–3): St Michael Bassishaw (1901) and St Aldhelm (1903), both at Edmonton, Middlesex: St Barnabas, Walthamstow, Essex (1902): St Edward's House, Gt. Smith Street, London (1906): the Bishop's Palace, Southwell, Notts. (1907–9): Dibden House, Maida Vale, London (1937: with Passmore): University College of South Wales and Monmouthshire, Cardiff: new buildings for the National Physical Laboratory, Teddington, Middlesex.

CARPENTER, Richard Cromwell: 1812–55
The son of a Deputy Lord Lieutenant of Middlesex: educated at Charterhouse: articled to John Blyth. He was a friend of A. W. N. Pugin: associated with the Cambridge Camden Society: and a member of the consulting committee of architects of the Incorporated Church Building Society: in partnership with William Slater. His work included the design of Lonsdale Square, Islington, London (1842–5): St Paul, Brighton, Sussex (1846–8: the tower and spire by his son, R. H. Carpenter): St Peter, West Street, Chichester, Sussex (1848): St Mary Magdalene, Munster Square, London (1849–52): St John's College, Hurstpierpoint, Sussex (1851–3: chapel by R. H. Carpenter): SS Mary and Nicholas

58

College, Lancing, Sussex (begun 1854: completed by William Slater and R. H. Carpenter). His son, Richard Herbert, FSA, FRIBA (1841–93), was a member of the Council of the Institute, associated with William Slater after his father's death, and later in partnership with Benjamin Inglelow. His work included Elles-mere College, Ellesmere, Salop (1879–83: with Inglelow): the chapel of St Chad's College, Denstone, Staffs. (1888): St Hugh, Charterhouse Mission, Bermondsey, London (1892–8: with In-glelow).

CARR, John: 1723–1807
The son of Robert Carr, a mason and quarry-owner of Horbury, Yorks.: educated at the village school: then worked with his father: in 1750 carried out the building of Kirby Hall, Yorks., designed by Lord Burlington. In 1754, Carr himself designed the grandstand at Knavesmire Racecourse, York (dem.): and set up in private practice in York: he became a prosperous and fashion-able architect, enjoying considerable patronage from the local nobility. He was an alderman of the City, and Lord Mayor in 1770 and in 1785: a West Riding Magistrate: and in 1791 became a member of the Architects' Club in London. From 1779–84 he assisted the 5th Duke of Devonshire in the development of Buxton, Derbys., where he laid out the Crescent, and Hall Bank, and built the Stables (later the nucleus of the Devonshire Royal Hospital). His work included Harewood House, Yorks. (1759–71: in collabor-ation with Robert Adam: alterations later by Sir Charles Barry): the rebuilding of Harewood village, Yorks. (1760): the Town Hall, Newark, Notts. (1773): the County Assize Courts, York Castle, York (1773–7): Basildon Park, Berks. (1776): Colwick Hall, Notts. (1776): Grimston Garth, Holderness, Yorks. (1781–6): the Gaol, Lincoln Castle, Lincoln (1787: with William Lumby): SS Peter and Leonard, Horbury, Yorks. (1791).

CARTER, John, FSA: 1748–1817
The son of Benjamin Carter, a London mason and monumental sculptor: worked at first for his father: in 1766 studied architecture under Joseph Dixon: in 1768 started his career as an antiquarian draughtsman, working for Henry Holland, and later providing drawings for the *Builder's Magazine*, and Gough's *History of Croyland* and *Sepulchral Monuments*. He was also an amateur musician and

composed two operas. His patrons included Horace Walpole and the Society of Antiquaries. In 1798 he began a long association with the *Gentleman's Magazine*, and the articles he contributed did much to improve methods of church restoration and to rectify the neglected state of many churches. He published *Specimens of Ancient Sculpture and Painting* (1780–94): *Views of Ancient Buildings in England* (1786–93): and *The Ancient Architecture of England* (1795–1814). His small output of architectural work included the old Middlesex Sessions House, Clerkenwell Green, London (1774: built by Thomas Rogers, who is alleged to have appropriated the design as his own): St Peter's Chapel, Winchester (1792): and the east Chapel of St Mary the Virgin and All Saints, Debden, Essex (1793).

CASSELS (or CASTLE), Richard: *c.* 1690–1751
Born at Hesse-Cassel, in Germany: began to practise as an architect in Dublin, in 1729, having been brought to Ireland in 1727 by an Irish gentleman, Sir Gustavus Hume, in order to build him a country house. Cassels was a military engineer, and designed the first stone lock in Ireland: he became one of the best known of Irish architects, working chiefly in Dublin, but he also built many large country houses, including Carton, Co. Kildare (1739), and Powerscourt and Russborough (1741) in Co. Wicklow. In Dublin his work included No. 80 St Stephen's Green (1730: now part of Iveagh House): the Rotunda Lying-in Hospital (built by John Ensor after Cassels' death): Nos. 9 and 10 Henrietta Street (*c.* 1730): the Printing House, New Square (1734): Tyrone House (1740–5): Leinster House (1745): the staircase of Trinity College Library (1750). He was the author of *Essay towards Supplying the City of Dublin with Water* (1736).

CATES, Arthur, FRIBA: 1829–1901
Born in London, the son of James Cates: educated King's College School: a pupil of Sydney Smirke: a member of the Institute's Council, and a Vice-President 1888–92. He had much to do with creating the Institute's examination system, and was Chairman of the Board of Examiners 1882–96. From 1859–92 he was Hon. Secretary of the Architectural Publication Society, and assisted Wyatt Papworth in the production of the *Dictionary of Architecture*. He was a Fellow of the Surveyors' Institution: Hon. Treasurer of

the Architects' Benevolent Society: Hon. Secretary to the Council of the Society of Biblical Archaeology: Surveyor to the Honourable Society of the Middle Temple: in 1870 he succeeded Sir James Pennethorne as Architect to the Land Revenues of the Crown under the Commissioners of Woods and Forests. His work included the Gatehouse from Tudor Street to King's Bench Walk, London (1887).

CHAMBERS, Sir William, FRS: 1726–96 (Portrait: Plate V)
Born at Gothenburg, Sweden, the son of John Chambers, a merchant: educated at Ripon: returned to Sweden: and from 1740–49 worked for the Swedish East India Company, making voyages to the Far East. In 1749 he began to study architecture seriously, first in Paris, then in Italy, and in 1755 returned to England and set up in practice in London. His appointment as architectural tutor to the Prince of Wales (later George III) led to continued royal patronage and commissions. In 1761 he became Architect of the King's Works jointly with Robert Adam, and in this capacity designed the Royal State Coach which is still used for coronations. He was Comptroller of the Board of Works in 1769: and the first Surveyor-General of H.M. Office of Works when this came into existence in 1782. Because of the honour conferred on him in 1770, when he received the Order of the Polar Star from the King of Sweden, George III permitted him to assume the rank and title of knighthood. Chambers did much to further the foundation of the Royal Academy, whose first Treasurer he became: took part in the meetings of the Architects' Club: designed furniture, interior decoration, landscaping, and many buildings in the Classic and Chinese style. He published various works on gardening, design and architecture, including *Designs of Chinese Buildings, Furniture, Dresses, Machines and Utensils* (1757): *A Treatise on Civil Architecture* (1759): *Plans, Elevations, Sections and Perspective Views of the Gardens and Buildings at Kew in Surrey* (1763): *A Dissertation on Oriental Gardening* (1772). His work included Manresa House, Roehampton Lane, Wandsworth, London (1750): the Stables at Goodwood House, Sussex (1757–63): planning of the Gardens, and the Orangery, Temples and Pagoda at Kew Gardens, Surrey (1759–62): the Clontarf Casino, Marino, nr. Dublin (*c.* 1762 onwards): the Temple of Romulus and Remus, Coleby Hall, Lincs. (1762): Peper Harow House, Surrey (1763–75: additions since): Walcot,

nr. Lydbury North, Salop. (after 1763): Melbourne House, Piccadilly, London (1770–4: additions later by Henry Holland, when it became the Albany Chambers): Royal Bank of Scotland, St Andrew Square, Edinburgh (1771–2): Wick House, Richmond Hill, Surrey (1772): Somerset House, London (1776 onwards: extensions later by Sir Robert Smirke and Sir James Pennethorne): Poston Lodge, Vowchurch Herefs. (*c.* 1780: wings added since).

CHAMPNEYS, Basil: 1842–1935
Son of the Dean of Lichfield: educated Charterhouse, and Trinity College, Cambridge: articled to John Prichard of Llandaff: set up in private practice 1867: Royal Gold Medallist 1912. He was the author of *A Quiet Corner of England* (1875): *Henry Merritt: Art Criticism and Romance* (1879): *Memoirs and Correspondence of Coventry Patmore* (1900). Much of his large practice consisted of educational buildings. His work included St Luke, Kentish Town, London, and the Vicarage (1868–70): Harwood Road School, Eel Brook Common, Fulham, London (1873): Newnham College, Cambridge (1875–1935): Selwyn Divinity School, Cambridge (1878–9): the Indian Institute, Oxford (1880s): St Bride's Vicarage, Bridewell Place, London (1885): the Butler Museum, Harrow School, Middlesex (1886): Mansfield College, Oxford (1888): Rylands Library, Manchester (1890): SS Andrew and Michael, Blackwall Lane, Greenwich, London (1900–2): King Edward VII Grammar School, King's Lynn, Norfolk (1903): Bedford College, Regent's Park, London (1910–13: additions since).

CHATWIN, Julius Alfred, FRIBA: 1829–1907
Born in Birmingham: educated King Edward's School there, and at London University: worked for a firm of building contractors: articled to Sir Charles Barry 1851. He built up a very large and important private practice in Birmingham, carried on by his descendants: he was Architect to the Governors of King Edward's School: and a Fellow of the Society of Antiquaries of Scotland. His work in Birmingham included Lloyds Bank, Temple Row (1864): Greek Orthodox Church, Summer Lane (1873: built as a Catholic Apostolic church): the complete rebuilding of St Martin, Bull Ring (1873–5: restored after war damage by his son, P. B. Chatwin): Grand Hotel (1875): St Paul, Lozells, Aston (1880):

SS Mary and Ambrose, Edgbaston (1897–8): other work in War-wickshire included the Grammar School, Solihull (1879–82): Church of the Holy Ascension, Mappleborough Green (1888).

CHAWNER, Thomas: 1774–1851
A pupil of Sir John Soane 1788–94: studied at the Royal Academy Schools 1797. After some years of working at the Land Revenue Department, he became Surveyor there in 1809: in 1832 was appointed (with Henry Rhodes) one of the Joint Architects and Surveyors to the newly constituted Woods and Forests Board, and held this post till 1845. His work included the completion of St Peter, Chertsey, Surrey (1807–8: begun by Richard Elsam): Richmond Terrace, Whitehall, London (1822–5): and an entrance from Duke Street to St James's Park, London (1834: with Rhodes).

CHRISTIAN, Ewan, FRIBA: 1814–95
Educated Christ's Hospital: articled to Matthew Habershon c. 1830: and contributed sketches to Habershon's *Half-Timbered Houses*: worked in the offices of John Brown of Norwich, and William Railton: toured Italy 1837, before setting up in private practice. He served on the Council of the Institute; was a Vice-President; and from 1884–6 President: Royal Gold Medallist 1887: Consulting Architect to the Ecclesiastical Commissioners 1850–95: and to the Charity Commissioners 1887–95: a member of the committee of architects of the Incorporated Church Building Society: and Consulting Architect to the Diocesan Church Building Societies at Carlisle and Lichfield. His extensive practice was largely devoted to church restorations, and the building of new churches, schools and parsonages. His work included St John the Evangelist, Hildenborough, Kent (1884): St Thomas, Douglas, I.O.M. (1849): Manor House, Market Lavington, Wilts. (1865): Nos. 4–9 Amen Court, London (1879): Holy Trinity, Scarborough, Yorks. (1880): National Portrait Gallery, London (1890–5): Surrey Convalescent Home, Seaford, Sussex (1891).

CHUTE, John: 1701–76
The son of Edward Chute: educated at Eton: travelled abroad till 1754 when he succeeded to his father's estate at The Vyne, Hants. A friend of Horace Walpole, and a talented amateur architect, he designed a large part of Strawberry Hill, Twickenham,

63

Middlesex (1749–63), including the Library and Gothic Chapel. His work included Chalfont House, Chalfont St Peter, Bucks. (*c.* 1755): considerable alterations to his own house, The Vyne, Hants (*c.* 1765): and Donnington Grove, Donnington, Berks. (before 1772).

CLARKE, Dr George: 1661–1736
The son of Sir William Clarke, secretary at war to Charles II: educated Brasenose College, Oxford: a DCL: a Fellow of All Souls, Oxford, in 1680; from 1717–36 he was M.P. for Oxford University. His political career included government appointments: he was Joint Secretary to the Admiralty; and from 1710–14 a Lord of the Admiralty. A gifted amateur architect, he possessed considerable taste and talent; and at Oxford, where he was often associated with Hawksmoor, his advice on designs and buildings was widely sought by the University authorities. His work at Oxford included the Warden's House, All Souls (1706): the Library of Christ Church (1716): the new buildings of Worcester College (*c.* 1720: assisted by Hawksmoor): rebuilding of the hall of All Souls (1729). Outside Oxford, the design of the Rectory at Kingston Bagpuize, Berks. (1723) is attributed to him.

CLARKE, George Somers, FRIBA: 1825–82
A pupil of Sir Charles Barry: travelled widely in England and on the Continent. He was an accomplished draughtsman and architectural artist; and established a considerable private practice, designing country houses, warehouses and office buildings in London. In 1849, in collaboration with J. Johnson, FSA, he illustrated *The New Palace of Westminster*. His work included the Turkish Baths, Jermyn Street, London; Cowley Manor, Oxon. (1854–62): Wanstead Hospital, Hermon Hill, Wanstead, Essex (1861: built as the Merchant Seamen's Orphan Asylum): the Bank of Australasia, Lothbury, London (1866: built as the Auction Mart).

CLARKE, Joseph, FSA, FRIBA: 1819–88
A pupil of John Griffith: he was an early promoter of elementary schools, and the author of *Schools and School-Houses*. His large practice lay chiefly in church restorations and ecclesiastical and school building. He was a founder and Vice-President of the Architectural Museum, from which the AA grew, and for which

III

JAMES GIBBS
1682–1754

[*National Portrait
Gallery, London*

WILLIAM KENT
c. 1685–1748

*National Portrait
Gallery, London*]

IV

RICHARD BOYLE, 3rd
Earl of Burlington
1694–1753

[RIBA

LANCELOT BROWN
1716–83

*National Portrait
Gallery, London*]

he designed premises in Westminster, with Ewan Christian. Clarke was President of the Ecclesiastical Surveyors' Association: a member of the Institute's Council and a Vice-President 1867–9: Diocesan Surveyor for Canterbury, Rochester and St Albans: Consulting Architect to the Charity Commissioners, and to the Incorporated Church Building Society: Joint Architect to the Bakers' Company. His work included the Mental Hospital, Burwood, Surrey (1840: built as the Metropolitan Convalescent Institution: enlarged later): Hockerill Training College, Bishops Stortford, Herts. (1852): St Mary the Virgin, Farnham, Essex (1859): St Philip, Whitwood, Yorks. (1865): Bishops Stortford College, Herts. (1867: additions since).

CLARKE, Somers, FSA: 1841–1926

Born in Brighton, the son of Somers Clarke, a solicitor: a pupil of Sir George Gilbert Scott, as was J. T. Micklethwaite, with whom Clarke was in partnership 1876–92. They collaborated so closely that individual identification of their work is often impossible, and together they carried out many restorations of old churches. Clarke was well known as an antiquary and ecclesiologist: he was Surveyor to the Fabric of St Paul's Cathedral 1897: Architect to Chichester Cathedral 1900–2: author of *Christian Antiquities in the Nile Valley*: for health reasons he spent a good deal of time in Egypt, where he did much on the repair of ancient temples; he retired to that country and died there. His work included the installation of electric lighting at St Paul's Cathedral: St Martin, Brighton, Sussex (1874–5): St Mary, Stretton, nr. Tutbury, Staffs. (1877: with Micklethwaite): St Paul, Putney, London (1877: with Micklethwaite): St John the Divine, Gainsborough, Lincs. (1881–2: with Micklethwaite): Holy Trinity, Ardington, Berks. (1887: except tower and spire).

CLIFTON, E. N., FRIBA: 1817–89

Born in Islington, London, the son of Dr Nathaniel Clifton: educated Charterhouse: articled to William Inwood and remained as his assistant till 1837: set up his own practice 1838: later was in partnership for many years with Sir William Tite. Clifton did much railway survey and valuation work, and built many railway stations on the old London & South Western line: he was a Fellow of the Surveyors' Institution: an Associate of the Institute of Civil Engineers:

E

District Surveyor of Bethnal Green: Architect to the Holborn Viaduct Land Company: and Surveyor to the Liverpool & London & Globe Insurance Co., the London & Westminster Bank, the Tallow Chandlers' Company, the London & Blackwall Railway, the East London Railway Co., the London & South-Western Railway Co. His work included St James, Chillingworth Road, Islington, London (1837–8: with Inwood): Epsom College, Surrey (1853: built as the Royal Medical Benevolent College): additions to Mann, Crossman & Paulin's Brewery, London (1853–5): the Imperial Hotel, Torquay, Devonshire.

CLUTTON, Henry, FRIBA: 1819–93
A pupil of Edward Blore: in partnership with William Burges for a time: together they won the competition for Lille Cathedral in 1856, but their design was not used. Clutton was the author of *Domestic Architecture of France in the Middle Ages*: much of his work was ecclesiastical, for the Roman Catholic Church. In 1875 he was appointed architect to the proposed new Roman Catholic Cathedral at Westminster, for which he prepared designs, but which was later designed and built by his pupil, J. F. Bentley. Clutton's work included St Mary, Ewell, Surrey (1848): Balcombe Place, Sussex (1856: additions later): restoration of the chapter house at Salisbury Cathedral, Wilts. (1857: with Burges): Quantock Lodge, Over Stowey, Som. (1857: later a Chest Clinic): Battle Abbey School, Sussex (1857: constructed from the domestic premises of Battle Abbey): the Welsh Charity School, Ashford, Middlesex (1857): the clock tower at Cliveden, Bucks. (1861): the chapel of the Sacred Heart in the Church of the Immaculate Conception, Farm Street, London (c. 1863): St Mary Magdalene, Tavistock, Devon (1865): St Mary, Woburn, Beds. (1865–8): Welcombe House, nr. Stratford-upon-Avon, Warwicks. (1867): the New School, St Mary's College, Spinkhill, Derbys. (1876): Church of our Lady of Consolation, Lynford, Norfolk (1879).

COATES, Wells Wintemute, OBE, RDI, FRIBA: 1895–1958
Born in Tokio: educated in Canada: came to London 1924 as an engineering research student, and gained his degree of PH.D. He was in private architectural practice in London 1929–39: in 1933 played a large part in the creation of the MARS Group (Modern Architectural Research), and was a pioneer of what was known in

the 1930s as the modern movement in architecture. He practised with success as an industrial designer, and worked on town planning projects. He served in both World Wars: moved to Vancouver, where he started to practise, in 1956. His work included interiors of a number of Studios at Broadcasting House, London (1930–2): Lawn Road Flats, Hampstead, London (1934): Embassy Court, Bedford Square, Brighton, Sussex (1934–5): Flats at No. 10 Palace Gate, Kensington, London (1938): the Telecinema at the South Bank Exhibition of 1951, in London.

COCKERELL, Charles Robert, RA: 1788–1863
Born in London, the second son of S. P. Cockerell: educated Westminster School: from 1804–9 trained in his father's office: toured Wales and the West of England: was for a time assistant to Sir Robert Smirke, before making a continental tour devoted to archaeological and antiquarian studies, in Asia Minor, Greece, Malta, Sicily and Italy. Set up in practice 1817: succeeded his father as Surveyor to St Paul's Cathedral 1819, and Sir John Soane as Architect to the Bank of England 1833. Was appointed Professor of Architecture 1840: awarded the first Royal Gold Medal of the RIBA 1848: and became the first professional President of the Institute, succeeding Earl de Grey in 1860. He was a member of the Society of Dilettanti, an HON.DCL of Oxford, a Chevalier of the Legion of Honour, a Member of the Institute of France, and of the Academy of St Luke, Rome, and was awarded many other foreign academic honours. His skill as a draughtsman was exceptional: he was the author of *The Temples of Jupiter Panhellenius at Egina and of Apollo Epicurus at Bassae* (1860): *The Antiquities of Athens and other places of Greece, Sicily, etc.* (1830): *The Temple of Jupiter Olympius at Agrigentum* (1830): *The Iconography of the West Front of Wells Cathedral* (1851): and contributed many papers to the *Archaeological Journal*. His work included additions at Oakley Park, Salop (1820): a new ball and cross on the lantern of St Paul's Cathedral, London (1820): the enlargement of Old School, Harrow, Middlesex (1820): chapel at Bowood House, Wilts. (1822–4): St David's College, Lampeter, Cards. (1822–7): Bank of England, Courtney Street, Plymouth (1835): Seckford Hospital, Woodbridge, Suffolk (1836–40): Old University Library, Cambridge (1836–42): Sun Life Assurance Office, 63 Threadneedle Street, London (1839–42): Ashmolean Museum and Taylorian

Institute, Oxford (1839–42): Bank of England, Broad Street, Bristol (1844–7): Bank of England, King Street, Manchester (1845): Bank of England, Castle Street, Liverpool (1845–48): St George's Hall, Liverpool (1851–4: completion of H. L. Elmes's design, with Sir Robert Rawlinson): Liverpool, London & Globe Insurance Company's offices, Dale Street, Liverpool (1855–7: with F. P. Cockerell).

COCKERELL, Frederick Pepys, FRIBA: 1833–78

Born in London, the second son of Charles Robert Cockerell: educated Winchester and King's College, London. In 1850 he visited France on a sketching tour, did some work connected with the Great Exhibition, and in 1853 went to France to study architecture: was a pupil of P. C. Hardwick from 1854–5: then toured France and Italy. He set up in practice about 1858: was Hon. Secretary of the Institute in 1871: and a Trustee of Sir John Soane's Museum. He built many country houses, and his work included No. 25 Old Bond Street, London (1865): St Mark, Marske-by-the-Sea, Yorks. (1865–7): Highgate School, London (1865–8: additions since): Memorial Column in the grounds of Castle Howard, Yorks. (1869–70): Lythe Hill House, Haslemere, Surrey (c. 1870): Woodcote Hall, Salop (1875): Nos. 1 and 2 South Audley Street, London (c. 1878–9: completed by George Aitchison the younger).

COCKERELL, Samuel Pepys: c. 1754–1827

The son of John Cockerell of Bishop's Hull, Somerset: his mother was related to the family of Samuel Pepys, the diarist. He became a pupil of Sir Robert Taylor: was Clerk of the Works at the Tower of London 1775–82: and at Newmarket 1780–82: Surveyor to the Admiralty 1786: and to the Foundling and Pulteney Estates 1788: Surveyor to the Sees of Canterbury and London: the East India Company 1806–24: and St Paul's Cathedral 1811–19. His work as Surveyor to the Foundling Hospital in London was the subject of much criticism of his efficiency, and a surveyor-in-charge (Joseph Kay) was appointed in 1807: Cockerell was however responsible for the layout of Brunswick and Mecklenburgh Squares (1790–1807), and later for part of residential Bayswater between Edgware and Bayswater Roads. His work included Admiralty House, Whitehall, London (1786–8): restoration and rebuilding of St Peter, Tickencote, Rutland (1792): rebuilding of St Mary,

Banbury, Oxon. (1793): the tower of St Anne, Soho, London (1802–6): interiors at Sezincote House, nr. Moreton-in-the-Marsh, Glos. (c. 1805): No. 32 St James's Square, London (1819–21: with C. R. Cockerell).

COE, Henry Edward: 1826–85

The son of Henry John Coe, a solicitor: a pupil of Sir George Gilbert Scott: awarded the first premium for his Foreign Office design in the competition for Government offices, 1856, for which Scott was ultimately commissioned. Coe was in partnership at different times with Goodwin, Frederick Peck of Maidstone, Stephen Robinson, and Arthur Catt: Peck designed the Royal Albert Almshouses, Cambridge (1859: with Stevens): the Prison, Greetwell Road, Lincoln (1872): and the old Workhouse (now a Hospital), Maldon, Essex (1873). Coe's work included Holy Trinity, Bracknell, Berks. (1851 and 1859: with Goodwin): Christ Church, Coatham, Yorks. (1854: with Goodwin): Christ Church, Ugthorpe, Yorks. (1855–7: with Goodwin): All Saints, Garsdon, Wilts. (1856: with Goodwin): the Agricultural Hall, Islington, London (1861–2: with F. Peck): Framlingham College, Suffolk (1864: with F. Peck: built as one of the Albert Memorial Colleges): Crown Point Hall, Trowse Newton, Norfolk (c. 1865): Trent College, Long Eaton, Derbys. (1866–8): St Paul's, St John's Hill, Battersea, London (1868): Holy Trinity, Worthing, Sussex (1882: with Robinson).

COLCUTT, Thomas Edward, FRIBA: 1840–1924

Born in Oxford: educated Oxford Diocesan School at Cowley, and at Mill Hill School: articled to R. E. Armstrong: worked in the office of Miles and Murgatroyd: became assistant to G. E. Street. He travelled extensively on the Continent: after a short partnership with Woodzell, he set up in independent practice c. 1872: later, he was in partnership with Stanley Hamp for many years. Colcutt was President of the RIBA 1906–8: Royal Gold Medallist 1902: and received many foreign architectural honours. He designed the decoration of many P. & O. Line vessels: four houses at Eton, Waynflete and Westbury (1899–1900), Wotton (1903), and Walpole (1906): and his work included the Town Hall, Wakefield, Yorks. (1877–80): Savoy Hotel, London (1889) and Savoy Court (1903–4): Nos. 38 and 40 Wigmore Street, London

69

(1890): Palace Theatre, Cambridge Circus, London (1890): Nos. 45–47 Ludgate Hill, London (1890): Wraysbury Hall, Bucks. (1892): Frascati's Restaurant, Oxford Street, London (1893: dem.): Imperial Institute, Kensington, London (1893: dem. except for the tower): The Croft, Totteridge, Herts. (1895): Lloyd's Shipping Register, Fenchurch Street, London (1900): extensions at Mill Hill School, Middlesex (1907).

COLLING, James Kennaway, FRIBA: 1816–1905
His father was Clerk of Works at Covent Garden and Hungerford Market in London. Delicacy in childhood debarred him from a normal education: from 1828–9 he worked in the London office of William Brooks: spent four years training as an engineer: from 1832–6 worked for Matthew Habershon: and from 1836–40 for John Brown of Norwich: later he spent some months with Scott and Moffatt. In his early years of practice he found a patron in Richard Naylor, a wealthy Liverpool banker. Colling's brother, William (d. 1886), also studied under Habershon and Brown, and from 1846–86 worked for William Burn and J. Macvicar Anderson. James Colling was a draughtsman of great ability: a talented water-colour artist: well known for his drawings from nature of flowers and foliage; and contributed drawings to the *Illustrated London News*. He published *Details of Gothic Architecture from existing examples* (1852–6): *Gothic Ornament* (1846–50): *Art Foliage* (1865): *Examples of English Mediaeval Foliage and Coloured Decoration* (1874). He was a founder of the AA, and its Hon. Secretary 1850–1. His work included St Paul, Hooton, Cheshire: Albany Building, Old Hall Street, Liverpool (1856): Coxwold Hall, Lincs. (1861): restoration of St Withburga, Holkham, Norfolk (1870): interior detail at St Andrew, Scole, Norfolk (1874) and at St Dionysius, Kelmarsh, Northants (1874).

COMPER, Sir Ninian: 1864–1960
Born in Aberdeen: educated at the Ruskin School of Art, Oxford, and Royal College of Art, London: articled to Bodley and Garner. He was well known for his church restorations, and had a very large practice, devoted to ecclesiastical work, in the style of the Gothic Revival, and which included interior design, stained glass windows, and church furnishings and fittings. He was knighted 1950. He was the author of *Of the Christian Altar and the Buildings*

Which Contain It (1950), and his work included St Cyprian, Clarence Gate, London (1903): Holy Trinity, Southchurch, Essex (1906: chancel by F. C. Eden): St Mary, Wellingborough, Northants (1908): St Martin's Chapel, Heritage Crafts School, Chailey, Sussex (1913): the Chapel of St George, Westminster Abbey, London (1925): Parliamentary War Memorial, Westminster Hall, London (1952): Royal Window, Canterbury Cathedral, Kent (1954): the East Window, Holy Trinity, Coventry, Warwicks. (1955).

COOLEY, Thomas: 1740–84
Generally considered an Irish architect, but he was in fact an Englishman by birth, and may have been the son of William Cooley, who worked as a mason in London in the 1730s. Thomas Cooley was apprenticed as a carpenter to a Mr Reynolds in London: worked as a clerk to a carpenter at the Board of Works; and became assistant to Robert Mylne on the building of Blackfriars Bridge. Encouraged by Mylne, he entered a design for the Royal Exchange in Dublin, in 1769, which was awarded the first prize, and set up in practice there, remaining in Ireland till his death. From 1775–84 he was Clerk and Inspector of the Civil Buildings. He is best known for his work in Dublin which included the Royal Exchange (1769–79: now the City Hall): the Hibernian Marine School (1770–3): Chapel of the Hibernian Military School (1771): Newgate Prison (1773: dem.): additions to Swift's Hospital (1778: side wings and extension to rear wings): Public Offices on the Inns Quay (1779: later incorporated into the Four Courts by James Gandon). He also built Caledon Castle, Co. Tyrone (1779: colonnade by John Nash).

COOPER, Sir Edwin, RA, FRIBA: 1873–1942
Born in Scarborough: travelled extensively in France and Italy: articled to, and later in partnership with Hall and Davis: after a further period of partnership with S. B. Russell, he set up in private practice, and became highly successful and very well known. He served on the Institute's Council and committees: was knighted 1923: an Hon. Member of Lloyd's: Royal Gold Medallist 1931. His work included the Guildhall, Hull, Yorks. (1903–14): Royal Grammar School, Newcastle-on-Tyne, Northumb. (1907): Town Hall (1914) and Public Library (1939), Marylebone, London:

Port of London Authority Building, Trinity Square, London (1912–22): Star and Garter Home, Richmond, Surrey (1921–4): College of Nursing, Henrietta Street, London (1922–6): Baggage Hall and Offices, Tilbury Docks, Essex (1925–30): Lloyd's, Leadenhall Street, London (1928): Medical School and Nurses' Home, St Mary's Hospital, Paddington, London (1933): rebuilding of Gatton Park, Surrey (1936).

CORSON, George: 1829–1910
The fourth son of the Provost of Dumfries, where he was born. Educated Dumfries Academy: apprenticed to a local architect, Walter Newall: in 1849 set up in practice in Leeds where he was in partnership with his brother William till *c.* 1860. He was the founder and first President of the Leeds Architectural Association (1877: later the West Yorkshire Society of Architects), and from 1864–1904 was architect to Tetleys, the brewers. His work in Leeds included the Municipal Buildings (1876) and Education Department (1879), Calverley Street: Sun Fire Offices, Park Row (1877): Spenfield, Otley Road (1877): the Grand Theatre, New Briggate (1877–8).

COTTINGHAM, Lewis Nockalls, FRS: 1787–1847
Born at Laxfield, Suffolk, the son of a farmer: apprenticed to an Ipswich builder: then became an architect's clerk in London, where he set up in practice 1814. Appointed Surveyor to the Cook's Company 1822, and was commissioned to carry out repairs and rebuilding at Rochester Cathedral 1825. He was the author of a number of books on mediaeval architecture, among them *Plans, etc., of Westminster Hall* (1822): *Plans, etc., of King Henry VII Chapel* (1822–9): *Working Drawings of Gothic Ornaments, etc., with a Design for a Gothic Mansion* (1824): *The Smith and Founders' Director, containing a series of Designs and Patterns for Ornamental Iron and Brass Works* (1824). His son, Nockalls Johnson (1823–54), a designer of stained glass, collaborated in much of his later work, particularly at Hereford Cathedral, where he designed the reredos in 1852. L. N. Cottingham designed Snelston Hall, Derbys. (1827), but he was mostly engaged in restoration and rebuilding: included in work of this kind carried out by him were the chapel at Magdalen College, Oxford (1830–5): St Mary, Bury St Edmunds, Suffolk

(1840): Hereford Cathedral (1841 onwards): St Mary, Market Weston, Suffolk (1844).

COUSE, Kenton: 1721–90
A pupil of Flitcroft, and much associated with James Paine. His first official post was as Clerk of the Works at Newmarket in 1750: he subsequently held the appointments of Clerk of the Works at Charing Cross (1750–66), Whitehall, Westminster and St James's (1766–75), and at Buckingham House (1775–82). In 1782 he became the first Examining Clerk, holding this post till his death; he was also Surveyor to the Goldsmith's Company for many years. In 1774–7 he assisted James Paine in the design and building of Richmond Bridge, Surrey. His work included Botleys, nr. Ottershaw, Surrey (1765): refacing the fronts of Nos. 10–12 Downing Street, London (1766): Holy Trinity, Clapham, London (1775).

COWPER, John: c. 1438–84
A Master Mason, who served his apprenticeship and worked at Eton College 1460. Later, he also became a contractor. He worked for Bishop Waynflete of Winchester, and is believed to have been his Master Mason at Holy Trinity, Tattershall, Lincs. (1440 onwards): Esher Place, Surrey (c. 1460: gatehouse remains): and Wainfleet School, Lincs. (c. 1484). He superintended the building of Kirby Muxloe Castle, Leics., where he was Master Mason, in 1480–84. Much of his work was carried out in brick.

CRESY, Edward, FSA: 1792–1858
Born at Dartford, Kent: educated at Rawes's Academy, Bromley: a pupil of James Parkinson: worked for two years in the office of George Smith. Between 1816 and 1819 he travelled extensively in England and on the Continent, in company with G. L. Taylor, making numerous sketches and measured drawings, which formed the basis of *The Architectural Antiquities of Rome* (1821–2), and *Architecture of the Middle Ages in Italy* (1829), of which they were the joint authors. Publication of a projected third work was never completed. From 1829–30 Cresy worked in Paris, then established a private practice in England. He became a sanitary engineer of repute: a superintending inspector under the Board of Health: a member of the British Archaeological Association: wrote professional papers and reports: and was the author of *A Practical*

Treatise on Bridge Building (1839): *Illustrations of Stone Church, Kent* (1840): *On the Cottages of Agricultural Labourers, with economical Working Plans* (1847: with C. W. Johnson): and the editor of *An Encyclopaedia of Civil Engineering* (1847). Details of his architectural work are sparse, but he superintended the building of the Dartford Gas Works (1826–7): and built for himself No. 6 Suffolk Street, London (1824), and The Towers, Dartford, Kent (1828).

CRUNDEN, John: 1740–*c.* 1828
Born in Sussex. Associated with Henry Holland the elder, and employed as a surveyor by him: became District Surveyor for St Pancras (1774–1824), and for Paddington and St Luke's, Chelsea (1774–1828). He was the author of a number of books, among them *Designs for Ceilings* (1765): *Convenient and Ornamental Architecture, consisting of Original Designs for Plans, Elevations and Sections from the Farm House to the most grand and magnificent Villa* (1768): and *The Joiner's and Cabinet-Maker's Darling, or Pocket Director* (1770). His work included Boodle's Club, St James's Street, London (1775): Busbridge Hall, nr. Godalming, Surrey (1775: dem.): Assembly Rooms at the Castle Hotel, Brighton, Sussex (1776: dem., but the ballroom re-erected in Montpelier Place, Brighton, *c.* 1850).

CUBITT, Lewis: b. 1799 (Portrait: see Plate IX)
The youngest son of Jonathan Cubitt: a pupil of H. E. Kendall, and from 1824 in partnership with his brothers, Thomas and William. He designed many of the houses built by the brothers Cubitt, in Belgravia and Bloomsbury, notably those in Eaton Square (1825–6) and Lowndes Square (1837–9) in London. His work included Bricklayers' Arms Station, Bermondsey, London (1842–4): King's Cross Railway Station, London (1851–2).

CUBITT, Thomas: 1788–1855
The eldest son of Jonathan Cubitt, a farmer of Buxton, Norfolk. He worked at first as a journeyman carpenter and ship's carpenter, and in 1809 set up as a master in this trade in London. About 1815 he started his own building firm – the first of its kind – with workmen in the different trades on a permanent payroll. In order to keep his men constantly employed, he entered the field of speculative building, and with his brothers William and Lewis designed, laid

out, and built large parts of Bloomsbury, Belgravia, Pimlico and Clapham Park in London, and Kemp Town in Brighton, between 1820 and 1850. He was a man of exceptional vision and energy: his work was of a high standard: and he became extremely prosperous and successful. He was associated with the preparation of the Metropolitan Buildings Act of 1855: was a member of the Committee of Management which organized the building of Kemp Town, Brighton: gave evidence before House of Commons committees, and took an active interest in such matters as smoke control, sewage disposal, public parks, and the Great Exhibition of 1851. Apart from his speculative building schemes, his work included a Model Laundry for the Royal Households, in Kew Foot Road, Richmond, Surrey: Polesden Lacey House, Surrey (1824: enlarged since): mansions on the east and west of Albert Gate, Knightsbridge, London (1845): remodelling of east front of Buckingham Palace, London (1846–7: to the designs of Edward Blore): Osborne House, I.O.W. (1848): Denbies, Ranmore Common, Surrey (1850: dem.).

CUNDY, Thomas, the elder: 1765–1825
The son of Peter Cundy, of St Dennis, Cornwall: apprenticed to a Plymouth builder before going to London. He became Clerk of Works to S. P. Cockerell at Normanton Park, Rutland, c. 1793: then set up in private practice in London: appointed Surveyor to Lord Grosvenor's London Estates 1821. His sons, Thomas (1790–1867) and Joseph (1795–1875), were associated with him in his practice. His work included the remodelling of Coventry House (later the St James's Club), Piccadilly, London: stables and farm buildings at Normanton Park, Rutland: Tottenham House, Wilts. (1825), and the stables (1818): and the tower and portico of St Matthew, Normanton (1826–9: with his son, Thomas Cundy).

CUNDY, Thomas, the younger: 1790–1867
Born in London, the eldest son of Thomas Cundy: trained by his father, and worked with him till his death: then succeeded to his practice and to the Surveyorship of the Grosvenor Estates in London, which he held from 1825–66. He was responsible for much of the layout of Grosvenor Gardens and Grosvenor Place, including an early block of flats – Belgrave Mansions in Grosvenor Gardens. His work included St Paul, Wilton Place, London

75

(1840–3): Holy Trinity, Bishop's Bridge Road, Paddington, London (1843–6): St Michael, Chester Square, London (1846: War Memorial Chapel since): St Barnabas, Pimlico, London (1846–9: with Butterfield): St Gabriel, Warwick Square, London (1853: additions since): St Mark, Hamilton Terrace, Marylebone, London (1847). His son Thomas (b. 1820) succeeded to his practice and Grosvenor Estates Surveyorship.

CUNNINGHAM, John: 1799–1873

Born at Leitholm, Berwicks., the son of a builder, to whom he was apprenticed: studied as an architectural draughtsman in Edinburgh till 1833, when he went to New York, intending to settle there, but disliking the climate, he returned to England in 1834 and set up practice in Liverpool. He built many churches, institutions and mansions in the neighbourhood: was appointed consulting architect to the Liverpool Assembly Hall: for a time was in partnership with a Liverpool architect, Arthur Holme (1814–57), who had been a pupil of Thomas Rickman, and who built a number of local churches. Cunningham's work in Liverpool included St Anne, Aigburth (1837: with Holme): the Sailors' Home (1846–9): Canning Place (1846): the Philharmonic Hall (1848).

CURREY, Henry, FRIBA: 1820–1900

The son of Benjamin Currey, a solicitor who was Clerk of the Table, at the House of Lords: educated Dr Pinckney's, East Sheen, and at Eton: articled to Decimus Burton for five years: worked in the office of William Cubitt & Co. in London: travelled in Germany and Italy: set up in practice in London 1843. He was appointed Architect and Surveyor to St Thomas's Hospital in 1847, and held this post for many years. He was a Vice-President of the Institute in 1874–7 and 1889–93: an Associate of the Institute of Civil Engineers; a Fellow of the Surveyors' Institution: Architect to the 6th Duke of Devonshire: Architect and Surveyor to the Foundling Hospital, and the Magdalen Hospital: a Trustee of the Architects' Benevolent Society. In his later years he was assisted by his son, Percivall, FRIBA. Henry Currey's work included the street front of the P. & O. Line offices, Leadenhall Street, London (1858): the Congregational Church, Buxton, Derbys. (1861): the Palace Hotel, Buxton, Derbys. (1868): St Thomas's Hospital, London (1868–71): Devonshire Royal Hospital, Buxton, Derbys.

(1868–82: converted from John Carr's Stables buildings): School House and Chapel, Eastbourne College, Sussex (1870, 1874, 1889): Holy Trinity, Buxton, Derbys. (1873): St Paul, Chiswick, London (1892): St Peter, Meads Road, Eastbourne, Sussex (1894–6): the layout of the Duke of Devonshire's estate at Eastbourne, including much work on sea walls and terraces.

DANCE, George, the elder: 1695 or 1700–68
The son of Giles Dance, a London mason, with whom he was in
partnership 1726–7. Appointed Clerk of the City Works in 1735, and
held the post till early in 1768. The acceptance of his design for the
Mansion House, in competition with a number of famous architects,
may have been due to his official position in the City. His work
included St. Leonard, Shoreditch, London (1736–40): The Mansion House, London (1739–52: attics removed 1842): St Botolph,
Aldgate, London (1741–44): St Matthew, Bethnal Green, London
(1743–6): rebuilding of the nave of Our Lady of Charity, Faversham,
Kent (1755).

DANCE, George, the younger, FRS, FSA: 1741–1825
The fifth son of George Dance: about 1758 he went to Italy with his
brother Nathaniel (later Sir Nathaniel Dance-Holland, RA), where
he studied architecture, was awarded the Gold Medal of the Academy of Arts at Parma, and became a member of the Arcadi. In 1765
he returned to England and succeeded his father as Clerk of the City
Works early in 1768, holding the post till 1815. He was one of the
original members of the Royal Academy, and from 1798–1805 Professor of Architecture: a member of the Architects' Club; a talented
musician, and a skilful draughtsman and artist. His pencil portraits
were engraved and published in 1808–14 under the title of *A Collection of Portraits sketched from the Life since the Year 1793*. He and Sir
Robert Taylor drafted the London Building Act (1774): in 1816
Dance published a *Report on Inspection, with a Committee of Aldermen,
of several Gaols of this Kingdom*, the result of a tour of prisons he had
made in 1815. Dance was responsible for much street layout and
planning in London: he made designs for the improvement of the
Port of London, which were published in 1800, but never carried out.
His work included All Hallows, London Wall, London (1765–7):
layout of St George's Circus, Southwark, London, and adjoining
roads (1769: built *c.* 1785): Newgate Prison, London (1770–8:
repaired by Dance after Gordon Riots damage 1780: dem. 1902):
layout of Finsbury Square, London (1777): St Luke's Hospital, Old
Street, London (1782–4: later the Bank of England Printing Works):
rebuilding of the south front of the Guildhall, London (1788–9):
layout of Alfred Place, Tottenham Court Road, London, and ad-
78

joining crescents (1790): Coleorton Hall, Leics. (1804–8: except the second floor): Royal College of Surgeons, Lincoln's Inn Fields, London (1806–13: with James Lewis: rebuilt since, but portico remains).

DARBYSHIRE, Alfred, FSA, FRIBA: 1839–1908
Born at Salford, Lancs.: his family were Quakers: educated at the Friends' School, Ackworth, and at Alderley: articled to P. B. Alley: set up practice in Manchester 1862: travelled on the Continent 1864. He was a Vice-President of the Institute 1902–5: President of the Manchester Society of Architects 1901–3: President of the Building Construction and Equipment section of the International Fire Congress held in London in 1903. He was much interested in theatre design, and published *The Irving-Darbyshire Safety Plan* (1884): and *An Architect's Experiences: Professional, Artistic and Theatrical* (1897): the former work advocated the use of an asbestos safety curtain between stage and auditorium. His work in and near Manchester included alterations at Prince's Theatre (1869): abattoir and meat market, Water Street (1870–2): the Comedy Theatre, and Palace of Varieties (1890–1): St Ignatius, Salford (1902–3): Free Library, Knutsford (1904): the Town Hall, Pendleton.

DAVIS, Arthur Joseph, RA, FRIBA: 1878–1951
Born in London: educated in Brussels and Paris: trained in the Godefroy Atelier and École des Beaux Arts in Paris. In 1900 he joined the French architect Charles Mewès (d. 1914), who had a large continental practice; a partnership which was very successful and became famous. Davis was interested in educational reform and was a member of the Faculty of Architecture to the British School in Rome: a member of the Royal Fine Art Commission: Consulting Architect for the Cunard Building, Liverpool: hon. architect for Dulwich Picture Gallery, London. He was responsible for the interior design of the Cunard liners *Aquitania*, *Laconia* and *Franconia*; and for Westminster Bank premises in Old Broad Street, Threadneedle Street and Throgmorton Street in London, and in Brussels and Antwerp. His work included Inveresk House, Strand, London (1903–7: with Mewès: built as the offices of the *Morning Post*: additions since): the Ritz Hotel, Piccadilly, London (1904–6: with Mewès): Royal Automobile Club, Pall Mall, London (1908–11: with Mewès): Morgan, Grenfell & Co.'s premises, 23 Gt Winchester

Street, London (1925): Hasilwood House, Bishopsgate, London (1928: built as the Hudson's Bay Company Building): Cunard House, Leadenhall Street, London (1930).

DAWBER, Sir Guy, RA, FSA, FRIBA: 1861–1938
Born at King's Lynn, Norfolk: educated there, and at the Royal Academy Schools. Articled to Sir Thomas Deane in Dublin, subsequently worked in the offices of Sir Ernest George and of Messrs George Peto, before setting up in practice at Bourton-on-the-Hill, Glos., and in 1891 in London. He was President of the AA 1904–6: President of the RIBA 1925–7: Royal Gold Medallist 1928: Chairman of the Council for the Preservation of Rural England: knighted in 1936. Though his practice was largely domestic, he designed many war memorials, numerous London and provincial branches of the Westminster Bank, and undertook commissions for the Armourers and Braziers', Carpenters' and Leathersellers' Companies. At Hampstead Garden Suburb, built largely before the First World War, Dawber designed 38–48 Temple Fortune Lane; 20 Hampstead Way; and 5–6 Ruskin Close. His work included St David, Moreton-in-the-Marsh, Glos. (1889): Westhope Manor, Salop (1901–2): Conkwell Grange, Winsley, Wilts. (1907): Hamptworth Lodge, Landford, Wilts. (1910–12): Eyeford Park, Glos. (1912): transept, screen, panelling and reredos of St George's Chapel, Ely Cathedral, Cambs. (1922): Stowell Court, Somerset (1925): Foord's Almshouses, Rochester, Kent (1925–35): Eyewell House, Queen Camel, Somerset (1926): Tuesley Court, nr. Godalming, Surrey (1928): dining hall at Overstone Park, Northants (1935).

DAWKES, Samuel Whitfield: 1811–80
Born in London: articled to an architect in York named Pritchard: and set up in practice in Gloucester and Cheltenham. He specialized in the building of railway stations, at a time when their growth was increasing rapidly. His work included St Peter, Cheltenham, Glos. (1840–9): St Andrew, Kingsbury, Middx. (1847: with Hamilton: built in Wells Street, London, and re-erected at Kingsbury 1933): Colney Hatch mental hospital, Friern Barnet, Middlesex (1849–51): Horsted Place, Little Horsted, Sussex (1850–1): Christ Church, Hampstead, London (1852): Freemasons' Asylum, Croydon, Surrey (1852): St James, Gravesend, Kent (1852).

DEANE, Sir Thomas: 1792–1871
The son of a builder in Cork: he carried on the family business: became very prosperous: was Mayor of Cork in 1830, and knighted the same year. He then set up in private practice in partnership with Benjamin Woodward (1815–61), an Irishman who had been articled to a civil engineer, and later with his son Thomas Newenham. He was for many years President of the Institute of Irish Architects: his work at Cork included the Old and New Savings Banks, the Bank of Ireland, and the Courthouse: at Killarney, he built the mental asylum. The work of the partnership included the Museum Building at Trinity College, Dublin (1853–7): the University Museum, Oxford (1854): Crown Life Insurance Offices, Bridge Street, London (1855: dem.): the Meadow Building, Christ Church, Oxford (1862–5): the Kildare Street Club, Dublin (1860).

DEANE, Sir Thomas Newenham: 1828–99
Born in Cork, the son of Sir Thomas Deane: studied under his father: about 1850 joined him and Benjamin Woodward in partnership, and continued the practice after the retirement of his father, and the death of Woodward. He was a Royal Hibernian Academician: a Member of the Royal Irish Academy: Superintendent of the National Monuments and of Ancient Monuments of Ireland: knighted 1890. After Woodward's death, his work in Dublin included the Munster Bank, and the Scottish Widows' offices in Dame Street. In 1878 he took into partnership his son, Thomas Manly, who had been a pupil of William Burges, and had gained the Royal Academy Travelling Scholarship in 1876. Their work together included the Town Hall, Bray, Co. Wicklow: branch offices throughout Ireland of the Munster Bank and the Provincial Bank of Ireland: the Physiological Laboratory and Anthropological Museum at Oxford: and in Dublin the Royal Exchange and Commercial Union offices, and the Science and Art Museum and National Library of Ireland (1887–90).

DEERING: See GANDY, J. P.

DENHAM, Sir John: 1615–69
An Irishman, the son of a judge. During the Civil War he took part in the defence of Farnham Castle for the Royalists. He lived in retirement in Oxford until the Restoration, when he was appointed

Surveyor-General of the King's Works, over the head of John Webb, a post he held till his death. He had some reputation as a poet, but his practical knowledge of architecture and building was sparse. He was a member of the Commission appointed for the repair of St Paul's Cathedral before the Great Fire, and is alleged to have designed and built the original Burlington House in Piccadilly, London (1663–8).

DEREHAM, Elias de: d. 1245
Born sometime in the second half of the twelfth century, the son of a Norfolk squire. Probably educated at the Cluniac Monastery at Lewes: was personal clerk to Hubert Walter, who became Archbishop of Canterbury in 1193, and to whom Elias was Seneschal in 1197. From 1199–1209 he was in the service of King John, described as 'King's architect'. Disagreements with the King led to his absence abroad till 1219, though he was present at the signing of Magna Carta. From 1220–41 he was continuously engaged in England: he is reputedly the architect of Salisbury Cathedral (1220–58: except the spire, begun 1334): of the hall of Winchester Palace (1222–35): and is believed to have advised on building at Wells, Canterbury and Lewes. He was a Canon of Salisbury, and held a number of Church livings.

de SOISSONS, Louis, CVO, OBE, RA, FRIBA: 1890–1962
Born in Montreal: articled to J. H. Eastwood: studied at Royal Academy Schools and the École des Beaux Arts, Paris. He was well known as an architect and town planner; was in partnership for some years with G. Grey Wornum, and later worked with Peacock, Hodges and Partners. Before the Second World War he designed and planned Welwyn Garden City, Herts. (with A. W. Kenyon), and in 1948 was Consultant Architect for the plan to link Welwyn with Hatfield New Town. He carried out housing schemes in London, Devonshire and Hertfordshire, and after the Second World War planned and laid out war cemeteries in Italy and Greece for the Imperial War Graves Commission. His work included the Shredded Wheat Factory, Welwyn Garden City, Herts. (1925): Earl Haig Memorial Homes at Meadow Head, Sheffield, Yorks. (1928–9), and at Morden, Surrey (1931 and later: both with G. Grey Wornum): housing estate at Dittisham, Devonshire (1937): St James's Priory Estate, Exeter (1938): Broom Park and Huxham's Cross Estates,

Dartington, Devonshire (late 1940s): Hobbs Memorial Gates, Kennington Oval, London: King George VI monument, The Mall, London (statue by William McMillan).

DEVEY, George, FRIBA: 1820–86

Born in London, the son of Frederick Devey, a solicitor: educated King's College, London: articled to a London surveyor named Little: travelled in Greece and Italy: set up in practice in the 1840s. He became a successful architect, with a large practice, building mainly country houses and mansions, many now demolished, and cottages and lodges on country estates. Devey was an exceptionally able artist and draughtsman. His work included Sendholme, Send, Surrey: addition of a lodge to Titsey Place, Titsey, Surrey (*c.* 1855): additions to Betteshanger House, Kent (1856): Wickwar parsonage, Glos. (*c.* 1870): Goldings House, Herts. (*c.* 1870): Broomfield Manor, nr. Jacobstowe, Devonshire (1870s): additions to Ascott, Bucks. (1874): additions to Durdans, Epsom, Surrey (1878): Blakesware, nr. Widford, Herts. (1878): the remodelling of No. 41 Grosvenor Square, London (1884–5).

DOBSON, John, FRIBA: 1787–1865

Born in humble circumstances at Chirton, North Shields: attended the village school, and started work when he was about twelve years old, making designs for a local damask weaver. From 1802–10 he was apprenticed to David Stephenson of Newcastle-on-Tyne; then spent some time in London, studying under the artist, John Varley: about 1813 set up in architectural practice in Newcastle. He travelled extensively in England and France during the early years of his practice, and by 1830 was successfully established. He was the first President of the Northern Society of Architects, in 1859. His practice, confined to the North of England, was immense: he built many large country houses, schools, churches, docks and staithes, and was also an able landscape gardener and town planner. He worked in close collaboration with Richard Grainger, a speculative builder of Newcastle, during the 1830s and 1840s, and within this partnership Dobson replanned much of Newcastle's street layout, including Grainger, Grey, Clayton and Market Streets, and Eldon Square, and designed a number of the city's public buildings. His work in Northumberland included the Scotch Church, North Shields (1811): Linden House, nr. Long Horsley (1812–13):

83

Doxford Hall (1818): Nunnykirk Hall (1825): Northern Academy of Art, Blackett Street, Newcastle-on-Tyne (1828): Longhirst, nr. Morpeth (1828): Lilburn Tower (1828–43): the Royal Arcade, Newcastle-on-Tyne (1831–2): Meldon Park (1832): the Vicarage, Chatton (1834): entrance gates to the General Cemetery, Newcastle-on-Tyne (1839): the Town Hall, North Shields (1844): the High Level Bridge, Newcastle-on-Tyne (1847: with Robert Stephenson): the Central Railway Station, Newcastle-on-Tyne (1846–50): the Collingwood Monument, Tynemouth (1847): St John, Otterburn (1858): Jesmond Parish Church, Newcastle-on-Tyne (1858–61).

DOLLMAN, Francis Thomas, FRIBA: 1812–99

A pupil of Augustus Pugin the elder, to whom he was articled: in 1833 became assistant to Basevi, and remained with him till the latter's death in 1845. He then set up in private practice, which consisted largely of churches and rectories. He was better known for his literary work than for his buildings, and was the author of *History and Illustrations of the Grand Old Priory Church of St. Mary Overie, Southwark,* and, in collaboration with a Mr Jobbins, of a number of archaeological works, including *Ancient Pulpits,* and *Ancient Domestic Architecture.* His work included the addition of a steeple to Basevi's Church of St Matthew, Eye, Northants (1846): the chancel and transepts to Basevi's Church of Holy Trinity, Twickenham, Middlesex (1863): St Saviour, Walthamstow, Essex (1874).

DONALDSON, Thomas Leverton, FRIBA: 1795–1885

The younger son of James Donaldson, a district surveyor who had been a pupil of Thomas Leverton, had exhibited at the Royal Academy in 1777, and was later clerk to Robert Mylne. (His elder son, James, became an architect, but died in 1806 before his career was established.) Thomas Leverton Donaldson was born in London, educated at King Edward VI Grammar School, St Albans, and at fourteen went to South Africa to start work with a merchant there: he joined a military expedition against the French in Mauritius, as a volunteer, and returned to England when he was sixteen. He then studied architecture under his father and at the Royal Academy Schools, where he obtained the Silver Medal in 1817: toured Greece and Italy 1818–23, and was elected a member of the Academy of St Luke, Rome. He set up in practice in London: was for many years Professor of Construction and Architecture at University College,

London: was one of the founders of the Institute of British Architects, of which he was a Life Member, Hon. Secretary, and President 1863–5, and Royal Gold Medallist 1851. He had many architectural contacts with foreign architects, notably in France; was a member of the Commission of Sewers, and District Surveyor of South Kensington. He delivered and published a large number of lectures and technical papers: contributed to Stuart and Revett's *Athens*: and was the author of *Architectura Numismatica: Handbook of Specifications*: and *Maxims and Theorems*. His work included Dr Williams's Library, Gordon Square, London (1848): Great Hall interior and Library at University College, London (1848): the German Hospital, Dalston Lane, Hackney, London (1865: enlarged since): Holy Trinity, Brompton Road, London (1826–9): Royal Scottish Corporation offices, Crane Court, Fleet Street, London (1877).

DONTHORNE, W. J.: nineteenth century
A pupil of Jeffry Wyatt 1817–20: exhibited at the Royal Academy 1817–53: was one of the founders of the Institute of British Architects. He built a number of country houses, rectories and workhouses in the provinces, chiefly in Norfolk and Sussex. His work included Cromer Hall, Cromer, Norfolk (1827–9): Howdale Home, Downham Market, Norfolk (1836: built as a workhouse): Workhouses at Gayton (1836), Aylsham (1849) and Beckham (1851), all in Norfolk: Peasmarsh House, Peasmarsh, Sussex (1839): Holy Trinity, Upper Dicker, Sussex (1843): St Mary, Bagthorpe, Norfolk (1853–4).

DREW, Sir Thomas, FRIBA: 1838–1910
Born in Belfast, the son of the Rev. Thomas Drew: educated in Belfast: articled to Sir Charles Lanyon 1854: went to Dublin 1862, where he worked in the office of W. G. Murray, with whom he remained for some years before setting up independent practice. He had many influential clients, and became very well known. He was President of the Royal Institute of Irish Architects 1892–1901: President of the Society of Antiquaries (Ireland) 1895–7: a Vice-President of the Georgian Society 1908: served on the RIBA Council: was President of the Royal Hibernian Academy: Consulting Architect to St Patrick's and Christ Church Cathedrals, Dublin, and to St Patrick's Cathedral, Armagh: Diocesan Architect of Down and Dromore: the first President of the Ulster Society of Architects: the

85

Chair of Architecture at the National University of Ireland was offered to him a few weeks before his death. He was knighted in 1900. His work included general restoration of St Patrick's Cathedral, Dublin (1864–9): the Graduates' Memorial Building, Library Square, Dublin (1899–1902): Masonic Boys' Schools, Clonskeagh, Co. Dublin: St Kevin, South Circular Road, Dublin.

DUBOIS, Nicholas: *c.* 1665–1735
A Frenchman who served with the British Army 1706–14: was then employed at the Board of Ordnance: and was appointed Master Mason at the Office of Works in 1719. His translation of Giacomo Leoni's *The Architecture of Andrea Palladio* was published in 1715: he designed and built Stanmer House, near Brighton, Sussex (1722–7): and designed the bridge at Lewes, Sussex, in 1727.

DYER, Charles: 1794–1848
The son of a Bristol surgeon: a pupil of William Brooks: exhibited at the Royal Academy 1818–47: a member of the Institute of Architects. His practice was largely in Bristol and Clifton, and his work included the Female Orphan Asylum, Ashley Hill, Bristol, Som. (1825–9: now a Salvation Army Home): Litfield House (*c.* 1830) and Camp House (1831), Clifton, Bristol: Dyers' Hall, Dowgate Hill, London (1838–40: front altered since): the Victoria Rooms, Clifton, Bristol (1839–41): St Mark, Easton, Bristol (1848–9).

EASTLAKE, Charles Locke: 1836–1906
Although trained as an architect, and articled to P. C. Hardwick, he never built anything, but was the founder of the so-called Eastlake style of furniture design: as a furniture designer, he was better known in America than in England. He was Secretary to the RIBA 1866–78; from 1878–98 was Keeper and Secretary of the National Gallery. He was the author of *Hints on Household Taste* (1868): *History of the Gothic Revival* (1872): some guide books to the Louvre, Paris, and to the Brera Gallery, Milan, and was a contributor to *Building News* for many years.

EBBLES, Robert: nineteenth century
He lived at Wolverhampton during the 1830s and 1840s. His practice consisted almost entirely of church building, and his work included St Peter, Priorslee, Salop (1836): the central tower of SS Peter and Paul, Ewhurst, Surrey (1837–8), and the Rectory: St James, Handsworth, Birmingham, Warwicks. (1838–40: a second church added by J. Chatwin 1894–5): St Peter, Coventry, Warwicks. (1840–1): St Mary, Stourbridge, Worcs. (1842).

EDEN, Francis Charles, FSA, FRIBA: 1884–1944
The son of F. M. Eden, Agent to the Duke of Buccleuch: educated Wellington College, and Keble College, Oxford: articled to Bodley and Garner. He travelled widely on the Continent, had a considerable knowledge of Italian art, and was well known for his restorations of old buildings, in which he specialized: he was outstanding as an artist in stained glass. His work included the restoration of the Treasury of Canterbury Cathedral: restoration of St Mary the Virgin, Elham, Kent: restoration of St Lawrence, Ardeley, Herts., where he also designed the Village Hall and adjacent cottages: St John, Harpenden, Herts. (*c.* 1920): St George, Wash Common, Newbury, Berks. (1933).

EDIS, Colonel Sir Robert William, CB, KBE, FRIBA: 1839–1927
Born at Huntingdon, the son of Robert Edis: educated Aldenham School: set up in architectural practice in London 1861. He was President of the AA; a member of the LCC; DL and JP for Norfolk: a Colonel of the Artists' Corps of Volunteers with which he served for

twenty years, having joined in 1859: he travelled widely, and was a big-game hunter. In 1881 he published *Decoration and Furniture of Town Houses*: he was knighted in 1919. His work included No. 31 Tite Street, Chelsea, London: Nos. 59–61 Brook Street, London: Nos. 91–3 Southwark Street, London (1872): No. 70 Marine Parade, Brighton, Sussex (1879–80): Warren House, Iver Heath, Bucks. (1881): Nos. 100 and 101 Piccadilly, London (1883 and 1890): the ballroom at Sandringham House, Norfolk (1883), and additions to York Cottage, Sandringham: Constitutional Club, Northumberland Avenue, London (1883–6): No. 10 Fleet Street, London (1885): Great Central Railway Hotel, Marylebone Road, London (1897–9).

EDWARDS, Francis: 1784–1857

Born in London, where he was apprenticed to a cabinet-maker. From 1806–11 worked in Sir John Soane's office: was awarded the Royal Academy Silver Medal 1808, and Gold Medal 1811: set up practice in London, and until 1823 also gave part-time assistance to H. H. Seward. Edwards did much arbitration and valuation work, and was responsible for all building and engineering carried out by the Imperial Gaslight Company from 1823, eventually becoming their consultant architect. He was also employed by Goding & Co. on their breweries and public houses. His work included the offices of the Imperial Gaslight Company at Hoxton, London (1823): Holmbush, nr. Cuckfield, Sussex (1823): St John the Baptist, Hoxton, London (1825–9): additions to Wotton House, Surrey (1830): the Workhouse, Romford, Essex (1838: now incorporated into Oldchurch Hospital).

EGINTON, Harvey: 1809–49

The son of Raphael Eginton, the glass painter. Acquired a knowledge of architecture from his father, studied in Worcester Cathedral, and was helped and sponsored by a Wiltshire magistrate. He did much church restoration work, and built some schoolhouses and police stations, his practice being in Worcestershire and neighbouring counties. He was County Surveyor of Worcestershire: architect to the Incorporated Society for Building Churches and Chapels for the Worcester District: and architect to the Worcester Diocesan Church Building Society. His work included All Saints, Broseley, Salop, and Holy Trinity, Dawley, Salop, both in 1845.

ELLIOT, Archibald: 1761–1823
A Scottish architect who began his career in London, but returned
to practise in Edinburgh, where his work included Waterloo Place,
and the Regent Bridge (1815): St Paul's Episcopal Chapel (1816–
18): Dr John Brown's Chapel (1821: later Broughton Place Church).

ELMES, Harvey Lonsdale: 1814–47
Born at Oving, nr. Chichester, the son of James Elmes: studied
architecture under his father and uncle, H. J. Elmes (also an architect), and with John Elger, a builder: entered the Royal Academy
Schools 1831. He was articled to H. E. Goodridge of Bath 1834–7:
then returned to London, where he assisted his father in his practice.
He designed a number of private houses in Liverpool and London,
and in 1839 and 1840 won the competitions for the design of St
George's Hall and the Assize Courts, Liverpool: he united these
later into one design, which was completed after his early death by
C. R. Cockerell and Sir R. Rawlinson. His work included St
George's Hall and Assize Courts, Liverpool (1842–54: completed
after his death): Lancashire County Lunatic Asylum, Rainhill, nr.
Liverpool (1847: completed after his death).

ELMES, James: 1782–1862
Born in London: educated at Merchant Taylors' School: a pupil of
George Gibson: entered Royal Academy Schools 1804 and won the
Silver Medal 1805. He practised in London and West Sussex: was
Surveyor to the Port of London: and Vice-President of the London
Architectural Society. A friend of Keats, he was a writer of some
distinction on architectural and artistic matters; he edited *Annals
of the Fine Arts* (1816–20): and *Metropolitan Improvements* (1827–9):
and was the author of *Memoirs of the Life and Works of Sir Chr. Wren*
(1823): *A General and Bibliographical Dictionary of the Fine Arts* (1824):
*A Scientific, historical and commercial survey of the Harbour and Port of
London* (1838), and a number of other books. His work, in some of
which he was assisted by his son, Harvey Lonsdale, included Oakwood House, Sennicotts, Sussex (1809–12): St John, Chichester,
Sussex (1812–13): the House of Correction, Waterford, Ireland
(1820): Nos. 6–12 Queen Anne's Gate, London (1836–8: with
Harvey Lonsdale Elmes).

ELSAM, Richard: nineteenth century
A pupil of Robert Browne, Clerk of the Works at Kew: exhibited at the Royal Academy 1797–1807: practised for a time in London, and was appointed Surveyor to the Corporation of Dover: during his career he was involved in a series of professional disputes. He was the author of *An Essay on Rural Architecture* (1803): *Hints on Improving the Condition of the Peasantry* (1816): and *The Practical Builder's Perpetual Price-Book* (1825). His work included St Peter, Chertsey, Surrey (1806–7: completed by T. Chawner): the Gaol at Dover, Kent (1820–1).

EMBERTON, Joseph, FRIBA: 1889–1956
Trained at the Royal College of Art: worked in the offices of Sir John Burnet and Partners: was in partnership with P. J. Westwood 1922–6: then set up independent practice. He served on the RIBA Council 1933–9, and on many Institute committees; during the Second World War he was Housing Officer to the Ministry of Air-craft Production: architectural adviser on hostels to the Ministry of Works: and consultant on the design of steel prefabricated houses to the Ministry of Supply. He was a pioneer in the so-called modern style of architecture in England, and in the use of ferro-concrete and stainless steel for building, and an ardent supporter of flats as opposed to individual houses. His work included the refacing of Olympia, Hammersmith, London (1930), and extensions there (1936): The Royal Corinthian Yacht Club, Burnham-on-Crouch, Essex (1931): Universal House, Southwark Bridge Road, London (1933): flats in Lower Chapman Street, Stepney, London (1934): Simpson's, Piccadilly, London (1935): Nos. 363–7 Oxford Street, London (1938–9): flats and commercial buildings on the Stafford Cripps Estate, Finsbury, London.

EMLYN, Henry: 1729–1815
Believed to have been connected with a family of builders named Emblin or Emlyn, of Maidenhead, Berkshire. He worked first as a carpenter, then practised as an architect, and devised what was known as an 'English' or 'British' Order of Architecture, which he described in *A Proposition for a new Order of Architecture, with rules for drawing the several parts*, published 1781. His work included super-vision of the restoration of St George's Chapel, Windsor, Berks. (1782–92: conversion of Edward IV's chantry to the Royal Pew,

additions and carving to the Stalls, Edward IV Monument, and Organ Gallery): Beaumont College, Old Windsor, Berks. (1790: built as Beaumont Lodge: the portico an example of his 'English' Order): he is believed to have designed the Kederminster Chapel screen at St Mary, Langley Marish, Bucks. (1792).

ESSEX, James, FSA: 1722–84

The son of James Essex, a carpenter who worked in Cambridge during the first half of the eighteenth century, and who was associated there with James Gibbs. The younger Essex was educated at King's College Grammar School, Cambridge: and became a pupil and then a collaborator of Sir James Burrough. When his father died in 1749 he carried on the family carpentry and joinery business for a time, and built the wooden bridge at Queen's in that year. Essex was one of the first architects of his time to appreciate Gothic construction and design: he was a frequent contributor to *Archaeologia*: wrote an unpublished *History of Gothic Architecture in England*: and was the author of *Journal of a Tour through part of Flanders and France in August 1773*, published by the Cambridge Antiquarian Society in 1888. Many well-known antiquaries were his friends, and he was consulted by Horace Walpole on the design of Strawberry Hill, Twickenham. The greater part of his career was devoted to additions and restorations to the University buildings at Cambridge, where he worked closely with Burrough, and later independently. He also carried out restorations at Ely and Lincoln Cathedrals. His work at Cambridge included Ramsden Building, St Catherine's Hall (1757): stone bridge at Trinity College (1763–5): Chapel at Clare Hall (1764–9: he completed Sir James Burrough's design): Combination Rooms at Trinity College (1770–4).

EVELEIGH, John: eighteenth century

Worked in Bath during the last two decades of the eighteenth century, in association with Thomas Baldwin and other speculative builders, and also in private practice. Like Baldwin, he became bankrupt in 1793, and left the city. His work in Bath included Camden Crescent (*c.* 1788): Sion Row (*c.* 1790): Somerset Place (*c.* 1790): Grosvenor Place (1791): he designed and built the Guildhall at Plymouth (1800: now dem.).

FAWCETT, William Milner, FSA, FRIBA: 1833–1909
Born at Woodhouse, nr. Leeds, the son of the Rev. James Fawcett, Vicar of Knaresborough: educated Leeds Grammar School, and Jesus College, Cambridge: established a large and successful practice in Cambridge: from 1906 was in partnership with T. D. Atkinson. He was a Vice-President and member of the Council of the RIBA: County Surveyor to Cambridgeshire: Surveyor to Cambridge County Council: Diocesan Surveyor to Ely: he published an edition of Paley's *Gothic Mouldings*. The considerable amount of work he did at the University included restoration at Queen's; additions at Peterhouse, Emmanuel and King's; the Cavendish Laboratory; the Curator's House at the Botanic Gardens; and the Syndicate Building at the Pitt Press. His work also included All Saints, Knapwell, Cambs. (1866: except tower): the Vicarage, Schools and School-master's house at Barton, Cambs. (1885): Perse School for Boys, Cambridge (1890): Hughes Hall, Cambridge (1894–5).

FERGUSSON, James, FSA, FRIBA: 1808–86
Born at Ayr, the son of Dr William Fergusson, Inspector-General of Military Hospitals: educated Edinburgh High School, and at Hounslow: spent some ten years in a commercial family concern in India, where he first became interested in Oriental architecture. On his return to England he was General Manager of the Crystal Palace Company 1856–8, and for a short time architectural adviser to the Office of Works: in 1857 he was a member of a royal commission enquiring into the defences of the United Kingdom. He became famous as a writer of standard works of reference on architecture, archaeology and antiquities in Europe and Asia: he delivered many professional papers to the Institute, and was Royal Gold Medallist in 1871. Included in his vast literary output were *The Palaces of Nineveh and Persepolis Restored* (1851): *The Illustrated Handbook of Architecture* (1855): *A History of the Modern Styles of Architecture* (1862): *A History of Architecture in all Countries from the Earliest Times to the Present Day* (1865–7): *The History of Indian and Eastern Architecture* (1876): *Temples of the Jews* (1878): *Cave Temples of India* (1880: with James Burgess): *The Parthenon: an Essay on the Mode in which Light was introduced into the Temples of the Greeks and Romans* (1883).

FERREY, Benjamin, FSA, FRIBA: 1810–80

Born at Christchurch, Hants, the youngest son of Benjamin Ferrey: educated Wimborne Grammar School: a pupil of the elder Pugin for some years: toured the Continent: and after further study under William Wilkins, set up in practice in London in 1834. He was one of the earliest members of the Institute, of which he was twice Vice-President, and Royal Gold Medallist in 1870: he was Honorary Secretary to the Committee of Architects for the competition for the Houses of Parliament: one of the consulting architects of the Incorporated Church Building Society: Diocesan Architect to Bath and Wells from 1841 till his death. Ferrey was an exceptionally fine draughtsman; an amateur of church music; and invented and patented a method of stamping plaster: he was the author of *Antiquities of the Priory Church of Christchurch, Hants* (1834), and *Recollections of A. N. Welby Pugin, and his father Augustus Pugin* (1861). He laid out and designed the older part of Bournemouth, including the Bath Hotel, about 1838, and did much restoration work at Wells Cathedral and the Bishop's Palace there. Ferrey built up an enormous architectural practice in which in his later years he was assisted by his son, Benjamin Edmund, FSA, FRIBA (1845–1900). The work of the elder Ferrey included St James, Morpeth, Northumb. (1843–6): St Stephen, Rochester Row, London (1845–7): St Peter's College, Selly Oak, Birmingham (1847–52): Holy Trinity, Penn Street, Bucks. (1849): All Saints, Blackheath, London (1857–67): The Grammar School, Morpeth, Northumb. (1859): St Peter, Slinfold, Sussex (1861): Bulstrode Park, Bucks. (1862): Bagshot Park, Surrey (1877).

FLETCHER, Banister, FRIBA: 1833–99

The son of Thomas Fletcher: educated privately: began to practise architecture at Newcastle-on-Tyne, *c.* 1853. He came to London about 1870, where he established a large and successful practice as an architect and surveyor, in which his sons, Banister Flight and Herbert Phillips, assisted him: he was appointed District Surveyor of West Newington and part of Lambeth 1875: was a member of the Common Council of the City of London: Surveyor to the Board of Trade: Chairman of the Trades' Training Schools Committee: President of the architectural section of the Congress of the British Institute of Public Health: Colonel of the Tower Hamlets Volunteer Brigade: M.P. for North-West Wilts. 1885–6: Master of the Carpenters' Company 1889: a Fellow of King's College, London, where he became Professor of Architecture 1890. He was the author of many books, including *Houses for the Industrial Classes*: *Quantities, Arbitrations*: *The London Building Act 1894*: and in collaboration with his son, later Sir Banister Fletcher, the first edition of *A History of Architecture on the Comparative Method*, published 1896.

FLETCHER, Sir Banister Flight, FSA, FRIBA: 1866–1953
The son of Professor Banister Fletcher: educated King's College and University College, London: articled to his father 1884: studied at the AA, at the École des Beaux Arts in Paris, in the practical carpentry and woodwork workshops at King's College, and under Alfred Waterhouse, Norman Shaw, J. L. Pearson and Sir Arthur Blomfield. He travelled widely: was called to the Bar of the Middle Temple 1908: knighted as a Senior Sheriff of the City of London 1919: served on the Court of Common Council of the City of London: was a member of the Tribunal of Appeal under the London Building Act for many years: was an FRICS and FRSL, and received many foreign honours. At the RIBA he served on committees, was a member of the Council, a Vice-President, and President 1929–31. He assisted his father in his practice, and later was in partnership with Herbert G. Tilley. His monumental standard work of reference, *A History of Architecture on the Comparative Method*, was first published in collaboration with his father, in 1896. Since then it has been reprinted, rewritten, reillustrated, and translated into most European languages: the 17th edition was published in 1961. Sir Banister Fletcher's architectural work included Nos. 20 and 46 Harley Street, and No. 30 Wimpole Street, London: Gosletts' premises, Charing Cross Road, London (1897): extensions to King's College School, Wimbledon, Surrey (1899): St Ann's Vestry Hall, Carter Lane, London (1905): No. 23 The Avenue, and The Gables, in The Avenue, Potters Bar, Middlesex (1909): the Roan School, Blackheath, London (1926: with Dunnett): the Gillette factory, Great West Road, Osterley, Middlesex (1937).

FLITCROFT, Henry: 1697–1769
The son of Jeffery Flitcroft, William III's gardener at Hampton Court. From 1711–19 he was apprenticed to a London joiner, and was admitted to the freedom of the Joiners' Company in 1719. An

accidental injury brought him to the notice of Lord Burlington, and by 1720 was an assistant and draughtsman in his employ: Lord Burlington, who sponsored the publication of *The Designs of Inigo Jones* edited by William Kent in 1727, commissioned Flitcroft to carry out the drawings for this work. In 1726 Flitcroft entered the Office of Works, and remained in this public service till his death, first as Clerk of the Works at Whitehall, Westminster and St James's; as Master Carpenter 1746: Master Mason 1748: and finally as Comptroller of the Works from 1758–69. His work included Bower House, Havering-atte-Bower, Essex (1729: wings added 1800): St Giles-in-the-Fields, Holborn, London (1731–3): and the Vestry Room: the east façade of Wentworth Woodhouse, Yorks. (*c.* 1734–70), and, in the grounds, the Hoober Stand (1748): Nos. 9–10 St James's Square, London (1736): No. 105 Frognal Grove, Hampstead, London (*c.* 1745: since altered and remodelled): the south front, offices and interiors at Milton House, Northants (1745–50): the rebuilding of Woburn Abbey, Beds. (1747–61): St Andrew, Wimpole, Cambs. (1749: much altered since): the Hercules Temple (1755) and the Temple of the Sun (1765), both at Stourhead, Wilts.

FLOCKTON, Thomas James: FRIBA: 1824–99
The son of William Flockton (1804–64), who practised as an architect in Sheffield, where he designed The Mount (*c.* 1830–35): King Edward VII Grammar School (1837–40: built as the Wesley Proprietary Grammar School): Nether Edge Hospital (1842–3: built as the Workhouse): and the New Chapel at the General Cemetery (1848). He also laid out the Ferham Estate, near Rotherham, Yorks. *c.* 1840. Thomas Flockton was trained in his father's office: worked for Sir George Gilbert Scott: joined his father in practice. In 1862 he set up independently in partnership with Abbott, and the firm later became Flockton, Gibbs and Flockton. He was the first President of the Sheffield Society of Architects and Surveyors, and had a large practice in that part of Yorkshire. His work in Sheffield included Williams Deacon's Bank, Church Street (1866–7: with Abbott): the Hall of Cutlers' Hall (1867: with Abbott): Firth College (1877–9: with E. R. Robson: later part of the Central Schools): Mappin Art Gallery, Weston Park (1886–8: with Gibbs): St John, Ranmoor Park Road (1887–8: with Gibbs).

95

FLORENCE, Henry Louis, FRIBA: 1841–1916

The eldest son of J. H. Florence: studied at the Atelier Questel in Paris: travelled in Italy: awarded a Royal Academy Travelling Studentship and Gold Medal 1870, and the Soane Medal 1869: served on the RIBA Council, and was a Vice-President 1897–9. He practised in London, in partnership with Lewis Henry Isaacs (d. 1908). His work included Holborn Viaduct Hotel and Railway Station, London (1876: since refronted): Northumberland House, Northumberland Avenue, London (1882–5: with Isaacs: built as the Victoria Hotel): Institute of Journalists, Tudor Street, London (1893): Connaught Hotel, Carlos Place, London (1896: with Isaacs): St Luke's Hospital, Lowestoft, Suffolk (1901: with Isaacs: built as the Empire Hotel: dem.).

FOSTER, James: early nineteenth century

A pupil and assistant of William Paty, of Bristol: set up private practice there about 1820, in partnership with his son, James, and later with Thomas Foster and William Okeley: the firm thus founded was still in existence early in the twentieth century, under the title of Foster and Wood, and was responsible for much nineteenth-century building in Bristol: the firm of Foster and Okeley built the arcade of shops in Horsefair, Bristol (1824–5), and the terraces of New Mall and Caledonia Place in Clifton (c. 1840–43). The work of James Foster the elder included the rebuilding of the Palace of the Bishop of St David's, Carmarthen (1803–25): St Andrew, Clifton, Bristol (1819–22: dem. except tower): Holy Trinity, Kingswood, Glos. (1819–21: with his son, James). The work of Thomas Foster included SS Mary and Thomas of Canterbury, Much Birch, Herefs. (1837): and Holy Trinity (1838) and St Paul (1841) both at Stroud, Glos.

FOSTER, John: c. 1786–1846

The second son of John Foster, a Liverpool builder who was Surveyor and Architect to the Corporation: studied under James Wyatt and in his father's office: travelled in Greece in company with C. R. Cockerell: on the death of his father, in 1824, succeeded him in his Corporation post, which he held till 1835. He had a large practice in Liverpool, where many of the public buildings he designed have been destroyed. His work there included St Luke (1811–31: with his father): St Andrew of Scotland (1823): the

JAMES PAINE,
c. 1716–89,
and his son

[RIBA

SIR WILLIAM
CHAMBERS
1726–96

*National Portrait
Gallery, London*]

VI

ROBERT ADAM
1728–92

[*National Portrait
Gallery, London*

HENRY HOLLAND
1745–1806

RIBA]

Infirmary, Brownlow Hill (1824: dem.): the Customs House (1828: dem.): the entrance façade screen to Lime Street Railway Station (1835–6: dem.): Gambier Terrace (1836): the Huskisson Memorial, St James's Cemetery: he also designed St Mary, Cardiff (1842).

FOULSTON, John: 1772–1842
A pupil of Thomas Hardwick, he started practice in London in 1796, but moved to Plymouth in 1811, when he was commissioned to build the Hotel, Assembly Rooms and Theatre there. He built up a large local practice, which included street layout and planning in Plymouth, Devonport and Stonehouse, but much of his work was destroyed during the Second World War. He was in partnership with George Wightwick towards the end of his career, and in 1838 published *The Public Buildings Erected in the West of England as designed by J. Foulston*. His work included Union Street and Wyndham Square, Stonehouse, Plymouth (1815): the Athenaeum (1818–19), Windsor Villas (1821) and St Catherine (1823), all in Lockyer Street, Plymouth: County Mental Hospital (1818–20) and Workhouse (1826), Bodmin, Cornwall: Town Hall (1821), Ker Street, the Civil and Military Library (1823) and the Naval Column (1824), in Devonport, Plymouth: the Workhouse, Liskeard, Cornwall (1830).

FOWKE, Captain Francis: 1823–65
Born in Belfast: educated Dungannon College, and at the Royal Military Academy, Woolwich: commissioned in the Royal Engineers 1842, and spent some time in Bermuda. Became an Inspector of the Science and Art Department, 1853: Secretary of the English Commission attached to the Paris Exhibition, 1855: and a member of the International Technical Commission, 1858. He was a gifted engineer, and an inventor of ability: his inventions included a collapsing canvas pontoon, a military fire engine, a travelling scaffold, and a folding indiarubber bath. He was joint designer, with Major-General H. G. D. Scott, of the Royal Albert Hall, Kensington, London (1867), but died before building began. His work included the Raglan Barracks, Devonport, Plymouth (1853–6): National Gallery, Dublin (1859–60): Museum of Science and Art, Edinburgh (1860–1): buildings and galleries for the International Exhibition of 1862, in Kensington, London.

G

FOWLER, Charles: 1791–1867
Born at Cullompton, Devonshire: from 1806–14 apprenticed to John Powning, of Exeter: then went to London, where he worked first in the office of David Laing, and then set up in private practice. He was one of the founders of the Institute of British Architects, was for many years Honorary Secretary, and later a Vice-President. He was the author of *Description of the plan for the revival of Hungerford Market, with some particulars of the buildings proposed to be erected* (1829): and *On the proposed site of the new Houses of Parliament* (1836). He built markets, many country houses, and carried out restorations at Powderham Castle, Devonshire. His work included the bridge over the River Dart at Totnes, Devonshire (1826): St Paul, Honiton, Devonshire (1837–8): Covent Garden Market, London (1828–31): Higher Market, Queen Street, Exeter (1838: with George Dymond): the London Fever Hospital, Islington, London (1848): Hungerford Market, London (1863: Charing Cross Railway Station now occupies the site).

FOWLER, Charles Hodgson, FSA, FRIBA: 1840–1910
The son of the Rev R. Fowler, Vicar of Rolleston, Notts.: a pupil of Sir George Gilbert Scott. He established a large practice in the North of England, almost entirely devoted to church building and restoration, and became well known for this type of work. He was Architect to Rochester Cathedral 1898: to Lincoln Cathedral 1900: for many years Diocesan Architect to Durham and York: Hon. Consulting Architect to the Incorporated Society for Promoting the Enlargement, Building and Reparation of Churches and Chapels. His work included St Paul, West Hartlepool, Co. Durham (1885–6): St Barnabas, Middlesbrough, Yorks. (1888–91): the restoration of St Mary, Scrawton, Yorks. (1892): St Bartholomew, Marsden, Yorks. (1895): St Andrew, Bishopthorpe, Yorks. (1898–1902): All Saints, Lincoln (1903): the Dean Wickham Library, Lincoln Cathedral (1909–14): rebuilding of the central tower of Rochester Cathedral.

FOWLER, James, FSA, FRIBA: 1828–92
Educated at the Diocesan School, Lichfield, Staffs.: articled to Joseph Potter, a Lichfield architect. In 1849 he settled in Louth, Lincs., and practised there as an architect, in partnership with Joseph Maughan from 1851–59, and then independently. He was a

member of the AA, and served on the RIBA Council. His practice in Lincolnshire, East Anglia and neighbouring counties was very large, consisting mainly of church building, though he also designed parsonages, country houses and a few office buildings. His work included The Rectory, Amcotts, Lincs. (1862 and 1880): The Rectory, Utterby, Lincs. (1863): St Matthew, Skegness, Lincs. (1879–80): Holy Trinity, Wanstead, Essex (1887–90).

FOWLER, William: 1761–1832
Born at Winterton, Lincs., where he became a master-builder and architect of local importance. His clients were mainly farmers and local clergy and gentlemen. He was an antiquary and artist of considerable repute, he specialized in Roman pavements and mediaeval glass, and volumes of his coloured engravings were published in 1804, 1809 and 1824. His eldest son, Joseph (1791–1882), assisted him, and eventually took over his practice. William Fowler's work included the stables at Cleatham Hall, Manton, Lincs. (1802): No. 35 West Street, Winterton, Lincs. (1827: his own house): the Vicarage, Caythorpe, Lincs. (1827).

GARNER, Thomas: 1839–1906
Born at Wasperton Hill, Warwicks.: articled to Sir George Gilbert
Scott 1856: practised for a few years in Warwickshire before joining
G. F. Bodley in 1869, a partnership which lasted till 1897. They
collaborated closely and it is not easy to attribute their work specific-
ally. (See Bodley for some of their achievements in partnership.)
Independently, Garner's work included the North Block, Marlborough College, Wilts. (1893): Moreton House, Hampstead, London (1896): the chancel at Downside Abbey, Somerset (1901–5):
the Empire Hotel, Buxton, Derbys. (c. 1906).

GANDON, James: 1743–1823
Born in London, the son of Peter Gandon, whose father had been a
Huguenot refugee: educated at a boarding school in Kensington:
then became a pupil at Shipley's Drawing Academy, at the same
time working under Sir William Chambers; set up in practice 1764.
He was the winner of the first Gold Medal for Architecture awarded
by the Royal Academy, where he entered the Schools in 1769. In
1776, he won the competition for the new Bethlehem Hospital, in
which he was assisted by John Howard, the prison reformer, but his
design was not used. In 1781 Gandon moved to Ireland where he
continued to practise in Dublin till 1808, when he retired to Lucan
near the city, where he died. In addition to his considerable architectural contributions to Dublin, it is probable that he also assisted
in the street planning carried out there by the Commissioners for
Making Wide and Convenient Streets, between 1757 and 1840.
Gandon was an Honorary Member of the Architects' Club in
London, and one of the original members of the Royal Irish Academy. In 1767–71 (with John Woolfe) he published a continuation of
Colen Campbell's *Vitruvius Britannicus*. His work included the Shire
Hall, Nottingham (1770: altered since): the Court House and Gaol,
Waterford (1784): and, in Dublin, the Custom House (1781–91):
extensions to Parliament House (1782–89: later the Bank of Ireland):
the Four Courts (1786–1802): old Carlisle Bridge (1791–4: now
replaced by O'Connell Bridge): the King's Inns (1795–1808: with
H. A. Baker).

GANDY (later DEERING), John Peter, RA: 1787–1850

The younger brother of Joseph and Michael Gandy: a pupil of James Wyatt: entered the Royal Academy Schools: won the Silver Medal in 1806: in 1808 he had a post in the Barrack Office which he retained when he joined a small expedition to Greece to study antiquities, organized by the Society of Dilettanti in 1811–13. The results were published as *The Unedited Antiquities of Attica* (1817). With Sir W. Gell, who was a member of the party, Gandy published *Pompeiana* (1817–19). About 1828 Gandy inherited an estate from a friend, Henry Deering, whose surname he then assumed, and thereafter ceased to practise architecture, but lived as a country gentleman: he was High Sheriff of Bucks. in 1840 and M.P. for Bucks. in 1847. His work included St Mark, North Audley Street, London (1825–8): the Infirmary, Stamford, Lincs. (1826–8: later the Stamford and Rutland Hospital): University College, Gower Street, London (1827–9: with William Wilkins): the Pimlico Literary Institute, Ebury Street, London (1830).

GANDY, Joseph Michael: 1771–1843

The son of an employee at White's Club, London: *c.* 1786 he started work in the office of James Wyatt: in 1789 entered the Royal Academy Schools and won the Silver and Gold Medals in 1789 and 1790 respectively: toured in Italy 1794–8: worked as a draughtsman in the office of Sir John Soane: began independent practice 1801. He became an ARA in 1803: was in Liverpool for a short time: acted as tutor to Soane's eldest son: illustrated topographical works: and became increasingly involved in financial difficulties, spending some time in the Fleet Prison. He is better known for his numerous drawings and paintings of architectural fantasies, and for his two books, both published in 1805, *The Rural Architect* and *Designs for Cottages*, than for his buildings which were few: they included St Anne's House, Kennington Lane, Lambeth, London: the Public Bath, Bath Street, Lancaster (1806): Doric House, Sion Hill, Bath, Som. (*c.* 1810). Gandy's brother and pupil, Michael (1778–1862), was an assistant to James Wyatt: spent some time in the Indian naval service: and finally worked as an architectural draughtsman to Edward Holt, Francis Goodwin, and Sir Jeffry Wyatville. In 1842 he published *Architectural Illustrations of Windsor Castle*, in collaboration with Benjamin Baud, who had been a pupil of Francis Goodwin and Sir Jeffry Wyatville, and laid out the Brompton Cemetery,

Kensington, London (1839–40), where he also designed the Chapel.

GEARY, Stephen: *c.* 1797–1854

He was Architect to the London Cemetery Company, and is chiefly known for his work in laying out cemeteries during the mid-nineteenth century. These included Highgate (1838): Peckham: Nunhead: Brighton. He designed a statue of George IV (known as King's Cross) that was set up at Battlebridge, St Pancras, London (1830: dem. 1845), the lower part being used as a police station, and later as a public house with a camera obscura in the upper storey.

GEORGE, Sir Ernest, RA, FRIBA: 1839–1922

The son of a wholesale iron dealer in Southwark, London: educated at a small school at Clapham Common, and at Brighton and Reading: articled to Samuel Hewitt in London: awarded Royal Academy Gold Medal 1859. He set up practice in partnership with Thomas Vaughan, and later with Harold Peto (1828–97), and then with Alfred Yeates. He was Royal Gold Medallist 1896: knighted 1907: President of the RIBA 1908–10: had a large and successful practice which included commissions in India, and was a water-colour artist of great ability. His work included St Pancras, Rousdon, Devonshire (*c.* 1870: with Vaughan): No. 8 Stratton Street, London (1871: with Vaughan): Nos. 6–7 St Mary-at-Hill, London (1873: with Vaughan): Rousdon House, Devonshire (*c.* 1880: with Vaughan): houses in Harrington Gardens and Collingham Gardens, Kensington, London (1881: with Peto): Nos. 5, 105–6, 110–13 Mount Street, London (1885–90: with Peto): St Andrew, Guildersfield Road, Wandsworth, London (1886: with Peto): Claridge's Hotel, Brook Street, London (1894–7: with Yeates: enlarged since): the Crematorium, Golders Green, London (1905: with Yeates): Busbridge Hall, Surrey (1906: with Yeates): Royal Exchange Buildings, Cornhill, London (1907–10: with Yeates): Royal Academy of Music, Marylebone Road, London (1910–11: with Yeates): the design of Southwark Bridge, London (1915–19).

GERBIER, Sir Balthasar: *c.* 1591–1667

Of Dutch birth, he joined the entourage of the Duke of Buckingham in 1613: came to England with him, and became his Surveyor.

Gerbier was a painter and courtier: and was involved in various secret political activities. He became a British subject in 1641: a Royalist sympathizer, he spent the period of Puritan ascendancy in Holland and Cayenne, returning to England in 1660. In 1648 he attempted to found an academy of elocution in Bethnal Green, but this failed within a year. He was the author of *A Brief Discourse Concerning the three chief Principles of Magnificent Building* (1662) and *Counsel and Advice to all Builders* (1663). He was almost certainly the designer of the York Water Gate (1626) in the Victoria Embankment Gardens, London: and designed the house of Hamstead Marshall, Berks. *c.* 1660, completed after his death by William Winde, and since destroyed.

GIBBS, James: 1682–1754 (Portrait: see Plate III)
The younger son of Peter Gibbs, a gentleman of Footdeesmire, near Aberdeen. He spent some time travelling through Europe, and studied architecture in Italy, where he met influential British visitors, who commissioned drawings from him and assisted him when he re- turned to England in 1709. His patron, the Earl of Oxford, helped him to a Surveyorship to the Commissioners for Building Fifty New Churches, and he held this post till 1715. He had a large and successful practice, much helped by his patrons among the nobility and gentry; designed several monuments; and held the sinecure post of Architect to the Office of Ordnance. He published *A Book of Architecture* (1728): *Rules for Drawing the Several Parts of Architecture* (1732): and *Bibliotheca Radcliviana* (1747). His work included, in London: St Mary-le-Strand (1714–17): St Peter, Vere Street, Marylebone (1721–4): St Martin-in-the-Fields (1722–6): St Bar- tholomew's Hospital (1730–59): and the Senate House, Cambridge (1722–30): the rebuilding of All Saints, now the Cathedral, Derby (1723–5: except the w. tower): Fellows' Building, King's College, Cambridge (1724–9): Sudbrooke House, Petersham, Surrey (1726– 8): Kelmarsh Hall, Northants (*c.* 1727–32): No. 16 Arlington Street, Piccadilly, London (1736: later part of the Overseas League): the Radcliffe Camera, Oxford (1737–49: adaptation and completion of Hawksmoor's design): in the grounds of Stowe House, Bucks., the Gothic Temple (*c.* 1740): the Boycott Pavilions (*c.* 1730: altered later): the Temple of Friendship (1739): the Cobham Monument (1747): alterations and interior work, including the Great Hall, Ragley Hall, Warwicks. (1750–5).

GIBSON, John, FSA, FRIBA: 1814–92
Was a pupil of J. A. Hansom at Birmingham: and later of Sir Charles
Barry, whose assistant he was for three years. Set up independently in
1844 and established a large and successful private practice. He
served on the RIBA Council: was a Vice-President: and Royal Gold
Medallist 1890. Became Architect to the National Provincial Bank
in 1864, and built about forty of their branches in London and the
provinces. His work included Bloomsbury Central Baptist Church,
Shaftesbury Avenue, London (1845–8): St John the Baptist, Shenstone, Staffs. (1853): Dobroyd Castle, Todmorden, Yorks. (1865:
later a school): the National Provincial Bank, Bishopsgate, London
(1865): the Unitarian Church (1869) and the Town Hall (1870) at
Todmorden, Yorks.: Nutfield Priory, Surrey (1871): SPCK Building,
Northumberland Avenue, London (1876–9): Child's Bank, Fleet
Street, London (1879).

GODWIN, Edward William: 1833–86
The son of a Bristol decorator: trained in the office of a local archi-
tect, and practised there himself until about 1862 when he went to
London. He contributed regularly to professional journals, particu-
larly to *The British Architect*: was a designer of theatrical costumes and
scenery: and published *Temple Bar Illustrated* (1877) and *Artistic
Conservatories and other Horticultural Buildings* (1880). One of his clients
was Oscar Wilde, for whom he re-designed No. 33 Tite Street,
Chelsea, London (1884–5). His work included the Town Hall,
Northampton (1861–4): premises for Anderson's Rubber Co.,
Stokes Croft, Bristol, Som. (1862): the Town Hall, Congleton,
Cheshire (1864): the Guildhall, Plymouth (1870–4: he was con-
sultant to Norman and Hine): No. 148 New Bond Street, London
(c. 1876): No. 35 Swan Walk, Chelsea, London (1879).

GODWIN, George, FSA, FRS, FRIBA: 1815–88 (Portrait: see
Plate XI)
Born in Brompton, London, the son of George Godwin, an architect: entered his father's office, and practised himself and with his
younger brother, Henry. He was District Surveyor for South Islington for some time: a Vice-President of the Institute: Royal Gold
Medallist 1881. He took over the Editorship of *The Builder* in 1844,
and retained it until he retired in 1883. He read papers before the
Institute: wrote pamphlets: was the author of *The Churches of London*

(1838), and of a number of books concerned with the housing and sanitary conditions existing among the working classes of that time. His work included St Mary Boltons, Kensington, London (1850): the Drinking Fountain, Clifton Down, Bristol (1861: with Henry Godwin): Chiddinglye, West Hoathly, Sussex (1866: with Henry Godwin: built as Rockhurst): St Jude, Collingham Road, Kensington, London (1870): St Luke, Redcliffe Square, Kensington, London (1874).

GOLDICUTT, John: 1793–1842

Studied at the Royal Academy Schools, where he gained the Silver Medal 1814: from 1815–19 he was in Paris, where he studied architecture; then in Italy. He was a pupil of Henry Hakewill, for whom he worked until 1830, and also practised independently: Hon. Secretary of the Institute of British Architects at its formation: Surveyor for the districts of St Clement Danes and St Mary-le-Strand: and the author of *Antiquities of Sicily* (1819): *Specimens of Ancient Decorations from Pompeii* (1825): and *Heriot's Hospital, Edinburgh* (1826). He was a draughtsman of great ability, but little of his architectural work is known or survives: it included a Casino on the front at Worthing, Sussex (1830), and St James, Sussex Gardens, Paddington, London (1841–3: with G. Gutch: since remodelled).

GOLDIE, George: 1828–87

Born at York: educated at St Cuthbert's College, near Durham: a pupil, and then assistant to Hadfield and Weightman of Sheffield. Set up his own practice in London, which later became the partnership of Goldie, Child and Goldie. He built a number of Roman Catholic Pro-Cathedrals, churches, and convents, and his work included St Peter, Castle Road, Scarborough, Yorks. (1858): the Church of the Assumption, Kensington Square, London (1875): St Anne's School, Seminary Street, Leeds (1877: formerly the R.C. Seminary): St James, Spanish Place, Marylebone, London (1885–90: with his partners): the Church of the Holy Redeemer, Cheyne Row, Chelsea, London (1895).

GOOD, Joseph Henry, FIBA: 1775–1857

The son of the Rev. Joseph Good, of Sambrook, Somerset: articled to Sir John Soane 1795–99, and became well known as a Surveyor: his clients included the Armourers' and Braziers' Company, the

Hope Assurance Company, and the Commissioners for Building New Churches. He was also Clerk of the Works at the Tower, Royal Mint, and Kensington Palace. He was an original member of the Institute of British Architects. His work included the Armourers' and Braziers' Hall, Coleman Street, London (1840).

GOODHART-RENDEL, Harry Stuart, CBE, MUS.B, FSA, FRIBA: 1887–1959
A grandson of Lord Rendel: educated at Eton, and Trinity College, Cambridge, where he studied music under Sir Donald Tovey: articled to Sir Charles Nicholson. He set up in practice in London in 1910, and also worked in the Var district of France: formed a partnership with H. L. Curtis in 1930, which F. G. Broadbent joined in 1945. Goodhart-Rendel was President of the AA 1924–5, and Director of its School of Architecture 1936–8: served on the Council of the Institute: was Vice-President 1933–5: President 1937–9: President of the Architects' Benevolent Society 1937–9, and Hon. Treasurer 1940–59: a Past President of the Franco-British Union of Architects: served on committees of a number of official bodies, including the Board of Architectural Education, the Advisory Council of the National Buildings Record, and (from 1945–59) the MHLG Advisory Committee on Buildings of Special Architectural or Historic Interest: was President of the Guild of Catholic Artists and Craftsmen 1946–52: and of the Design and Industries Association 1948–50. In addition to his architectural career, Goodhart-Rendel was recognized as a musician and pianist, and as an able writer: he was a Governor of Sadler's Wells 1934–59: Vice-President of the Royal Academy of Music 1953–59: his published works included *Nicholas Hawksmoor* (a monograph): *Vitruvian Nights*: *Fine Art*: *How Architecture is made*: *English Architecture since the Regency*: and he contributed many articles to professional journals. His practice included a good deal of country house remodelling, ecclesiastical work, and meticulous restoration of his predecessors' designs. His work included extensive additions to Tetton House, nr. Kingston, Som. (1924–6): alterations and remodelling at Bessborough House, Kilkenny, Eire (1926–30): Hay's Wharf head offices, Southwark, London (1929): St Wilfrid, Brighton, Sussex (1933–4): Alliance Building Society, North Street, Brighton, Sussex (1935): Council housing estate at East Clandon, Surrey (1949): Our Lady of Peace, Sheen Road, Richmond, Surrey (1953–4): SS Francis and Anthony,

Crawley, Sussex (1958–9): restoration of All Souls, Langham Place, London, and of St John the Divine, Kennington, London, after Second World War damage.

GOODRIDGE, Henry Edmund: *c.* 1800–63

The son of James Goodridge, who was a builder in Bath. The younger Goodridge exhibited at the Royal Academy 1828–48, and carried on a successful architectural practice in Bath, to which his son, A. S. Goodridge, succeeded. The work of H. E. Goodridge at Bath included the front of the Congregational Church, Argyle Street (1821): The Corridor (1825): the Lansdowne Tower (1825–6): Cleveland Bridge (1827): Holy Trinity, Combe Down (1832): the Congregational Church, Charlotte Street (1854). He also carried out extensions and the chapel at Downside Abbey, Som. (1823), and built Holy Trinity, Frome, Som. (1837), and Devizes Castle, Wilts. (1842: additions since).

GOODWIN, Francis: 1784–1835

Born at King's Lynn, Norfolk: pupil under J. Coxedge in London: exhibited at the Royal Academy: in 1833 his designs for the new House of Commons were printed by the Committee of the House, and published by Goodwin as *Plans of the New House of Commons*. He was also the author of *Domestic Architecture* (1833–4), re-titled *Rural Architecture* in 1835. He practised in the North and Midlands, and was in partnership for a time with Richard Lane. His work included the first Town Hall, Manchester (1819–34: dem. 1911, the central façades being re-erected in Heaton Park): Holy Trinity, Bordesley, Birmingham (1820–2): the Town Hall and Assembly Rooms, Macclesfield, Cheshire (1823–4): the County Gaol, Derby (1823–7: remodelled since): St Leonard, Bilston, Staffs. (1826) and the Parsonage (1830): St George, Manchester (1826–7): St John the Evangelist, Derby (1828): St Thomas, Pendleton, Lancs. (1830: with Richard Lane).

GOUGH, Alexander Dick: 1804–71

As a youth, he travelled on the Continent, and on his return to England, c. 1823, he entered the office of Benjamin Wyatt, where he remained as a pupil and then an assistant, till 1836, when he set up in partnership with R. L. Roumieu: they practised together till 1848. Gough's two sons, Charles and Hugh Roumieu, were associated with him professionally for many years. His practice consisted mainly of churches, schools and parsonages, and his work included the Literary Institute, Almeida Street, Islington, London (1837: with R. L. Roumieu): Milner Square, Islington (pre-1841: with R. L. Roumieu): St Mark (church and schools), Tollington Park, Islington, London (1854): Tollington Park, Islington, London (built 1860-70: with R. L. Roumieu): St Anne, Poole's Park, Islington, London (1871): St John (church and parsonage), Tunbridge Wells, Kent.

GOUGH, Hugh Roumieu: 1843-1904
The third son of A. D. Gough. On completion of his architectural training he spent some time on the Continent, and in 1864 entered the War Office, where he later became Chief Draughtsman at Woolwich Arsenal. He worked with his father for many years, before setting up his own practice in 1870. His work included Holy Saviour, Herne Hill, London (1866-7): St Paul, Hammersmith, London (1882: with J. P. Seddon): St Cuthbert, Philbeach Gardens, Kensington, London (1884-7).

GRAHAM, James Gillespie: 1777-1855
A Scottish architect, born in Dunblane of poor parents: his father's surname was Gillespie: apprenticed to a joiner: married an heiress, and took her surname of Graham. He practised in Edinburgh, where he collaborated with A. W. N. Pugin in the design of the Tolbooth Church, and built a number of Gothic Revival mansions in Scotland, including Murthley House, Perthshire. His work included the Roman Catholic Cathedral of St Andrew, Clyde Street, Glasgow (1816): Dr Jamieson's Chapel, Nicholson Street, Edinburgh (1819): laying out the Moray Estate, Edinburgh (c. 1822): the Deaf and Dumb Institution, Henderson Row, Edinburgh (1823).

GREEN, John: 1787-1852
A Newcastle-on-Tyne architect, with an extensive practice in Northumberland and Co. Durham, who was for some time much employed by the Duke of Northumberland on church building. His son, Benjamin (d. 1858), was in close partnership with him, and from c. 1830 it is difficult to attribute the work of father and son separately, but it is probable that in Northumberland, John Green's work included the Literary and Philosophical Society, Newcastle-

on-Tyne (1822–5): Bellingham Bridge (1834): St Mary, Alnwick (1836): Holy Trinity, Seghill (1849). The work of father and son together included St Alban, Earsdon (1836–7): the Tyne Master Mariners' Asylum, Tynemouth (1837): Holy Saviour Church, Tynemouth (1841): Holy Trinity, Cambo (1842). The work of Benjamin Green in Northumberland included the Theatre, Newcastle-on-Tyne (1837): Holy Saviour, Sugley (1837): All Saints cemetery entrance, Jesmond Road, Newcastle-on-Tyne (1853–7).

GREENWAY, Francis Howard: 1777–1837
The youngest son of Francis Greenway, a Gloucestershire mason: a pupil of John Nash in London, where he exhibited at the Royal Academy in 1800. In 1805 he joined his two brothers in Bristol as the architect member of their building and masonry business: in 1809 they were declared bankrupt, and in 1812 Francis Greenway was convicted of forgery, and sentenced first to death and then to transportation to Australia. There, the Governor, Lachlan Macquarie, befriended him, and employed him in the planning of Sydney, which was followed by a pardon for Greenway. He became Government Architect in 1816. His work included the Hotel, and Assembly Rooms, The Mall, Clifton, Bristol (1806–11: completed by Joseph Kay): in Australia, St Matthew, Windsor, N.S.W. (1817): the Macquarie Tower, Sydney (1818): St Luke, Liverpool, N.S.W. (1818–25): St James, Sydney, N.S.W. (1819): the Court House, Sydney.

GREGAN, John Edgar, FRIBA: 1813–55
Studied as a draughtsman under T. W. Atkinson of Manchester: then built up a good private practice there in 1840. He was Hon. Secretary of the Royal Institution in Manchester, and took much interest in the local School of Design, and the Free Library. His work there included Williams Deacon's Bank, St Ann Street (1848–9: built as Sir Benjamin Heywood's Bank): a Warehouse for Barbour & Ashton, Parker/Portland Streets (1850): the College of Commerce, Princess Street (1854: built as the Mechanics' Institution).

GRELLIER, William: 1807–52
Born in Surrey: articled to George Smith in 1823: awarded the Royal Academy Silver Medal 1826, and Gold Medal 1829: acted as

Honorary Secretary to the Architectural Society for four years from its formation in 1831. He was District Surveyor for Whitechapel in 1838, and in 1849 Master of the Tylers' and Bricklayers' Company, for whom he surveyed property, and designed, free of charge, Almshouses in Balls Pond Road, Islington, London, in 1835. His work included the rebuilding of the roof of St Ethelburga, Bishopsgate, London (*c.* 1835): the Royal Exchange Insurance Buildings, Dale Street, Liverpool (1846–9).

GRIBBLE, Herbert A.: 1847–94
Born at Plymouth: apprenticed there to the architect, J. Norman: came to London *c.* 1867: studied at the National Art Training Schools, South Kensington: and entered the office of J. A. Hansom, with whom he stayed for ten years, before setting up his own practice. His work included Brompton Oratory, Kensington, London (1880): the Artisans' Dwellings, Notte Street, Plymouth (1883): the Armada Monument, Plymouth (1888: with W. C. May).

GRIFFITH, William Pettit, FSA, FRIBA: 1815–84
The son of John William Griffith (d. 1855), who was Surveyor to St Botolph's, Aldersgate, and to the London Estates of St John's College, Cambridge, and who built a number of villas in the northern suburbs of London. William Griffith was trained as an architect, and built up a sound practice in London. He was an Honorary Member of the Bedfordshire and Liverpool Architectural Societies, and of the Surrey Archaeological Society: contributed papers to the proceedings of architectural and archaeological bodies, and was the author of a number of books including *Grecian Architecture*: *Natural System of Architecture*: and *Mediaeval Architecture*. His work included a number of parochial schools, some church restoration, and the Royal Hospital for Incurables, West Hill, Wandsworth, London (1864–5: constructed round the original house, Melrose Hall, built 1804).

GRIMTHORPE, Lord: See BECKETT

GUNDULPH, Bishop: d. 1107
A Norman: Bishop of Rochester in 1077: Surveyor and Architect to William the Conqueror. His work included a fortification called St Leonard's Tower, at West Malling, Kent, where he founded a

Benedictine nunnery (the present convent incorporates the ruins): a church in Rochester (*c.* 1080) which later became the Cathedral: a large part of Rochester Castle: the White Tower, Tower of London (1081–1090).

GWILT, George: 1746–1807

Born in London, the son of Richard Gwilt, a wig-maker: apprenticed as a boy to a London mason: became architect to the West India Dock Company: Surveyor to the County of Surrey: St George's, Southwark: the Commissioners of Sewers for Surrey: and the Clink Paving Commissioners: he was Master of the Masons' Company in 1790. His work included the bridges at Cobham (1782), Leatherhead (1782), Godalming (1782–3), all in Surrey: and in London the tower and west end of the church of St Mary-at-Hill (1787–8). His elder son, George, FSA (1775–1856), was born in Southwark, and apprenticed to his father. He was an antiquary, and an authority on antiquities: a regular contributor to professional publications: three times Master of the Masons' Company: carried out much restoration work at Southwark Cathedral.

GWILT, Joseph, FSA: 1784–1863

Born in Southwark, the younger son of George Gwilt the elder: educated St Paul's School: studied in his father's office and at the Royal Academy Schools, where he was awarded the Silver Medal 1801. He set up in independent practice while still a young man: made a four-year tour of France and Italy 1814–18: was Surveyor to the Commissioners of Sewers for Surrey and Kent; to the Grocers' and Waxchandlers' Company, and to the Imperial Fire Assurance Company. He was a Fellow of the Royal Astronomical Society, and an acknowledged authority on architectural and antiquarian subjects. Among his numerous published works were *A Treatise on the Equilibrium of Arches* (1811): a new edition of Chambers' *Treatise on the Decorative Part of Civil Architecture* (1825): a translation of *The Architecture of Vitruvius* (1826): *Rudiments of Architecture* (1826): *Encyclopaedia of Architecture* (1842): and a new edition of P. Nicholson's *Principles of Architecture* (1848). His younger son, John Sebastian Gwilt (1811–90), made the drawings for the *Encyclopaedia*. Gwilt's architectural work included St Margaret, Lee, Lewisham, London (1813: dem.): St Thomas, Charlton, Greenwich, London (1847–50).

GWYNN, John: d. 1786

He came from Shrewsbury, and is believed to have begun his career as a carpenter: he acquired a knowledge of architecture probably more by his own efforts than by any training. He was a friend of Dr Johnson; a prolific writer on architectural subjects: and an able draughtsman. He was among those who attempted to launch an academy for improvement of the arts, in 1755: this was not accomplished, but when the Royal Academy was founded in 1768, Gwynn was a founder member. His published works included *An Essay on Harmony as it relates chiefly to Situation and Building* (1734): *An Essay on Design* (1749): and *London and Westminster Improved* (1766), the last-named being a suggested replanning of the metropolis, extraordinarily prophetic and showing much foresight and ability. He carried out some building in Oxford, which has now disappeared, and designed the reredos at Holy Trinity, Bledlow Ridge, Bucks., but it is as a bridge builder that he is chiefly known. His work included the Severn Bridge, Atcham, Salop (1769–71): the English Bridge, Shrewsbury, Salop (1769–74): the Severn Bridge, Worcester (1771–80: widened and lengthened since): Magdalen Bridge, Oxford (1772–82). His pupil and assistant, William Hayward (*c.* 1740–82), designed and built a bridge in the grounds of Attingham Hall, Salop (1780), and designed the bridge at Henley-on-Thames, Oxon. (completed in 1786 after his death).

HABERSHON, Matthew: 1789–1852

A Yorkshireman: in 1806 articled to William Atkinson, for whom he worked later as an assistant: entered the Royal Academy Schools 1808. In 1842 was commissioned by the London Society for Promoting Christianity among the Jews to design the Anglican Cathedral in Jerusalem. Was the author of *The Finest Existing Specimens of Ancient Half-Timbered Houses of England* (1836), and of books on Biblical prophecies. His work included St Peter, Belper, Derbys. (1824): the Town Hall, Derby (1828): Christ Church, Derby (1839–40): St Catherine, Burbage, Leics. (1842): St Thomas, Kimberworth, Yorks. (1842): the Cathedral of St James at Jerusalem was built by J. Johns in 1844. His sons, Edward and William Gillbee, practised for a time in partnership, and built the Harecourt Congregational Church, Balls Pond Road, Islington, London (1855). When their association was dissolved, Edward went into partnership with a former pupil, E. P. L. Brock (1833–95): their work included Holy Trinity, Wallington, Surrey (1867): Holy Trinity Chapel, Ebernoe, nr. Petworth, Sussex (1867): St Andrew, Queen's Road, Hastings, Sussex (1869): St John the Evangelist, Copthorne, Sussex (1877). Independently, Edward Habershon built Highbury Park Presbyterian Church, Islington, London (1863). When he retired, Brock continued to practise alone, his independent work including the Rectory, West Deeping, Lincs. (1869): St Stephen, Hammerwood, Sussex (1879–80): Christ Church, Newhaven, Sussex (1881). William Gillbee Habershon (1818–91) joined A. R. Pite, with whom he built St James, Warter, Yorks. (1862). He then went into partnership with Fawckner: their work included an extension to the Royal School, Lansdown, Bath, Som. (1884): St Peter, Shelley, Essex (1888): St Helen and All Saints, Beckham, Norfolk (1890–1).

HADFIELD, Matthew Ellison, FRIBA: 1812–85

Born at Lees Hall, Glossop, Derbys., the eldest son of Joseph Hadfield: articled to Woodhead and Hurst of Doncaster, 1831: in 1834 entered the office of P. F. Robinson, in London. Set up practice in Sheffield in 1837, taking into partnership in 1838 John Grey Weightman (1801–72), who retired in 1858: Hadfield's son, Charles, joined the firm in 1864. Hadfield served on the Council of the Institute: his practice in the northern counties was extensive: he built many public and commercial buildings in Sheffield; hotels, railway stations, and works for the Manchester, Sheffield and Lincolnshire Railway (with their engineer, John Fowler), and for the Great Northern Railway Company. His work included the Town Hall, Glossop, Derbys. (1838: with Weightman): St Bede, Rotherham, Yorks. (1843): the Roman Catholic Cathedral of St John, Salford, Manchester (1845: with Weightman): St Mary, Burnley, Lancs. (1846: with Weightman): the Victoria Hotel, Sheffield (1860): the Royal Hotel, Grimsby, Lincs. (1863–5): the Corn Exchange, Sheffield (1878: with Charles Hadfield).

HAGUE, Daniel: *c.* 1736–*c.* 1816
The son of Daniel Hague, a Wiltshire yeoman: apprenticed to Thomas Manley, a Bristol mason: and remained there to become a prosperous builder and surveyor, till *c.* 1805 when his son took over his business. His work at Bristol included the Royal Infirmary (1784, with Thomas Paty: much altered and enlarged since): St Paul, Portland Square (1789–94): the laying out of Portland Square (1790).

HAKEWILL, Edward Charles: 1812–72
The younger son of Henry Hakewill: a pupil of Philip Hardwick from 1831 to 1838, when he set up in practice. He was District Surveyor for St Clement Danes and St Mary-le-Strand, and later for the District of Hanover Square: in 1851 he published *The Temple: an Essay on the Ark, the Tabernacle, and the Temples of Jerusalem.* His work included St Leonard, Beaumont-cum-Moze, Essex (*c.* 1854): St Andrew, Rushmere, nr. Ipswich (1861): St Peter, Thurston, Suffolk (1861–2).

HAKEWILL, Henry: 1771–1830
The eldest son of John Hakewill, a painter and decorator: a pupil of John Yenn: studied at the Royal Academy Schools, where he won the Silver Medal in 1790. He was Architect to the Radcliffe Trustees at Oxford, to the Benchers of the Middle Temple and, from 1809 till his death, to Rugby School: in 1823 he wrote *An Account of the Roman Villa discovered at Northleigh, Oxfordshire in the years 1813–14–15–16.* His work included the Old Buildings, Headmaster's House, and Arnold Library at Rugby School, Warwicks. (1809–42): The Judge's

114

Lodging, Warwick (1814–16): Holy Trinity, Wolverton, Bucks. (1815): Stisted Hall, Essex (1823): St Peter, Eaton Square, London (1824–7: burnt in 1836, but rebuilt to his designs by his son J. H. Hakewill): Hakewill's brother, James (1778–1843), who carried on the family decorating business, also practised as an architect, but to a very limited extent, and is known for his published works and drawings, which included *The History of Windsor and its Neighbourhood* (1813): *A Picturesque Tour of Italy* (1818–20): *A Picturesque Tour in the Island of Jamaica* (1825): and *An Attempt to determine the exact character of Elizabethan Architecture* (1835).

HAKEWILL, John Henry, FIBA: 1811–80
The elder son of Henry Hakewill: articled to his father. He practised mainly in Wiltshire, Suffolk and Essex, and built many churches, schools and parsonages: he was one of the consulting architects to the Incorporated Church Building Society, and a founder of the Architects' Benevolent Fund. His work included St James, Stert, Wilts. (1846): St Mary, Seagry, Wilts. (1849): St Peter, Bury St Edmunds, Suffolk (1858): Stowlangtoft Hall, Suffolk (1859): SS Philip and James, Neston, Corsham, Wilts. (1866).

HALFPENNY, William (also known as MICHAEL HOARE): d. 1755
A carpenter working at Richmond, Surrey, during the 1730s, and associated in the following decade with architectural work at Bristol. He was a prolific and well-known writer of architectural pattern books, some issued in collaboration with his son, John. Between 1722 and 1753 he produced some twenty of these publications, which included *Practical Architecture* (1724): *The Art of Sound Building* (1725): *Builder's Pocket Companion* (1728): *A New and Complete System of Architecture* (1749): *Rural Architecture in the Chinese Taste* (1750): *Six New Designs for Farmhouses* (1751): *Rural Architecture in the Gothic Taste* (1752): *The Country Gentleman's Pocket Companion and Builder's Assistant* (1753). In 1741–3 he completed the building of Redland Chapel, Bristol, which may have been designed by John Strahan, and his architectural work included Holy Trinity, Leeds (1722–7): Coopers' Hall, Bristol (1743–4).

HALIBURTON: see BURTON, James.

HAMILTON, David: 1768–1843

Born in Glasgow in humble circumstances: self-taught to a large degree, he built up a large and successful practice in Glasgow, and the neighbourhood. He was the only Scottish architect to compete in the design for the new Houses of Parliament, for which he was awarded a premium. He built a number of country houses and mansions, including Dunlop House, Ayrshire: Lennox Castle: and Hamilton Palace. His work in Glasgow included Hutcheson's Hospital, Ingram Street (1802–5): the Royal Exchange (1828–30: later Stirling's Library): the Bridge of Sighs (1833), the Gates (1838) and the Lodge (1839) at the Glasgow Necropolis: the British Linen Bank (1840): the Western Club, Buchanan Street (1840–1).

HAMILTON, Thomas: 1784–1858

Born in Edinburgh, the son of a carpenter and builder: apprenticed to his father, later becoming his assistant. He won the competition for the Burns Memorial (1818) and thus started a prosperous and extensive architectural practice in Edinburgh. He was one of the founders and the first Treasurer of the Royal Scottish Academy, and a member of the Institute of British Architects 1838–46. He laid out part of Edinburgh, including the George IV Bridge and Johnson Terrace in 1827, and his work included the Burns Memorial, Alloway, near Ayr (1818–23): the Royal High School, Calton Hill, Edinburgh (1825–9): the Burns Monument, Calton Hill, Edinburgh (1830).

HANSOM, Joseph Aloysius: 1803–82

Born in York, the son of a joiner, to whom he was apprenticed: he later became the pupil and then the assistant of a York architect named Philips: in 1825 he went to Halifax, where he worked in the office of a local architect named Oates, and in 1828 went into partnership with Edward Welch. In 1834 Hansom was involved in bankruptcy over the building of Birmingham Town Hall, which he and Welch had designed, and he became business manager to Dempster Hemming, who had many financial and industrial interests. With Hemming's encouragement, he perfected and registered his invention, the 'Patent Safety Cab', and having left Hemming's employ, devoted himself to the administration of the company to whom he had sold his patent rights. In 1842 he founded and published the first number of *The Builder*. He was in partnership at different times with his brother, Charles (the architect of Clifton College, Bristol, 1860–80), his son, Henry, and with E. W. Pugin: another son, Edward John (1842–1900), later went into partnership with Archibald Mathias Dunn (d. 1917): the firm eventually became Dunn and Fenwicke, and carried out much Roman Catholic church building in the north of England. The work of J. A. Hansom included the Town Hall, Birmingham (1832–4: with Welch: continued by Charles Edge): St Scholastica's Priory, Atherstone, Warwicks. (1837–41): St Mary, Studley, Warwicks. (1853): the Roman Catholic Cathedral of SS Mary and Boniface, Plymouth, Devonshire (1858): St Augustine's Priory (1863) and nunnery (1871), at Abbotskerswell, Devonshire: St Philip Neri, Arundel, Sussex (1868–73): the Church of the Holy Name, Oxford Road, Manchester (1869): St Mary's Priory (a Servite church), Fulham Road, London (1876).

HARDWICK, Philip, RA, FRS, FSA: 1792–1870

The son of Thomas Hardwick: educated at Dr Barrow's School in Soho: attended the Royal Academy Schools and studied architecture in his father's office: visited France and Italy 1815–19: then started independent practice in London. He was appointed Architect to the Bridewell and Bethlehem Hospitals 1816: St Katharine's Dock Company 1825: St Bartholomew's Hospital 1827: the Goldsmiths' Company 1828: he was architect to the Duke of Wellington, and Surveyor to the Portman Estate: a member of the Institute of Civil Engineers; an original member and Vice-President of the Institute of British Architects, and Royal Gold Medallist 1854. In 1847 his health failed, and from then till his retirement in 1861 his son, Philip Charles, took over much of his practice, so that the buildings of father and son are often difficult to identify individually. The work of Philip Hardwick included Christ Church, Cosway Street, Marylebone, London (1824–5): Babraham Hall, Cambs. (1829–32: enlarged since): the Free Grammar School, Stockport, Cheshire (1829–32): Goldsmiths' Hall, Foster Lane, London (1829–35): No. 19 Old Broad Street, London (1833–4): the Arch, Portico, Lodges, and Hotel at Euston Station, London (1836–9: dem.): Curzon Street Goods Station, Birmingham, Warwicks. (1838): Seaford House, Belgrave Square, London (1842): the New Hall and Library, Lincoln's Inn, London (1843: built by P. C. Hardwick).

HARDWICK, Philip Charles, FSA, FRIBA: 1822–92
The son of Philip Hardwick: trained under Edward Blore: joined
his father's practice in 1842 and virtually took it over in 1847 when
the elder Hardwick's health declined. He was Architect to the Bank
of England: St Bartholomew's Hospital: the Goldsmiths' Company:
the Merchant Taylors' Company: Greenwich Hospital: Charterhouse: and Surveyor to the Portman Estate. His work included the
Great Hall at Euston Station, London (1846–9: dem.): Aldermaston
Court, Berks. (1848–51): the G.W.R. Hotel, Paddington Station,
London (1850–2): the Australia and New Zealand Bank, Threadneedle Street, London (1854): St John, Lewisham Way, Deptford,
London (1855): the Bank of England, South Parade, Leeds, Yorks.
(1862–4): Hassobury House, Farnham, Essex (1868): Charterhouse
School, Surrey (1872).

HARDWICK, Thomas, FSA: 1752–1829
The son of Thomas Hardwick, a mason of Brentford, Middx.: a
pupil of Sir William Chambers: entered the Royal Academy
Schools, where he won a Silver Medal in 1769: from 1776–9 he
travelled in Italy. He built up a successful practice as an architect
and surveyor: was architect to St Bartholomew's Hospital (1808):
Clerk of the Works at Hampton Court (1810), and at Richmond
(1815): a founder member of the Architects' Club; and the author
of a memoir of Sir William Chambers. His work included St Mary,
Wanstead, Essex (1790): the rebuilding of St Paul, Covent Garden,
London (1795: as nearly as practicable to Inigo Jones's design, after
its destruction by fire): the Nelson Column, Castle Green, Hereford
(1809): St John's Chapel, St John's Wood, London (1813): St
Mary, Marylebone Road, London (1813–17).

HARE, Henry Thomas, FRIBA: 1860–1921
Educated at Sheffield and Harrogate: articled to C. A. Bury of
Scarborough, 1876: studied at the École des Beaux Arts in Paris:
was an assistant to King and Hill in London, before setting up in
independent practice. He served on the RIBA Council for many
years; was a Vice-President, and President 1917–19: Technical
Adviser to the Building Works Section 1917–18: President of the AA
1902. He built many large public buildings, worked much in collaboration with other architects; was in partnership with Bertram Lisle.
His work included the Town Hall, Oxford (1892): Westminster

College, Cambridge (1899): the Technical College (1900) and Central Public Library (1906), Southend-on-Sea, Essex: the Public Library, Wolverhampton, Staffs. (1902): Ingram House, Strand, London (1902): University College of North Wales, Bangor (1907): the Public Library, Fulham Road, Fulham, London (1908–9).

HARRIS, Thomas, FRIBA: 1830–1900
Little is known of his early life: he was an Associate of the Institute in 1852: his patrons included Titus Salt, the industrial magnate, and Harry Batsford, the bookseller. Harris was the author of *Victorian Architecture* (1860): *Three Periods of English Architecture* (1894): and of a pamphlet 'A Historical and Descriptive Sketch of Marylebone Gardens' (1887). He produced the latter in conjunction with a reproduction setting of Old Marylebone Gardens, which he made and displayed publicly in order to help defray the cost of his additions to Marylebone Parish Church in 1883–4. He designed several large houses and mansions, and a number of shop and office buildings in London, now mostly demolished. His work included Nos. 58 and 60 Shaftesbury Avenue: No. 45 Wardour Street: and Batsford's bookshop at No. 94 High Holborn, London: Milner Field, Bingley, Yorks. (1871–3: Titus Salt's house): Bedstone Court, Salop (1884): Stokesay Court, Salop (1889).

HARRISON, Thomas: 1744–1829
Born at Richmond, Yorks., the son of a carpenter. With the help of his patron, Lord Dundas, he spent the years 1769–76 in Italy, where he designed the decoration of the Belvedere Cortile at Rome for Pope Clement XIV, and was elected a member of St Luke's Academy. On his return to England he set up practice in Chester. His work included the rebuilding of Lancaster Castle as a Gaol (1788–1802: completed by J. M. Gandy): Chester Castle, including County Courts, Prison, Armoury, Exchequer and Gateway (1793–1820): Portico Library, Mosley Street, Manchester (1802): Lyceum Club, Bold Street, Liverpool (1802): Lord Hill's Column, Shrewsbury (1814–16: based on a design by E. Haycock): Grosvenor Bridge, Chester (1827–32: carried out by J. Hartley).

HARTLEY, Jesse: 1780–1860
Born at Pontefract, Yorks., the son of a West Riding Bridgemaster: apprenticed as a stone-mason: succeeded to his father's post. From

1824–60 he was Dock Surveyor and Engineer at Liverpool, where he was responsible for the design and construction of Brunswick Dock (1832): Waterloo Dock (1834): Clarence and Albert Docks (1839–45): the Victoria Tower at Salisbury Dock (1848): Stanley and Wapping Dock warehouses (1850–7), and for many of the swing bridges and stone walls around the dock area. He became Consulting Engineer for the Dee Bridge at Chester, and Engineer for the Bolton and Manchester Railway and Canal. He designed a fireproof warehouse at the junction of Humber and Prince's Docks, Kingston-upon-Hull (1844).

HAWKINS, Major Rhode (or Rohde): 1820–84
The third son of Edward Hawkins, Keeper of Antiquities at the British Museum: apparently 'Major' was a Christian name and not a military title: educated at Charterhouse: studied architecture under Edward Blore: in 1841 became travelling architect attached to the Fellowes expedition to Caria and Lycia: several antiquities were reconstructed from the drawings and measurements he made then. He was later appointed Architect to the Committee of Council on Education, a post he retained for thirty-one years. He built many small churches, schools and parsonages, and his work included Swarcliffe Hall, Birstwith, Yorks. (1848: additions since): St Andrew, Gargrave, Yorks. (1852): Hunt's House, Guy's Hospital, Southwark, London (1853): the Royal Victoria Patriotic School, Trinity Road, Wandsworth Common, London (1857: later a Training College): All Saints, Hovingham, Yorks. (1860: except the tower): St John, Holmwood, Surrey (1875): Christ Church, Fairwarp, Sussex (1881: enlarged since).

HAWKSMOOR, Nicholas: 1661–1736
Born in Nottinghamshire, of farming stock. About 1679 he began his long career in the public service: first as a clerk in Wren's office, then his Deputy Surveyor at Chelsea Hospital (1682). In 1690, he was Clerk of the Works at Kensington Palace: 1698 Clerk of the Works at Greenwich, becoming Deputy Surveyor 1705: in 1711 he was appointed one of the Joint Surveyors to the Commissioners for Building Fifty New Churches: in 1715 he was Clerk of the Works at Whitehall, St James's and Westminster: in 1715, Secretary to the Board of Works: in 1723, on the death of Wren, he was appointed Surveyor of Wesminster Abbey. Hawksmoor was Assistant Surveyor

to Vanbrugh at Blenheim Palace: assisted him at Castle Howard: was the author of *Account of the Buildings of Greenwich Hospital* (1728) and *A Short Historical Account of London Bridge* (1736). During his many years under Wren, and later under Vanbrugh, Hawksmoor must certainly have collaborated with both, and opinions differ about the extent to which he was responsible for some of the works usually attributed to these famous architects. He certainly contributed much to the design and building of St Paul's Cathedral (completed 1711): Chelsea Hospital (1682–90): Blenheim Palace (1705–25): and to work at Kensington Palace and Wesminster Abbey: the design of Queen's College, Oxford (1700–33), is generally believed to have been his, though authorities differ about this. His own work included Easton Neston, Northants (1702): St Alphege, Greenwich, London (1712–14: with John James): the Clarendon Building, Oxford (1712–15): the north Quadrangle, Hall, Buttery and Codrington Library at All Souls College, Oxford (1715–40: in association with Dr George Clarke): St Mary Woolnoth, London (1716–27): new buildings at Worcester College, Oxford (*c.* 1720: with Dr George Clarke): St George, Bloomsbury, London (1720–30): the Mausoleum, at Castle Howard, Yorks. (1729–36): the twin west towers of Westminster Abbey, London (1734: completed by John James): the Radcliffe Camera, Oxford (1737–49: his design adapted and completed by James Gibbs).

HAYWARD, Charles Forster, FSA, FRIBA: 1830–1905
Studied at the Royal Academy Schools: was a pupil of Philip Hardwick and his son. He set up practice in London in partnership with Professor T. R. Smith: from 1871–1905 was a District Surveyor in London, mainly in Bloomsbury: in 1894 became Architect of Harrow Local Board Offices and Fire Station. He was responsible for much street planning and design of buildings in Bloomsbury. His work included The Garlands (1863): The Druries (1864): and Laboratories (1874) at Harrow School, Middx.: St Andrew, Malden Road, St Pancras, London (1866): the Public Hall, Harrow-on-the-Hill, Middx. (1875): the Thackeray Hotel, Bloomsbury, London (1895).

HERBERT, Henry, 9th Earl of Pembroke, FRS: 1693–1751
The eldest son of the 8th Earl of Pembroke: succeeded his father in 1733. He was an amateur architect of some ability and taste, and in accordance with eighteenth-century custom, devoted his position and

wealth to the pursuit and patronage of this art. It is probable that Roger Morris was responsible for much of the practical side of his work: their collaboration included Marble Hill, Twickenham, Middx. (*c.* 1720): the central part of White Lodge, Richmond Park, Surrey (1727–9): the Palladian Bridge, Wilton, Wilts. (1737).

HINE, James, FRIBA: 1830–1914
Practised in the West of England for many years with Alfred Norman (d. 1893), with whom he went into partnership in 1869: later the firm became Hine, Odgers and May: Hine was an original member of the Devon and Exeter Architectural Society. His independent work included All Saints, Harwell Street, Plymouth (1874): Alfred Norman was the architect of the Library and Museum, Devonport, Plymouth (1844 and 1852: built as the Mechanics' Institute) and of the Market House, Ashburton, Devonshire (1850): together, they designed the Guildhall and Assize Court, Plymouth (1870–4: with E. W. Godwin as Consultant): the Town Hall, Launceston, Cornwall (1887: with O. B. Peters). With Odgers, Hine's work included St Mathias, Tavistock Road, Plymouth (1887).

HINE, Thomas: 1813–99
Articled to Habershon and Patterson, and later went into partnership with Patterson: in 1849 set up independent practice, working in the Midlands and Notts. He was Surveyor to the Newcastle Estates 1854: built many churches, parsonages, and warehouses and factories for the lace industry in Nottingham. In 1867 his son, George Thomas, joined him in partnership, and later specialized in designing asylums and similar buildings. The work of Thomas Hine included the laying out of Nottingham Park Estate (1850 onwards): additions to Ogston Hall, Derbys. (1864): the restoration of Nottingham Castle (1875–8: his proposal to convert it into a municipal art museum was accepted, and it became the first of its kind in England): Victoria Railway Station, Nottingham (1898–1900: built for the Great Northern Railway).

HIORNE (or HIORN), William: 1712–76
The son of John Hiorne of Great Tew, Oxon., a member of a well-established local family of masons. William Hiorne and his brother, David, practised in Warwickshire and the neighbouring counties, as

architects and masons, and together built the Shire Hall, Warwick (1753–8: designed by Sanderson Miller). William Hiorne was Mayor of Warwick in 1765–6. He was employed as mason-architect at Arbury Hall, Warwicks. (1748–55), and his work included rebuilding of the spire at Holy Trinity, Stratford-upon-Avon, Warwicks. (1763). The work of David Hiorne included Holy Cross, Daventry, Northants (1752–8): St Mary, Great Houghton, Northants (1754: with John Hiorne): Foremark Hall, Derbys. (c. 1760). William Hiorne's son, Francis, FSA (1744–89), succeeded to his father's business, and became a well-known architect, practising in the Gothic style. He was Mayor of Warwick three times between 1773 and 1788: Corporation Treasurer: and County Bridgemaster 1781–9. His work included St Giles, Stony Stratford, Bucks. (1776): the Chapel of St Peter, East Gate, Warwick (1788: later incorporated into a school): Hiorn's Tower, Arundel Castle, Sussex (1790).

HIORT, John William: 1772–1861
Born in London: his father was Swedish, his mother English: educated at a school in Kensington: studied first under a miniaturist, then in the office of C. A. Craig: in 1799 entered the Office of Works where he held various posts until the Office was merged with that of Forests and Woods in 1832, when he retired. He invented and patented a system of circular flues, and in 1825 founded the London, Surrey and Kent Safety Brick Company which produced the special bricks used: in 1826 his *Practical Treatise on the Construction of Chimneys, etc.* was published; and in 1852 his *Report of the Aeronomic Association*: he designed a floating bath for George III at Weymouth, and an apparatus for lowering a coffin into a vault. Hiort specialized in the planning of official ceremonies, festivities and royal and diplomatic occasions: among these, he was responsible for arrangements at Lord Nelson's funeral, including the design of the funeral car, and for temporary buildings and the triumphal arch at the Coronation of George IV. He was Architect to Princess Charlotte: made a valuation of the Claremont Estate when she married Prince Leopold: assisted by J. B. Papworth, he built the Cobham Road Lodges there, and some cottages, kennels, and an aviary in the grounds, and a 'retreat' which was later adapted to a memorial cenotaph.

HOARE, Michael: See HALFPENNY.

HOLDEN, Charles, RDI, FRIBA: 1875–1960
Born at Bolton, Lancs.: educated Manchester Technical College,
and Manchester School of Art: articled to E. W. Leeson of Manchester, and worked with J. Simpson of Bolton, and as assistant to
C. R. Ashbee: studied at the Royal Academy School of Architecture. Set up in practice in London, in partnership with H. Percy
Adams, c. 1907: they were joined by Lionel Pearson in 1912. Holden
was an Architectural Adviser to the Imperial War Graves Commission during the First World War: Royal Gold Medallist 1936: a
member of the Fine Art Commission: a Member of the Town
Planning Institute: Planning Consultant to the Cities of Canterbury
and Tynemouth, to Edinburgh University, and to the LCC for the
South Bank. With Lord Holford, he produced the report on the
development of the City of London, published 1947. He was an
architect and town planner of vision and great reputation: an outstanding industrial designer: and in collaboration with Frank Pick,
he evolved a new style of transport architecture, and designed and
built some fifty underground railway stations for London Transport
(many between 1932–3), as well as designing shelters, equipment
and posters. His large output of work with his partners included
King Edward VII Sanatorium, Midhurst, Sussex (1903–6): Nos.
127–29 High Holborn, London (1904): the Municipal Library,
Bristol (1906): additional building for the Royal Infirmary, Bristol
(1906–11): Queen Mary's Hostel (King's College), Kensington,
London (1914): War Cemeteries at Boulogne, Wimereaux, Corbie,
Louvencourt, Forceville (1918–22): Mansion House underground
station, London (1926): London Transport HQ, No. 55 Broadway,
London (1927–9): Piccadilly Circus underground station, London
(1929): the Senate House and ancillary buildings of the University
of London, Bloomsbury, London (1932–53): Chiswick Park and
Cockfosters underground stations, London (1933): extension to the
Cavendish High Tension Laboratory, Cambridge (1939–40):
Offices of the English Electric Company, Strand, London (1955).

HOLLAND, Henry, FSA: 1745–1806 (Portrait: see Plate VI)
The son of Henry Holland of Fulham, a prosperous builder, who
worked for a number of well-known architects, among them Lancelot 'Capability' Brown, with whom the family was on terms of
personal friendship. The younger Holland worked in his father's
business: in 1771 became assistant to Brown, then his partner, and

124

son-in-law. He was District Surveyor of the Liberties of Hatton Garden, Ely Rents, Saffron Hill, St Mary-le-Strand, the Duchy of Lancaster and the Precincts of the Savoy: Surveyor to the East India Company, and a founder member of the Architects' Club. In 1771 he leased a large acreage of land on the Cadogan Estate in London, and developed the area known as Hans Town, including Sloane Street, Cadogan Place and Hans Place, as well as Sloane Place, the house he designed for himself and which has now disappeared. He was the author of two papers published in the Communications of the Board of Agriculture (1797), and of a Report dealing with fire prevention (1793). His work included Brooks's Club, St James's Street, London (1776–8): the Marine Pavilion, Brighton, Sussex (1786–7: later remodelled by Nash): considerable additions, including Riding School, Conservatory and Chinese Dairy, at Woburn Abbey, Beds. (1787–8): recasing, alterations and reconstruction at Althorp Park, Northants (1787–9): the Swan Hotel, and Rose Inn, Bedford (c. 1790): Southill, Beds. (1795): at Albany, Piccadilly, London, Holland built the side wings in the forecourt, the covered way to Vigo Street, and Nos. 10 and 12 Burlington Gardens, at the Vigo Street entrance (1804).

HOOKE, Robert, FRS: 1635–1703
Born at Freshwater, I.O.W.: received his early education from his father, who was a curate there: in 1648 became a pupil of Sir Peter Lely for a time: then went to Westminster School, and in 1653 to Christ Church, Oxford, where he met Wren and Robert Boyle, and began his scientific career. He was appointed Curator of Experiments to the Royal Society in 1662: Professor of Geometry at Gresham College 1665: and was Secretary to the Royal Society 1677–82. He was a distinguished scientist, particularly in the fields of experiment and invention, and also a horologist of great ability: he published a number of scientific works and treatises, notably *Micrographia* (1665), a work on the microscope. His proposed plan for rebuilding the City of London after the Great Fire led to his appointment as one of the three City Surveyors required by the Act for Rebuilding the City of London, in 1667, and in this capacity he was closely associated with Wren in the design and rebuilding of the City churches: he was concerned in the building of the Monument in Fish Street Hill, London (1671–6), and authorities are divided as to whether he or Wren designed the column. Hooke was

Surveyor to the Dean and Chapter of Westminster from 1690–6. His architectural work, much of which has disappeared, included the Royal College of Physicians, Warwick Lane, London (1672–8: dem.): Bethlehem Hospital, Moorfields, London (1675–6: dem.): Writing School, Christ's Hospital, Newgate Street, London (1675–6: with John Oliver: dem.): St Mary Magdalene, Willen, Bucks. (1679–80: apse added since): Ragley Hall, Warwicks. (1679–83: alterations later by James Gibbs, and portico by James Wyatt): Shenfield Place, Shenfield, Essex (1689).

HOPE, Alexander James Beresford, HON.FRIBA: 1820–87
The youngest son of Thomas Hope: educated Harrow, and Trinity College, Cambridge. He was a politician of standing in his day: M.P. for Maidstone in 1841, 1852 and 1857: for Stoke-upon-Trent 1865: for the University of Cambridge 1868: a Privy Councillor 1880: a Trustee of the National Portrait Gallery: HON.LL.D of Cambridge: the author of over thirty published works, including *Public Offices and Metropolitan Improvements* (1857): *The English Cathedral of the Nineteenth Century* (1861): and *The Condition and Prospects of Architectural Art* (1863). He inherited his father's wealth, and interest in architecture, of which he was a generous patron, and an ardent champion of the Gothic Revival: one of the earliest members of the Ecclesiological (formerly Cambridge Camden) Society, of which he became President: President of the Architectural Museum: President of the Institute in 1865 (as an HON.FIBA he was the first amateur to hold this office since Earl de Grey). He contributed numerous papers, lectures and addresses to professional journals and bodies: supervised the design and building of Christ Church, Kilndown, Kent (1841): and restored at his own expense St Augustine's Abbey at Canterbury, as a Missionary College (1844).

HOPE, Thomas: *c.* 1770–1831
The son of John Hope, a rich Amsterdam merchant, whose forbears came from Scotland. Thomas Hope was brought up in Holland: travelled widely in Europe and the Near East: settled in England about 1795, where he lived as a wealthy amateur of the arts, the possessor of valuable collections of pictures, pottery, sculpture and furniture: as an amateur architect he stimulated interest in the Greek Revival, and was the author of several books, notably *Household Furniture and Decoration* (1807). He accommodated his

collections in a house in Duchess Street, Portland Place (built by Robert Adam), which he remodelled himself; and in the mansion of Deepdene in Surrey, where he employed William Atkinson on extensive additions (1819–26). *An Historical Essay on Architecture*, illustrated by his drawings made in Italy and Germany, was published posthumously, in two volumes.

HOPPER, Thomas: 1776–1856
The son of a Rochester surveyor, and trained in his father's office. A commission from the Prince Regent to make some alterations at Carlton House helped him to establish and build up a very large and fashionable practice: he was County Surveyor of Essex for forty years, and Surveyor to the Atlas Fire Assurance Company. He carried out additions and alterations to many large country houses, and his work included Leigh Court, Abbotsleigh, Som. (1814): the County Gaol, Chelmsford, Essex (1822–8): the Carlton Club, St James's Street, London (1826–7: built as Arthur's Club): Penrhyn Castle, North Wales (1827–47): Atlas Fire Assurance office, Cheapside, London (1839): Holy Trinity, Bromley Common, Kent (1842): St Mary's Hospital, Paddington, London (1845–51: he gave his services gratuitously): Wivenhoe Hall, Essex (1846).

HORDER, Percy Richard Morley, FSA, FRIBA: 1870–1944
Educated at the City of London School: articled to George Devey: practised in London. He designed many important educational buildings, also village halls and country houses: Lloyd George was one of his clients. His work included Nos. 121–3 Hampstead Way, Hampstead Garden Suburb, Middx.: the Village Hall, Pitsford, Northants: Hen Grove, St Leonards, Bucks. (1910): Cheshunt College, Cambridge (1913–14): National Institute of Agricultural Botany, Cambridge (1921): Periton Mead, Minehead, Som. (*c.* 1922): Nottingham University buildings, and layout of Highfields Park, Nottingham (1922–8): School of Hygiene and Tropical Medicine, Keppel Street, Holborn, London (1926–8: with V. Rees).

HOSKING, William: 1800–61
Born at Buckfastleigh, Devonshire, he was taken as a child to New South Wales, and was apprenticed there to a builder and surveyor: returned to England 1819, and until 1822 was articled to a London architect: then spent a year in Italy and Sicily. He contributed

articles on architecture and building to the 7th edition of the *Encyclopaedia Britannica*: was the author of *An Essay on the Construction of Bridges*, and *A Guide to the Proper Regulation of Buildings in Towns*: and was Professor of Architecture at King's College, London, from 1840 until his death. He did a small amount of architectural work, which included the entrance and chapel to Abney Park Cemetery, Stamford Hill, London (1840).

HUNT, Thomas Frederick: *c.* 1791–1831
He was Clerk of the Works at Whitehall, Westminster and St James's, and at Kensington for the last two years of his life. He was a serious student of the revival of interest in mediaeval and Tudor architecture, and is best known for his literary works, which included *Half-a-dozen Hints on Picturesque and Domestic Architecture* (1825): *Designs for Parsonage Houses, Almshouses, etc.* (1827): *Exemplars of Tudor Architecture with illustrative details selected from Ancient Edifices, and observations on the Furniture of the Period* (1830): and *A Series of Designs for Gate Lodges, Gamekeeper's Cottages, and other Rural Residences* (1836). His architectural work included the Burns Mausoleum, Dumfries (1816): and Danehurst, nr. Cuckfield, Sussex (1828).

HURST, William: 1787–1844
Born in Doncaster, where he was articled to William Lindley; he set up in practice there, first as a partner to Lindley and Woodhead, then with Woodhead alone, and eventually with W. L. Moffatt. The partners enjoyed a large local practice in ecclesiastical and secular building in and around Sheffield. Independently, William Hurst designed Christ Church, Doncaster, Yorks. (1827–9): the work of the partnerships included St George, Portobello Street, Sheffield (1821–5: with Woodhead): Christ Church, Ardsley, Yorks. (1841: with Moffatt): St James, Rawcliffe, Yorks. (1842: with Moffatt): St John, Goole, Yorks. (1843–8: with Moffatt).

VII

JOHN NASH
1752–1835

[RIBA

SIR JOHN SOANE
1753–1837

*National Portrait
Gallery, London*]

VIII

SIR ROBERT SMIRKE
1781–1867

[RIBA

JOHN CLAUDIUS LOUDON
1783–1843

*From the frontispiece of
Self-Instruction for Young
Gardeners*]

I'ANSON, Edward, the elder: 1775–1853
Born in London: articled to an architect there: studied at the Royal
Academy Schools. Practised independently as a measuring surveyor: then became the assistant, and subsequently partner and
successor, to D. A. Alexander. I'Anson built commercial premises
and houses in the City, and warehouses in Southwark, and was well
known as a prosperous London surveyor. From 1804–46 he was
Surveyor to the Commissioners of Sewers for Surrey and Kent, and
the drainage and preparation for building on large areas south of the
Thames was carried out by him in this capacity: he was associated in
this post with Joseph Gwilt and J. Newman, and *Reports relating to
the Sewage, etc.* was issued jointly by them in 1843.

I'ANSON, Edward, the younger, FRIBA: 1812–88
Born in London, the son of Edward I'Anson, a prosperous architect
and surveyor in the City. The younger I'Anson was educated at the
College Henri Quatre in France: articled to his father: spent some
time with John Wallen, a quantity surveyor in the City of London:
made a European tour which included Turkey and Greece: joined
his father in practice 1837. He was Surveyor to the Merchant
Taylors' Company and to St Bartholomew's Hospital: District
Surveyor for Clapham: a Fellow and President of the Surveyor's
Institution: Fellow of the Geological Society: J.P. for Surrey: an
early member of the Institute, and its President 1886–8: in 1867 he
visited Russia, Norway, Cyprus and Rome. I'Anson was a pioneer
in the design of office premises built for that specific purpose, and the
author of a paper entitled 'Office Building in the City', which he
delivered to the Institute in 1864. His work included No. 13 Chelsea
Embankment, London: Pavilion Buildings, Brighton, Sussex:
Assembly Hall at Merchant Taylors' School, Charterhouse, Finsbury, London (*c.* 1856): British and Foreign Bible Society, Queen
Victoria Street, London (*c.* 1869): the Library, St Bartholomew's
Hospital, London (1878–9): Corn Exchange, Seething Lane,
London (1881: Seething Lane front survives). His son, E. B. I'An-
son, was later in partnership with him.

INWOOD, Henry William, FSA: 1794–1843
The eldest son of an architect, William Inwood (*c.* 1771–1843), with
whom he worked so closely that nearly all the work of both was in

I   129 fact done in partnership. William Inwood, who acted as Surveyor to a number of landowners, and was Lord Colchester's Steward, was the author of a standard work of reference, *Tables for the Purchasing of Estates* . . . first published in 1811. He was the architect of Westminster Hospital, Broad Sanctuary, London (1832–3: dem. 1951). Henry Inwood was trained in his father's office, travelled in Greece, and published *The Erectheion at Athens, with Marble and Terra-Cotta Fragments of Athenian Architecture and a few remains in Attica, Megara and Eleusis* (1827), and *The Resources of Design in the Architecture of Greece, Egypt, and other Countries obtained by the studies of the Architects of those Countries from Nature* (1834). The work of father and son included St Pancras, Euston Road, London (1819–22): All Saints, Camden Town, London (1822–4): St Peter, Regent Square, Holborn, London (1824–6): St Mary, Somers Town, St Pancras, London (1824–7): an Ionic temple in the grounds of Clandon Park, Surrey (1838). William Inwood's second son, Charles Frederick (1798–1840), studied at the Royal Academy Schools: assisted his father in the design and building of Westminster Hospital: and himself designed All Saints, Marlow, Bucks. (1832–5: spire added since).

IRESON, Nathaniel: 1686–1769

A mason and architect, born in Warwicks., who moved to Wiltshire and later (1726) to Wincanton, in Somerset, where he lived and practised till his death. In addition to designing buildings, he was a sculptor, mason, master-builder, quarry-owner, and made bricks and pottery. His work included Ireson House, Wincanton, Som. (*c.* 1726: altered since): alterations to Rodber House (*c.* 1730), 'The Dogs', Tout Hill (*c.* 1745), and Balsam House, all in Wincanton, Som.: White Horse Hotel, Wincanton, Som. (1733): Crowcombe Court, Som. (1734: he continued the house begun by Thomas Parker).

IVORY, Thomas: *c.* 1720–86

An Irishman, born in Cork. He was at first a carpenter of considerable skill, and designed the bridge at Lismore over the River Blackwater, before coming to Dublin, where he worked for a gunsmith, studied drawing, and became an architectural draughtsman of outstanding ability. From 1759 till his death he was Master of the Dublin Society's Architectural School: he was also Surveyor of the Revenue Buildings. His work included the Blue-Coat School,

Dublin (1773–80: completed by John Wilson): the layout of Blackhall Place and Blackhall Street, Dublin: Municipal Buildings,
Castle Street, Dublin (1781: built as Newcomen's Bank: additions
since): he was almost certainly the designer of Kilcarty House, Co.
Meath.

IVORY, Thomas: 1709–79
His career in Norwich began when he was appointed carpenter to
the Great Hospital there in 1751, a post he held till his death. He
became a prosperous builder and timber merchant, owning several
properties in Norwich, where he designed many of the City's buildings. His work there included the Methodist Meeting House,
Bishopsgate (1751–2): house in entrance court of Great Hospital
(1752–3): the Assembly Rooms, Theatre Street (1754): Octagon
Chapel, Colegate (1754–6): the Theatre (1757: dem.): Nos. 25–35
Surrey Street (1761–71): Artillery Barracks (1771–2). In 1767–9,
Thomas Ivory, assisted by his sons, Thomas and William, carried
out alterations at Blickling Hall, Norfolk.

IVORY, William: c. 1746–c. 1801
The son of Thomas Ivory of Norwich, whom he assisted and to
whose practice in Norwich he succeeded: he built the Norfolk and
Norwich Hospital there (1770–5: additions since). About 1785 he
left Norwich, apparently because of some private misfortune. He
should not be confused with William Ivory, an architect of Saffron
Walden, Essex, who died in an almshouse there in 1837, aged
ninety-one.

JACKSON, Sir Thomas Graham, RA, FSA, FRIBA: 1835–1924
Born in Hampstead, London, the son of Hugh Jackson, a solicitor:
educated Brighton College, and Wadham College, Oxford, of
which he became an Hon. Fellow in 1882: articled to Sir George
Gilbert Scott 1858: set up practice in London 1862: in 1864
travelled abroad in company with J. Oldrid Scott. In 1891 Jackson
was estranged from the Institute over his disagreement with its
policy on official registration, but was reconciled later, and became
Royal Gold Medallist in 1910. He was an HON. LL. D of Cambridge:
HON. DCL of Oxford: an Associate of the Académie Royale de
Belgique: a member of the Board of Architectural Education:
made a baronet 1913: the author of numerous books, notably
Modern Gothic Architecture (1873): *Byzantine and Romanesque Archi-
tecture* (1913): *Gothic Architecture in France and Italy* (1915): *The
Renaissance of Roman Architecture* (1921–2). He did much work at
Oxford and Cambridge: also restorations of many ancient build-
ings, among them Winchester Cathedral (1905–12), where he was
associated with Sir Francis Fox, the engineer. His work included
the restoration of St Nicholas, Pyrford, Surrey (1869): All Saints,
Annesley, Notts. (1873–4): St John, Spencer Hill, Wimbledon,
Surrey (1875): the Examination Schools, Oxford (1876): entrance
and staircase, Drapers' Hall, Throgmorton Street, London (1878–9),
Girls' High School (1879) and Boys' High School (1881), both at
Oxford: No. 1 Kensington Court, London (1883): new buildings
at Trinity College (1883–7), at Brasenose College (1886–9 and
1909–11) and at Hertford College (1887–90 and 1903–13), all at
Oxford: Nos. 2–3 Hare Court, Temple, London (1893): the Cricket
Pavilion on Agar's Plough, and Club-House on Queen's Eyot, at
Eton College, Bucks. (1901–2): Law School, Museum of Geology
and Museum of Archaeology and Ethnology, Cambridge (1904–11):
No. 54 Ridgway, Wimbledon, Surrey (1908): Temple Speech
Room, Rugby School, Warwicks. (1908–9).

JAMES, Charles Holloway, RA, FRIBA: 1893–1953
Born in Gloucester: educated Rich's School and Taunton School:
articled to W. B. Wood of Gloucester: an assistant to Sir Edwin
Lutyens, and later to Sir Raymond Unwin and Barry Parker:
served in the First World War, and then set up independent practice

in partnership with various architects, and finally with S. Rowland Pierce and James Bywaters. He was Architect to All Souls College, Oxford: Vice-President of the RIBA and AA: with F. R. Yerbury, he published *The Modern Small English House*, and *Small Houses for the Community*, and with S. Rowland Pierce *A Plan for Norwich* and *Royal Leamington Spa*. He built many public buildings, and was concerned with a number of municipal housing schemes, particularly after 1945. His work included the City Hall, Norwich (1932–8: with S. R. Pierce): Town Hall, Slough, Bucks. (1934–6: with Bywaters and Pierce): County Hall, Hertford (1939: with Bywaters and Pierce): Crescent Lane Council Flats, Clapham, London: Pevensey Garden Estate, West Worthing, Sussex (1958–60: with Bywaters).

JAMES, John: *c*. 1672–1746
The eldest son of the Rev. John James, who later became Vicar of Basingstoke. It is believed that James, who began his career as a carpenter, was a pupil of Matthew Banckes, Master Carpenter to the Crown: he became Assistant Clerk of the Works at Greenwich in 1699, and for the rest of his life worked in official posts, in which he was associated with Hawksmoor, Gibbs and Wren. He was Clerk of the Works at Greenwich 1736–46: at St Paul's Cathedral he was Master Carpenter 1711–15, Assistant Surveyor 1715–23, and Surveyor 1723: he succeeded James Gibbs as a Surveyor to the Commissioners for Building Fifty New Churches 1715–33: was Surveyor to the Dean and Chapter of Westminster 1724: and Surveyor to the Fabric of Westminster Abbey 1736–45: he was Master of the Carpenters' Company in 1734. He became involved in disputes over dilapidations at the Archiepiscopal Palaces of Lambeth and Croydon (1715–17) and the design of Westminster Bridge (1736), and contributed pamphlets to these controversies; he also published *Rules and Examples of Perspective, proper for Painters and Architects* (1707: from the Italian): *A Treatise of the Five Orders of Columns in Architecture* (1708: from the French): and *The Theory and Practice of Gardening* (1709: from the French). In 1714–15, James worked at Canons House, Stanmore, Middx.: he was one of many architects employed there, but the design of the house (now dem.) is attributed to him. His work included St Mary, Twickenham, Middx. (1714–15): St Lawrence, Whitchurch, Middx. (1715): St George, Hanover Square, London (1721–4):

rebuilding of the tower of St Margaret, Westminster, London (1735–7).

JANYNS, Henry: fl. 1453–83
A mason, the son of Robert Janyns, the builder of the tower of Merton College, Oxford, in 1448–50, and Warden of the masons working at Eton College, where Henry Janyns was apprenticed in 1453–4. He worked at St George's Chapel, Windsor, Berks. (1478–84). His son, Robert, became a Master Mason under Henry VII and also worked at Windsor (1498–1500).

JARMAN (or JERMAN), Edward: d. 1668
A member of the Carpenters' Company, and one of the Surveyors appointed by the Corporation of London to deal with rebuilding after the Great Fire of 1666. His work included the rebuilding of the Royal Exchange, Threadneedle Street, London (1667–9: rebuilt since): Drapers' Hall, Throgmorton Street, London (1668–71: rebuilt since): Vintners' Hall, Upper Thames Street, London (1671: altered since, but now restored to original): Mercers' Hall, Cheapside, London (1672–82: rebuilt since).

JEARRAD, Robert William: nineteenth century
He exhibited at the Royal Academy in 1813–14, and was in practice until about 1846, some of his work being done in collaboration with C. Jearrad. In 1815, the two were living at the same London address, but later they seem to have practised largely in the West of England. R. W. Jearrad was responsible for laying out the Lansdowne Estate at Cheltenham, Glos., and designed large houses and villas in Lansdowne Place. His work included the Literary and Philosophical Institution, Cheltenham (1835–6): the Queen's Hotel, Cheltenham (1838): Christ Church, Cheltenham (1838–40: with C. Jearrad: St Martin, Hereford (1845): Christ Church, Birkenhead, Cheshire (1846).

JELFE, Andrews: d. 1759
Born probably in Essex, the son of William Jelfe. He was a Free-mason of the Masons' Company 1711, and was in partnership with other masons, including members of the Strong family, Cass, and Mercer. He was Clerk of the Works at Newmarket: Clerk Itinerant at the Office of Works: and employed by the Board of Ordnance as Architect and Clerk of Works on military buildings of all kinds.

In addition, he had a flourishing private business as a master mason: he and Samuel Tufnell were the masonry contractors for the building of Westminster Bridge, London, in 1738–50. Jelfe designed Exning House, Suffolk (1734), and the Town Hall, Rye, Sussex (1743).

JELLY, Thomas: eighteenth century
An architect and master-builder of Bath, associated with John Palmer. Jelly and Palmer competed with Thomas Warr Atwood for Corporation contracts and work, and submitted a rival plan for the Guildhall, markets and shops. This was rejected, but was the cause of a long and violent public controversy. Jelly designed the Kingston Baths (1763–6: dem.): and, with John Palmer, the Masonic Hall, Manvers Street (1750): the Church of St James (1768–9: dem.): and houses in North Parade and Milsom Street.

JOHNSON, John: 1732–1814
Born at Leicester, the son of John Johnson: went to London as a young man, apparently with few resources, but by *c.* 1775 his designs were being exhibited at the Society of Arts. He was County Surveyor of Essex 1782–1812, and also built up a considerable and lucrative private practice in London and the provinces. In Leicester, he built and endowed his 'Consanguinitarium' in Southgate Street (*c.* 1795, now dem.), where he established his poor relations in five small houses. His work included Terling Place, Terling, Essex (1772–80: wings and conservatory added since): Woolverstone Hall, Suffolk (1776): Bradwell Lodge, Bradwell-Juxta-Mare, Essex (1781–6): Moulsham Bridge, High Street, Chelmsford, Essex (1787): Shire Hall, Chelmsford, Essex (1790–2): County Rooms, Leicester (1792): Nos. 9–15 Southgate Street, Leicester (1795): Ingram's, Felsted, Essex (1800): interior restoration at the Cathedral of St Mary, Chelmsford, Essex (1801–3).

JOHNSTON, Francis: 1760–1829
An Irishman, born in Co. Armagh, he worked as a young man under Thomas Cooley in Dublin: became Architect to the Board of Works there, and during a distinguished career, designed buildings all over Ireland: founded the Royal Hibernian Academy of Arts in 1823, and was a friend of James Gandon. His work in Dublin included Daly's Club House, College Green (1790: since

135

much altered): alterations to Parliament House when it became the Bank of Ireland (1802): St George, Hardwicke Place (1802-3: the General Post Office, O'Connell Street (1814-18): adaptation of a house in Phoenix Park to become the Viceregal Lodge (1816). He was Consultant Architect for the Nelson Pillar in O'Connell Street (erected 1808-9: destroyed 1966). Johnston's elder brother, Richard, was responsible for the elevations and execution of the New Assembly Rooms, Cavendish Row, Dublin (1784-6: now the Dublin Gate Theatre and palais de danse): and designed Green Street Courthouse, Dublin (1792-7).

JONES, Sir Horace, FRIBA: 1819-87

Born in Bucklersbury, in the City of London, where his father practised as a solicitor: articled to John Wallen, a City architect and surveyor: travelled in Italy and Greece: set up independent practice in London 1846. He was Surveyor to the Tufnell Park Estate: City Architect and Surveyor to the Corporation of London 1864-87: an early member of the Institute: President of the RIBA 1881-4: knighted 1886. He had a very large and prosperous practice, mostly devoted to public buildings, large markets, offices and shops, and is best known for his work in London, which included Smithfield Market (1866): Marshall and Snelgrove, Oxford Street (1870: completed by Octavius Hansard): Guildhall Free Library and Museum, Basinghall Street (1873): Billingsgate Market, Lower Thames Street (1875): Temple Bar Memorial (1880: this replaced Wren's Temple Bar, transferred to Theobalds, Herts. 1878): Leadenhall Market (1881): Guildhall School of Music, John Carpenter Street, Victoria Embankment (1885-7: additions since): Tower Bridge (1886-94: with the engineer, J. Wolfe Barry).

JONES, Inigo: 1573-1652 (Portrait: see Plate I)

The son of a Smithfield clothworker. As a young man his resources were sparse, but, possibly with the help of a patron, he visited Italy in 1601. This visit awakened a deep interest in design and a determination to study architecture: he was employed till 1605 in Denmark, by Christian IV (the brother-in-law of James I), and returned to England with a reputation as a painter and designer. For James I, he became a designer of court masques, of which he produced a number, including the costumes, scenery and stage effects. He was appointed Surveyor to the Prince of Wales in 1611,

Surveyor of the King's Works in 1615, and made further visits to Italy. During the Commonwealth, his Royalist and Catholic loyalties brought him into conflict with the Puritan régime, who inflicted severe fines on him. He worked closely with John Webb, who was his pupil and assistant and who married his niece, and it is probable that Webb completed and co-ordinated many designs roughly indicated by Jones. From 1634 he was put in charge of restoration work at Old St Paul's Cathedral, and in 1649 he advised on rebuilding at Wilton House, Wilts. His work included The Queen's House, Greenwich Park, London (1616–37: work on it ceased during the years 1619–25): The Banqueting House, Whitehall, London (1619–25): Queen's Chapel, Marlborough Gate, Pall Mall, London (1623–7): Piazza and Church of St Paul, Covent Garden, London (1631–8: the church was damaged by fire in 1795, and restored to the original design by Thomas Hardwick): almost certainly Lindsey House, Nos. 59–60 Lincoln's Inn Fields, London (1640).

JONES, Owen: 1809–74

Probably of Welsh descent: a pupil of Lewis Vulliamy: travelled in Greece, Egypt and Spain, where he spent three years studying Moorish architecture. He was an early industrial artist, employed by firms to design their manufactured products, and a pioneer in new ways to use colour: Royal Gold Medallist of the Institute 1857: the author of a number of professional papers and books including *Plans, Elevations, and Sections of the Alhambra*: *Grammar of Ornament*: *Examples of Chinese Ornament*. He did much interior decoration, and his work included No. 8a Kensington Palace Gardens, London (*c*. 1850): the design of the Egyptian, Greek, Roman and Alhambra Courts at the Great Exhibition of 1851, and decoration of the Crystal Palace, both in Hyde Park and when it was re-erected at Sydenham: Nos. 49–50 New Bond Street, London (*c*. 1851): alterations to No. 16 Grosvenor Street, London (1862).

JONES, William: d. 1757

An architect and furniture designer: the author of *The Gentlemen's or Builder's Companion containing Variety of Usefull Designs for Doors, Gateways, Peers, Pavilions, Temples, Chimney-Pieces, etc.* (1739): and Surveyor to the East India Company 1752. His work included the

Rotunda in Ranelagh Gardens, Chelsea, London (1742: dem.): Edgcote House, Northants (1747–52: probably designed by William Smith who d. 1747): offices and warehouses at East India House, Leadenhall Street, London (1754: dem.).

JOYNES, Henry: *c.* 1684–1754

He was Comptroller of the Works under Sir John Vanbrugh at Blenheim Palace (1705–15), and assisted Nicholas Hawksmoor at the Clarendon Building, Oxford (1712–13): from 1715 till his death, was Clerk of the Works at Kensington Palace, and was Surveyor of Sewers in Westminster for many years. He also had a private architectural practice, in which his work included possibly the Water Tower in the grounds of Carshalton House, Surrey (1719–20): Nos. 57–58 Lincoln's Inn Fields, London (1730): Normanton Hall, Rutland (*c.* 1740: dem.): Linley Hall, Salop (1742).

JUPP, Richard: d. 1799

The younger son of Richard Jupp, Master of the Carpenters' Company in 1768. The younger Jupp was Surveyor to the East India Company from *c.* 1769 till his death, and in 1799 was Master of the Carpenters' Company. Between 1796 and 1799 he was involved in a serious professional dispute with Sir John Soane, arising from Jupp's design for the rebuilding of East India House in Leadenhall Street, London: the work was eventually begun in 1799 just before his death, and completed by Henry Holland in 1800: dem. 1861–2. Jupp's work included probably Painshill Park, nr. Cobham, Surrey (*c.* 1778: much altered since): Severndroog Castle (a memorial tower), Castlewood Park, Shooter's Hill, Woolwich, London (1784): Wilton Park, nr. Beaconsfield, Bucks. (*c.* 1790). His elder brother, William (d. 1788), was a Warden of the Carpenters' Company: rebuilt the London Tavern, Bishopsgate Street Within, London (1765: with William Newton: dem.), and designed the entrance hall and main staircase of Carpenters' Hall, London (1780: dem.).

JUPP, William: d. 1839

The elder son of William Jupp, and nephew of Richard Jupp. He had a flourishing practice as an architect and surveyor in London, and in this capacity acted for the Skinners', Merchant Taylors', Ironmongers' and Apothecaries' Companies. He was

District Surveyor for Limehouse, Blackwall, Wapping, Mile End Old Town, Poplar, and Ratcliff: and in 1831 was Master of the Carpenters' Company. His work included the façade of Skinners' Hall, Dowgate Hill, London (*c.* 1790): and the Merchant Taylors' Almshouses in Lee High Road, Lewisham, London (1826).

JURDAN, Thomas: d. 1482

Appointed King's Master Mason by Edward IV on his accession. Previously, he had worked as a mason at Eton College, and a master mason of London Bridge. He designed and built the Great Hall of Eltham Palace, Kent, *c.* 1475, the timber roof of which was carried out by the chief carpenter, Edmund Graveley.

KAY, Joseph: 1775–1847
A pupil of S. P. Cockerell: from 1802–5 he travelled abroad: in 1807 was appointed Surveyor to the Foundling Hospital Estate: in 1814 Architect to the Post Office: in 1823 Surveyor of Greenwich Hospital. He was Secretary of the Architects' Club, and helped to found the Institute of British Architects, of which he was a Vice-President. His clients included the Earl of Chichester, the Earl of Radnor and Marquis Camden: he was helped in his practice by his son, William Porden Kay (b. 1809). His work included assistance to his father-in-law, William Porden, at Eaton Hall, Cheshire (1804–12): completion of the Hotel and Assembly Rooms, The Mall, Clifton, Bristol (1809–11: following the bankruptcy of F. H. Greenway): the layout of garden and east side of Mecklenburgh Square, London (1812–21): planning of Pelham Crescent, Hastings, Sussex (1824–8): St Mary-in-the-Castle, Hastings, Sussex (1828): the layout of Nelson Street, Greenwich, London (1829).

KECK, Anthony: 1726–97
Practised as an architect, builder and surveyor in the West Midlands, of which he was a native. His work included Beveré Hall, nr. Worcester: the County Infirmary (1767–70) and St Martin (1768–72), both in Worcester and both subsequently altered by W. J. Hopkins): Moccas Court, Moccas, Herefs. (1775–81: to the designs of Robert Adam): Longworth House, Lugwardine, Herefs. (c. 1788).

KEELING, Bassett: 1836–86
Articled to C. L. Dresser of Leeds: a Fellow of the Surveyors' Institution: designed a large number of churches and cemetery chapels in a debased Gothic style which did not find favour with the Ecclesiological Society. His work included St George, Campden Hill, Kensington, London (1864): St Mark, St Mark's Road, Paddington, London (1864): St Paul, Upper Norwood, London (1866): St John, Killingworth, Northumb. (1869).

KEENE, Henry: 1726–76
The son of Henry Keene, believed to have been a carpenter and builder, who was Surveyor to the Dean and Chapter of Westminster

in 1746, and to the Fabric of Westminster Abbey in 1752. In 1761 the younger Keene accompanied his patron, Lord Halifax, to Ireland, and held an official appointment there under what was later to become the Irish Board of Works, till *c.* 1766. He was much employed at Oxford, where his design for the Radcliffe Observatory was begun in 1772, but a year later the design of another architect (possibly James Wyatt) was substituted, to which Keene worked till his death in 1776. His son, Theodosius, also an architect, was commissioned to complete the Radcliffe Observatory after his father's death. Little is known of his other work, apart from a design for Racton Tower (a Folly), Racton, Sussex (1772), and one for the Town Hall, Maidenhead, Berks. (1777: since remodelled). Henry Keene's work included No. 4 South Square, Gray's Inn, London (1750): Bowood House, Wilts. (1755–60: much altered since): Nos. 17–18 Cavendish Square, London (1756–7): the Guildhall, High Wycombe, Bucks. (1757): the Anatomy School, Christ Church, Oxford (1766–7: later the Chemical Laboratory): Fisher Buildings, Balliol College, Oxford (1769): the Provost's Lodgings and north range of Worcester College, Oxford (1773–6): Vandalian Tower in the grounds of Uppark House, Sussex (1774).

KEMP, George Meikle: 1795–1844

Born at Moorfoot, Midlothian, the son of James Kemp, a shepherd: attended the local school at Penicuik: as a boy, worked at the farm where his father was employed: apprenticed to a master carpenter near Peebles 1809–13. From then until *c.* 1830, he worked in Scotland, London and France, employed as a millwright and journeyman carpenter, at the same time studying drawing and architecture, much of it self-taught from books. On his return to Edinburgh, he became assistant to William Burn, and in 1838, under an assumed name, won the competition for the Scott Memorial, erected 1840–46. Of great potential promise, Kemp was accidentally drowned in 1844.

KEMPTHORNE, Sampson: d. *c.* 1842

Studied at the Royal Academy Schools in 1833, and in 1833–4 visited Rome. He set up practice in London *c.* 1835, and about the same time was appointed Architect to the Poor Law Commissioners. He was one of the early Associates of the Institute of

141

British Architects. In 1841 he went to New Zealand, where it is believed he died. He prepared a number of designs for schools for the Committee of the Council on Education, and designed and built many workhouses. His work included Holy Trinity, Bermondsey, London (1834–8: severely war-damaged): the Town Hall, Wantage, Berks. (1835: dem.): Holy Trinity, Buckhold, Berks. (1836): Furze House, Ticehurst, Sussex (1836: built as the Workhouse): Bath Poor Law Institution, Odd Down, nr. Bath, Som. (1836): St Leonard, Misterton, Som. (1840): St James, Holywell, Northants (1840).

KENDALL, Henry Edward: 1776–1875
Born in York, the son of a banker: a pupil of Thomas Leverton and John Nash: worked in the Barrack Department of the War Office, before setting up practice: from 1823–73 was Surveyor to St Martin-in-the-Fields, and St Anne, Soho. He was one of the founders of the Institute of British Architects: he had a large practice, and among his clients were many members of the nobility whose mansions he altered or rebuilt. His work included the Sessions House, Spilsby, Lincs. (1824): St George, Ramsgate, Kent (1825–7: Kendall completed this after the death of H. Helmsley, the designer): the Rectory, Fishtoft, Lincs. (1827): the Esplanade, Tunnel, and Reading Room, Kemp Town, Brighton, Sussex (1828–40: with his son): No. 24 Belgrave Square, London (c. 1830: now the Spanish Embassy): Sessions House (1831), Carre's Almshouses (c. 1832), and Sleaview (1838: built as the Workhouse), all at Sleaford, Lincs.: Haverholme Priory, Anwick, Lincs. (1835): St George's Hospital, Semington, nr. Melksham, Wilts. (1836–9: built as the Workhouse): Highview House, Uckfield, Sussex (1839: built as the Workhouse): St John the Evangelist, Kensal Green, London (1844): Mental Hospital, Brentwood, Essex (1853: additions since). His son, H. E. Kendall (1805–85), who studied at the Royal Academy Schools, and in his father's office, became District Surveyor for Hampstead, and set up in partnership with Frederick Mew. His work included St Patrick, Hove, Sussex (1858), and St Francis's Hospital, Haywards Heath, Sussex (1859).

KENDALL, John: c. 1766–1829
He is believed to have been a pupil of James Paine: he held the appointment of Surveyor to the Dean and Chapter of Exeter for

many years, and extensive restorations and repairs were carried out there by him between 1805 and 1827. He was the author of *An Elucidation of the Principles of English Architecture, usually denominated Gothic* (1818): he designed church monuments, and his architectural work included Holy Trinity, Exeter (1820).

KENT, William: *c.* 1685–1748 (Portrait: see Plate III)
Born at Bridlington, Yorks.: believed to have been a coachmaker's apprentice. His parents were not wealthy, and he was fortunate enough to find patrons who financed his Continental visit in 1709–19: he returned to England with Lord Burlington, whom he had met in Rome, and who remained his patron for the rest of his life. Kent was at first a 'History Painter', working at Burlington House and Kensington Palace, and did not begin his architectural career until the early 1730s. He held a number of official posts: Master Carpenter 1726: Master Mason and Deputy Surveyor 1735: Inspector of Paintings at the Royal Palaces 1727: and Portrait Painter to the King 1739. He lived mostly at Burlington House; was largely responsible for translating Lord Burlington's Palladian ideals into realities; designed sculpture; illustrated books; played an important part in the creation of English landscape-gardening as opposed to formal layout; and was a designer of interiors and internal decoration of outstanding architectural merit and beauty. He edited *Designs of Inigo Jones, with some additional Designs* (they were by Lord Burlington and himself) in 1727. His work included interior remodelling of Raynham Hall, Norfolk (1720–30): internal decorations at Chiswick House, Middx. (*c.* 1726): Holkham Hall, Norfolk (*c.* 1731–4: carried out by Matthew Brettingham): Treasury Buildings, Whitehall, London (1733–6): Devonshire House, Piccadilly, London (1734–5: dem.): No. 22 Arlington Street, London (*c.* 1740–55: completed by S. Wright: altered since): No. 44 Berkeley Square, London (1742–4): the Horse Guards, Whitehall, London (1750–60: built by John Vardy, after Kent's death).

KERR, Robert, FRIBA: 1823–1904
Born and educated in Aberdeen. He was one of the founders and the first President of the Architectural Association, 1847–8: served on the Council of the Institute: was a Fellow of King's College, London, and for many years Professor of the Arts of Construction

there: from 1862–1902 District Surveyor of St James's, West-minster. He was the author of many professional papers, articles, and books, including *Newleafe Discourses on the Fine Art Architecture* (1846): *The English Gentleman's Country House* (1864): *The Consulting Architect* (1894): *Town Houses*. As a designer of monumental, High Victorian style mansions, he was outstanding. His work included the National Provident Institution, Gracechurch Street, London (1863: dem. and since rebuilt): Bear Wood House, Berks. (1865–70): Ascot Heath House, Ascot, Berks. (1868): Ford Manor, nr. Lingfield, Surrey (1868).

KIRBY, John Joshua, FRS, FSA: 1716–74
Born at Wickham Market, Suffolk, the eldest son of John Kirby: apprenticed to a house painter in Ipswich, but then turned to landscape painting and perspective: lectured at St Martin's Lane Academy in London, and *c.* 1754 was appointed drawing master to the Prince of Wales, later George III. He was Secretary, and for a short time President, of the Incorporated Society of Artists: with his son, he was made Joint Clerk of the Works at Richmond and Kew Palaces in 1761, and *c.* 1770 made some additions to the Church of St Anne, Kew Gardens, Surrey, but he is known more for his writings than for his architectural work. He was the author of an *Historical Account* (of Suffolk) (1748): *Dr Brook Taylor's Method of Perspective made Easy, both in Theory and Practice* (1754): *The Perspective of Architecture deduced from the principles of Dr Brook Taylor* (1761): and *Dr Brook Taylor's Method of Perspective compared with the examples published as Sirigatti's by Isaac Ware. . . .* (1767).

KNIGHTLEY, Thomas Edward, FRIBA: 1823–1905
Articled to John Wallen in the City of London: set up his own practice there *c.* 1853: went into partnership with Thomas Batterbury in 1901. Knightley was Surveyor to the Birkbeck Building Society 1851–1905: District Surveyor for Hammersmith 1866–1904: Architect to the Edmonton Board of Guardians 1850–1904. He built offices, warehouses, workhouses, almshouses and schools, his practice being largely confined to London. In 1891 he was involved in a professional quarrel with C. J. Phipps over the design of the Queen's Hall, London. Knightley's work included the London Master Bakers' Benevolent Institution, Leyton, Essex (1857):

St Paul (Presbyterian), West Ferry Road, Millwall, London (1859): Birkbeck Schools, Hackney, London (1862): the Cavendish Hotel, Eastbourne, Sussex (1866): the Queen's Hall, London (1891–3: destroyed in the Second World War): Westminster Bank, Southampton Buildings, Holborn, London (1895–6: built as the Birkbeck Bank).

KNOTT, Ralph, FRIBA: 1878–1929
Educated at the City of London School: articled to Woodd and Ainslie: worked in the office of Sir Aston Webb. He set up in partnership with E. S. Collins in London in 1921. His work included County Hall, Lambeth, London (1911–33: additional wing since): the Northern Ireland Parliament House, Belfast (in association with Arnold Thornely): Nos. 1 and 21 Upper Grosvenor Street, London: observation wards at the Actors' Orphanage, Langley, Bucks.: a factory for Messrs W. T. Henley at Gravesend, Kent: Mallord House, Chelsea, London.

KNOWLES, Sir James, KCVO, FRIBA: 1831–1908
The son of James Knowles, a London architect: educated University College: trained in his father's office. He founded the Metaphysical Society (1869), and *The Nineteenth Century and After Review*, and was the editor of the *Contemporary Review* 1870–7: he was a close friend of Lord Tennyson, for whom he designed a house at Blackdown, Sussex. He was knighted in 1903. His work included Cedar Terrace, Thornton Terrace, and St Augustine, Cedars Road (dem.), Clapham Common, London (1860): the Grosvenor Hotel, Victoria Station, London (1860–1): Union Club, St James's Street, London (1862: built as the Thatched House Club): Aldworth House, Blackdown, Sussex (1869).

LAING, David, FSA: 1774–1856
The son of D. Laing, a merchant in the City of London, articled
to Sir John Soane. Appointed Architect and Surveyor to the Board
of Customs *c.* 1810, and between 1813 and 1817 built the new
Custom House in Lower Thames Street, London: a few years after
completion the building showed signs of decay, and in 1825 the
central front was demolished and rebuilt by Sir Robert Smirke.
Much litigation took place, Laing was suspended, and then retired,
and suffered much financial distress. In 1800 he published *Hints
for Dwellings, consisting of original designs for Cottages, Farm Houses,
Villas, etc.*, and in 1818 *Plans, etc. of Buildings, Public and Private,
executed in various parts of England, including the Custom House.* He was
Master of the Tylers' and Bricklayers' Company 1815–16. His work
included the New Custom House, The Parade, Plymouth, Devonshire
(1810): rebuilding at St Dun stan-in-the-East, Great Tower Street,
London (1817–21: with Sir William Tite): Essex and Suffolk Equitable Insurance, Colchester, Essex (1820: built as the Corn Exchange).

LAMB, Edward Buckton, FRIBA: 1805–69
The son of James Lamb, an amateur artist and government
official: articled to L. N. Cottingham. He had an extensive private
practice: much of his work, examples of which may be found all
over the country, was of the same 'rogue' Victorian, debased
character as that of Bassett Keeling, and, like Keeling, Lamb was
not *persona grata* with the Ecclesiological Society. He is well known
for the number of illustrations he contributed to the published
works of J. C. Loudon: he also illustrated for the *Builder.* His work
included lodge and chapel at the cemetery, Cambridge (1842):
Wadhurst Castle, nr. Wadhurst, Sussex (1842): Holy Trinity,
Prestwood, Bucks. (1849): the Rectory, Aston Clinton, Bucks.
(1850): St Margaret, Leiston, Suffolk (1853): Wayland Hall,
Watton, Norfolk (1853: built as the Corn Hall): Christ Church,
West Hartlepool, Co. Durham (1854): St Mary, Braiseworth,
Suffolk (1857): SS Simon and Jude, Englefield Green, Surrey
(1859): restoration of Hughenden Manor, Bucks. (1862): St Mary,
Bagby, Yorks. (1862): St Martin, Vicars Road, Gospel Oak,
London (1866): St Mary Magdalene, Canning Road, Addiscombe,
Surrey (1868: except tower).

LANCHESTER, Henry Vaughan, FRIBA: 1863–1953
Born in St John's Wood, London, the son of H. J. Lanchester, an architect who practised in London and Brighton: a pupil of his father: assistant in the offices of George Sherrin and other architects: set up in private practice 1894. From 1899 he was in partnership with James Stewart (d. 1904) and E. A. Rickards (d. 1920) and subsequently with T. A. Lodge and Lucas. He was a Vice-President of the RIBA: a founder of and President of the Town Planning Institute: the first President of the South-Eastern Society of Architects: Editor of the *Builder* 1910–12: Royal Gold Medallist 1934: an HON.LITT.D of Leeds: his published works included *The Art of Town Planning*: *Talks on Town Planning*: and *Fischer von Erlach*. He did much town planning in India, Rangoon and Zanzibar: advised the Maharajah of Baroda: and in India his partnership built the Palace of the Maharajah of Jodhpur, the Post Office at Lucknow, and the Birkmyre Hotel at Calcutta. Their other work included the Civic Centre, Cardiff: the Horticultural Research Station, East Malling, Kent: premises of Bovril Ltd., City Road, Finsbury, London (1892–1923): the Town Hall, Deptford, London (1900–3): the Central Hall, Westminster, London (1905–11): Third Church of Christ, Scientist, Curzon Street, London (1910–12): Nos. 144–6 New Bond Street, and No. 11 Old Bond Street, London (1911): extensive additions to the University, Leeds, Yorks. (1926–50): the Town Hall, Beckenham, Kent (1932): Queen Elizabeth Hospital and Medical School, Birmingham, Warwicks. (1933–8).

LANE, Richard: nineteenth century
He practised in Manchester, and was the first President of the Manchester Architectural Society: exhibited at the Royal Academy in London and Manchester, 1815 and 1826: Land Surveyor to the Manchester Police Commissioners 1821: in partnership with Francis Goodwin for a time. His work in Manchester included the Friends' Meeting House, Mount Street (1828): Town Hall and Dispensary, Chorlton (1830): the Deaf and Dumb and Blind Asylum, Old Trafford (1834–7): the Corn Exchange (1837): Richmond Chapel, Blackfriars Road (1845). He also built St Mary, Oldham, Lancs. (1823–7): St Thomas, Pendleton, Lancs. (1830: with F. Goodwin): the Infirmary, Stockport, Cheshire (1832): façade of the Boys' Grammar School, Wakefield, Yorks. (1833–4).

LANGLEY, Batty: 1696–1751

The son of a gardener, David Langley of Twickenham. He and his brother, Thomas, who was an engraver, conducted a school of architectural drawing in Soho, London, which they established about 1740. Batty Langley advertised himself as able to carry out the duties of an architect and surveyor: he was employed at Wrest Park, Beds. (*c.* 1735), and designed the Gothic Temple in the grounds of Painshill Park, Surrey (*c.* 1740). He is best known as the author of numerous books for the guidance of builders and workmen: these included *The City and Country Builder's and Workman's Treasury of Designs* (1740): and *The Builder's Director or Bench-Mate* (1746).

LANYON, Sir Charles: 1812–89

Of English parentage, he was apprenticed to the Dublin Board of Works, and lived and practised in Northern Ireland, where he became well known as an architect and civil engineer. From 1835–60 he was County Surveyor of Antrim, where he laid out many roads and railways. He was President of the Royal Institute of the Architects of Ireland, and was knighted during his spell in office. His private practice included many churches in Down, Connor and Dromore, and in Belfast he designed and built the Ulster Institute for the Deaf, Dumb and Blind (1845): Queen's College (1849: with his partner, Lynn): the County Courthouse and Gaol (1850): the Northern Bank.

LAPIDGE, Edward, FIBA: 1793–1860

The son of Samuel Lapidge, Chief Gardener at Hampton Court, who had been an assistant to Lancelot 'Capability' Brown. Edward Lapidge exhibited at the Royal Academy 1808–50, and was County Surveyor of Surrey. His work included probably Hildersham Hall, Cambs. (1814): Kingston Bridge, Surrey (1825–8: widened 1914): St Peter, Hammersmith, London (1827–9): St Andrew, Ham Common, Surrey (1830–1: south aisle and chancel added later): St Mary, Hampton, Middx. (1831): St James, Ratcliff, Stepney, London (1837–8): the old Rectory, Skirbeck, Lincs. (1847): the County Asylum, Fulbourn, Cambs. (1851).

LATROBE, Benjamin: 1764–1820

Born near Leeds, Yorks., the son of the Rev. Benjamin Latrobe, a prominent Moravian minister: educated at the Moravian College, Nisky, Saxony: and on his return to England in 1783 worked in the Stamp Office till 1786, when he became a pupil of S. P. Cockerell, and later of Smeaton, the engineer. Set up in private practice, and in 1796 emigrated to the United States. He carried out much important work there, became Surveyor of Public Buildings to the Federal Government; and his commissions in America included the Bank of Pennsylvania at Philadelphia, Baltimore Cathedral, and the south wing of the Capitol at Washington, D.C. He did little work in England, but was employed at Frimley Park, Surrey (*c.* 1780), and designed Hammerwood House, nr. East Grinstead, Sussex (*c.* 1793), and Ashdown House, nr. Forest Row, Sussex (*c.* 1794).

LEADBETTER, Stiff: d. 1766

A carpenter and builder of Eton, Bucks., who was Surveyor to St Paul's Cathedral in 1756. His work included Langley Hall, nr. Slough, Bucks. (*c.* 1755–8: additions since): Shardeloes, nr. Amersham, Bucks. (1758–60: his design was altered and completed by Robert Adam): the Radcliffe Infirmary, Oxford (1759–70: completed by John Sanderson): St Paul, Baker Street, London (1766: considerably remodelled since).

LEE, Thomas: 1794–1834

The son of Thomas Lee of Barnstaple, an architect who retired from practice when only twenty-one, after inheriting a private fortune. Thomas Lee the younger was educated at Barnstaple Grammar School: worked in the office of Sir John Soane, and for David Laing: entered the Royal Academy School 1812: was awarded the Silver Medal 1816, and in the same year the Gold Medal of the Society of Arts. His work included the Wellington Memorial, Blackdown Hill, Som. (1817–18: the obelisk was intended to support a statue of the Duke, which was never erected): Arlington Court, nr. Combe Martin, Devonshire (1820–3): the Guildhall, Barnstaple, Devonshire (1826).

LEONI, Giacomo: *c.* 1686–1746

A Venetian, architect to the Elector Palatine, who came to England sometime before 1715 in order to superintend the publication of an English edition of his book, *The Architecture of A. Palladio, Revis'd, Design'd, and Publish'd by Giacomo Leoni, a Venetian: Architect to his most Serene Highness, the Elector Palatine.* Translated by Nicholas Dubois, it was first published in 1715–16, and there were subsequent editions in 1721 and 1742. Leoni was also the author of an MS treatise, *Compendious Directions for Builders,* and the translator of *The Architecture of L. B. Alberti* (1726). Leoni remained in England where he practised as a private architect: among his patrons were Lord Fitzwalter, and the Duke of Kent, for whom he did much remodelling at Wrest Park, Beds. His work included Clandon Park, Surrey (1713–29): Lyme Hall, Cheshire (*c.* 1720–30: altered since): No. 7 Burlington Gardens, London (1721: reconstructed 1792): Argyll House, King's Road, Chelsea, London (1723): Lathom Hall, Lancs. (1725: dem.). No. 4 St James's Square, London (1725–6) is believed to have been designed by Leoni, but Moor Park, Herts. (1720), often attributed to him, is now declared to be the work of Sir James Thornhill.

LETHABY, William Richard, FSA, FRIBA: 1857–1931

Born at Barnstaple, Devonshire, where his father carried on business as a picture framer and gilder, and was a member of the Bible Christians sect: educated at the Grammar School, and Art School, Barnstaple: articled to a local architect, Alexander Lauder. In 1879 he was awarded the Soane Medallion of the RIBA: entered the Royal Academy Schools: and spent some time in Northern France, drawing and measuring cathedrals and monuments: he worked in the office of Norman Shaw from 1879–91. In 1893 he visited Constantinople, and with Harold Swainson, who accompanied him, produced a scholarly study of the church of Sancta Sophia. With a few other architects, he founded and worked for a time in a furniture-designing firm, Kenton & Co.: he was a member of the Society for the Protection of Ancient Buildings: of the Art Workers' Guild: and, after it was formed in 1915, of the Design and Industries Association. From 1896–1911 Lethaby was Principal of the LCC Central School of Arts and Crafts, and from 1900–18 Professor of Design at the Royal College of Art: he was the author of many articles, papers, and books on art, architecture and design, notably *Architecture, Mysticism and Myth* (1892): *The Church of Sancta Sophia Constantinople* (1894: in collaboration with Harold Swainson): *Mediaeval Art* (1904): *Westminster Abbey and the King's Craftsmen*

(1906): *Architecture – An Introduction to the History and Theory of the Art of Building* (1911): *London before the Conquest* (1911): *Form in Civilization* (1922): *Londinium: Architecture and the Crafts* (1923): *Westminster Abbey Re-Examined* (1925). He was Surveyor of Westminster Abbey 1906–28: his work included Melsetter House, Isle of Hoy, Orkney (1898): Orion Insurance, Colmore Row, Birmingham, Warwicks. (1900: with C. L. Ball: built as Eagle Insurance Co.): All Saints, Brockhampton-by-Ross, Herefs. (1901–2).

LEVERTON, Thomas: 1743–1824

Born at Woodford, Essex, the son of a local builder, Lancelot Leverton. Worked for his father, and acquired other architectural training: began to exhibit at the Royal Academy 1771. He was Surveyor to the Phoenix Fire Insurance Company, and to the Theatres Royal, in London: with Thomas Chawner, was Joint Architect to the Land Revenue Authorities: and a J.P. for Surrey and Kent. He was closely concerned in the laying out of Bedford Square, London: he designed the interiors of many of the houses there, and lived at No. 13 from 1796–1824. His work included No. 65 Lincoln's Inn Fields, London (1772): Boyles Court, Great Warley, Essex (1776): Woodhall House, nr. Watton-at-Stone, Herts. (1777): Triumphal Arch at Parlington Park, Aberford, Yorks. (1785).

LEWIS, Hayter, FSA: 1818–98

Studied at the Royal Academy Schools: was a pupil of Sir William Tite: travelled on the Continent for two years: went into partnership with Finden. He was Hon. Secretary of the Institute of British Architects in 1860: and later became Professor of Architecture at University College. He contributed to the *Encyclopaedia Britannica* and published *The Holy Places of Jerusalem*. His work included the North and South wings of the Court, at University College, London (1869–81).

LEWIS, James: c. 1751–1820

Believed to have been born at Brecon, in Wales: travelled in Italy 1770–72. Was a founder member of the Architects' Club: Surveyor to Christ's Hospital 1792–1816: and Surveyor to the Bridewell and Bethlehem Hospitals 1793–1816. He was the author of *Original Designs in Architecture, consisting of Plans, etc. for Villas, Mansions,*

Town Houses, etc. and a new Design for a Theatre, published in two volumes in 1779–80 and 1797. His work included Eydon Hall, Northants (*c.* 1790): Lavington Park, East Lavington, Sussex (1790–94): Hackthorn Hall, Lincs. (1792): No. 14 New Bridge Street, London (*c.* 1805: later the Chartered Institute of Secretaries): The Bethlehem Hospital, Southwark, London (1812–15: now the Imperial War Museum: enlarged later by P. Hardwick and S. Smirke, and portio and dome added: wings dem. since).

LIGHTHOLDER (or LIGHTOLER), Thomas: eighteenth century
A carver of Bath, who also practised as an architect, and contributed to *The Modern Builder's Assistant,* by R. Morris and W. and J. Halfpenny (1742). He published *The Gentleman's and Farmer's Architect, being correct Plans and Elevations of Parsonage and Farm Houses,* in 1762. His work included the Octagon Chapel, Milsom Street, Bath, Som. (*c.* 1763–7): St Paul (1763–9) and St John (1775–83) in Liverpool, now both dem.: redecoration and additions at Burton Constable, Yorks. (*c.* 1760).

LOCKWOOD, Henry Francis: 1811–78
Born at Doncaster: articled to P. Robinson of London: set up in practice at Kingston-upon-Hull 1834: moved to Bradford 1849, where he joined William and Richard Mawson (1834–1904), in a partnership that lasted for many years, and was responsible for many buildings in Bradford. Lockwood was arbitrator to Bradford Corporation for their street improvement programme, and he and William Mawson were architects to Sir Titus Salt, the philanthropic industrialist. Lockwood moved to London in 1874: he built Dent Cottage, Winterton, Lincs. (1830): Barclays Bank, Market Place, Boston, Lincs. (1835): and the City Temple, Holborn Viaduct, London (1873–4: virtually rebuilt after war damage). His work in Bradford, with Mawson, included St George's Hall (1851–3): The Exchange, Market Street (1864–7): the Victoria Hotel (1867): the Town Hall (1873: extended since): Manningham Mills, Lister Park (1873): monument to Sir Titus Salt, Lister Park (1874): Yorkshire United Independent College (1874–7: built as the Airedale College): the Bradford Club, Bank Street (1877): Kirkgate, Darley Street and Godwin Markets (1877): they also designed Victoria Chambers, Leeds: the Saltaire Housing Estate,

nr. Shipley, Yorks. (*c.* 1850–76): Congregational Church, Saltaire, Yorks. (1858–9): Methodist Church, Harrogate, Yorks. (1862): Baptist Church, Scarborough, Yorks. (1867): Mechanics' Institute, Keighley, Yorks. (1868): St Stephen, Cambridge Park, Twickenham, Middx. (1874): the Civil Service Stores, Strand, London (1876–7: alterations since).

LOUDON, John Claudius: 1783–1843 (Portrait: see Plate VIII) Born at Gogar, nr. Edinburgh, the son of a Scottish farmer: educated privately in Edinburgh: *c.* 1798 began work as a draughtsman with John Mawer, an Edinburgh landscape gardener and nurseryman: then with another, Mr Dickson, at the same time studying agriculture under Dr Coventry, Professor of that subject at Edinburgh University. Loudon went to London in 1803, and set up as a landscape gardener. He became interested in farming; from 1808–11 took over the management and improvement of Tew Park, Oxon., and started a school of agriculture there. From 1813–14 he travelled in Europe: on his return he encountered financial misfortunes, and ill-health, and in 1816 began a career as an editor and writer on horticulture and architecture, that continued till his death. His wife, Jane Loudon, was also well known as a horticultural writer. Loudon was a Fellow of the Geographical, Horticultural, Linnean and Zoological Societies: he introduced the plane tree to London squares: invented a channelled iron sash bar for use in hothouses: designed and laid out the Botanical Gardens, Edgbaston, Birmingham, Warwicks. (*c.* 1832): the Derby Arboretum (1840): laid out the cemetery in Histon Road, Cambridge (1842): and the Abbey Cemetery, Prior Park Road, Bath (1843). Among his numerous published works (the immense length of the titles make it impracticable to give them in full here) were *Observations on the Formation and Management of Useful and Ornamental Plantations* (1804): *A Short Treatise on several Improvements recently made in Hot-houses* (1805): *A Treatise on Forming, Improving and Managing Country Residences* (1806): *Designs for laying out Farms and Farm-Buildings* (1811): *Hints on the Formation of Gardens and pleasure grounds* (1812): *Remarks on the Construction of Hothouses* (1817): *Sketches of Curvilinear Hothouses* (1818): *An Encyclopaedia of Gardening* (1822): *An Encyclopaedia of Agriculture* (1825): *An Encyclopaedia of Plants* (1829): *A Manual of Cottage Gardening, Husbandry and Architecture* (1830): *Illustrations of Landscape-Gardening and Garden Architecture*

LUGAR, ROBERT

(1830): *An Encyclopaedia of Cottage, Farm and Villa Architecture and Furniture* (1833): *The Suburban Gardener and Villa Companion* (1838): *The Landscape Gardening and Landscape Architecture of the late Humphry Repton Esq.* (1840): *The Derby Arboretum* (1840): *On the Laying Out, Planting and Managing of Cemeteries* (1843). He was the founder and editor of the *Architectural Magazine* (1834–38).

LUGAR, Robert: *c.* 1773–1855
He exhibited at the Royal Academy 1799–1841: practised in London: appointed Essex County Surveyor in 1812: and was the author of a number of books including *Architectural Sketches for Cottages, Rural Dwellings, and Villas* (1805): *The Country Gentleman's Architect; Designs for Farm Houses and Yards* (1807): and *Villa Architecture, a collection of Views, with Plans, of Buildings executed in England, Scotland, etc.* (1828). His work included The Turrets, Lexden Road, Colchester, Essex (1818): internal alterations and extensive additions to Swinton Park, Yorks. (1821–4): the Rectory, Yaxham, Norfolk (1822): Newlaithes Hall, Horsforth, Yorks. (before 1828): Betteshanger House, nr. Sandwich, Kent (1829: enlarged since).

LUMBY, William: eighteenth century
The son of Thomas Lumby, a master carpenter at Lincoln Cathedral: learned his father's trade, but also practised as an architect after his appointment as Surveyor and Clerk of the Works to Lincoln Cathedral *c.* 1775. Both Lumbys were closely associated with James Essex, and did much work together in Lincs. William Lumby became Keeper of the Castle Gaol: he was carpenter for the staircase at Ormsby Hall, Lincs. (designed by James Paine 1752–5), and at Lincoln supervised the construction of the Infirmary (1776: later the Bishop's Hostel): and of a new Gaol (1786–8: enlarged since: later the County Record Office), both designed by John Carr. Lumby's work included St Peter, Doddington, Lincs. (1771–5: with Thomas Lumby): the Old Blue Coat School, Lincoln (1784: later the Lincoln School of Art).

LUTYENS, Sir Edwin Landseer, KCIE, OM, RA, FRIBA: 1869–1944
(Portrait: see Plate XII)
Born in London, the son of Captain C. H. A. Lutyens, whose forbears had come from Schleswig-Holstein in 1745: educated privately, and at the Royal College of Art in London: a pupil of

Sir Ernest George 1887: set up his own practice 1889. In 1908–9 he was a Consultant to Hampstead Garden Suburb: 1912 Joint Architect, with Sir Herbert Baker, to the New Delhi Government buildings: 1917 a Consultant to the Imperial War Graves Commission: knighted 1918: Royal Gold Medallist 1921: a Vice-President of the Institute 1924–5: Gold Medallist of the American Institute of Architects 1924: KCIE 1930: Legion of Honour 1932: President of the Royal Academy 1938: OM 1942: he was a member of the Royal Fine Arts Commission, an HON.LL.D of Liverpool, and HON.DCL of Oxford. Lutyens' mastery of architectural design was proved by his great reputation at home and abroad: he built many large country houses, advised Government Commissions, carried out schemes of civic planning, designed memorials, and was a landscape gardener of genius. The huge output of his practice included Crooksbury Lodge, nr. Farnham, Surrey (1890): Munstead Wood (1896) and Orchards (1899), both at Munstead, Surrey: the restoration of Lindisfarne Castle, Holy Island, Northumb. (1902): Little Thakeham, Thakeham, Sussex (1902–3): offices of *Country Life*. Tavistock Street, London (1904): Heathcote, Ilkley, Yorks. (1906): St Jude, Hampstead Garden Suburb, Middx. (1910): restoration of Great Dixter, Northiam, Sussex, and design of the gardens (1910): Viceroy's Palace and ancillary buildings, New Delhi, India (1912–30: with Sir Herbert Baker): the Cenotaph, Whitehall, London (1919–20): the Midland Bank, Piccadilly, London (1922): British Medical Association, Tavistock Square, London (1922–9): Britannic House, Finsbury Circus, London (1924–7): the British Embassy, Washington, DC, USA. (1926–9): layout of Page Street and Vincent Street Council Estate, Westminster, London (1928–30): the Metropolitan Cathedral, Liverpool (begun 1929): YWCA Building, Great Russell Street, London (1930–2): Hampton Court Bridge, Middx. (1933): Campion Hall, Oxford (1934): Reuters and Press Association, Fleet Street, London (1935): Halnaker House, Sussex (1938).

MACARTNEY, Sir Mervyn Edmund, FSA, FRIBA: 1853–1932
The fourth son of Maxwell Macartney of Co. Armagh: educated
Lincoln College, Oxford: a pupil of Norman Shaw: for a time was
a member of the furniture-designing firm of Kenton & Co., founded
c. 1899 by a group of young architects. He was a founder of the Art
Workers' Guild and its Master in 1900: Surveyor to the Fabric
of St Paul's Cathedral 1906–31: Editor of the *Architectural Review*
for many years. Knighted 1930. He resigned from the RIBA in
1891, over the question of its official registration and examination
policy, but rejoined in 1906. He did much to revive the relation
of garden design to architecture: designed many country houses
and gardens, and carried out church repairs and restorations:
assisted John Belcher on his book, *Later Renaissance Architecture in
England*: and was himself the author of *English Houses and Gardens
of the 16th and 17th Centuries*. His work included No. 167 Queen's
Gate, London (1889): Sandhills, Bletchingley, Surrey (1893):
Guinness Trust flats, Vauxhall Walk, Lambeth, London (1893):
Shalesbrooke, Forest Row, Sussex (c. 1900): Bussock Wood,
Winterbourne, Berks. (1907: later Phillip's Hill House): Kennet
Orleigh, and The Court, Woolhampton, Berks. (c. 1910–15):
houses in the South Avenue of the Whiteley Village, nr. Cobham,
Surrey (c. 1912): the Public Library, Essex Road, Islington,
London (1916).

MACKINTOSH, Charles Rennie, FRIBA: 1869–1928
A Scotsman: educated Allan Glen's School, and at the Glasgow
School of Art: articled to John Hutchinson of Glasgow: set up in
practice there in partnership with John Honeyman and John
Keppie. He won the Greek Thomson Travelling Studentship
1890: was a member of the Glasgow Institute of Architects, and
a pioneer of the modern movement in architecture. His work
in Glasgow included assistance to Keppie on the extension to the
Glasgow Herald buildings in Mitchell Street (1893–5): St Cuthbert
and Queen's Cross Church (1897–9): Glasgow School of Art
(1897–9 and 1907–9: with his partners): Tea Rooms at No. 211
Ingram Street (1901: later Zederbaum's): Scotland Street School
(1904): Willow Tea Rooms at No. 199 Sauchiehall Street (1904:
later Daly's).

MAIR, George James John, FIBA: 1810–89

Born in Aberdeen: articled to Decimus Burton 1826: entered the Royal Academy Schools 1830: travelled in Italy 1832: set up in practice as an architect and surveyor in London, 1833. He was a founder and Hon. Secretary of the Architectural Society, and became a Fellow of the Institute of British Architects when the two organizations merged in 1842: he served on the Institute's Council in 1842–4, 1848–50, 1853–5 and 1863–4: was a member of the Surveyors' Club, and one of the first Life Members of the Architects' Benevolent Society, of which he was Hon. Treasurer in 1873–85. His work included Northwood House, I.O.W. (1837): Welcombe House, nr. Stratford-upon-Avon, Warwicks. (1838: rebuilt 1867): Kneller Hall, Whitton, Middx. (1848: later the Royal Military School of Music).

MALTON, Thomas: 1748–1804

The elder son of Thomas Malton, an architectural draughtsman who settled in Dublin. Thomas Malton the younger worked in James Gandon's London office, studied architecture at the Royal Academy Schools, and was awarded the Silver and Gold Medals of the Academy in 1774 and 1782 respectively. He did not practise architecture, but is known as an expert draughtsman and engraver of topographical views of streets and buildings. Malton was among the early users of aquatinta, and his best-known work, *A Picturesque Tour through the Cities of London and Westminster* (1792), contains many aquatint plates. His younger brother, James (d. 1803), was a topographical artist in Ireland for most of his life; he published *A Descriptive View of Dublin* (1797), among other works. He returned to England *c.* 1792: it has been suggested that he may have been the author of a series of vicious letters attacking James Gandon, published anonymously in Dublin from 1786 onwards.

MANNERS, George Philip: nineteenth century

The City Architect of Bath in 1830: was in partnership with Charles Harcourt Masters. In Bath his work included St Catherine's Almshouses (1829): St Michael, Broad Street (1835–7): the Catholic Apostolic Church, Vineyards (1840): chapel at the Abbey Cemetery, Prior Park Road (1844): St Matthew, Widcome (1846–7: with J. Elkington Gill): Blue Coat School, Upper Boro' Walls (*c.* 1860: with Gill). Manners also built Holy Trinity, Cleeve, Som. (1840):

rebuilt the Market Cross, Shepton Mallet, Som. (1841): the Gaol, Lower Bristol Road, Twerton, Som. (1843: later the premises of an engineering firm): Holy Trinity, Clandown, Som. (1849).

MARRABLE, Frederick: 1818–72

The son of Sir Thomas Marrable, Secretary to the Board of Green Cloth under George IV and William IV. Frederick Marrable was articled to Edward Blore: travelled abroad: set up in private practice, and was Superintending Architect to the Metropolitan Board of Works 1856–62. His work included St Mary Magdalen, St Margaret's Road, Hastings, Sussex (1852: enlarged later): in London, the Old County Hall, Spring Gardens, Trafalgar Square (1860): the Garrick Club, Garrick Street (1864): St Peter, Deptford (1867–70).

MASTERS, Charles Harcourt: eighteenth century

Practised as an architect and surveyor in Bath, and published a Survey of the City in 1794: towards the end of his life he was in partnership with G. P. Manners, using the surname of Harcourt. He carried out much survey work, was concerned with the laying out of Widcombe Crescent and Sydney Place, and designed the Sydney Hotel, in Sydney Gardens (1796: later the Holburne of Menstrie Museum).

MAY, Hugh: 1622–84

The son of John May, a gentleman, of Mid Lavant. Sussex. For some twenty years Hugh May was in the service of the Duke of Buckingham: was a strong Royalist: and a friend of Sir Peter Lely and John Evelyn. At the Restoration he was appointed Paymaster of the Works; in 1668 Comptroller: and in 1673 Comptroller of the Works at Windsor. Most of his work there, which included the remodelling of St George's Hall and the King's Chapel, has now disappeared. May was appointed one of the King's Surveyors for rebuilding the City after the Great Fire. His work included rebuilding of the east front and design of stables and chapel at Cornbury House, Oxon. (1663–8): Eltham Lodge, Woolwich, London (1664): Berkeley House, Piccadilly, London (1664–6: dem.): additional wings at Cassiobury Park, Herts. (c. 1677–80: rebuilt later by James Wyatt).

MEDWORTH, Joseph: *c.* 1754–1827
A bricklayer of Wisbech, Cambs.: he set up as a builder in London, and became sufficiently prosperous to return to Wisbech, where he bought the old Castle and grounds in 1793, and developed the site, building the Crescent (1797–1808) and Castle House (*c.* 1811). He was Bailiff of Wisbech in 1819.

MEE, Arthur Patrick, FRIBA: 1802–68
The son of Joseph Mee of London: a pupil of Sir John Soane 1818–23: entered the Royal Academy Schools 1822: later travelled in Italy: served on the Institute's Council 1849–56. His work included the Town Hall, Wolverhampton, Staffs. (1844): the Fishmongers' and Poulterers' Almshouses, Wood Green, London (1847–9: with W. Webb): addition of an upper storey (1859) and a wing (1868) to St George's Hospital, London.

MICKLETHWAITE, John Thomas, FSA: 1843–1906
A pupil of Sir G. G. Scott in 1862: set up independent practice 1869, and from 1876–92 was in partnership with Somers Clarke, with whom he worked very closely, so that identification of their individual work is difficult. He was appointed Surveyor to the Dean and Chapter of Westminster 1898: Architect to St George's Chapel, Windsor 1900. He was a distinguished antiquary; a founder of the Alcuin Club; served on the Council of the Society of Antiquaries, and was Vice-President in 1902. Micklethwaite was a contributor to *The Church Builder*, the *Builder*, and the *Archaeological Journal*: he published *Modern Parish Churches* (1874), and was the author of the architectural section of *Westminster Abbey Historically Described* by H. J. Feasey (1899). His work included St Anne, Wrenthorpe, Yorks. (1873–4): St Hilda, Cross Green Lane, Leeds, Yorks. (1876–81): St Paul, Augustus Road, Putney, London (1877): St John the Divine, Gainsborough, Lincs. (1881–2: with Somers Clarke: enlarged since): St John, Horbury Bridge, Horbury, Yorks. (1884: with Somers Clarke): St Luke, Sharlston, Yorks. (1886): All Saints, Wimbledon, Surrey (1891–3: with Somers Clarke): St Mary, Stretton, nr. Tutbury, Staffs. (1897: with Somers Clarke): St Peter, Bocking, Essex (1897): St Saviour, Scarborough, Yorks. (1901): St Bartholomew, Barking Road, East Ham, London (1901: with Somers Clarke).

159

MIDDLETON, Charles Thomas: 1756–c. 1818
Studied under James Paine, and at the Royal Academy Schools, where he was awarded the Silver Medal 1779: in partnership for a time with James Bailey, and with him was Surveyor to Lambeth. He was the author of *Picturesque and Architectural Views for Cottages, Farm Houses and Country Villas* (1793): *The Architect and Builders' Miscellany . . . containing original Picturesque Designs in Architecture* (1799): *Decorations for Parks and Gardens* (1810): *Abstract of the Building Act* [of 1774] (1810): *Designs for Gates and Rails suitable to Parks, Pleasure Grounds, etc.* He supervised the reconstruction of Carlton House, London (dem.), designed by Henry Holland, in 1783–5.

MILLER, Sanderson: 1717–80
Born near Edgehill, Warwicks., the son of Sanderson Miller, a prosperous Banbury merchant: an undergraduate at St Mary Hall, Oxford 1734: in 1737, on the death of his father, he inherited his property and became a wealthy country squire, who also practised as an amateur architect. He specialized in designing sham ruins in Rococo Gothic style, for which he was an early enthusiast. He made Gothic additions to his own house, Radway Grange, Warwicks. (c. 1745), and built a thatched cottage (1744) and a sham castle (1746–7) in the grounds there. His work was done largely for his friends, the practical construction of his designs being carried out by professional builders from the sketches and drawings he provided. His work included a mock ruined castle in the grounds of Wimpole Hall, Cambs. (c. 1749): rebuilding of Hagley Hall, Worcs., and a sham Gothic castle in the grounds (1749–50: some damage by fire since): alterations at Belhus, Aveley, Essex (1751–60): the design of the Shire Hall, Warwick (1753–8: built by the Hiornses): reconstruction of the Great Hall, Lacock Abbey, Wilts. (1754–6): the sham castle on Bathwick Hill, Bath, Som. (c. 1755: built for Ralph Allen in 1762).

MOCATTA, David, FSA, FRIBA: 1806–82
The son of a wealthy Jew, Moses Mocatta: studied architecture in Italy: was a pupil of Sir John Soane before setting up in practice: among his more important clients was the London, Brighton & South Coast Railway. Mocatta was an early member of the Institute: a Vice-President: a Trustee of Sir John Soane's Museum:

an active supporter of the Architects' Benevolent Society: a founder member of the West London Synagogue of British Jews. His work included the railway viaduct near Haywards Heath, Sussex, and the Railway Station at Brighton, Sussex (1840).

MOORE, Temple Lushington, FRIBA: 1856–1920

The son of Maj.-Gen. G. F. Moore: articled to George Gilbert Scott the younger, in 1875: then became his assistant, and remained in close professional association with him throughout his career. Moore had intended to be an artist, and he was a superb draughtsman: he travelled widely in Europe, sketching and measuring mediaeval work, and did much church building and restoration: he also designed furniture and decoration for his buildings. He was later in partnership with his son, Richard, and his nephew-in-law, Leslie Moore. His work included stables and lodge, Kenwick Hall, nr. Louth, Lincs. (1888): the Church of the Good Shepherd, Lake, I.O.W. (1892): St Peter, Barnsley, Yorks. (1895): St Mark, Mansfield, Notts. (1897): the Manor House, Bilbrough, Yorks. (1901): St. Wilfrid, Harrogate, Yorks. (1904–14: additions later by Leslie Moore): All Saints, Franciscan Road, Tooting, London (1905–6): St Luke, Eltham, London (1906): the Chapel at the Bishop's Hostel, Lincoln (1906): Priory of St Wilfrid, Leeds, Yorks. (1908–28): St James, Clacton-on-Sea, Essex (1913): St Augustine, Gillingham, Kent (1916).

MORRIS, Roger: 1695–1749

The son of Owen Morris of Netherby, Yorks. The Duke of Argyll and the Earl of Pembroke were his principal patrons: he was made Carpenter and Principal Engineer to the Board of Ordnance, and in 1727 Clerk of the Works at Richmond New Park Lodge. Much of his work was done in collaboration with Henry Herbert, 9th Earl of Pembroke, himself an amateur architect. Examples of this partnership were Marble Hill, Twickenham, Middx. (c. 1728): White Lodge, Richmond Park, Surrey (1727–9): the Palladian Bridge, Wilton, Wilts. (1737). The work of Morris himself included Whitton Park, Twickenham, Middx. (1724–5): the Council House, Chichester, Sussex (1731–3): the central part of Standlynch House, Wilts. (1733: later Trafalgar House): Carne's Seat, in the grounds of Goodwood House, Sussex (1743): Inverary Castle, Argyllshire (1746–61: restoration since). Robert Morris, also an

L

architect, was related to Roger Morris who gave him some training and instruction. Robert is believed to have completed Inverary Castle after the death of Roger, and to have worked with him at other places, but is better known for his published works. These included *Essay in Defence of Ancient Architecture: or a Parallel of the Ancient Buildings with the Modern, shewing the Beauty and Harmony of the Former, and the Irregularity of the Latter* (1728): *Rural Architecture: consisting of Regular Designs of Plans and Elevations for Buildings in the Country* (1750): *The Architectural Remembrancer: being a collection of New and Useful Designs of Ornamental Buildings and Decorations* (1751): *Select Architecture* (1755): *Architecture Improved in a collection of modern, elegant and useful designs* (1755): *Lectures on Architecture Consisting of Rules founded upon Harmonick and Arithmetical Proportions in Building* (1759).

MOUNTAGUE, William: 1773–1843

A pupil of the younger Dance, whom he succeeded as Clerk of the Works to the Corporation of London, 1816. He was also Surveyor to the City Improvement Committee: District Surveyor for the Western division of the City: and Surveyor to the Estates of Sir Charles Morgan; of the Sons of the Clergy; and to the Thames Tunnel Company. He was responsible for much clearing of sites, replanning of streets, and preparing valuations of property in the City of London. There, he designed Faringdon Market (1828–9): enlarged Smithfield Market, and designed a new ceiling for the Ballroom at the Mansion House, having removed the attic storey above it. His younger brother, James (d. 1852), was District Surveyor for the Northern division of the City of London, and Surveyor to the Port of London, and of Blackfriars Bridge. William Mountague's son, Frederick William (d. 1841), was also a surveyor with a large private practice: he was his father's chief assistant and, in his capacity as Surveyor to a House of Commons Committee for Metropolitan Improvements, was responsible for laying out many streets in London, including New Oxford Street.

MOUNTFORD, Edward William, FRIBA: 1855–1908

The son of Edward Mountford of Shipston-upon-Stour, Worcs.: educated at Clevedon: articled to Habershon and Pite, in London 1872: set up in practice 1881. He served on the RIBA Council: was President of the AA 1893–5: had a very large practice in

London and the provinces. From 1907 he was in partnership with F. Dale Clapham. His work included the Battersea Polytechnic, London (1890–1): the Town Hall, Sheffield, Yorks. (1890–7): St Andrew, Garratt Lane, Wandsworth, London (1891): the Town Hall, Battersea, London (1892–3): St Olave's Grammar School, Tooley Street, Bermondsey, London (1893): the Northampton Institute, St John Street, Finsbury, London (1896): the Central Criminal Court, Old Bailey, London (1900–7): the premises of Willett & Co., Sloane Square, London (c. 1905): Northern Assurance, Moorgate, London (1906: with Gruning).

MYLNE, Robert, FRS: 1734–1811
A descendant of a famous family of Scottish master masons who had worked in the royal service since the end of the fifteenth century. Born at Powderhall, nr. Edinburgh, the son of Thomas Mylne, City Surveyor of Edinburgh: among his forbears was John Mylne (d. 1667), who designed the Tron Kirk, Edinburgh, c. 1633. Robert was apprenticed to an Edinburgh mason, then assisted his father in that trade: travelled on the Continent 1754–9: was awarded the Silver Medal for architecture of St Luke's Academy, Rome, and became a member of the Academy and of those at Florence and Bologna. He was an engineer as well as an architect: planned the Gloucester and Berkeley Ship Canal, and the drainage scheme at Eau Brink Cut, King's Lynn, Norfolk, and made numerous surveys and reports on bridges, harbours, canals and waterworks. In 1767 he was appointed Joint Engineer to the New River Company, which had been founded by Sir Hugh Myddelton between 1609 and 1613, and which gave London its first proper water supply. Mylne was also Surveyor to St Paul's Cathedral: Surveyor to Canterbury Cathedral: Clerk of the Works at Greenwich Hospital 1775–82: Surveyor to the Thames Commissioners from 1788: Surveyor to the Stationers' Company: an original member of the Architects' Club. He built many bridges, the best known Blackfriars Bridge, London (1760–9: dem. 1868), and his work included St Cecilia's Hall, Edinburgh (1763–5: much altered since): Wormleybury, Wormley, Herts. (1767–9): the New River Company's offices, Clerkenwell, London (1770): Addington Palace, nr. Croydon, Surrey (1773–9: later the Royal School of Church Music): The Wick, Richmond, Surrey (1775): rebuilding of the east front of Stationers' Hall, Ludgate Hill, London (1800):

at Great Amwell, Herts., a monument commemorating Sir Hugh Myddelton, and a mausoleum for the Mylne family (1800).

MYLNE, William Chadwell, FRS, FIBA: 1781–1863
Born in London, the second son of Robert Mylne: assisted his father from *c.* 1797: succeeded to his appointments as Engineer to the New River Company and Surveyor to the Stationers' Company, holding these posts from 1804–61 and from 1811–61 respectively. He practised as an engineer, surveyor, valuer and architect: was a member of the Institute of Civil Engineers and Treasurer of the Smeatonian Society of Civil Engineers. His son, Robert William, FRS, FSA, FRIBA (1817–90), succeeded him as Surveyor to the Stationers' Company. The work of William Mylne included laying out much of the property of the new River Company in Clerkenwell, including Myddleton Square, Amwell Street and Lloyd Square (*c.* 1819 and *c.* 1827): St Mark, Myddelton Square, Finsbury, London (1826–8): Garret Hostel Bridge, Cambridge (1837): the Waterworks Pumping Station, Green Lanes, Stoke Newington, London (1854–6).

NASH, John: 1752–1835 (Portrait: see Plate VII)

The son of William Nash, a Lambeth engineer and millwright. John Nash worked in the office of Sir Robert Taylor from *c.* 1766–77: he set up as an architect and speculative builder in London, but became bankrupt in 1783: he started again in Wales, in partnership with a builder named Saxon, and returned to London in 1796, and in partnership with Humphry Repton became established as a successful architect with a large and fashionable practice. From 1798 he enjoyed the patronage of the Prince Regent, was Architect to the Department of Woods and Forests 1806: Surveyor-General 1813: and from 1815–30 one of the three 'attached' architects directing Royal works. He laid out Regent's Park, London, and the adjacent terraces, and Regent Street from Portland Place to Carlton House in Pall Mall (1810–23), and remodelled the Royal Pavilion at Brighton, Sussex (1815–21). His very large practice which extended all over England and Wales, and also in Ireland and the Isle of Wight, included Longner Hall, Salop (*c.* 1805): West Grinstead Park, Sussex (*c.* 1806): Southborough House, Sur- biton, Surrey (1808): Caerhays Castle, Cornwall (1808): Knepp Castle, West Grinstead, Sussex (1809): the Royal Opera Arcade, Pall Mall, London (1816–18: with G. S. Repton): façade of the Haymarket Theatre, London (1821): All Souls, Langham Place, London (1822–4): Clarence House, London (1825): Buckingham Palace, London (1825–30: completed by Edward Blore and rebuilt by Sir Aston Webb): United Service Club, Pall Mall, London (1827): Carlton House Terrace, London (1827–33).

NEDEHAM, John: d. 1544

The son of Christopher Nedeham, a London carpenter. John Nedeham was himself a carpenter: a freeman of the Carpenters' Company: and Surveyor-General 1532–44. With the help of important patrons, who included Wolsey and Thomas Cromwell, he established a very successful practice as an architect and builder, became a large property owner, and finally Receiver-General in Yorkshire: he was Master of the Carpenters' Company three times. He designed the roof of the Great Hall at Hampton Court, Middx., and was in charge of many Royal Palaces and manors, including the Tower, Greenwich, Eltham, Petworth and Knole.

NESFIELD, William Eden: 1835–88

The son of William Nesfield, an artist with a large practice in landscaping, and the layout of gardens and ornamental parks: educated Eton: a pupil of William Burn 1851–3; of his uncle, Anthony Salvin, 1853–6; and for a short time of Viollet-le-Duc in Paris. Nesfield travelled in France and Italy, making measured drawings which he used later in his book, *Specimens of Mediaeval Architecture* (1862). He set up in practice in 1858, and though he shared office premises with Norman Shaw from 1863–76 and they were professionally associated, it is uncertain as to whether they were ever actually in partnership. Nesfield was a furniture designer as well as an architect. His work included Cloverley Hall, Salop (1862–70: dem.): a Lodge near the North Gallery in Kew Gardens, Surrey (1866): Kinmel Park, Denbighshire (1866–8): Farnham Park (built as Farnham Royal House) and St Mary, Farnham, Bucks. (1867–9): St Mary the Virgin, (1869–70), shops and cottages (1873), additions to the school (1877), and almshouses (1887), all at Radwinter, Essex: Lea Wood, Dethick, Derbys. (1870–6): Holy Trinity, Calverhall, Salop (1872 and 1878): Barclays Bank, Market Place, Saffron Walden, Herts. (1874): Loughton Hall, Loughton, Essex (1878: later a school): the Headmaster's House, Grammar School, Newport, Essex (1878).

NEWTON, Ernest, CBE, RA, FRIBA: 1856–1922

Educated Uppingham School: articled to Norman Shaw 1873: set up in private practice 1879. He was President of the RIBA 1914–17: Royal Gold Medallist 1918: was awarded a number of foreign architectural honours, and was made an Officier de l'Ordre de la Couronne, in acknowledgment of the assistance he gave to Belgian refugee architects during the First World War. He was a founder of the Art Workers' Guild: an early member of the Arts and Crafts Society: served on the Council of the Royal Academy: for some years was Joint Editor (with his son) of the *Architectural Review*: the author of *A Book of Country Houses*: was much interested in the problem of smoke abatement. He built many private houses, mostly in the Home Counties, and his large practice included St Barnabas Vicarage, Beckenham, Kent (1888): St Swithun, Hither Green, Lewisham, London (1892): Red Court, Haslemere, Surrey (1894): Glebelands, Wokingham, Berks. (1897): St George, Bickley, Kent (1905): Ardenrun Place, Crowhurst, Surrey (1906):

Oldcastle, Dallington, Sussex (1910): houses in East Avenue of the Whiteley Village, Surrey (c. 1912): St Nicholas Rectory, Stevenage, Herts. (1919): War Memorial Chapel at Uppingham School, Rutland (1920–1): and additions at the School (1923–4: carried out by W. G. Newton): the County Fire Office, Piccadilly Circus, London (completed 1924).

NEWTON, William: 1730–98
Probably a relative of Robert Newton, an architect and builder of Newcastle-on-Tyne, with whom he was collaborating in 1762. Newton had a large local practice in the vicinity of Newcastle, where he worked, and where he built St Ann, City Road (1768), and the Assembly Rooms (1774–6). His work included Backworth Hall, Backworth, Northumb. (1778–80): Howick Hall, Northumb. (1782: additions since): Castle Eden, Co. Durham (before 1786: additions since).

NEWTON, William: 1735–90
The son of James Newton, a Holborn cabinet-maker: educated Christ's Hospital: apprenticed to a London architect, William Jones: worked in the office of Matthew Brettingham: and was in independent practice by 1764: in 1766–7 he spent a year in Italy: he was Clerk of the Works at Greenwich 1782–90. Newton published the earliest English translation of the first five books of Vitruvius – *De Architectura libri decem, written by Marcus Vitruvius Pollio* – in 1771, and the complete work, including a translation of the remaining five books, was published in 1791 after his death. He was also the author of *Commentaires sur Vitruve* (1780), and assisted in the completion and editing of Volume II of James Stuart's *Antiquities of Athens*, published 1788. His work included Durdans, Epsom, Surrey (1764: additions later): Theobalds Park, nr. Cheshunt, Herts. (1765: additions since): Highnams, Walthamstow, Essex (1768: wings added since: later the County School for Girls): Hungerford Park, Berks. (1768: additions since): remodelling of the Chapel at Greenwich Hospital, London (1782–90: with James Stuart).

NICHOLSON, Sir Charles Archibald, FRIBA: 1867–1949
Born in London, the eldest son of Sir Charles Nicholson, 1st Baronet of Luddenham, who had been Speaker of the House of Assembly,

Sydney, Australia, and Chancellor of Sydney University. The younger Nicholson was educated at Rugby and New College, Oxford: articled to J. D. Sedding: worked with Henry Wilson: set up independent practice in London in 1893: from 1895–1914 was in partnership with H. C. Corlette (d. 1956), and from 1927–49 with Thomas J. Rushton. Nicholson succeeded to the baronetcy in 1903: he was Consulting Architect to the Cathedrals of Wells, Lichfield, Llandaff, Sheffield, Portsmouth and Belfast: Diocesan Architect to Wakefield, Winchester, Portsmouth and Chelmsford: Hon. Secretary and Vice-President of the Architects' Benevolent Society. With Rushton, he designed the conversion of the parish church of St Thomas à Becket to Portsmouth Cathedral when the See was created in 1927. He had a large practice, mostly in church building, cathedral and church restoration, and war memorials of the First World War. His work included St Alban, Westcliff-on-Sea, Essex (1898–1908: with Corlette): alterations to interior of the Chapel, Clifton College, Bristol, Som. (1909–10): War Memorial Chapel, Rugby School, Warwicks. (1922): at the Cathedral, Chelmsford, Essex, the east end (1923), Chapter House, Muniment Room and Vestries (1926) and Bishop's Throne with Gothic canopy: St John, Bromley Road, South End, Lewisham, London (1928): St Margaret, Leigh-on-Sea, Essex (1931): Screen and west gallery, St Mary, South Benfleet, Essex (1931), and the Parish Hall (1932).

NICHOLSON, Peter: 1765–1844

Born at Prestonkirk, East Lothian, the son of a stonemason, apprenticed to an Edinburgh cabinet-maker: worked in Edinburgh as a journeyman. About 1788 he went to London, where he continued this trade, at the same time teaching mechanics at an evening school in order to augment his finances, and assist him to publish his first book, *The Carpenter's New Guide*, in 1792. From 1800–8 he practised as an architect in Glasgow: was County Surveyor of Cumberland 1808–10, when he returned to London. In 1829 he suffered severe financial loss owing to the bankruptcy of his publishers, and retired to Newcastle-on-Tyne where a friend helped support him. He had great mathematical ability, and contributed much to the knowledge and growth of scientific building methods. His work in this field gained him the Gold and Silver Medals of the Society of Arts in 1814. He is known chiefly for his published

works, which included *The Carpenter's and Joiner's Assistant* (1792):
Principles of Architecture (1795–8): *The Architectural Dictionary* (1812–
19: since re-edited by Lomax and Gunyon): *A Treatise on Practical
Perspective* (1815): *Treatise on the Construction of Staircases and Hand-
rails* (1820): *Popular Course of Pure and Mixed Mathematics* (1822):
The New and Improved Practical Builder and Workman's Companion
(1823): *The Builder and Workman's New Director* (1824): *The Practical
Cabinet Maker, Upholsterer, and Complete Decorator* (1826: with his
son Michael Angelo): *The Carpenter, Joiner, and Builder's Companion*
(1846). Nicholson laid out the town of Ardrossan, Ayrshire; supervised the building of the Courts of Justice at Carlisle (designed by
Telford): and in 1802 built the early part of Carlton Place, in
Glasgow. His elder son, Michael Angelo (*c.* 1796–1842), studied
architectural drawing in London, was a pupil of John Foulston,
and entered the Royal Academy Schools in 1814. He conducted
a school of architectural drawing in London, engraved the plates
for his father's books, and was the author of *The Practical Cabinet
Maker* ... (1826: with his father): *The Carpenter and Joiner's Companion* (1826): *The Five Orders, Geometrical and in Perspective* (1834):
The Carpenter's and Joiner's New Practical Work on Handrailing (1836).

NICHOLSON, William Adams, FIBA: 1803–53
Born at Southwell, Notts., the son of a carpenter: articled to
J. B. Papworth in London 1821–24: started practice in Lincoln
1828. He was an antiquary of some reputation and standing, and
was a member of the local Archaeological, Literary and Topo-
graphical Societies. In 1830–40 he laid out the village of Blankney,
Lincs., and his work included the Rectory, Wrawby, Lincs. (1830):
Bayon's Manor, nr. Tealby, Lincs. (1836–42): the Workhouse,
Brigg, Lincs. (1837): St Peter, Raithby, Lincs. (1839): All Saints,
Haugham, Lincs. (1840): South Elkington Hall, Lincs. (*c.* 1841):
St John the Evangelist, Brigg, Lincs. (1842–3): the Corn Exchange,
Lincoln (1847).

NORTH, Roger: 1653–1734
Born at Tostock, Suffolk, the youngest son of the 4th Lord North.
Educated for the Law, which became his profession, he also studied
for his own enjoyment the scientific theories of the day, as well
as music, pictures, and building: he was an amateur architect of
considerable talent and skill, and a friend of Sir Christopher Wren

and Hugh May. Though he built very little, a number of his designs exist. He made alterations at Wroxton Abbey, Oxon. (1685–90): remodelled Rougham Hall, Norfolk (1693), where his work has practically disappeared: and designed Middle Temple Gateway, Fleet Street, London (1684).

OAKLEY, Edward: eighteenth century

He lived in Carmarthen before 1725: by 1730 he was in London, where he had set up as an estate surveyor and manager of building activities: the greenhouses and hothouses of the Chelsea Physic Garden were designed by him (1732–4): but he is known for his writings rather than his designs. *The Magazine of Architecture, Perspective and Sculpture* was published by him between 1730 and 1732, and his other works included *Every Man a Compleat Builder* (1738), and *Ornamental Architecture in the Gothic, Chinese and Modern Taste* (1758).

OLIVER, John: d. 1701

A surveyor by profession, and in 1667 one of those appointed by the Corporation of London to superintend the rebuilding of the City after the Great Fire. He was Assistant Surveyor of St Paul's Cathedral from 1675–c. 1700: Surveyor to the Skinners' Company: became Master Mason to the Crown in 1685: and was a Governor of Christ's Hospital. His architectural work included the design of Skinners' Hall, Dowgate Street, London (c. 1670): supervision of the building of Mercers' Hall and Chapel, Cheapside, London (1672–82: destroyed in the Second World War): wards and Writing School at Christ's Hospital, Newgate Street, London (1673 and 1675–6: dem. 1902): the design of the woodwork in Emmanuel College Chapel, Cambridge (1676: with Edward Pearce or Pierce, the sculptor): supervision of the building of Christ's Hospital School for Girls, Hertford (1695).

OLIVER, Thomas: 1791–1857

Born near Jedburgh, Roxburghshire, the son of a weaver: educated Jedburgh school. By 1821 he was established in practice as an architect in Newcastle-on-Tyne, where he worked on street planning for the City authorities, designed houses in Blackett Street, and designed Leazes Crescent and Leazes Terrace for Richard Grainger (1829–30). The design of the Londonderry Institute at Seaham Harbour, Co. Durham (c. 1830), has been attributed to Oliver, but he is best known for his maps and plans of Newcastle, published in 1830, 1844, 1849, 1851 and 1858; he was the author of *The Geographical Synopsis of the World: A Topographical View of Great*

Britain and Ireland: *A New Picture of Newcastle upon Tyne* (1831):
and *The Topographical Conductor, or Descriptive Guide to Newcastle and Gateshead* (1851). His son, Thomas (b. 1824), practised as an architect in Sunderland, and later in Newcastle-on-Tyne, where he founded the architectural partnership of Oliver, Leeson and Wood, well known in the north of England.

ORCHARD, William: d. 1504

One of the great architect-contractors of Tudor times. He was a master mason and quarrier of Headington, Oxon., and worked in the neighbourhood from 1475 till his death. He designed and executed buildings in Oxford and the vicinity, and conducted a flourishing business as contractor and supplier of building materials. His work at Oxford included the Chapel and Founder's Tower at Magdalen College (1475–90), the vault at the Divinity School (1480–83): and work at St John's College towards the end of his life. He is believed to have designed the ante-chapel at Eton College, Bucks. (*c.* 1479–82).

PAIN, James: 1780–1877
The son of James Pain, a builder and surveyor, and grandson of
William Pain, a joiner who was the author of a number of publica-
tions including *The Builder's Pocket Treasure* (1763): *Builder's Golden
Rule; or, Youth's Sure Guide in Architecture and Carpentering* (1782):
Carpenter's pocket Directory (c. 1786): and *British Palladio; or, Builder's
General Assistant* (1786: with his son, James). The younger James
Pain and his brother, George Richard, were pupils of John Nash,
and worked for him in Ireland. Later, they established their own
successful practice there, in the south and west. They built many
churches and country houses, two bridges over the Shannon,
prisons at Cork and Limerick, the Courthouse at Cork, and Dromo-
land Castle, Lough Castle, and Michelstown Castle (c. 1820).

PAINE, James: c. 1716–89 (Portrait: see Plate V)
Born in the south of England: believed to have studied drawing at
the School in St Martin's Lane, and architecture under Thomas
Jersey. He was a draughtsman of great ability, and while quite a
young man established a very large and prosperous architectural
practice, notably for large country houses. He was appointed Clerk
of the Works at Greenwich 1744: at Charing Cross Mews 1746: at
Newmarket 1750: at Richmond New Park Lodge 1758: and from
1780–2 was one of the two Board of Works Architects. He was
President of the Society of Artists of Great Britain in 1771: High
Sheriff of Surrey 1783: and was the author of *Plans, Elevations and
Sections of Noblemen and Gentlemen's Houses . . . executed in the counties of
Derby, Durham, Middlesex, Northumberland, Nottingham and York* (1767):
a second volume, covering other parts of the country, appeared in
1783. His son, James (1745–1829), was trained as an architect and
assisted his father: studied at the St Martin's Lane Academy:
travelled on the Continent, and was an original member of the
Architects' Club. He does not appear to have practised after his
father's death, when he was left well off, but he designed and
executed a number of monuments. The work of James Paine the
elder included Nostell Priory, Yorks. (1733): alterations to Cusworth Hall, nr. Doncaster, Yorks. (c. 1740): Heath House, Yorks.
(1744): the Mansion House, Doncaster, Yorks. (1745–8: attic
storey added since): internal additions and decoration at Felbrigg

Hall, Norfolk (1750): Dover House, Whitehall, London (1754–8: additions by Henry Holland 1787): Brocket Hall, Herts. (1775–80): Middlesex Hospital, London (1755–75: dem. 1928): Stockfield Park, Yorks. (1758–63): the central block of Kedleston Hall, Derbys. (1757–61): Gibside Chapel, Co. Durham (1760: built as a mausoleum for the Bowes family: consecrated as a church 1812): Sandbeck Hall, Yorks. (1763): Hare Hall, Romford, Essex (1768): Richmond Bridge, Surrey (1774–7: with Kenton Couse: widened since): Wardour Castle, Wilts. (1769–76): Shrubland Park, Suffolk (1770–2: remodelled by Gandy-Deering and Sir Charles Barry): Chertsey Bridge, Surrey (1780–5: alterations since): Kew Bridge, Surrey (1789: dem. and rebuilt 1903).

PALMER, John: 1738–1817
The son of Thomas Palmer, a prosperous Bath glazier, who was an associate of Thomas Jelly. John Palmer became a partner of Jelly *c.* 1765, and together they put forward an alternative to the official design for the Guildhall and markets in Bath: it was not accepted, but was the cause of bitter controversy with Thomas Atwood. About 1789 Palmer was associated with a wealthy coachbuilder and speculator, Charles Spackman: in 1792, Palmer was appointed Supervisor of Bounds, and then City Architect of Bath. His work there included St James (1768–9: with Jelly: dem.): St Swithin, Walcot (1777–88): the layout of Lansdown Crescent (1789–93): and of St James's Square (1794): Kensington Chapel, London Road, and neighbouring houses (1795–8): Christ Church, Montpelier Row (1798): the building of the Theatre Royal, Beauford Square (1804–5: designed by George Dance the younger).

PAPWORTH, John Buonarotti: 1775–1847
Born in Marylebone, London, the second son of John Papworth, a famous worker in stucco. Studied drawing under John Deare and Thomas Malton: spent two years in the office of John Plaw: for three years was apprenticed to a builder, Thomas Wapshott: worked for a year with a firm of decorators; was assistant to Michael Novosielski for a short time: entered the Royal Academy Schools 1798. By 1800 he had established his own private practice, chiefly in London and the south of England, which became very large and prosperous. Papworth, in addition to his architectural work, was an accomplished draughtsman, landscape gardener, writer, artist,

174

and what would now be called an industrial designer: a member of the Society of Arts: Hon. Secretary to the Associated Artists in Water-Colours 1808–10: Director of the Government School of Design 1836–7. He was one of the twelve architects responsible for the foundation of the Institute of British Architects in 1834: was Vice-President of the Institute eight times, and became an Honorary Member in 1846, when he retired from professional life. His work as a designer included a glass throne for the Shah of Persia: a sherbert service for the Pasha of Egypt: figurehead and decorations of the *London Engineer*, a paddle steamer: and the covers of *Forget-me-not Annual*. His literary work included *Essay on the Causes of Dry Rot in Timber* (1803): *Architectural Hints* (a series of papers, 1813–14): and a second series (1816–18) later republished as *Designs for Rural Residences* (1818): *Hints on Ornamental Gardening* (1832): the editorship of the 4th edition of Sir William Chambers's *Treatise on the Decorative Part of Civil Architecture* (1826), to which he added notes: *An Essay on the Principles of Design in Architecture*. He also contributed many papers, articles and chapters to technical journals and books by other architects. His brother, George (1781–1855), also an architect, practised successfully in Ireland, where he designed Kingsbridge, an iron bridge over the Liffey, in Dublin (1827–8), and the Church of the Calced Carmelites, Whitefriars Street, Dublin. J. P. Papworth built many shopfronts, warehouses and factories in London, most of which have disappeared, and his work included St Mary's Rectory, Woolwich, London (1809): Cobham Lodge, Cobham, Surrey (*c.* 1810): Gwynne House, in the grounds of Dr Barnardo's Homes, Woodford, Essex (1816): St Julien's, nr. Sevenoaks, Kent (1818–20: additions later): layout of the Montpellier Estate, the Montpellier Pump Room (1825–6), and Nos. 15–17 Lansdowne Terrace (1825), at Cheltenham, Glos.: layout of the Brockwell Estate, Lambeth, London (1825–32): St John, Berkeley Street, Cheltenham, Glos. (1827–9).

PAPWORTH, John Woody, FIBA: 1820–70
The elder son of J. B. Papworth. Born in Marylebone, London: educated at the University College School in Gower Street: in 1836 entered his father's office as a pupil, and remained as an assistant, taking over the practice when his father retired. Studied at the Royal Academy: awarded the Silver and Gold Medals of the Society for the Encouragement of Arts (1838 and 1840): served on

the Institute's Council: was for a short time Director and Secretary of the Government School of Design in London. Contributed papers and articles on architecture and antiquities to technical journals, and designed many exhibits for the Great Exhibition of 1851: was deeply interested in architectural education, particularly in the institution of examinations and diplomas in architecture. He is best known for his book, an *Ordinary of British Armorials*, a standard work of reference: and he collaborated with his brother, Wyatt, in the publication of *Museums, Libraries and Picture Galleries, Public and Private* (1853).

PAPWORTH, Wyatt Angelicus Van Sandau, FRIBA: 1822–94
The second son of J. B. Papworth: educated University College School, Gower Street: trained in his father's office: worked for a time for the Westminster Commissioner of Sewers: then for Sir John Rennie: and was Surveyor to the Alliance Fire Assurance Company *c.* 1848–88. He served on the Council of the Institute: was Master of the Clothworkers' Company: Curator of Sir John Soane's Museum. Wyatt Papworth is known chiefly as the founder of the Architectural Publication Society, and as the editor and chief contributor to the monumental work of reference which it published, *The Dictionary of Architecture*: he also edited three editions of Gwilt's *Encyclopaedia*: was the author of *Museums, Libraries and Picture Galleries, Public and Private* (1853: with John Woody Papworth): *Life and Works of J. B. Papworth* (1879): *Renaissance and Italian Styles of Architecture in Great Britain* (1883).

PARKER, Charles, FSA, FIBA: 1800–81
A pupil of Sir Jeffry Wyatville: studied at the drawing school run by George Maddox: and subsequently in Italy for some years. Began to practise in London in 1830: was an original Fellow of the Institute of British Architects in 1834: Surveyor to the Duke of Bedford's London Estates 1859–69. He was the author of *Villa Rustica* (1832). His work included Hoare's Bank, No. 37 Fleet Street, London (1829–30): St Raphael, Kingston-upon-Thames, Surrey (1846–7): Christ Church, St Albans, Herts. (1850).

PARKINSON, Joseph: 1783–1855
The son of James Parkinson, a solicitor: articled to William Pilkington: from *c.* 1811–*c.* 1853 Surveyor to the Union Fire Assurance Office. In 1788 his father had built the Leverian Natural History

Museum in Blackfriars, and in 1809 Joseph Parkinson converted this building to form the Surrey Institution. His work included the layout of Montagu and Bryanston Squares, London, and neighbouring streets, and the design of their façades (1811): St Peter, Frimley, Surrey (1825): Whitbread's Stores, Gray's Inn Road, London (1829): the rebuilding of St Leonard, Streatham, London (1831).

PATEY, Andrew: nineteenth century
He is believed to have worked as a mason in Yorkshire before going to Exeter, where he practised as an architect during the 1820s, and where he designed the West of England Fire Assurance Office and Commercial Union, destroyed in the Second World War. His work included St Michael, Teignmouth, Devonshire (1823: tower and chancel since): the layout of Den Crescent and building of the former Assembly Rooms, Teignmouth, Devonshire (1826): rebuilding of St Michael, Dawlish, Devonshire (1824).

THE PATY FAMILY
The name of a Bristol family of masons, statuaries and architects, who flourished there during the second half of the eighteenth century. James Paty designed the Theatre Royal, Bristol (1764–6), but Thomas (c. 1713–89) and his son, William (1758–1800), are the best known as architects. Thomas Paty carried out much carving and masonry work in Bristol and neighbourhood, including the carving at Redland Chapel (1741–3) and masonry and carving at Clifton Hill House (built 1746–50). He laid out Clare, High, Bridge, Union, and Bath Streets, and designed their building elevations and those of Berkeley Square, Berkeley Crescent and Upper Berkeley Place and Great George Street, among many others. His architectural work included the Library in King Street, Bristol (1739–40): the rebuilding of Bristol Bridge (1764–8: to the designs of James Bridges): Prospect House, Clifton, Bristol (c. 1765): St Michael, Bristol (1775–7). His son, William, studied at the Royal Academy Schools: carried on the family business; and became a City Surveyor at Bristol. Before his father's death he acted as his assistant and partner, notably in the street planning schemes carried out by the family firm. William Paty's architectural work included Christ Church, Bristol (1786–90): Blaise Castle House, nr. Bristol (1796: with some assistance from John Nash).

M   177

PAXTON, Sir Joseph: 1801–65 (Portrait: see Plate X)
Born at Milton Bryant, nr. Woburn, Beds., the son of William
Paxton, yeoman: educated at the Woburn Free School: apprenticed
to a gardener at Battlesden, Beds. He went to London, where he
worked for a gardening firm in Kensington, and then at the Horticultural Gardens in Chiswick, where he met his future patron, the
6th Duke of Devonshire, who appointed him as Superintendent to
the Gardens at Chatsworth, Derbys., in 1826, and later his confi-
dential adviser, House Steward, and Manager of the Devonshire
Estates in Derbyshire. Paxton became established as a landscape
designer of gardens and estates, and also of country houses, and his
suggested building to house the Great Exhibition of 1851 can be
related to his knowledge of glasshouses and conservatories. Paxton's
design, known as the Crystal Palace, was accepted in 1850, erected
in Hyde Park in 1851, and later transferred to Sydenham, London,
where it was reconstructed under Paxton's supervision, and where
it remained till its destruction by fire in 1936. Paxton was a
Fellow of the Horticultural and Linnean Societies: Vice-President
of the former: awarded the Russian Order of St Vladimir: was a
Director of the Midland Railway Company: had a genus of orchids
named after him: was one of the founders of the *Gardener's Chronicle*
(1841): knighted 1851. He designed a 'Great Victorian Way', a
continuous arcade of glass and iron which was intended to encircle
London and thus avoid congestion in the City, but his plan never
materialized. His work included the Great Conservatory, Chatsworth, Derbys. (1836–40: dem. 1920: erected under his supervision,
though the structural details were by Decimus Burton), and other
horticultural and garden buildings there, some of which survive:
planning of a new site for the village of Edensor, Derbys. (moved
there *c.* 1839): layout of the Cemetery, Cheylesmore, Coventry,
Warwicks. (*c.* 1843): layout of Birkenhead Park, Wirral, Cheshire
(1843): Barbrook House, Edensor, Derbys. (*c.* 1844): layout and
planning at Buxton, Derbys. (*c.* 1845): Mentmore House, Bucks.
(1852–4: with G. H. Stokes).

PEARCE, Sir Edward Lovett: 1699–1733
The son of Major-General Pearce: spent his early years as a Captain
in the Army, and may have visited Italy during this time: he
settled in Ireland, where he had close family ties, and in 1727
became Member for Ratoath. He was Deputy to Sir Thomas

Burgh, the Surveyor-General for Ireland, and succeeded him in this post when he died in 1730: Pearce was knighted in 1732, and received the Freedom of Dublin in 1733. He is believed by some authorities to have designed Speaker Conolly's mansion, Castletown, Kildare (1725–30): his work included the south front of Drumcondra House (1727): Parliament House, Dublin (1728–39: later the Bank of Ireland): and Cashel Place (*c.* 1731).

PEARSON, John Loughborough, RA, FSA, FRIBA: 1817–97
Born in Brussels, the son of William Pearson, of Durham, an artist: articled in 1831 to Ignatius Bonomi of Durham, where his interest in church buildings, furniture and fittings was fostered and developed. Went to London, where he worked in the offices of Anthony Salvin and Philip Hardwick, and set up private practice in 1843, designing and restoring churches throughout the country. He was Royal Gold Medallist 1880: a Consulting Architect of the Church Building Society: Surveyor of Westminster Abbey 1878–97. His work included St James, Weybridge, Surrey (1848): St Augustine, Kilburn, London (1870–80): St Michael, Croydon, Surrey (1871): St John, Red Lion Square, London (1874: ruined in Second World War): St Alban the Martyr, Bordesley, Birmingham, Warwicks. (1879–81): Truro Cathedral, Cornwall (1880–1910: completed by his son, F. L. Pearson): Westwood, Westwood Hill, Sydenham, London (1881): the Catholic Apostolic Church, Maida Avenue, Paddington, London (1891): the Incorporated Accountants' Hall, Victoria Embankment, London (1895): St Matthew, Douglas, I.O.M. (1895–1902): All Saints, Ascot, Berks. (1896–7).

PEMBROKE, Lord: See HERBERT

PENNETHORNE, Sir James, FRIBA: 1801–71
Born at Worcester, the son of Thomas Pennethorne, and a family connection of John Nash, from whom he received his early architectural training. Later, he studied under the elder Pugin: travelled on the Continent 1824–6: returned as assistant to Nash, for whom he completed Park Village East and West, Regent's Park, London. In 1838 he joined Thomas Chawner as one of the Joint Architects to the Commissioners of Woods, and in 1845, on Chawner's retirement, became the sole holder of the office: in 1840 he was made Joint

Surveyor to the Land Revenue Department. He carried out large
street planning and improvement projects in London, including the
layout of Kensington Palace Gardens (1843), and extensions east-
wards in Oxford Street (1845–7): and laid out Kennington Park,
Lambeth (1841–51), Victoria Park, Hackney (1842–5), and
Battersea Park (1858). He was Royal Gold Medallist 1865: knighted
1870: published *Elements and Mathematical Principles of the Greek
Architects and Artists* in 1844. His private practice was much res-
tricted by his public appointments: his work included extensive
alterations and rebuilding at Dillington House, nr. Ilminster, Som.
(1830s): No. 10 St James's Street, London (1832: built as the St
James's Bazaar): Christ Church, Albany Street, St Pancras, London
(1838): the Museum of Economic Geology, between Piccadilly and
Jermyn Street, London (1851: dem.): the Public Record Office,
Fetter Lane, London (1851–66: the Chancery Lane addition
1891–6 by Sir John Taylor): the Ballroom range at Buckingham
Palace, London (1853–5): the west wing of Somerset House, Lon-
don (1856): the back of the Royal Academy, in Burlington Gardens,
London (1866–9: built as the University of London).

PHIPPS, Charles John, FSA, FRIBA: 1835–97
Born in Bath: articled to local architects, Wilson and Fowler: set
up in practice 1857. He specialized in the design of theatres, and
built a great many in all parts of the country. In 1891 he became
involved in a serious professional dispute with T. E. Knightley
over the authorship of the design for the Queen's Hall, London
(1891: destroyed in the Second World War). Phipps's work included
the rebuilding of the Theatre at Bath, Som. (1863): Theatre Royal,
Nottingham (1865): Savoy Theatre, London (1881): Repertory
Theatre, Northampton (1884): Vaudeville Theatre, Strand (1887):
Lyric Theatre, Shaftesbury Avenue (1888): Her Majesty's Theatre,
Haymarket (1895), all in London: the Passmore Edwards Library,
Borough Road, Southwark, London (1898).

PICKFORD, Joseph: eighteenth century
Lived in Derby, where he built himself a house in Friargate, and
practised as an architect and builder in neighbouring counties.
Known chiefly as the designer and builder of Josiah Wedgwood's
Etruria Works, nr. Burslem, Staffs. (1767–73): Etruria Hall (1767–
9): and Bank House, Newcastle-under-Lyme, Staffs. (1767–9). He

undertook the erection of the Shire Hall at Nottingham, designed by James Gandon in 1770.

PILKINGTON, William: 1758–1848

Born at Hatfield, near Doncaster, the elder son of William Pilkington: a pupil of Sir Robert Taylor, whose assistant he became, and whom he succeeded in 1782 as Surveyor to the Board of Customs. He was also District Surveyor to the parishes of St Margaret and St John, Westminster (1784): to the Sun Fire Assurance Office (1792): to the Charterhouse (1792): and to the Earl of Radnor. His younger son, Redmond William (1789–1844), became an architect and succeeded to some of his father's Surveyorships. William Pilkington's work included the building of the Guildhall, Market Place, Salisbury, Wilts. (1788–95: to the designs of Sir Robert Taylor): Chilton Lodge, Chilton Foliat, Berks. (1800): improvements at Polstead Hall, Suffolk (1818–19). Attributed to him is St Nicholas Hospital, Great Yarmouth, Norfolk (1809–11: built as the Naval Hospital).

PINCH, John: 1770–1827

Worked as a builder in Bath, and though he became bankrupt *c.* 1800, he subsequently set up there as a successful architect and surveyor, and practised for about thirty years. Much building in Bath suggests his influence, though it cannot be certainly ascribed to him, but his work there included New Sydney Place (1807–8): Cavendish Place (1808–16): Cavendish Crescent (*c.* 1810): St Mary, Bathwick (1814–20): Sion Hill Place (1818–21): the Technical School, Beau Street (1824–6: built as the United Hospital). He also built St Lawrence, Hungerford, Berks. (1816). His son, John (d. 1849), continued his father's practice at Bath: his work included The Nunnery (a house), in the Isle of Man (1823): All Saints, Upper Weston, Som. (1832): St John the Baptist, Midsomer Norton, Som. (1830): the central part of the west side of Queen Square, Bath, Som. (1830): Christ Church, Stratton-on-the-Fosse, Som. (1837): St John the Baptist, Farrington Gurney, Som. (1843).

PITE, Arthur Beresford, FRIBA: 1861–1934

The son of Alfred Robert Pite (1832–1911), an architect: articled to W. G. Habershon and became his partner 1860–78: he had worked in the office of Philip Hardwick in 1851: became Architect to the Dom Pedro Railway in Brazil: later was Architect to the YMCA. A. B. Pite was educated at King's College School, and University College: articled to his father and W. G. Habershon: studied at the Royal College of Art in South Kensington, and at the Royal Academy Schools: worked in the office of John Belcher: was on the staff of the *Builder* for a time. He was President of the AA in 1896: Professor of Architecture at the Royal College of Art 1900–23: Architectural Director of the LCC School of Building at Brixton 1905–28: a member of the Board of Architectural Education, and of the Board of Architectural Studies at Cambridge: he also practised privately in London. His work included No. 32 Old Bond Street, London (1898): All Souls School, New Cavendish Street, London (1906–8): the London, Edinburgh and Glasgow Assurance Offices, Euston Road, London (1907): and the re-design of the Piccadilly entrance to the Burlington Arcade, London (1929–31).

PITT, Thomas, 1st Baron Camelford: 1737–93
The son of Thomas Pitt of Boconnoc, Cornwall, and nephew of William Pitt, 1st Earl of Chatham. Educated at Clare College, Cambridge: 1760–1 travelled on the Continent. On his father's death, he returned to England, became M.P. for Old Sarum, and was created 1st Baron Camelford in 1784. He was a friend of Horace Walpole and Sanderson Miller, a member of the Society of Dilettanti, and an amateur architect. His work included a Gothic cottage, bridge and conservatory at Park Place, nr. Henley-on-Thames, Oxon.: the Corinthian Arch at Stowe, Bucks. (1767): a wing at Boconnoc House, Cornwall, and an obelisk in the grounds there (1771).

PLATT, John: 1728–1810
The son of George Platt (1700–43), a master mason of Rotherham, Yorks., and the designer of Cusworth Hall, nr. Doncaster, Yorks. (1740: altered later by James Paine). John Platt, at an early age, took over his father's business, and established a prosperous practice as an architect and builder in Rotherham, Yorks.: he had a part interest in marble quarries in Derbyshire, and was in partnership with Samuel Walker in a pottery works. His work included Wortley Hall, Rotherham, Yorks. (1743–61): Moorgate Hall, Rotherham, Yorks. (1764): Canklow House, Yorks. (1767): The Crofts, Rother-

PLUMBE, ROWLAND

ham, Yorks. (1776): the building of Sheffield Royal Infirmary (1793-7: to the designs of John Rawsthorne).

PLAW, John: 1745-1820
He was in practice as an architect and builder in London in 1763: in 1795 he went to Southampton, and later emigrated to Canada: he was the last President of the Incorporated Society of Artists before it was dissolved in 1791: and the author of *Rural Architecture* (1785): *Ferme ornée or Rural Improvements* (1795): and *Sketches for Country Houses, Villas and Rural Dwellings* (1803). His work included Belle Isle, Lake Windermere, Westmorland (1774-5): Haresfoot House, nr. Berkhamsted, Herts. (1787): St. Mary, Paddington Green, London (1788-91): possibly Clare House, East Malling, Kent (1793).

PLAYFAIR, William Henry: 1789-1857
The son of James Playfair (d. 1794), a Scottish architect, who practised in London and Scotland, built a number of mansions for members of the Scottish nobility, and some houses in London. W. H. Playfair was born in London: educated in Edinburgh: studied under William Stark of Glasgow, worked for a time with Sir Robert Smirke and James Wyatt in London. He returned to Edinburgh, where he set up in private practice, and in 1815 won the competition for the completion of the University Buildings designed by Robert Adam. His work in Edinburgh included the Observatory, Calton Hill (1818): layout of streets and terraces in the Calton Hill area (1819): St Stephen (1828): Dugald Stewart Monument, Calton Hill (1832): Surgeons' Hall (1832): the Royal Institution (1833-6: later the Royal Scottish Academy): the National Gallery (1850).

PLUMBE, Rowland, FRIBA: 1838-1919
The son of Samuel Plumbe: educated privately and at University College: articled to N. J. Cottingham, then to Cooper and Beck: spent two years in the USA. He served on the Council of the Institute: was President of the AA 1871-2: he had a large practice, and made a special study of Polytechnic Institutes. His work included the Bank of Ceylon, Ludgate Hill, London: the Royal National Orthopaedic Hospital, Great Portland Street, London: Woodlands Park, Stoke d'Abernon, Surrey: St Nicholas, Remen-

ham, Berks. (1870): layout of part of the Queen's Park Estate, Paddington, London (1875): layout of Noel Park Estate, Wood Green, London, and the Church of St Mark there (1889): early council flats in Nile Street, Shoreditch, London (1896–9): St John the Baptist, Loxwood, Sussex (1898): Kneesworth Hall, nr. Bassingbourn, Cambs. (1901): the YMCA Building, Gt Russell Street, London (1911).

POCOCK, William Fuller: 1779–1849
The son of George Pocock, a London builder: studied under Charles Beazley, and at the Royal Academy Schools: was an early member of the Institute of British Architects: Master of the Carpenters' Company 1840: the author of *Architectural Designs for Rustic Cottages, Rural Dwellings, and Villas, with appropriate scenery* (1807): *Modern Finishings for Rooms* (1811): *Designs for Churches and Chapels* (1819): *Observations on Bond of Brickwork* (1839). His practice was widespread, and he designed the Ballroom and Supper Room at the Mansion House in Montreal: his work included Christ Church, Virginia Water, Surrey (1831): St Mary's Parsonage, Climping, Sussex (c. 1833): Carpenters' Almshouses, Twickenham, Middx. (1842). His son, William Wilmer, also an architect, designed Carpenters' Hall, Throgmorton Avenue, London (1877).

POPE, Richard Shackleton: nineteenth century
A District Surveyor in Bristol from 1831 to c. 1850. He rebuilt St Nicholas, Winsley, Wilts., in 1841, but most of his work was done in Bristol, and included the Wool Hall, St Thomas's Street (1830): the Royal Western Hotel, St George's Road (1837–9: later Brunel House): St Mary-on-the-Quay (1839): Buckingham Baptist Chapel, Clifton (1842): the Guildhall (1843–6): Stuckey's Bank, St Nicholas Street (1855: later the Westminster Bank).

PORDEN, Charles Ferdinand: 1790–1863
The son of Isaac Porden, a Birmingham architect, and nephew of William Porden: studied under George Wyatt, and at the Royal Academy Schools where he gained a Silver Medal in 1809, having won a Gold Medal of the Society of Arts in 1806. Was for many years with Sir William Tite, with whom he worked on the Royal Exchange, London: he supervised the building of the Church of St

184

Pancras, London, designed by the Inwoods in 1819–22, and designed the Church of St Matthew, Brixton, London (1822–4).

PORDEN, William: *c.* 1755–1822
Born at Hull, the son of Roger Pourden: studied under James Wyatt, then with S. P. Cockerell: became secretary to Lord Sheffield, and for a time was an army paymaster. He later became Surveyor to the London Estates of Lord Grosvenor – for whom he did much other work – and was commissioned to prepare Westminster Abbey for the Handel Festival in 1785–6. His work included Hampton Lodge, nr. Seale, Surrey (1798: much altered since): Mrs Fitzherbert's house, Old Steine, Brighton, Sussex (1804: altered externally since): the Stables (later the Dome) and Riding House at the Royal Pavilion, Brighton, Sussex (1804–8): Eaton Hall, Cheshire (1804–12: with Joseph Kay: additions, alterations and remodelling since).

THE POTTER FAMILY
Joseph Potter, a builder of Lichfield, was for many years County Surveyor of Staffordshire, and practised as an architect and builder in Lichfield, in partnership with his younger son, Joseph (*c.* 1797–1875). Their work included Plas Newydd, Anglesey (*c.* 1800–10): the Baths and Assembly Rooms at Caernarvon (1822): the Church of SS Peter and Paul, Newport, Salop (1832): and St Mary, Bramall Lane, Sheffield, Yorks. (1826–30). His elder son, Robert (*c.* 1795–1854), practised in Sheffield, where he was 'resident' architect during the construction of this church. Robert Potter's work at Sheffield included the Savings Bank (1832), and Christ Church, Fulwood (1837–9).

POYNTER, Ambrose: 1796–1886
Born in London, the son of Ambrose Lyon Poynter, descended from a family of Huguenot refugees. The younger Poynter was a pupil of Thomas Shotter Boys: articled to John Nash *c.* 1814–18: travelled in Italy, Sicily and the Ionian Islands 1819–21. He then established a successful practice in London, from which he was forced to retire in 1860 when his sight failed. He was a founder member of the Institute: served on the Council: was Secretary in 1840, 1841 and 1844: a member of the Arundel and Graphic Societies and of the

Archaeological Institute: was much interested in heraldry, and contributed illustrations to Sandford's *Genealogical History of England*, and to Charles Knight's *Shakespeare* and *Pictorial History of England*. Poynter played a large part in the introduction of drawing as a compulsory subject in national schools; and in the establishment of government schools of design. He was the first inspector for the provinces, appointed by the School of Design at Somerset House: in 1848 was a member of a committee appointed to supervise district design schools, and became an inspector of these in 1850. His work included St Katharine's Hospital, Regent's Park, London (1826): Christ Church, Cambridge (1839): Christ Church, Broadway, Victoria Street, London (1841–3: dem.): St Paul, Cambridge (1841): St Andrew the Great, Cambridge (1842–3).

PRATT, Sir Roger: 1620–84

The son of Gregory Pratt, a country gentleman of Ryston, Norfolk. Educated at Magdalen College, Oxford: entered the Inner Temple 1639: from 1643–49 travelled widely on the Continent, and met and became a friend of John Evelyn, the diarist. On his return, he practised as an architect, following the principles of classic design clarified by Inigo Jones, collecting architectural works, and compiling scholarly notebooks. He was a member of the Committee for the restoration of Old St Paul's Cathedral in 1663: and after the Great Fire was a Royal Commissioner for the rebuilding of the City. He was knighted in 1668. The design of Coleshill House, Berks. (*c.* 1650–64), has been attributed to him, but Inigo Jones was also concerned in it. Horseheath Hall, Cambs. (1663–5: dem.), may also have been the work of Pratt or John Webb. Pratt's work included Kingston Lacy House, Dorset (1663–5: later altered by Sir Charles Barry): Clarendon House, Piccadilly, London (1664–7: dem.): Ryston Hall, Norfolk (1669–72: much altered since).

PRICE, Francis: 1704–53

From 1737–53 he was Surveyor of the Works at Salisbury Cathedral: much repair work there was carried out by him, and he prepared an important Survey of the building. He was the author of *The British Carpenter, or a Treatise on Carpentry*, first published in 1733, and for many years a standard work of instruction: in 1753 he published *A Series of particular and useful Observations etc. on Salisbury Cathedral*.

PRICE, John: d. 1736

Practised as an architect at Richmond, Surrey, and with his son, John, built the Church of St George, Gt Yarmouth, Norfolk, in 1714–16. He was one of a series of architects employed by the Duke of Chandos, and worked for him at Canons House, Middlesex (dem.), in 1720–1. He designed and built the churches of St George (1734–6) and Christ Church (1738), in Southwark, London, and was the author of *Some considerations for building a stone Bridge over the Thames from Fulham to Putney*. The Church of St Mary-at-the-Walls, Colchester, Essex (1713–14 and since rebuilt), is attributed to him.

PRIOR, Edward Schroeder, FSA: 1852–1932

The son of John Venn Prior, a Chancery Division barrister: educated Harrow, and Caius College, Cambridge: articled to Norman Shaw. He was among those members of the Institute who, in the late 1880s, opposed its policy on official registration and examination: a founder of the Art Workers' Guild, and Master in 1906: Secretary of the Arts and Crafts Exhibition Society 1902–17, and Vice-President in 1918. Prior had a distinguished career in the field of architectural education, and was the author of standard works on mediaeval architecture. He was Lecturer to the Edinburgh Art Congress, the Newcastle Art Congress, and the Royal Institution: a Fellow of Caius College, Cambridge, and Slade Professor of Fine Arts at Cambridge University 1912–32. Among his published works were *A History of Gothic Art in England*: *The Cathedral Builders in England* : *The Mediaeval Figure Sculpture of England* (with Arthur Gardner). His work included the Henry Martyn Memorial Hall, Cambridge (1887): the New Music School, Harrow School, Middx. (1891): Pembroke College Mission Church, Southwark, London (1892): The Barn, Exmouth, Devonshire (1897): Zoology Laboratory, Cambridge (1901–4: later the School of Medicine): Home Place, Holt, Norfolk (1903–5: built as Voewood): St Andrew, Roker, Co. Durham (1906–7): The Small House, Mid Lavant, Sussex (1912).

PRITCHARD, Thomas Farnolls: d. 1777

A Shrewsbury architect, who had been a mason and statuary. He designed a bridge at Stourport, Worcs. (1775: later destroyed and rebuilt 1870), and the cast-iron bridge at Coalbrookdale, Salop, the first in the world to be built of this material (1777–9): also St

Julian, Shrewsbury (1749–50): and St Mary, Kinnerley, Salop (1769: built by James Bayle 1773–4).

PRITCHETT, James Pigott: 1789–1868

Born at St Petrox, Pembrokeshire, the son of Prebendary Charles Pritchett: a pupil of James Medland: then worked in the office of D. A. Alexander: studied at the Royal Academy Schools: worked in the Barrack Office: started to practise as an architect in London in 1812. In 1813 he moved to York, where he remained in practice, and in a successful partnership with William Watson. Pritchett was Architect and Surveyor to Earl Fitzwilliam at Wentworth Wood-house, Yorks., where he did much building on the estate. In the City of York, his work included the Deanery (1827–32): St Peter's School (later the School of Art): the Savings Bank: the Friends' Meeting House. In Yorkshire, he built the Court House and Gaol, Beverley (1804–14): St Peter, Huddersfield (1834–6): St John, Brearton (1836): Holy Trinity, Thorpe Hesley (1837): Huddersfield College (1838–9): St Mary, Rawmarsh (1839): St James, Meltham Mills (1845): Huddersfield Railway Station (1847–8): the Lion Building, Huddersfield (1852–4). His son, James Pigott, had a large practice in Darlington, Co. Durham. His work included the Mechanics' Institute, Darlington (1853): St Nicholas, Durham (1857–8): St James, Stockton-on-Tees, Co. Durham (1867–8): All Saints, Great Stainton, Co. Durham (1876): the Chapel at Armley Cemetery, Leeds, Yorks. (1887): St Mary, Denton, Co. Durham (1891).

PRYNNE, George Halford Fellowes, FRIBA: 1853–1927

Born at Plymouth, the son of the Rev. G. Rundle Prynne: educated Chard School and Haileybury. In 1891 he went to the United States, to study farming as a career, but abandoned this, and became a pupil of R. C. Windyer in Toronto: on his return to England he worked in the office of G. E. Street, studied at the Royal Academy Schools, and set up in practice c. 1882. His work was almost entirely confined to church building and restoration, and he became well known and extremely successful in this field. Prynne was President of the AA 1899 and 1900: Hon. Secretary of the Honorary Consulting Architects of the Church Building Society 1906–27: Diocesan Architect for Oxfordshire 1913–27. His work included St Peter, Plymouth (1882): All Saints, Rosendale Road,

Lambeth, London (1887–8: badly war damaged): Hadlow Grange, Kent (1895): Holy Trinity, Roehampton, London (1898): restoration and additions at Gifford House, Roehampton, London (1899): St John, Sidcup, Kent (1900): St Wilfrid, Bognor, Sussex (1908): St Alban, Bournemouth, Hants (1909): St Michael, Beaconsfield, Bucks. (1914–16).

PUGIN, Augustus Charles: 1762–1832

A Frenchman, who came to England in 1793 as a refugee from the French Revolution. He arrived in Wales, where he was employed as a draughtsman by John Nash, and developed great skill and ability in architectural drawing and colouring. He went to London, where he worked for Nash, exhibited independently at the Royal Academy, was commissioned to draw and engrave for many well-known topographical authors and publishers, and set up a successful school of architectural drawing. He was an Associate of the Old Water Colour Society in 1808. Among the works to which he contributed illustrations were *The Microcosm of London* (R. Ackermann, 1808): *Illustrations of the Public Buildings of London* (with J. Britton, 1825–8): *Specimens of the Architectural Antiquities of Normandy* (with J. Britton and Le Keux, 1826–8). Works which he published himself included *Specimens of Gothic Architecture* (1821–3): *Gothic Ornaments from Ancient Buildings in England and France* (1831): and *Ornamental Gables* (1831).

PUGIN, Augustus Welby Northmore: 1811–52 (Portrait: see Plate X)

The son of Augustus Charles Pugin: educated at home, and as a private pupil at Christ's Hospital, London: studied at his father's drawing school, and travelled with him in England and France: assisted him on his books, among them *Specimens of the Architectural Antiquities of Normandy* (1826–8). As a youth and young man, he studied and became expert in the design and painting of theatrical scenery: he prepared working drawings and designs of furniture for Windsor Castle: and attempted the commercial manufacture of Gothic furniture, but failed. In 1833 he began to write, and finding a patron in the Earl of Shrewsbury, he embarked on an architectural career, *c.* 1836: was converted to the Roman Catholic faith, and became very well known as a church architect, and designer of church furniture and fittings. He lived at Salisbury, and finally settled at Ramsgate. His capacity for work, and his incessant industry, were so prodigious as to be abnormal, and he became mentally deranged, and ended his life in a private asylum. He was an ardent worker for the establishment of Gothic Revival style in architecture and furniture, and a convinced believer in its relationship to religious truth as well as its artistic superiority. He was so closely associated with Sir Charles Barry on the designs of the new Houses of Parliament, that it has been suggested he was a collaborator rather than an assistant: for Barry, he executed numberless drawings, and made the original designs for countless fitments, over a long period, and often at high pressure. Among his literary works were *Examples of Gothic Architecture* (1831–8): *Gothic Furniture* (1835): *Contrasts: or a parallel between the noble edifices of the fourteenth and fifteenth centuries, and similar buildings of the present day: showing the present decay of taste* (1836): *The True Principles of Pointed or Christian Architecture* (1841): *The Present State of Ecclesiastical Architecture in England* (1843): *Glossary of Ecclesiastical Ornament and Costume* (1844). Pugin's great output of Roman Catholic ecclesiastical building included his own house, St Marie's Grange, nr. Alderbury, Wilts. (1835): St Mary's Cathedral, Derby (1838–9): St Chad's Cathedral, Birmingham, Warwicks. (1839–41): St Wilfrid, Hulme, Manchester (1842): St Peter, Marlow, Bucks. (1845–8): St Giles, Cheadle, Staffs. (1846): St Mary's Cathedral, Newcastle-on-Tyne, Northumb. (1844: except the spire, by Hansom later): the Chapel of St Edmund's College, Old Hall Green, Herts. (1845–53), and the Headmaster's house: St Thomas of Canterbury, Rylston Road, Fulham, London (1847–9): St Augustine, Ramsgate, Kent (1847–51), and his own house there, The Grange.

PUGIN, Edward Welby: 1834–75
The son of A. W. N. Pugin: educated at home: was a pupil and assistant of his father, and at his death in 1852, took over and completed his work. His own practice became very extensive, and he built many Roman Catholic churches, schools and convents, also some private mansions. He was involved in complicated and notorious litigation over his claim that his father rather than Sir Charles Barry had been the true designer of the Houses of Parliament. Edward Pugin's work included Our Lady of Help Cathedral, Shrewsbury, Salop (1856): St Mary the Immaculate, Warwick (1859–60): Convent of Our Lady of Charity and Refuge, Bartestree,

Herefs. (1863): St Francis, Gorton, Manchester (1863): St Gregory, Stratford-upon-Avon, Warwicks. (1866): additions to Garendon Hall, Leics. (1866): The Towers, Parklands Estate, Leeds, Yorks. (1867): Mayfield College and St Joseph's College, Mark Cross, Sussex (1868–9: additions since to the latter): completion of the Convent of the Christ Jesus, St Leonards-on-Sea, Sussex (1869: begun by A. W. N. Pugin): rebuilding at Carlton Towers, Carlton-in-Balne, Yorks. (1874).

RAILTON, William: *c.* 1801–77
Studied under William Inwood, and at the Royal Academy Schools: visited Greece in 1825–7, and his description of a newly discovered temple at Corfu appeared in Stuart and Revett's *Antiquities of Athens*. He was Architect to the Ecclesiastical Commissioners 1838–40, and had a large practice in London and the provinces. His work included Grace Dieu Manor and Chapel, Leics. (1833–4): St Peter, Copt Oak, Leics. (1837): the Nelson Column, Trafalgar Square, London (1839–42: statue by E. H. Bailey: lions by Landseer): St Mary, Wolverhampton, Staffs. (1842–3): All Saints, Thorpe Acre, Leics. (1845): Beaumanor Park, Leics. (1845–7): Holy Trinity, Meanwood, Leeds, Yorks. (1849): Holy Trinity, Shoreditch, London (1849).

RAWSTHORNE, John: eighteenth century
A pupil of James Wyatt: set up in architectural practice in Birmingham, where in 1790–95 he was associated with a speculative builder, Charles Norton, in the design of a proposed residential scheme, The Crescent: this was not a success, and five houses only were built. Rawsthorne's work included the Cavalry Barracks, Great Brook Street, Birmingham (1790): the Bluecoat School, Harborne, Birmingham (1792–4: dem.: rebuilt since): the Royal Infirmary, Sheffield, Yorks. (1793–7).

REBECCA, J. B.: nineteenth century
The son of the Italian painter Biagio Rebecca (1735–1808), who worked in England and was an ARA. J. B. Rebecca practised as an architect in the South of England, and exhibited at the Royal Academy between 1820 and 1827. He designed the Rectory at Crowell, Oxon. (1822), and his work in Sussex, where he seems to have practised most, included Castle Goring, nr. Arundel (*c.* 1790): St Paul, Worthing (1812): Beach House, Worthing (1820): Buckingham House, Shoreham (*c.* 1820).

REDMAN, Henry: d. 1528
The son of Thomas Redman, of Huntingdonshire, who was a Master Mason at Westminster Abbey. Henry Redman was closely

associated with William Vertue: succeeded his father at West-minster Abbey in 1516: became Joint King's Mason, with Vertue, in 1519: and Master Mason at Windsor Castle 1520. He designed the chancel and tower of St Margaret's, Westminster, London (1516–23): and from 1525–8 worked with John Lebons (d. 1537) on 'Cardinal College' at Oxford, a project of Cardinal Wolsey's, which was eventually taken over and rechristened Christ Church by Henry VIII, in 1546.

REID, Robert: 1776–1856

A Scottish architect, the last holder of the office of Master of the King's Works for Scotland, which was abolished in 1840. He practised mainly in Edinburgh, where, with William Sibbald, he planned the second New Town (1802–25), and Great King Street (1820). His work there included the completion of the Register House (1792–1822): the Bank of Scotland, The Mound (1806: with Richard Crichton: much altered later): Parliament House and westward extension, Parliament Square (1807–10): St George (1814).

REILLY, Sir Charles Herbert, OBE, FRIBA: 1874–1948

Born in London, the son of Charles Thomas Reilly, a City architect and surveyor: educated Merchant Taylors' School and Queen's College, Cambridge: a pupil of his father, and of John Belcher, for both of whom he worked: set up in partnership with Stanley Peach. In 1898 he was a Lecturer at King's College, London: from 1904–34 he occupied the Chair of Architecture at Liverpool University, and under his guidance the School of Architecture at Liverpool achieved its reputation as an influential centre of architectural training. In 1906 Reilly joined the Board of Architectural Education: in 1911 was co-opted by the Faculty of Architecture of the British School at Rome: he was Assistant Inspector of Munitions Areas during the First World War: served on the Council of the RIBA and was a Vice-President: instituted the Degrees of M.Arch and B.Arch: Royal Gold Medallist 1943: knighted 1944: a member of the Town Planning Institute. He was an active journalist, contributing to the *Liverpool Post, Westminster Gazette*, and *Strand Magazine*: was Consulting Editor for a time to the *Builder's Journal* (later the *Architect's Journal*): Architectural Editor to *Country Life* in 1922: his published works included a monograph on the work of *McKim,*

Mead and White: Some Manchester Streets and their Buildings: Some Architectural Problems of Today: and in 1938 his autobiography, *Scaffolding in the Sky*. His architectural practice included much consultancy work, notably on Devonshire House, Piccadilly, London (1924–6), and for the John Lewis Partnership, whom he advised on the design of the Peter Jones Store in Sloane Square, London (1936). His work included No. 28 Austin Friars, London (1897): Power Station, Lodge Road, St Marylebone, London (1904): Upminster Court, Essex (1906–8: later Education Offices): St Barnabas, Shacklewell Lane, Hackney, London (1910): the Students' Union, Liverpool.

RENNIE, John: 1761–1821

A Scotsman, born in East Lothian, the son of James Rennie, a farmer: worked as a millwright in his youth: studied at Edinburgh University for three years: set up as an independent millwright and engineer, and in 1784 assisted Boulton and Watt with the design of the power-driven Albion Flour Mills at Southwark. Rennie became a famous civil engineer of outstanding ability, and had a large practice which included much bridge and aqueduct building. In association with Robert Whitworth, he designed the Kennet and Avon Canal, connecting Newbury with Bath, built 1786–1810. His work included the Lune Aqueduct, nr. Lancaster: the bridge over the Avon–Kennet Canal at Bathampton, Bath, Som.: the Avon–Kennet Canal Aqueduct, Avoncliff, Wilts. (1804): Dundas Aqueduct, Limpley Stoke, Wilts. (1805): the Ladies' Bridge, Wilcot, Wilts. (1808): Vauxhall Bridge, London (1811: dem.: rebuilt): Plymouth Breakwater (1811–44: completed by his son): Chepstow Bridge, Mon. (1815–16): Southwark Bridge, London (1815–19: dem.: rebuilt): Waterloo Bridge, London (1817: dem.: rebuilt): London Bridge (1823–31: Rennie's designs for its rebuilding were carried out by his son: widened since).

RENNIE, Sir John: 1794–1874

Born in London, the second son of John Rennie, the civil engineer and bridge builder. The younger Rennie also became a civil engineer, continued his father's practice with great success, working, as he did, for the Admiralty, and completing his designs for Plymouth Breakwater and London Bridge. He was knighted in 1831, and was President of the Institution of Civil Engineers 1845–8. He had a long and distinguished engineering career, and was not a professional architect, but he designed and built the Royal William Victualling Yard, Stonhouse, Plymouth, Devonshire (1826–35).

REPTON, Humphry: 1752–1818

Born at Bury St Edmunds, Suffolk, the son of an Excise Collector. He started on a business career, but was unsuccessful, and after a period of studying botany and gardening, he became a landscape gardener. Working in collaboration with John Nash, and later with his own sons, he carried out commissions which involved architectural as well as landscape planning. He became very well known, built up an extremely large practice to which his sons, John Adey and George Stanley, made the architectural contribution, and examples of his work may be seen in every part of the country. He was the author of many published works on landscape gardening and architecture, and most of these were included by J. C. Loudon in *The Landscape Gardening and Landscape Architecture of the late Humphry Repton*, published 1840. Repton's 'Red Books' were beautifully compiled reports of his more important commissions, which he prepared for his clients: the drawings incorporated an ingenious flap system which enabled a 'Before and After' comparison to be made. Repton's landscape and gardening works included Panshanger House, Herts.: Attingham Hall, Salop: Rivenhall Place, Essex: Longleat House, Wilts. (1790): Cobham Hall, Kent (1790): Scrivelsby Court, Lincs. (pre-1791): Port Eliot House, Cornwall (1792–3): Sheffield Park, Sussex (pre-1794): Finedon Hall, Northants (pre-1794): Bloomsbury Square, and Russell Square, London (c. 1800): West Wycombe Park, Bucks. (pre-1803): Endsleigh Cottage, Endsleigh, Devonshire (c. 1810): Sheringham Hall, Norfolk (1812–17): Ham House, Surrey (pre-1816).

REPTON, John Adey, FSA: 1775–1860

Born at Norwich, the eldest son of Humphry Repton: a pupil of William Wilkins the elder, of Norwich: from 1796–1802 was assistant to John Nash: then joined his father, to whose landscape gardening practice he contributed his architectural knowledge, and for which he carried out many country house alterations and additions. He travelled in Germany and Holland in 1821–2, where he had received commissions from Continental clients. He was a contributor to archaeological journals, and a supporter of the Cambridge Camden Society. In addition to assisting his father in many of his commissions, John Repton's work included Laxton Hall, Northants (1811: altered since): Sheringham Hall, Norfolk (1812–17): Holy Trinity, Springfield, Chelmsford, Essex (1843). His brother George Stanley (d. 1858), the fourth son of Humphry Repton, was a pupil of John Nash: became his assistant: worked with his father and elder brother, and set up in independent practice *c.* 1820. He became well known as a designer of country houses: his work included the Assembly Rooms, Aberystwyth (1820): Kitley House, Devonshire (1825): Follaton House, nr. Totnes, Devonshire (pre-1827): Widworthy Court, nr. Honiton, Devonshire (1830): Middleton Manor, Westmeston, Sussex (*c.* 1830): Dumbleton Hall, nr. Evesham, Worcs. (*c.* 1830): Camerton Court, Som. (1835).

REVELEY, Willey: 1760–99
Entered the Royal Academy Schools in 1777: became a pupil of Sir William Chambers. From 1784–9 he toured Italy, Greece and Egypt in the capacity of draughtsman to Sir Richard Worsley: he edited the third volume of Stuart's *Antiquities of Athens* in 1794. His early death terminated a potentially promising career, but his work included Windmill Hill Place, nr. Herstmonceux, Sussex (*c.* 1790): All Saints, Southampton, Hants (1792–5: destroyed in Second World War).

REVETT, Nicholas: 1720–1804
Born at Brandeston Hall, nr. Framlingham, Suffolk, the son of John Revett. In 1742 went to Rome to study painting: from 1751–5 he worked with James Stuart in Athens, measuring and drawing the city's chief antiquities, the expedition having been sponsored by the Society of Dilettanti, of which both were members. Their work was published in four volumes under the title of *The Antiquities of Athens measured and delineated by James Stuart FRS and FSA, and Nicholas Revett, Painters and Architects*, and the first appeared in 1762. From 1764–6 Revett accompanied Richard Chandler and William Pars on another expedition sponsored by the Society, to make measurements and drawings in Asia Minor: he was Editor of the resulting work, *The Antiquities of Ionia*, published 1769–97 in two volumes. Revett became an Honorary Member of the Architects' Club in 1791: his architectural output was limited, but included the porch at Standlynch House, nr. Charlton, Wilts. (*c.* 1766: later Trafalgar House): at West Wycombe Park, Bucks., the portico to the west

front (1771): portico to the east front, and Temple on the island in the lake (1778–80): St Lawrence, Ayot St Lawrence, Herts. (1778–9).

RICHARDSON, Sir Albert Edward, KCVO, RA, FSA, FRIBA: 1880–1964

Born in London, the son of a journalist: educated at a private school in North London: articled to Thomas Page 1895: was assistant to E. Hellicar, Leonard Stokes, F. T. Verity: entered into partnership with C. Lovett Gill 1908, and later with E. A. S. Houfe. Richardson served with the Royal Flying Corps during the First World War: he was Professor of Architecture at the Bartlett School of Architecture, University College, 1919–46: a member of the Royal Fine Art Commission 1939–56: Royal Gold Medallist 1947: President of the Royal Academy 1954–6: knighted 1956: a member of the Royal Commission on Historical Monuments: of the Central Council for the Care of Churches: of the Diocesan Advisory Committees of London, St Albans, Ely, Smethwick: an Hon. Fellow of St Catherine's College, Cambridge. His published works included *London Houses* (with Gill): *Regional Architecture of the West of England* (with Gill): *The Art of Architecture* (with H. O. Corfiato). Richardson was a leading figure in the Georgian Group, and served on its Council and Executive Committee: he possessed a remarkably fine collection of period furniture and antiques at his house at Ampthill, and in his later years lived, as far as he was able, in the manner of a Georgian gentleman. With Houfe, he did much restoration to buildings damaged in the Second World War, and carried out council housing schemes at Barnardiston, Hundon and Wickhambrook, in Suffolk. His work included the restoration of Tor Royal, and rebuilding of the Duchy Hotel, Princetown, Devonshire (1912): Ramsay Laboratory and Anatomy Building, University College, London (1918): No. 136 Bishopsgate, London (1927: with Gill): the Jockey Club, Newmarket, Suffolk (1933: with Gill): The House in the Fields, Wendover, Bucks. (1935: with Gill): Holy Cross (new church), Greenford, Middx. (1939): Chancellor's Building (1948) and Memorial Building (1952) at Christ's College, Cambridge: additions in Garret Hostel Lane, to Trinity Hall, Cambridge (1949–51): the restoration of St. James's, Piccadilly, London (1953: with Houfe): St Cuthbert, Colburn, Yorks. (1957): Bracken House, Cannon Street, London (1959: with Houfe).

RICHARDSON, Charles James: 1806–71

A pupil of Sir John Soane: in 1845–52 he was a Lecturer in Architecture at the School of Design at Somerset House. He possessed a large and valuable collection of architects' original drawings and designs for buildings, furniture and ornament, and was the author of several books, including *Observations on the Architecture of England during the Reigns of Queen Elizabeth and James I* (1837): *A Popular Treatise on the Warming and Ventilation of Buildings* (1837): *Architectural Remains of the Reigns of Elizabeth and James I* (1840): *Studies from Old English Mansions* (1841–8): *Studies of Ornamental Design* (1851): *The Smoke Nuisance and its Remedy* (1869): *The Englishman's House, from a Cottage to a Mansion* (1870). His architectural work included No. 13 Kensington Palace Gardens, London (1852).

RICHARDSON, George: d. *c.* 1813

Known chiefly for his books on architectural design, much material for which he gathered during a tour of France, Italy and Dalmatia in 1760–3. He began to practise in London *c.* 1765: became a Fellow of the Society of Artists in 1771: exhibited at the Royal Academy between 1774 and 1793: worked for the Adam Brothers: and gave lessons in drawing. Among his published works were *A Book of Ornamental Ceilings in the style of the Antique Grotesque* (1776): *A New Collection of Chimney Pieces* (1781): *Treatise on the Five Orders of Architecture and Observations on the Antiquities at Rome, Pola, and South of France 1760–63* (1787): *New Designs in Architecture* (1792): *Original Designs for Country Seats or Villas* (1795): *The New Vitruvius Britannicus* (1802–10). He found a patron in the 4th Earl of Harborough, for whom he built Holy Trinity, Teigh, Rutland (1782): St Mary Magdalene, Stapleford, Leics. (1783): St Peter, Saxby, Leics. (1789).

RICKMAN, Thomas, FSA: 1776–1841

Born in Maidenhead, the son of a Quaker druggist: worked as an assistant in his father's shop: qualified and practised as a doctor for two years: then spent five years working for a corn merchant in London: became an insurance broker's clerk in Liverpool in 1808. He continued in this occupation till 1813, but during these five years he taught himself to draw: studied: examined and recorded numbers of mediaeval buildings: and became an earnest student of church architecture. He was the author of the first systematic study

of Gothic architecture in England, published in 1817 under the title
of *An Attempt to Discriminate the Styles of Architecture in England from
the Conquest to the Reformation*. The terminology he suggested, i.e.
'Early English', 'Decorated' and 'Perpendicular', has been used
ever since. In 1818, Rickman began to practise architecture in
Liverpool, finding a patron and supporter in Thomas Cragg, a local
ironfounder. Later, he extended his practice to Birmingham, and
was in partnership with Henry Hutchinson, Edwin Rickman (his
brother) and finally with R. C. Hussey. His work included St
George, Everton, Liverpool (1814): St Michael-the-Hamlet,
Liverpool (1814): St George, Chorley, Manchester (1820): St
Barnabas, Erdington, Birmingham (1822-3): St Peter, Hampton
Lucy, Warwicks. (1822-6: with Hutchinson): St David, Ingram
Street, Glasgow (1824): St Andrew, Ombersley, Worcs. (1825):
New Court, St John's College, Cambridge (1825-31: with Hutchin-
son, who designed the Bridge of Sighs): St Thomas, Bath Row,
Birmingham (1826-9: with Hutchinson: severe war damage):
Matfen Hall, Northumb. (1828-32): The Midland Bank, Waterloo
Road, Birmingham (1830: with Hutchinson): Drapers' Hall,
Coventry, Warwicks. (1832: with Hutchinson): All Saints, Birming-
ham (1832-3: with Hutchinson): St Matthew, Kingsdown, Bristol
(1833-5): Holy Ascension, Settle, Yorks. (1835): Emmanuel
Church, Loughborough, Leics. (1835): All Saints, Stretton-on-
Dunsmore, Warwicks. (1835-7): Christ Church, Clevedon, Som.
(1839).

RIPLEY, Thomas: *c.* 1683-1758
A Yorkshireman, who came to London in poor circumstances, and
set up as a carpenter in the City: was admitted to the Freedom of the
Carpenters' Company in 1705. Through the patronage of Sir
Robert Walpole, he obtained the appointment of Clerk of the Works
at Charing Cross Mews 1716: Master Carpenter to the Crown 1721:
Comptroller of the Office of Works 1726: Surveyor to Greenwich
Hospital 1729: and Surveyor of the King's Private Roads 1737. In
1722 he and Richard Holt were partners in patenting the manu-
facture of an artificial stone, believed to be the forerunner of Coade
Stone. Ripley's work included the building of Houghton Hall,
Norfolk (1721-35: to the designs of Colen Campbell): the Admiralty,
Whitehall, London (1722: screen later by Robert Adam): Wolterton
Hall, Norfolk (1727-41: additions later).

ROBERTS, Henry: 1803–76
A pupil of Charles Fowler: entered the Royal Academy Schools
1825: worked in Sir Robert Smirke's office: travelled on the
Continent. He set up in practice in London, and in 1844 was
appointed Architect to the joint companies concerned in the
building of the new Brighton, Croydon, Dover and Greenwich
Railway terminus at London Bridge. He is remembered as a
pioneer for improved working-class housing: he was Hon. Architect
to Lord Shaftesbury's Society for Improving the Condition of the
Labouring Classes: Hon. Architect to the Windsor Royal Society
formed in 1852 to improve working-class housing in Windsor: and
he visited France and Italy in 1853–8 investigating Continental
working-class housing conditions, and making personal appeals to
the authorities there for improvement. He retired *c.* 1855 to Italy,
where he died. Roberts published, among other books, *The Dwellings
of the Labouring Classes* (1850): *House Reform: or, what the Working
Classes may do to improve their dwellings* (1852): *The Essentials of a
Healthy Dwelling, and the extension of its benefits to the Labouring Population*
(1862): *The Physical Condition of the Labouring Classes resulting from the
State of their Dwellings* (1866): *Efforts on the Continent for improving the
dwellings of the Labouring Classes* (1874). Among his working-class
buildings in London are blocks of flats (Model Dwellings) in
Streatham Street, Holborn (1849), and Thanksgiving Model Buildings, Theobald's Road, Holborn (1850–7). He designed two model
working-class cottages for the Great Exhibition of 1851, and these
were re-erected in the form of a lodge at the entrance to Kennington
Park, Lambeth, London. Roberts's other work included Fishmongers' Hall, London (1831–4): Escot House, nr. Ottery St Mary,
Devonshire (1837): the first Railway Station at London Bridge
(1844–6: dem. 1851: rebuilt): St Paul, East Smithfield, London
(1846).

ROBERTSON, Sir Howard Morley, MC, RA, FRIBA: 1888–
1963
Born at Salt Lake City, Utah, USA, the son of Casper Ludovic Van
Uytrecht Robertson of Liverpool: educated Malvern College:
trained at the AA and École des Beaux Arts, Paris: served in the
First World War: travelled extensively on the Continent. He began
practice in 1919 with Edwin Stanley Hall (who was later P.RIBA),
and John Murray Easton: by 1962, the partnership consisted of

Easton and Robertson, Cusdin, Preston and Smith. Howard Robertson was Principal of the AA 1920–9: Director 1929–35: President 1947–8: he served on the RIBA Council: was Royal Gold Medallist 1949: President 1952–4: knighted 1954: an Hon. Fellow of the American Institute of Architects, and was awarded many foreign architectural honours. He was a member of the Royal Fine Art Commission: Adviser to the Secretary-General of the League of Nations on the completion of the Geneva Building: UK Member of the Board of Design for the United Nations Building in New York: in 1949 served on the Council for Architecture, Town Planning and Building Research of the Festival of Britain. Robertson was an amateur musician of exceptional ability, and an experienced writer: his published works included *Principles of Architectural Composition* (1924): *Architecture Explained* (1927): *Modern Architectural Design* (1932): *Architecture Arising* (1944). His extremely large practice embraced much consultancy work, notably on the extension to Broadcasting House, London: the Television Studios at White City: and the University of Keele, Staffs. The work of his partnership included the British Pavilions at the Paris Exhibition (1925), Brussels Exhibition (1935), Johannesburg Exhibition (1936) and New York World Fair (1939): the New Hall of the Royal Horticultural Society, Westminster, London (1936): Research Building, Metropolitan Water Board Offices, Finsbury, London (1938): Technical College (1951–2) and Secondary Modern School, Hatfield New Town, Herts.: Bank of England Printing Works, Debden, nr. Chigwell, Essex (1953–6): Watling House, Cannon Street, London (1955–6): Buildings of Faculty of Letters, Physics, Sedimentology, Chemistry, Library and Windsor Hall, at Reading University, Berks. (1957–64): the Shell Centre, South Bank, London (1961).

ROBINSON, Peter Frederick, FSA: 1776–1858

A pupil of Henry Holland: assistant to William Porden: travelled on the Continent: a founder member of the Institute of British Architects, and an early Vice-President. His practice consisted largely of country houses and cottages, designed in any style required by his clients; and he published a number of works, including *Rural Architecture : a series of designs for ornamental Cottages* (1823): *Designs for Ornamental Villas* (1825–7): *Designs for Village Architecture* (1830): *Designs for Gate Cottages, Lodges and Park Entrances* (1833): *An Attempt to ascertain the Age of Mickleham Church in Surrey* (1824). His work included the Egyptian Hall, Piccadilly, London (1811–12: dem.): Millfield, nr. Gt Bookham, Surrey (1814: many additions since): Fernacres, Fulmer, Bucks. (1815): Trellissick House, nr. Penzance, Cornwall (*c.* 1825): Christ Church, Leamington, Warwicks. (1825: dem.): Coolhurst, nr. Horsham, Sussex (1833–5): the Chalet at Swiss Cottage, St John's Wood, London (1829–32).

ROBINSON, Samuel: 1752–1833
Entered the Royal Academy Schools 1775, and exhibited at the Royal Academy between 1775 and 1821. He did much valuation work, notably with D. R. Roper on the construction of Regent Street; was Surveyor to the estates of St Thomas's Hospital; St Olave's Grammar Schools, Southwark; the Cordwainers' Company; St Magnus Martyr; and St Margaret, Lothbury. Little of his work survives, but he built the anatomical theatre at the original St Thomas's Hospital in Southwark (1814–15) and did other work there with J. Field: almshouses and other building in Hackney; and the premises of the British and Foreign Bible Society in Borough Road, Southwark, London (1817: later part of the Borough Polytechnic).

ROBINSON, Sir Thomas: *c.* 1700–77
The son of William Robinson, gentleman, of Rokeby, Yorks. He travelled on the Continent as a young man and developed a taste for and interest in architecture. He was M.P. for Morpeth in 1727: created a baronet in 1730: an Excise Commissioner 1735–42. His enjoyment of fashionable social life and the extravagant entertainments he gave, involved him in financial trouble: he left the country, and from 1742–7 was Governor of Barbados. On his return, he became Master of Ceremonies and Entertainment Manager at Ranelagh Gardens, in Chelsea. He practised as an amateur architect, in the manner of the wealthy dilettanti of the time: rebuilt the family mansion at Rokeby, and laid out and enclosed the park: built the west wing of Castle Howard after Vanbrugh's death (but not to his designs): and was almost certainly the architect of St Mary, Glynde, Sussex (1763–5): he designed Claydon House, Middle Claydon, Bucks. (*c.* 1760), of which only one wing of his work remains.

ROBSON, Edward Robert, FSA, FRIBA: 1836–1917
The son of Robert Robson, a J.P. of Durham. Edward Robson
spent three years in practical building work: then became a pupil
of John Dobson, and of Sir G. G. Scott: travelled on the Continent,
and in North America. He was in partnership with J. J. Stevenson
1870–5: was Architect to the Dean and Chapter of Durham
Cathedral: Surveyor to the Corporation of Liverpool: Architect to
the School Board for London (the first one appointed) 1870–89:
Consulting Architect to the Education Department and its successor,
the Board of Education, 1889–1904. He was the author of *School
Architecture* (1874), and framed and revised the building rules for
elementary schools, published by the Board of Education 1884–
1904. Robson was responsible for the building of many hundreds of
elementary schools, and was an authority on the principles of school
design and construction of his day. His work included Blackheath
Road School, Greenwich, London (1874: with J. J. Stevenson):
LCC School, Bromley High Street, Poplar, London (1875): Girls'
High School, Wemyss Road, Greenwich, London (1879): the
western side of Queen Anne Mansions, Broadway, London (1880):
Royal Institute of Painters in Water Colours, Piccadilly, London
(1881): the People's Palace, Mile End Road, London (1886–7).

ROCHEAD, John Thomas: 1814–78
Born in Edinburgh: a pupil of David Bryce: worked as a draughts-
man for David Hamilton, and for Hurst and Moffatt at Doncaster.
He had a large private practice in Glasgow from 1841–70, was very
successful, and his reputation for ecclesiastical work was high. He
designed the Wallace Monument at Stirling, and his work in
Glasgow included the Davidson of Ruchill Monument at the
Necropolis (1851): the re-design of Grosvenor Terrace (1855):
Park Church, Lynedoch Place (1858): John Street Church (1859–
60): the Bank of Scotland, Gt Vincent Place and George Square
(1865–9).

ROPER, David Riddal: *c.* 1773–1855
He exhibited at the Royal Academy 1797–1822, and practised in
London as an architect and surveyor. With Samuel Robinson, he
carried out valuation work involved by the construction of Regent
Street. His work in London included Brockwell Hall, Brockwell
Park, Lambeth (1816): Grove Chapel, Camberwell (1819):

Haberdashers' Almshouses, Shoreditch (1825: later a Technical College): the Shot Tower, Lambeth (1826: dem.). The design of St Mark, Kennington (1822), is often attributed to him, but is believed by some authorities to have been the work of another architect, A. B. Clayton.

ROUMIEU, Robert Lewis: 1814–77
A pupil of Benjamin Wyatt, and in partnership with A. D. Gough from 1836–48. He was Surveyor to the Gas, Light and Coke Company's estate at Beckton, to the French Hospital, and other estates in and near London: he did much work for Crosse & Blackwell, and built many offices, warehouses, and commercial premises in London. His work included No. 70 The Ridgway, Wimbledon, Surrey (1860): the French Hospital, Hackney, London (1865): The Priory, Roehampton, London (1866): Nos. 33–35 Eastcheap, London (1877).

ST AUBYN, James Piers, FRIBA: 1815–95

Born at Powick, Worcs.: educated in Gloucester, where he became a pupil of a local architect named Fulljames: set up in practice in Devonport and London. He was Surveyor to the Manor of Stoke Damerel: Surveyor to the Middle Temple: a member of the Incorporated Church Building Society's Committee of Architects. He practised mostly in the West of England, and was an active restorer of churches, particularly in Cornwall, due perhaps to his relationship to the St Aubyn family of St Michael's Mount. His work included St Agnes, St Agnes, Cornwall (1848): additions at St Michael's Mount, and All Saints, Marazion, Cornwall (1850 and 1875–8): the Market, Devonport, Plymouth (1852): Goldsmith Building, Inner Temple, London (1861): St Mary, Widford, Essex (1862): All Saints, Reading, Berks. (1865): St Clement, Paddington, London (1867–9): St Mary, Tyndalls Park, Bristol (1870–81): Dunster School, Som. (1871): St Michael and All Angels, Galleywood Common, nr. Chelmsford (1873): Pencalenick, nr. St. Clement, Cornwall (1881): Garden Court Building, Middle Temple, London (1884–5): St Peter, Rose Ash, Devonshire (1888: with Wadling).

SALVIN, Anthony, FSA, FRIBA: 1799–1881

Born in Co. Durham, the son of General Anthony Salvin: educated at Durham School: worked for John Nash in London: set up his own practice 1828. He was an authority on mediaeval military architecture, carried out much restoration of castles, fortresses and mansions, built large country houses, and had a big and flourishing practice. He was a Vice-President of the Institute, and in the 1860s Architect to the Zoological Society, for whom he designed the original Antelope and Elephant Houses in Regent's Park. His work included Mamhead, nr. Exeter (1828): Harlaxton House, Lincs. (1831–8: he was replaced there by William Burn): Scotney Castle, nr. Lamberhurst, Kent (1837–43): the Barracks Building, Tower of London (1845): St Paul, Alnwick, Northumb. (1846): St Mary Magdalene, Torquay, Devonshire (1846: alterations since): Peckforton Castle, Cheshire (1846–50): St Stephen, Hammersmith, London (1850) and the Parsonage: considerable alterations and rebuilding at Alnwick Castle, Northumb. (1854 onwards): Thoresby,

SANDBY, THOMAS

Notts. (1864–75): Paddockhurst, Worth, Sussex (1869–72): St John, Perlethorpe, Notts. (1876).

SANDBY, Thomas, RA: 1721–98
Born at Nottingham, the son of a local gentleman, Thomas Sandby. Came to London with his brother, Paul, in 1742, and took a post in the Tower of London military drawing office, which he held almost till his death. In 1743 he was appointed to the suite of the Duke of Cumberland, with whom he served in the field, till c. 1748: became his Draughtsman in 1750: Steward and Clerk of the Stables at Windsor, 1764: and Deputy Ranger of Windsor Great Park, 1765: under George III he was Architect of the King's Works, and Master Carpenter at the Office of Works. He was a Professor of Architecture at the Royal Academy: a committee member of the Society of Artists: an honorary member of the Architects' Club. With his brother, he designed the lake, grottoes and 'ruins' of Virginia Water in Windsor Great Park (c. 1750–85). Here, too, he made additions to Cumberland Lodge: designed the mansion of St Leonard's Hill near Windsor (c. 1771: since largely rebuilt): and designed Norbury Park, nr. Mickleham, Surrey (1774).

SANDERS, John: 1768–1826
The son of Thomas Sanders, a London tallow chandler: a pupil of Sir John Soane in 1784: studied at the Royal Academy School: awarded the Academy Gold Medal 1788: in 1790 began independent practice. With two others, he was appointed Architect to the Barrack Department of the War Office in 1805: after early retirement, he travelled on the Continent 1817–c. 1820, partly in company with G. L. Taylor and E. Cresy, on a tour of architectural drawing and measuring. Sanders was the first President of the Architects' and Antiquaries' Club: his work included the Duke of York's HQ, King's Road, Chelsea, London (1801: formerly the Royal Military Asylum): the Royal Military Academy, Sandhurst, Berks. (1807–12).

SANDERSON, John: d. c. 1783
Lived in Hampstead: known chiefly as the architect of St John's Church there (1745–7). He completed the building of the Radcliffe Infirmary, Oxford, after the death of Stiff Leadbetter, who designed it: re-fronted St Peter's Rectory, Chalfont St Peter, Bucks. (1780):
206

and executed the building of the Church of St John the Evangelist, Wicken, Northants, designed by Thomas Prowse, an amateur architect.

SANDS, William: d. 1751
William Sands and his son, William, were architects and masons at Spalding, Lincs., the former a local Master Freemason and a member of Spalding Gentlemen's Society. The work of William Sands the elder included St James, Moulton Chapel, Lincs. (1722): possibly Fydell House, Boston, Lincs. (1726): No. 12 High Street, Spalding. That of the younger Sands included Westbourne Lodge (c. 1760–70) and Holland House (1768), both in Spalding.

SANDYS, Francis, FSA: eighteenth/nineteenth century
An Irishman by birth, he visited Italy c. 1796, and then came to England under the patronage of the 4th Earl of Bristol. He practised in Bury St Edmunds, Suffolk, till 1808, then in London. His work included Finborough Hall, Gt Finborough, Suffolk (1795): Ickworth House, nr. Bury St Edmunds (1796 onwards): the remodelling of Worlingham Hall, Suffolk (c. 1800): the Athenaeum, Bury St Edmunds (1804: built as the Assembly Rooms).

SAVAGE, James: 1779–1852
Born in Hackney: educated at a private school: a pupil of D. A. Alexander to whom he later became Clerk of Works. In 1798 entered the Royal Academy Schools: exhibited at the Royal Academy 1799–1832. In 1830 Savage became Architect to the Middle Temple: was President of the Surveyors' Club 1825: a Vice-President of the London Architectural Society: a member of the Institute of British Architects for a short time, but resigned after a disagreement: a member of the Institution of Civil Engineers; of the Graphic Society; and of the Skinners' Company: Chairman of the committee of fine arts of the Society for the Promotion of Arts, Manufacture and Commerce. He was the author of *Observations on the proposed new London Bridge* (1823): *St Saviour's Church, reasons against pulling down the Lady Chapel* (1832: with L. N. Cottingham): *Observations on Style in Architecture, with Suggestions on the best Mode of procuring Designs for Public Buildings and promoting the Improvement of Architecture; especially in reference to a Recommendation in the Report of the Commissioners on the Designs for the new Houses of Parliament*

207

(1836). His work included Richmond Bridge over the river Liffey, Dublin (1813–16): St Luke, Chelsea, London (1820–4): St James, Bermondsey, London (1827–9): All Saints, Beulah Hill, Upper Norwood, Surrey (1827–9): Holy Trinity, Tottenham, Middx. (1828–30): Clock Tower (1830–1) and Plowden Buildings (1831–3), Middle Temple, London: St Mary the Virgin, Ilford, Essex (1831): church schools at Ilford (1831) and Brentwood (1835), Essex: St Paul, Addlestone, Surrey (1836).

SCOLES, Joseph John, FIBA: 1798–1863

Born in London, the son of a joiner: educated at a Roman Catholic school at Baddesley Green: in 1812 became a pupil of Joseph Ireland, a distinguished Roman Catholic architect of the day, who designed All Saints, Hassop, Derbys., in 1818. Scoles entered the Royal Academy Schools 1820: from 1822–6 he travelled on the Continent, in Egypt and Asia Minor, in company with the younger Joseph Bonomi and others interested in archaeology and architecture; and later contributed plans and drawings to contemporary journals and books. He was in practice in London in 1826: and, in collaboration with John Nash, planned much of Gloucester Terrace and Gloucester Gate, Regent's Park, London (1827–8). Scoles was Hon. Secretary and a Vice-President of the Institute of British Architects: his work consisted mostly of Roman Catholic churches, and included St Peter, Gt Yarmouth, Norfolk (1831–3): Our Lady, Lisson Grove, St Marylebone, London (1836): St George, Edgbaston, Birmingham (1836–8: many additions since): St James the Less, Colchester (1837): St John the Evangelist, Islington, London (1843): St Paul, Prior Park, Bath (Scoles designed this c. 1844, and it was completed after his death by his son): Church of the Immaculate Conception, Farm Street, London (1844–9): the Oratorians' House, Brompton Oratory, London (1853).

SCOTT, Sir George Gilbert, RA, FRIBA: 1811–78 (Portrait: see Plate XI)

Born at Gawcott, Bucks., the son of the Rev. Thomas Scott, the incumbent: his education was haphazard until he was articled to James Edmeston, a London architect, in 1827: he also studied drawing under George Maddox in London. Scott worked for a time for Messrs Peto and Grissell, London builders: then in the office of Henry Roberts: and assisted Sampson Kempthorne in a programme of workhouse building. In 1835, on the death of his father, he set up in practice, with a former fellow-pupil, William Bonython Moffatt (1812–87), a partnership that lasted many years. Scott was appointed Architect to the Dean and Chapter of Westminster in 1849: knighted 1872: was President of the Institute in 1873: his published works included *Remarks on Secular and Domestic Architecture, Present and Future*: and *Personal and Professional Recollections*. He built up an enormous and very successful private practice, almost entirely of ecclesiastical building and restoration, and institutions, and has since acquired a reputation for widespread and Philistine destruction of the architecture of previous periods, which he replaced with the Gothic Revival designs of his own taste. It has been suggested that the output of Scott and Moffatt totalled more than seven hundred and fifty commissions: they included Cambridge House Hospital, Flax Bourton, Som. (1837–8: built as the workhouse): St Nicholas, Newport, Lincoln (1838: chancel added since): St Andrew's Hospital, Billericay, Essex (1840: built as the Poor Law institution): St Mary, Hanwell, Middx. (1841): the Martyrs' Memorial, Oxford (1841): Reading Gaol, Berks. (1842–4): Royal Wanstead School, Wanstead, Essex (1843: built as the Hackney Orphan Asylum): Christ Church, Turnham Green, Chiswick, London (1843: chancel added since): Brighton College, Sussex (1848: additions since): houses at the entrance to Dean's Yard, Westminster, London (1854): Chapel and Library of Exeter College, Oxford (1856–9): St Mathias, Richmond, Surrey (1858): Kelham Hall, Northants (1858–62): restoration at Bath Abbey, Som. (1858–74): the Albert Memorial, Kensington, London (1863–72): Home Office, and Foreign Office, Whitehall, London (1868–73): St Pancras Station Hotel, London (1868–74): St Mary's Episcopal Cathedral, Glasgow (1871–84: completed by J. Oldrid Scott). W. B. Moffatt carried out much independent work for Poor Law Authorities, and designed the Earlswood Asylum, Redhill, Surrey (1853).

SCOTT, George Gilbert, the younger: 1837–97

The eldest son of Sir George Gilbert Scott: he was a Fellow of Jesus College, Cambridge, where he had an academic career of some distinction, and where he carried out restorations at Peterhouse and Christ's College, and additions at St John's, and Pembroke. He was associated with Bodley and Garner in establishing the firm of Watts

o

& Co. in Baker Street, London, which produced church fittings of pre-Raphaelite design. Scott assisted his father, and brother, John Oldrid, but later withdrew from the practice. He was the author of *History of English Church Architecture* (1884), and edited his father's book, *Personal and Professional Recollections*. His work included St John the Baptist, Busbridge, Surrey (1865–7): Garboldisham Manor, Norfolk (1873: dem.): St Agnes, Kennington, London (1877: bombed): St Mark, Leamington, Warwicks. (1879): All Hallows, Southwark, London (1880: bombed): the New Building, Pembroke College, Cambridge (1883).

SCOTT, Sir Giles Gilbert, OM, RA, FRIBA: 1880–1960
The second son of George Gilbert Scott the younger, and grandson of Sir George Gilbert Scott: educated Beaumont College, Windsor: articled to Temple Lushington Moore: set up in practice 1903. In the same year he won the competition for the design of the Anglican Cathedral at Liverpool: the building of this (begun in 1903 and in association with G. F. Bodley till 1907) continued throughout his life, and was still incomplete at his death. Scott had a distinguished architectural career: he was President of the AA 1920–1: knighted 1924: Royal Gold Medallist 1925: President of the RIBA 1933–5: he received Honorary Degrees from the Universities of Oxford, Cambridge, Liverpool, and Trinity College, Toronto: was a Knight of the Norwegian Order of St Olaf. His work included the Église de Notre Dame, Northfleet, Kent (1915): the War Memorial Chapel, Charterhouse School, Surrey (1922–7): New Court, Clare College, Cambridge (1924–5): St Francis, High Wycombe, Bucks. (1930): William Booth Memorial Training College, Denmark Hill, London (1929: with Gordon and Vince): New University Library, Cambridge (1931–4): Battersea Power Station, London (1932–4): the new Bodleian Library, Oxford (1936–47): the Guinness Brewery, Willesden, London (1936): Waterloo Bridge, London (1939–45): rebuilding of the House of Commons, London (1950): Bankside Power Station, London (1952–3, and 1962–3).

SCOTT, Major-General Henry Young Darracot, CB, FRS: 1822–83
Born in Plymouth, the fourth son of Edward Scott: educated privately, and at the Royal Military Academy, Woolwich: in 1840

was commissioned as a second-lieutenant in the Royal Engineers: in 1855 he became an instructor in field works and surveying, and was given charge of a military chemical laboratory near Chatham. He invented a form of selenitic lime, and a technique of military sketching, and assisted in establishing the Luton Valley Waterworks. Scott was Secretary of the Commission for the Great Exhibition of 1851, from 1865–82: he retired from the Army in 1871: became an Associate of the Institution of Civil Engineers, contributed to professional journals, and specialized in the design and construction of exhibitions in London and on the Continent. He carried out the building of the Royal Albert Hall, London (1867–71: to the designs of Captain Francis Fowke), and designed and built the Imperial College of Science, Kensington, London (1868–73: built as the Huxley Building).

SCOTT, John Oldrid, FSA, FRIBA: 1841–1913
The second son of Sir George Gilbert Scott: educated at Bradfield College: entered his father's office 1860, was closely associated with his work, and succeeded to his practice on his death in 1878. For a time he was assisted by his elder brother, George Gilbert, whose work he completed when he retired. J. Oldrid Scott did much church building and restoration, and identified himself with his father's architectural beliefs: he also designed ironwork, woodwork, and embroidery. His work included St Mary, North Common, Chailey, Sussex (1876): St Sophia, Moscow Road, Bayswater, London (1877): Hollyhill, Coleman's Hatch, nr. Forest Row, Sussex (1885): the Chapel, Bradfield College, Berks. (1890–1): All Saints, Newborough, Staffs. (1901): Offices and Chapter Hall, the Priory of St John of Jerusalem, Clerkenwell Green, London (1903).

SCUNE, Christopher: fl. 1505–21
A master mason who worked in the provinces: he completed the spire of St James, Louth, Lincs. (1505–15: begun by John Cole): was Master Mason at Durham and Ripon Cathedrals: and at Ripon he designed the nave and tower (1503–21). The nave and tower of St Mary, Beverley, Yorks. (1520–4), and Abbot Huby's Tower at Fountains Abbey, Yorks. (c. 1510–25), may also have been his work.

SEARLES, Michael: 1750–1813
The son of Michael Searles, a Greenwich surveyor, whose profession he followed. Searles was Surveyor to the Rolls estate in London: from *c.* 1771 he practised in Bermondsey, and by 1792 was working as an architect as well. His work included the Paragon, Blackheath, London (1792), and possibly Colonnade House at Blackheath: Clare House, East Malling, Kent (1793): the layout of Surrey Square, Southwark, London (1794).

SEDDING, John Dando, FRIBA: 1838–91
Articled to G. E. Street 1858–65: then joined his brother, Edmund (d. 1868), who practised as an architect in Penzance. John Sedding worked in Cornwall and the West of England: in 1875 he set up a practice in London, and did much church restoration: he was Diocesan Architect to Bath and Wells: designed furniture, embroidery, and ornaments: Henry Wilson, a former pupil, worked with him, and completed some of his work after his death. Sedding was the author of *Garden Craft, Old and New* (1891), and *Art and Handicraft* (1893): his work included St Martin, Low Marple, Cheshire (1870): St Clement, Boscombe, Hants (1873–93): All Saints Vicarage, Plymouth (*c.* 1880): the Church of the Holy Redeemer, Clerkenwell, London (1887–8): All Saints, Falmouth, Cornwall (1887–90): Holy Trinity, Sloane Square, London (1888–90): St Peter, Ealing, London (1892: with Henry Wilson): the House of Charity, Redcatch Road, Bristol (completed shortly before 1896: built as the Industrial Schools).

SEDDON, John Pollard, FRIBA: 1827–1906
Born in Aldersgate, London, the son of Thomas Seddon the cabinet-maker: educated Bedford Grammar School: articled to Thomas Leverton Donaldson 1847: visited the Continent. From 1852–62 he was in practice at Llandaff with John Prichard, whom he succeeded as Diocesan Architect there: he was a Consulting Architect to the Incorporated Church Building Society, and Surveyor for the Archdeaconry of Monmouth. In 1862, he moved to London and was in partnership there from 1885–1904 with John Coates Carter. Seddon served on the Council of the RIBA: was Hon. Secretary there for ten years, with C. F. Hayward: was an original member of the AA in 1847: he published a number of books, including *Progress in Art and Architecture* (1852), and *Memoirs and Letters of the*

Late Thomas Seddon (1859). His work included the Southerndown Hotel, Bridgend, Glam. (1852–3): Ettington Park, Warwicks. (1858–62: with John Prichard): All Saints, Chigwell Row, Essex (1867): the Powell Almshouses, Fulham, London (1869): St James Gt Yarmouth, Norfolk (1870–8): St Mary, Ullenhall, Warwicks. (1875): St Andrew, Adforton, Herefs. (1875): extensive additions and remodelling to St Catherine, Hoarwithy, Herefs. (1880–5): St Paul, Hammersmith, London (1882: with H. R. Gough): Christ Church Vicarage, Victoria Street, London (*c.* 1888).

SELLARS, James: 1846–88
Born in Glasgow: a pupil of a local architect, Hugh Barclay, and then of Campbell Douglas, whose partner he became later. Sellars was President of the Institute of Architects in Glasgow, where he practised. His work there included St Andrew's Hall (1873–7): the Greek Orthodox Church of St Luke (1877): Kelvinside Academy (1877–9): Cornhill House (1879–81): the design of the International Exhibition (1881): No. 56 Dumbarton Road (1888–9: completed by his draughtsman, John Keppie: built as Anderson's College of Medicine).

SELLERS, James Henry: 1861–1954
Born at Oldham, Lancs., of humble parentage: educated at the local Board School: started his career as an office boy in the employment of an Oldham architect. He became a skilled draughtsman: worked as an assistant to other architects and surveyors: and was appointed Assistant County Architect at Carlisle. He started his own practice in Oldham in 1900, and shortly after went into partnership with Edgar Wood of Manchester, continuing to practise alone after Wood's retirement in 1922. He was a distinguished designer of furniture: his architectural work included Dronsfields' office block, Oldham (1906–7): schools in Durnford Street and Elm Street, Middleton, Lancs. (1910).

SEWARD, Henry Hake: *c.* 1778–1848
A pupil of Sir John Soane in 1794, and remained with him till 1808: in partnership with George Byfield 1810–13. Seward was District Surveyor of the parishes of St Martin-in-the-Fields and St Anne, Soho: Joint Surveyor, with Byfield, of the Estates of the Dean and Chapter of Westminster: Clerk of Works and then Surveyor of

213

Greenwich Hospital: Assistant Surveyor-General of the Board of Works: and from 1832–44 the first Surveyor of Works and Buildings. His work included the reconstruction, in the Gothic style, of New Court, Lugwardine, Herefs. (1809–10): rebuilding of the west façade of King Charles Block, Greenwich Hospital, London (1811–14): in Northumb. the churches and parsonages of St Michael, Wark-on-Tyne (1814–18): St Luke, Greystead (1818): St Aidan, Thorneyburn (1818): and St Peter, Humshaugh (1819): St Martin's Almshouses, Bayham Street, Camden Town, London (1818).

SHARP, Richard Hey: d. *c.* 1853
Studied under Peter Atkinson the younger: travelled on the Continent 1816–19: was in partnership with Atkinson till 1828, when he began to practise independently in York. His younger brother, Samuel (d. *c.* 1860), was also an architect; worked in Atkinson's office at York; and was awarded the Soane Medal of the Institute of British Architects in 1838. R. H. Sharp's work included the Concert Room, York (with Atkinson): All Saints, Wainfleet, Lincs. (1820–1: with Atkinson): St Mark, Woodhouse Moor, Yorks. (1823–6: with Atkinson): the Museum (1828–30) and Spa Buildings (*c.* 1835) at Scarborough, Yorks.: rebuilding of Holy Trinity, Low Moor, Bradford, Yorks. (1836–7: with S. Sharp): St Mary, Roecliffe, Yorks. (1843): St John Bowling, nr. Bradford (1842).

SHARPE, Edmund: 1809–77
Born in Knutsford, Cheshire: educated at Dr Burney's Academy, and St John's College, Cambridge, where he obtained the Travelling Bachelorship of the University, enabling him to spend three years in France and Germany. He was articled to Thomas Rickman in 1836: practised in Lancaster in partnership with Edwin Graham Paley (1823–95) from 1841 to 1851, when he retired in order to practise railway engineering, and devote himself to the production of books on mediaeval architecture. He was an amateur musician of great ability: Mayor of Lancaster 1848: Royal Gold Medallist 1875: Bridgemaster for Lonsdale South: Architect to the Justices of Lancaster County Asylum and Court: and in 1870 organized and personally conducted the first series of architectural tours for members of the Architectural Association. Among his published works were *Architectural Parallels* (1848): *The Rise and Progress of Decorated Window Tracery* (1849): *Seven Periods of Gothic Architecture*

(1851): *The Architecture of the Cistercians* (1874). He was responsible for a number of railways, some street tramways in Geneva; and many churches, including Holy Trinity, Howgill, Yorks. (1838): St Stephen and All Martyrs, Lever Bridge, nr. Bolton, Lancs. (1844: with E. G. Paley): and Holy Trinity, Platt Lane, Manchester (1845).

SHAW, John, the elder, FSA, FRS: 1776–1832
Born at Bexley, Kent: articled to George Gwilt the elder: began practice 1798. He was appointed Architect and Surveyor to Christ's Hospital, London, 1816, and was also Architect to the Trustees of Ramsgate Harbour: a Fellow of the Linnean Society, and a member of the Architects' Club. Between 1820 and 1832 he carried out much additional building at Christ's Hospital in Newgate Street, London (now all dem.), and his other work included the clockhouse, steps, and obelisk at Ramsgate Harbour, Kent: St Dunstan-in-the-West, Fleet Street, London (1829–33: completed by his son, John): and Ouborough, Godstone, Surrey (built as Rooksnest).

SHAW, John, the younger: 1803–70
Born in London, the son of the architect John Shaw: a pupil of his father, and succeeded him as Surveyor of Christ's Hospital, London. The younger Shaw was also Surveyor to Eton College, and an official referee of metropolitan buildings 1844–55. He built much at Christ's Hospital, Newgate Street, London, including the Grammar School designed by his father (now all dem.), and built houses in Adelaide Road, Provost Road, and Eton Rise, in Hampstead, London. His other work included the Phoenix Assurance office, 191 Fleet Street, London (1834: built as the Law Life Assurance office): Christ Church, Watney Street, Stepney, London (1841: severely war damaged): Goldsmith's College, Deptford, London (1843–4: formerly the Royal Naval School): New Buildings, Eton College, Bucks. (1844–6): Wellington College, nr. Sandhurst, Berks. (1855–9).

SHAW, Richard Norman, RA: 1831–1912
Born in Edinburgh: educated at Hill Street Academy there: articled to William Burn *c*. 1846: studied at the Royal Academy Schools where he was awarded the Gold Medal and the Travelling Scholarship in 1854: visited the Continent, and published the results of his travels in 1858 under the title of *Architectural Sketches*

from the Continent. He worked for a short time in Salvin's office: in 1858 became a draughtsman with G. E. Street: in 1862 set up in practice in London, sharing an office with W. E. Nesfield. They collaborated very closely till 1868, when Shaw began to work independently, and established a very big and flourishing private practice, specializing in large town and country houses. Shaw was a member of the RIBA for a time, but did not become a Fellow, and resigned in 1872: he was not in sympathy with the policies of the Institute, and twice refused the offer of the Royal Gold Medal. He made many improvements to the inadequate systems of sanitation of the period, and modern methods are based on his ideas. His work included Leys Wood, Groombridge, Kent (1868): Grimsdyke, Harrow Weald, Middx. (1872): Albert Hall Mansions, Kensington, London (1873): the layout and planning of Bedford Park, London (1875–8): Wispers, Midhurst, Sussex (1876: later a school): Merrist Wood, Worplesdon, Surrey (1877): the Royal Geographical Society, Kensington, London (1879: built as Lowther Lodge): Adcote, Salop (1879): Alliance Assurance premises, Pall Mall, London (1882): No. 39 Frognal, Hampstead, London (1885): All Saints, Leek, Staffs. (1886): Holy Trinity, Latimer Road, London (1887–9): New Scotland Yard, London (1888): No. 170 (1888) and No. 185 (1890) Queen's Gate, London: Bryanston, nr. Blandford, Dorset (1890): No. 5 Kennington Park Place, Southwark, London (1895): White Star Line offices, Liverpool (1896): Alliance Assurance premises, St James's Street, London (1903: with Ernest Newton): the Piccadilly Hotel, London (1905–8).

SHEPHERD, Edward: d. 1747
An architect and builder whose patron, the 1st Duke of Chandos, employed him at Canons House, Middx. (dem.), on two houses in Cavendish Square, London (dem.), and on his other properties. In 1735–46, as a private speculation, Shepherd built Shepherd's Market and the adjacent streets in Mayfair, London (rebuilt since). His other work included the building of Boreham House, Essex (1728): houses on the north side of Grosvenor Square, London (*c.* 1730): No. 71 South Audley Street, London (1736–7).

SHERRIN, George, FRIBA: 1843–1909
He practised in London and south-east England, and did much work for the Metropolitan Railway, including underground

stations at Moorgate, Kensington High Street, Gloucester Road, South Kensington, and Victoria, where he also built the arcade. He was Joint Architect, with John Clarke, to the Margate and Southend Kursaals Committee. Much of his work was done in Essex, where several houses designed by him at Ingatestone are typical of the style he used. His work included The Tiles, Ingatestone, Essex (*c.* 1870): the Cottage Hospital, Halstead, Essex (1884): No. 51 Carey Street, London (1888): St Mary Moorfields, Shoreditch, London (1899–1902): The Kursaal, Southend-on-Sea, Essex (1902): Alexandra House, Dovercourt, Essex (1904: built as the Alexandra Hotel): Pontings, Kensington High Street, London.

SHUTE, John: d. 1563
The date of his birth is unknown, but it is believed he was born at Cullompton, Devonshire: was probably a member of the Painters' and Stainers' Company: in 1550, the Duke of Northumberland sent him to Italy to study architecture. No evidence exists that he designed or erected any building, but he is famous as the author of the first English book on the classic orders of architecture, *The First and Chief Groundes of Architecture*, published in 1563, of which five known copies exist. In the 1633 edition of the *Survey of London* (p. 221), Stow records Shute's epitaph on 'a hansome small Monument' in the Church of St Edmond the King, Lombard Street, London.

SIMONS, see SYMONS

SIMPSON, Archibald: 1790–1847
Born in Aberdeen, the son of William Simpson, a clothier: educated Aberdeen Grammar School, and Marischal College: apprenticed to an Aberdeen builder, James Massie. From 1810 to 1813 he worked in the office of Robert Lugar in London: then visited Rome: set up practice in Aberdeen in 1813, where he became very successful. He was an able amateur musician and violinist. He built mansions and country houses, and carried out street replanning in Aberdeen. His work there included the Assembly Rooms (1820): the Athenaeum (1823): the Royal Infirmary (1832): Girls' High School (1840): North of Scotland Bank (1844): rebuilding of Marischal College

and University (1844). He also built St Giles, Elgin (1828), and the Duchess of Gordon's Schools, Huntly (c. 1840).

SLATER, William: 1819–73
His childhood was spent in Northants: in 1835 he came to London and was articled to R. C. Carpenter, with whom he remained as an assistant: he was in partnership for a short time with William Smith, but when R. C. Carpenter died he joined his son, R. H. Carpenter, in partnership from 1863–73. He completed many of the works of the elder Carpenter, succeeded him as Architect to Chichester Cathedral, and, with R. H. Carpenter, designed and built Denstone School, Staffs., and Ardingly, Sussex. Slater also carried out church building restoration independently. His work included the Town Hall, Loughborough, Leics. (1855): restoration of SS Peter and Paul, Coleshill, Warwicks. (1859): St Nicholas, Harpenden, Herts. (1862): St Michael, Stockton, Warwicks. (1863–73).

SMIRKE, Sir Robert, RA, FSA, FRS, HON.FRIBA: 1781–1867
   (Portrait: see Plate VIII)
Born in London, the second son of Robert Smirke, RA: educated Apsley School, Beds.: a pupil of Sir John Soane, and of Bush, the surveyor: entered the Royal Academy Schools 1796: was awarded the Gold Medal there in 1799. Between 1801 and 1805 he made two visits to the Continent, travelling in France, Italy, Germany, Sicily and Greece. His architectural career began in 1806, and by his retirement in 1845 he had become a very successful architect, widely known, and with an extensive public and private practice. He was Architect to the Board of Trade 1807: one of the three Board of Works Architects 1813: Surveyor to the Inner Temple 1814: Treasurer of the Royal Academy 1820–50: knighted 1832: a member of the London Improvements Commission 1845–c. 1848: Royal Gold Medallist 1853. He published *Specimens of Continental Architecture* in 1806, and *A Review of a Battalion of Infantry* in 1809, which he had written while a captain in a volunteer defence corps in London: this manual was still in use by the Regular Army in 1840. Smirke is said to have been the first English architect to use concrete in large quantities, and cast iron for beams and girders: he introduced the employment of quantity surveyors into building practice, measuring having been done previously by architects' clerks. His immense output of work included Walberton House, Sussex (1803):

218

Lowther Castle, Westmorland (1806–11): Eastnor Castle, Herefs. (1812): the Old Council House, Corn Street, Bristol (1822–7): St Philip, Salford, Lancs. (1822–5): St Mary, Wyndham Place, St Marylebone, London (1823): the British Museum, London (1823–47: the Reading Room by Sydney Smirke): St Anne, Wandsworth, London (1824): the Royal College of Physicians, Trafalgar Square, London (1824–7: additions since: now Canada House): rebuilding of central part of the Custom House, Lower Thames Street, London (1825): the Portuguese Embassy, Belgrave Square, London (*c.* 1830: built as a private mansion): the east wing of Somerset House, London (1830–1): the Oxford and Cambridge Club, Pall Mall, London (1835–8: with Sydney Smirke): Paper Buildings, King's Bench Walk, London (1838 and 1848: with Sydney Smirke).

SMIRKE, Sydney, RA, FSA, FRIBA: 1798–1877
The fifth son of Robert Smirke, RA, and younger brother of Sir Robert Smirke, in whose office he was trained, and with whom he later worked in close collaboration. Sydney Smirke succeeded his brother as Surveyor of the Inner Temple 1828: was Clerk of the Works at St James's Palace 1828–32: Royal Gold Medallist 1860: Professor of Architecture at the Royal Academy 1861–5: Treasurer there 1871: a Trustee of the Soane Museum: Surveyor to the Duchy of Lancaster: Architect to Woking Cemetery: established the Architects' Benevolent Society in 1852, and was its President till his death. He published *Suggestions for the Architectural Improvement of the Western Part of London* (1834): *A Mode of Assisting the Eye in the Right Perception of Colour in Pictures* (1856): *The Professional Life of C. R. Cockerell* (1863). His work included the Town Hall, Shoreham, Sussex (1830: built as the Custom House): portico and domes at the Imperial War Museum, Lambeth Road, Southwark, London (1838–40: built as the Bethlehem Hospital in 1812–15 by J. Lewis): The Rocks, nr. Uckfield, Sussex (1838): the Conservative Club, No. 74 St James's Street, London (1843–5: with George Basevi): the Turner Mausoleum, St Mary, Northiam, Sussex (1846): St John the Baptist, Loughton, Essex (1846: additions since): the Reading Room, British Museum, London (1852–7): Brookwood Cemetery, Surrey (1854): with Sir William Tite): Dr Johnson's Buildings, Inner Temple, London (1857–8): additions to Burlington House, Piccadilly, London (1867): King Edward's School, Wormley, Surrey (1867).

THE SMITH FAMILY

The name of a family of master builders who flourished in Warwickshire and the neighbourhood during the late seventeenth and early eighteenth centuries. William (1661–1724) and Francis (1672–1738) were the sons of Francis Smith, a bricklayer of Tettenhall, Staffs., and practised in partnership from *c.* 1697 to 1724. Much of their work consisted in building to the designs of others, but it is probable that they also practised as architects. Together, the brothers rebuilt the churches of St Mary, Warwick (1698–1704), designed by Sir William Wilson, and of All Saints, Derby (1723–5), designed by James Gibbs. William Smith designed Stanford Hall, Leics. (1697–1700), and was the builder of St Alkmund, Whitchurch, Salop (1712–13). Francis Smith built the west range of Stoneleigh Abbey, Warwicks. (1714–26): Sutton Hall, Sutton Scarsdale, Derbys. (1724): Davenport House, nr. Worfield, Salop (1726): Kinlet Hall, Salop (1727–9): Buntingsale House, nr. Market Drayton, Salop (*c.* 1730). William Smith the younger (1705–47), the son of Francis Smith, succeeded to the practice, designing and building large country houses. His work included the building of Kirtlington Park, Oxon. (1742–6: to the designs of John Sanderson): rebuilding the chancel, outer walls of nave, and south porch of All Saints, Lamport, Northants (1743): remodelling at Stanford Hall, Leics. (1745): stables at Edgcote House, Northants (1745–7).

SMITH, George, FSA, FIBA: 1783–1869

Born at Aldenham, Herts.: articled to R. F. Brettingham in London, 1797–1802: entered the Royal Academy Schools 1801: worked in the offices of James Wyatt, D. A. Alexander, and C. Beazley: then established his own practice in the City. He was District Surveyor of the southern division of the City of London 1810–69: Surveyor to the Mercers' Company 1814–69: for a time Surveyor to the Coopers' Company, and to the Trustees of Morden College, Blackheath: served on the Council of the Institute of British Architects, of which he was an early member: also a member of the Surveyors' Club. His work included St Peter, London Colney, Herts. (1825): Whittington's Almshouses, Archway Road, Highgate, London (*c.* 1825): No. 103 St Peter's Street, St Albans, Herts. (*c.* 1829): the Town Hall, St Albans, Herts. (1829): St Michael, Blackheath Park, London (1830): St Thomas, Stepney, London (1838): the Primary School, Horsham, Sussex (1840: built as

Collyer's School): Newlands, Copthorne, Sussex (1848–9). He may have been related to George Smith, the cabinet-maker, upholsterer and furniture designer who flourished in the early nineteenth century: published various works on furniture: and described himself as 'Upholder Extraordinary to H.R.H. the Prince of Wales'.

SMITH, Thomas: 1799–1875
The County Surveyor of Hertfordshire, 1832–75, and also of Bedfordshire for some years: Surveyor to the Marquis of Salisbury's and Baron Dimsdale's London estates: Mayor of Hertford 1868. His work included the central part of the Herts. County Hospital, Hertford (1833): Clock Tower, Hoddesdon, Herts. (1835): Holy Trinity, Wareside, Herts. (1841): St Thomas, West Hyde, Herts. (1844). In collaboration with his son, he designed villas on the Riviera; the English Hotel at Nice; and Protestant churches at Nice, Cannes, Stuttgart, and Naples (the latter in 1863).

SMITHSON or SMYTHSON
A family of mason-architects who flourished during the late sixteenth and early seventeenth centuries. Robert (1535–1614) was employed at Longleat House, Wilts., in 1568–80, and at Wardour Castle, Wilts., c. 1570. The design and building of Wollaton Hall, Notts. (1580–8), and Hardwick Hall, Derbys. (1590–7), are attributed to him, and it is probable that he was connected with the design and construction of many other Elizabethan mansions in the Midlands. His son, John (d. 1634), supervised the works at Bolsover Castle, Derbys. (1613–16). He, or his son Huntingdon (d. 1648), probably designed and built the Riding House and Stables at Welbeck Abbey, Notts. (1623–5). Huntingdon Smithson, who visited Italy at the expense of his patron, the Duke of Newcastle, was responsible for considerable work at Bolsover Castle, Derbys., including the Riding School and Stables (c. 1634).

SNELL, Henry Saxon, FRIBA: 1830–1904
The son of George Blagrave Snell of London: articled to Sir James Pennethorne: was assistant to Sir Joseph Paxton, and then to Sir William Tite: c. 1866 he became Architect to the St. Marylebone Board of Guardians. He was an original member of the Architectural Association, which he joined in 1850. He published *Charitable and Parochial Institutions:* and *Hospital Construction and Management*

(with Dr F. J. Mouatt). Snell worked mainly in London, and specialized in hospital building. His work included Archway Hospital, Islington, London (1869–79): Dr Barnardo's Home, Kingston-upon-Thames, Surrey (1875: built as the Metropolitan Convalescent Home for Young Girls): St Charles Hospital, Paddington, London (1881: additions since): the Victoria Hospital for Children, Chelsea, London (1885): Luxborough Lodge, St Marylebone, London (1900: built as the workhouse).

SOANE, Sir John, RA: 1753–1837 (Portrait: see Plate VII)
Born near Goring-on-Thames, Berks., the son of a bricklayer: attended a school in Reading: in 1768 entered the office of George Dance the younger, in London: in 1770 transferred to the office of Henry Holland: in 1771 admitted to the Royal Academy Schools. There, he won the Silver Medal in 1772, the Gold Medal in 1776, and was awarded the King's Travelling Studentship, and from 1776–1780 travelled in France, Italy and Sicily, a tour which introduced him to influential persons who proved a considerable help in his career. He established a practice in London in 1781, and became increasingly active, prosperous and well known. He was appointed Architect to the Bank of England 1788: Clerk of the Works at Whitehall, Westminster and St James's 1790: Deputy Surveyor of Woods and Forests 1797: Clerk of the Works at Chelsea Hospital 1807: and one of the three 'attached' architects at the Board of Works, 1814. He became Professor of Architecture at the Royal Academy 1806: was knighted in 1831. Soane bought No. 13 Lincoln's Inn Fields, London, in 1812, and it was his home from 1813–37: he made extensive alterations there, and left it, and the collections it contained, to the nation: it is now the Soane Museum. He was the author of a number of controversial pamphlets, and among his published books were *Plans, Elevations and Sections of Buildings erected in the Counties of Norfolk, Suffolk, etc.* (1788): *Sketches in Architecture, containing Plans and Elevations of Cottages, Villas and other Useful Buildings* (1793): and *Designs for Public and Private Buildings* (1828). His very extensive practice included Blackfriars Bridge, Norwich (1783): St Mary's Parsonage, Saxlingham Nethergate, Norfolk (1784): Shotesham Park, Norfolk (c. 1785): rebuilding of the Bank of England (1788–1833: since dem. and rebuilt): the Stables, Chelsea Hospital, London (c. 1810): Seven Bridges House, Bridge Street, Reading (1790: formerly the house of W. B. Simmonds, the brewer): Wiston

Hall, Wissington, Suffolk (1791): Pitzhanger Manor, Ealing, London (1801–2: now the Public Library): the Simeon Monument, Reading (1804): Dulwich Art Gallery, West Dulwich, London (1811–14: restored after war damage): St John, Bethnal Green, London (1825–8: interior remodelled since): Holy Trinity, Marylebone Road, London (1828).

SPILLER, James: d. 1829

A pupil of James Wyatt: exhibited at the Royal Academy 1780: Surveyor to the Royal Exchange Assurance Company c. 1790: he was involved in some professional disagreements with Sir John Soane and S. P. Cockerell. His work included additions to the London Hospital, Whitechapel Road, London (1781–3: designed by Boulton Manwaring in 1751): St John, Hackney, London (1792–7): the Library and Repository of the Royal Institution, Albemarle Street, London (1800–1: later refronted by L. Vulliamy): the porch at Drury Lane Theatre, London (1820).

STEPHENSON, David: 1756–1819

The son of John Stephenson, a Newcastle-on-Tyne carpenter: studied at the Royal Academy Schools: became Surveyor to the Duke of Northumberland. He built up a large practice in Newcastle, and his work included the design of Cale Cross (1783: formerly in Newcastle and re-erected at Blagdon in 1807): rebuilding of All Saints, Newcastle (1786–96): design of the buildings on the north side of New Quay, North Shields, Northumb. (built 1816): the Percy Tenantry Column, Alnwick, Northumb. (1816).

STEUART, George: d. 1806

A Scotsman, who came to London in 1770 under the patronage of the Duke of Atholl, and set up in practice as an architect. His work included Attingham Hall, Salop (1783–5): Erlestoke Park, Wilts. (1786–91): All Saints, Wellington, Salop (1790): St Chad, Shrewsbury (1790–2).

STEVENSON, John James, FSA, FRIBA: 1832–1908

A pupil of David Bryce and Sir G. G. Scott: travelled on the Continent. He practised in London: was in partnership with E. R. Robson from 1870 to 1875, and with him did much elementary school building for the London School Board. He also built large houses, and designed saloons, fittings, and so forth for the ss 'Orient', and then for other vessels, being the first architect to be commissioned for this type of work. He published *House Architecture* in 1879. His work included No. 140 Bayswater Road, London (1871): Munstead House, Surrey (1878: additions since by Sir E. Lutyens): No. 1 Fitzjohn's Avenue, Hampstead, London (1883): the Chemical Laboratory, Cambridge (1886–8: additions since).

STOKES, Leonard Aloysius, FRIBA: 1858–1925
The son of Scott Nasmyth Stokes, an Inspector of Schools: articled to S. J. Nicholl 1871–4: worked for James Gandy, a quantity surveyor: for G. E. Street: T. E. Colcutt: and for Bodley and Garner: set up in practice 1883. He was President of the AA 1889: a Member of the Historical Monuments Royal Commission 1908: President of the RIBA 1910–12: Royal Gold Medallist 1919. He built Roman Catholic churches, and many telephone exchanges in London and the provinces for the National Telephone Company. His work included St Clare, Sefton Park, Liverpool (1888): Corpus Christi Schools, Miles Platting, Manchester (1890): the Church of the Holy Ghost, Wandsworth, London (1897): All Saints Convent, London Colney, Herts. (1899): No. 2 West Drive, Streatham, London (1899): Shooter's Hill House (1898), Church Cottage (*c.* 1900) and houses and shops in Whitchurch Road (*c.* 1900), all in Pangbourne, Berks.: Grammar School, Lincoln (1905): the Telephone Exchange, Minster Street, Reading, Berks. (1908): St Wilfrid's Hall, Brompton Oratory, London (1910): North Court, Emmanuel College, Cambridge (1910–14): Nos. 34–36 Golden Square, London (1913–14).

STOKOE, William: nineteenth century
Practised at Newcastle-on-Tyne, possibly in partnership with his son, John, also a local architect. Very little is known of them, and it is not easy to a attribute their work. William Stokoe was the designer of the Moot Hall, Newcastle-on-Tyne (1810–12), and the Exchange, Sunderland, Co. Durham (1812): Hartford House, nr. Bedlington, Northumb., and Elswick Hall, nr. Newcastle (1803), may have been his work or that of John Stokoe. The latter was the architect of St Mary, Heworth, Co. Durham (1822).

x

SIR CHARLES BARRY
1795–1860

[*National Portrait
Gallery, London*

LEWIS CUBITT
b. 1799

*National Portrait
Gallery, London*]

X

SIR JOSEPH PAXTON
1801–65

[RIBA

AUGUSTUS WELBY
NORTHMORE PUGIN
1811–52

RIBA]

STONE, Francis: 1775–1835
The City Architect of Norwich and County Surveyor of Norfolk for many years: exhibited at the Royal Academy 1821. He did much repair and rebuilding work at Norwich Cathedral and Castle, including lodges and railings (1811) at the latter. His work in Norwich included St Andrew's Hospital, Thorpe (1811–14: said to be the first mental hospital to be built in England): the Fye Bridge (1829).

STOWELL, Robert: fl. 1452–1505
Master Mason at Windsor Castle from 1452 to 1462, and at Westminster Abbey from 1471 to 1505. He also practised privately as a mason-contractor. He built the south chapel of St Augustine, Broxbourne, Herts. (1476), and the nave of St Margaret, Westminster, London (1488–1504).

STRAHAN, John: eighteenth century
He started to practise as an architect in Bristol, c. 1725, and was introduced to Bath by his patron, John Hobbs, a Bristol timber merchant with interests in Bath, where, in 1727, he commissioned Strahan to lay out and design Kingsmead and Beauford Squares, the New Quay, and Kingsmead, Monmouth and Avon Streets: much of the latter has since been destroyed by war damage. Strahan's other work included the refronting of No. 59 Queen Charlotte Street, Bristol (c. 1730): Redland Court, Redland, Bristol (c. 1735): Rosewell House, Kingsmead Square, Bath (1736).

STREET, George Edmund, RA, FSA, FRIBA: 1824–81
Born at Woodford, Essex, the son of Thomas Street: articled to Owen Carter of Winchester, 1841: worked for Scott and Moffatt 1844: set up in practice at Wantage, 1848. He moved to Oxford c. 1851, and finally to London, in 1855. He travelled widely on the Continent, particularly in Spain, which he visited three times. Street was a member of the Ecclesiological Society: A Vice-President of the Institute: Diocesan Architect of Oxford 1850: Diocesan Architect at York, Ripon and Winchester: Royal Gold Medallist 1874: Professor of Architecture at the Royal Academy, and Treasurer there, 1879: awarded foreign architectural honours: a member of the Council of the English Church Union: a churchwarden of All Saints, Margaret Street, London. He published *Brick and Marble*

P

Architecture in Italy (1855), and *Some Account of Gothic Architecture in Spain* (1865). His practice was extremely large: he built many churches, and was a deeply religious man, a firm believer in the ability of Gothic architecture to assist the spiritual life. His work included St Mary, Par, Cornwall (1848–9): the School at Inkpen, Berks. (1850): All Saints, Boyne Hill, Maidenhead, Berks., and parsonage, school and church buildings (1854–7: west bays added since): Theological College, Cuddesdon, Oxon. (1853): St James-the-Less, Thorndike Street, Vauxhall Bridge Road, London (1860–1): All Saints, Denstone, Staffs. (1862): St Saviour, Eastbourne, Sussex (1867–8): All Saints, Clifton, Bristol (1868: severely war-damaged): the Royal Courts of Justice, Strand, London (1868–81): All Saints, Bolton, Lancs. (1870): St John the Divine, Vassall Road, Kennington, London (1870–4: war damaged and restored since): Holmdale, Holmbury St Mary, nr. Dorking, Surrey (1813), and the Church of St Mary there (1879).

STUART, James, FSA, FRS: 1713–88
Born in the City of London, the son of a Scottish sailor. As a young man, with little money, and his widowed mother and her other children to support, he worked as a fan-painter for Lewis Goupy, at the same time studying mathematics, drawing, Latin and Greek. He visited Rome in 1742, travelling rough, and working his way there: and Naples in 1748 in company with Nicholas Revett and others. In 1751, sponsored by the Society of Dilettanti, he and Revett went to Greece, where they remained till 1755, gathering material for their book, *The Antiquities of Athens measured and delineated by James Stuart, FRS and FSA, and Nicholas Revett, Painters and Architects*: the first volume appeared in 1762, the second in 1788–9, the third in 1795, and supplements in 1816 and 1830. On his return to England, Stuart became Painter to the Society of Dilettanti: Surveyor to Greenwich Hospital 1758–88: and Serjeant-Painter 1764–82. He designed monuments and medals, but his architectural practice was small: it included the Dreadnought Hospital, Greenwich, London (1763–4): buildings in Shugborough Park, Staffs., including the Temple of the Winds (1764): Lichfield House, No. 15 St James's Square, London (1764–6): Portman House, Portman Square, London (1777–82: formerly Montagu House: destroyed in the Second World War): the rebuilding of Greenwich Hospital Chapel (1779–88: with William Newton).

SYMONDS, Robert Wemyss, FSA, FRIBA: 1889–1958
The son of the artist, W. R. Symonds: educated at St Paul's School,
London: trained as an architect, though he is far better known as
an authority on English furniture and clocks, and as an enemy of
the makers of fake antiques. He was the author of many books,
including *The Present State of Old English Furniture* (1921): *Old
English Walnut and Lacquer Furniture* (1923): *Masterpieces of English
Furniture and Clocks* (1940): *Chippendale Furniture Design* (1948): *The
Ornamental Designs of Chippendale* (1949): *Thomas Tompion: His Life
and Work* (1951): *Furniture Making in Seventeenth and Eighteenth
Century England* (1955): and posthumously, in collaboration with
B. B. Whineray, *Victorian Furniture* (1962). His architectural work
included consultancy on the rebuilding of the Middlesex Hospital,
Mortimer Street, London (1931–4), and on St Swithin's House,
Walbrook, London (built on the site of Salter's Hall, destroyed in
the Second World War).

SYMONS (or SIMONS), Ralph: sixteenth century
Born at Berkhamsted, Herts. He practised as a mason-architect in
Westminster, and is chiefly known for his work at Cambridge. He
was associated there with Gilbert Wigge, a local mason: the two
were involved in financial trouble of some kind, which is believed to
be the reason for Symons's somewhat precipitate departure from
Cambridge in 1605. His work there included Emmanuel College
(1584): Hall Court at Sidney Sussex College (1596–8): the Second
Court of St John's College (1598–1602: with Gilbert Wigge):
alterations to Trinity College, instigated by Dr Thomas Nevile
(1604–5).

TALMAN, William: 1650–1719

The son of William Talman, the owner of a small property near Devizes, Wilts. He was in practice as an architect by 1671: was Comptroller of the King's Works 1689–1702: in 1700 was elected Steward of the Society of Virtuosi of St Luke. He was a connoisseur of antiquarian prints, drawings and books, and much of his large collection was contributed by his son, John (1677–1726), who spent many years abroad, at his father's expense, for this purpose. John Talman became the first Director of the Society of Antiquaries. William Talman's work included Thoresby House, Notts. (1671: destroyed by fire 1745: rebuilt by A. Salvin): Uppark, nr. Harting, Sussex (c. 1685–90): the south and east fronts at Chatsworth, Derbys. (1687–96): Swallowfield Park, Berks. (1689–91: refaced since): Dyrham Park, Glos. (1698–1700): remodelling at Drayton House, Northants (1702): Fetcham Park, Surrey (1705–10: remodelled externally since).

TATHAM, Charles Heathcote: 1772–1842

Born in Westminster, the son of Ralph Tatham of Co. Durham: educated Louth Grammar School: worked for a short time in the office of S. P. Cockerell: then, after a period of private study, was employed by Henry Holland, who helped finance Tatham's stay in Rome (1794–7), where he continued his studies, and met his most important patron, the Earl of Carlisle. He was in private practice in London till c. 1836: a member of the London Architectural Society, and of the Academies of St Luke in Rome, and Bologna. He wrote descriptions for architectural books including Coney's *Cathedrals*, and published a number of his own works including *Etchings of Ancient Ornamental Architecture drawn from the originals in Rome and other Parts of Italy* (1799): *Designs for Ornamental Plate* (1806): and *The Mausoleum at Castle Howard* (1812). His work included decoration of rooms in the west wing of Castle Howard, Yorks. (c. 1800): additions to Wilton Park, nr. Beaconsfield, Bucks. (1803–5): Roche Court, Winterslow, Wilts. (1804).

TATTERSALL, Richard: c. 1803–44

Born at Burnley, Lancs.: a pupil of, and then employed by, William Hayley of Manchester. Set up in independent practice c. 1830, and

228

designed and built cotton mills at Carlisle and Gloubourne, Lancs. His work included St Paul, Stalybridge, Cheshire (1832–3): the Manchester and Salford Bank, Mosley Street, Manchester (1838): St Barnabas, Oldham Road, Manchester (1842–4): the Moral and Industrial Training Schools, Swinton, nr. Manchester (1842–5: completed after his death by his partner, T. Dickson, and W. H. Brakspear).

TAYLOR, George Ledwell, FSA, FRIBA: 1780–1873
Born in London: educated at Rawes's Academy, Bromley, Kent: a pupil of J. T. Parkinson, 1804. With Edward Cresy, he made a walking tour of England in 1816, and of the Continent, including Greece, Malta and Sicily, in 1817–19: together, they published *The Architectural Antiquities of Rome measured and delineated by G. L. Taylor and E. Cresy*, in 1821–2, and *The Architecture of the Middle Ages in Italy*, in 1829. Taylor was Civil Architect to the Naval Department 1824–37: then in independent practice. He was District Surveyor of Westminster 1848: a Fellow of the Institute of Civil Engineers, and a member of the Architects' Club: President of the Architects' and Antiquaries Club 1822–3: he contributed papers to technical and professional journals; visited Italy again in 1856: published *Stones of Etruria and Marbles of Ancient Rome* (1859), and *The Auto-Biography of an Octagenarian Architect* (1870–2). Between 1843 and 1848 he laid out and designed houses in Hyde Park Square, Gloucester Square, Westbourne Terrace and Chester Place, all part of the Bishop of London's Paddington estate: and worked at the naval dockyards of Sheerness, Chatham and Gosport. In 1849 he suffered considerable financial loss owing to the failure of a North Kent railway extension project in which he was professionally involved. His work included No. 5 Suffolk Street, Haymarket, London (1820s): the Melville Hospital, Chatham, Kent (1827): Belmont House, Lee, Lewisham, London (1830): St Martin's National Schools, Adelaide Street, London (1830): the tower of Hadlow Castle Folly, Kent (*c.* 1835): the Custom House, 298 Clyde Street, Glasgow (1840).

TAYLOR, John Henry: d. *c.* 1865
He exhibited at the Royal Academy 1827–41, and in 1834 was one of the committee which formed the Institute of British Architects. He practised in London: laid out Nichols Square, Shoreditch, in 1841; and his work included St John, Walham Green, London

(1827): All Saints, Sidmouth, Devonshire (1837): Infirmary at the Infant Orphan Asylum, Wanstead, Essex (1854).

TAYLOR, Sir Robert: 1714–88

Born at Woodford, Essex, the son of Robert Taylor, a well known mason-contractor and statuary. Apprenticed to Henry Cheere, the sculptor, in 1728: visited Rome. His father died, bankrupt, in 1743, and Taylor returned to England, and with the help of influential friends became well known, first as a sculptor, and then as a highly successful architect. He built up an exceptionally large and lucrative architectural practice; was elected Sheriff of London in 1782, and knighted the same year: became Surveyor to the Bank of England 1765: Architect of the King's Works 1769: Master Carpenter 1777: Deputy Surveyor and Master Mason 1780: Surveyor of Greenwich Hospital 1788: other Surveyorships he held were those of the Admiralty, H.M. Customs, the Foundling Hospital, and Lincoln's Inn. The Taylorian Institute at Oxford was established from a large bequest made by him to the University, for the study of modern European languages. His work included Asgill House, Richmond, Surrey (1758): extensive additions at the Bank of England (1766–83: most of his work now replaced by that of other architects): No. 37 Dover Street, London (1772): Maidenhead Bridge, Berks. (1772–7): Stone Buildings, Lincoln's Inn, London (1774–80: south wing completed by Philip Hardwick): exterior of Heveningham Hall, Suffolk (1778–88).

TAYLOR, Thomas: c. 1778–1826

Began his career in the establishment of a London builder; then for eight years worked for James Wyatt. Started his own practice in Leeds c. 1805, and became well known in Yorkshire as an ecclesiastical architect. The majority of his buildings were churches or schools: his work in Yorkshire included Christ Church, Liversedge (1812–16): Holy Trinity, Huddersfield (1816–19): St Lawrence, Pudsey (1821): St John, Dewsbury (1823–7): St John, Roundhay, Leeds (1824–6): Holy Trinity, Ripon (1826–8).

TELFORD, Thomas: 1757–1834

Born in Dumfriesshire, the son of a shepherd: apprenticed to a mason: worked on the building of Edinburgh New Town: went to London in 1782 and was employed as a journeyman mason at

THOMAS, WILLIAM

Somerset House: he found a patron in William Pulteney, who was
later M.P. for Shrewsbury. In 1788 Telford became County Surveyor of Shropshire; and practised as a surveyor, architect and
bridge builder until his appointment as Surveyor and Engineer to
the Ellesmere Canal in 1793 turned his activities entirely to civil
engineering. He became the first President of the Institute of Civil
Engineers in 1820. His work included the building of the County
Gaol at Shrewsbury (1787–93: to the designs of J. H. Haycock, and
in conformity with the reforms of John Howard): Laura's Tower,
Shrewsbury Castle (1790): St Mary Magdalene, Bridgnorth, Salop
(1792–4): the Aqueduct carrying the Ellesmere Canal over the River
Tern at Longdon, Salop (1794): St Michael, Madeley, Salop
(1796): the Onny Bridge, Stokesay, Salop (1823): St Katharine's
Dock, London (1825–8).

TEULON, Samuel Sanders, FIBA: 1812–73
Of French descent, born at Greenwich, London, the son of Samuel
Teulon: articled to George Legg: worked in the office of George
Porter in Bermondsey. Set up in private practice c. 1840: one of the
early members of the Institute, and served on the Council. He had a
large and successful practice which included much church building
and restoration in the High Victorian Gothic Revival style: his work
has acquired a reputation for extreme ugliness. He designed, laid out,
and built the village of Hunstanworth, Co. Durham (1863), including
the Church of St James, the Vicarage and Schools: his other work
included Tortworth Court, Glos. (1850–2): Christ Church, Croydon,
Surrey (1851–2): Holy Trinity, Hastings, Sussex (1851–9): St
James, Edgbaston, Birmingham (1852): Almshouses (1858) and
School (1860) at South Weald, Essex: St Mark, Silvertown, London
(1861–2): Bestwood Lodge, Notts. (1862): St Mary, Ealing, London
(1866–73): St Stephen, Rosslyn Hill, Hampstead, London (1876).
His brother, William Mitford, FRIBA (1823–1900), founder of the
City Church and Churchyard Protection Society, also practised as
an architect: his work included Overstone Park, Northants (c. 1860:
later a school).

THOMAS, William: d. 1800
The son of William Thomas of Pembrokeshire. In that county he
built Brownslade House, much of Stackpole Court, and Upton, nr.
Carew. He was the author of *Original Designs in Architecture* (1783),

and is best known as the designer of Willersley Castle, Cromford, Derbys. (1782–8), built for Sir Richard Arkwright, whose first cotton-spinning mill was set up at Cromford in 1771.

THOMASON, Yeoville, FRIBA: 1826–1901
Born in Edinburgh: articled to Charles Edge of Birmingham: worked in the architectural department of the Borough Surveyor there: travelled in Italy. He established a large practice in Birmingham, where he was well known, and where his work included the Congregational Chapel, Edgbaston (1855–6): the Synagogue, Blucher Street (1856): City Temple, Acock's Green (1860): Barclays Bank, Temple Row/Colmore Row (1873): the Council House, Colmore Row (1874–9): City Museum and Art Gallery (1881–5): Jaffray Hospital, Erdington (1884–5).

THOMSON, Alexander: 1817–75
Sometimes known as 'Greek' Thomson, born at Balfour in Stirlingshire. He went to Glasgow c. 1824, and there worked in the offices of Robert Foote, and John Baird the elder: in 1847 he went into partnership with John Baird the younger, and later with his own brother, George. He was President of the Glasgow Institute of Architects for two years; his practice, which was almost entirely in Glasgow, included street planning: his work there included the Caledonia Road Free Church (1856–7): Holmwood House, Cathcart (1856–8: later a Convent): the layout of Walmer Crescent (1859–62) and Great Western Terrace (c. 1870): the Egyptian Halls, Union Street (1871–3).

THOMSON, James: 1800–83
The son of David Thomson, of Melrose: apprenticed to John B. Papworth, in London, and later became his assistant: he was one of the earliest members of the Institute. He was much employed in Wiltshire by a wealthy and rather eccentric client, Joseph Neeld, M.P. for Chippenham. Thomson's work included St Giles, Alderton, Wilts. (1845), and probably the Vicarage: rebuilding of St Margaret, Leigh Delamere, Wilts., and Parsonage and Almshouses (c. 1846): School at Sevington, Wilts. (1847): Grittleton House, Wilts. (c. 1848–60: begun by Clutton, whom Thomson succeeded): the Royal Hotel, Tenby, Pem. (1848): the Town Hall, Chippenham, Wilts. (1848): additions to Charing Cross Hospital, London (1877 and 1881).

THORNHILL, Sir James: 1675–1734

Born at Melcombe Regis, Dorset, a member of the local Thornhill family. He is best known for his decorative paintings at Greenwich Hospital, Blenheim Palace, and other great houses: he was History Painter to George I in 1718, and became his Serjeant-Painter in 1720. His architectural work included advice and consultancy: he may have contributed to the design of the west façade at Chatsworth, Derbys. (1700–3): and the design of Moor Park, Herts. (1720), is now attributed to him rather than to Leoni.

THORPE, John: *c.* 1563–*c.* 1655

The son of Thomas Thorpe, a Northamptonshire mason. He went to London *c.* 1583, and became a Clerk in the Queen's Works, employed at Eltham Palace, Whitehall, Hampton Court, the Tower, Greenwich and Richmond. From about 1600 he was a successful land surveyor, his commissions including Crown property. He compiled a book of drawings and plans of well-known houses (now in the Soane Museum), which is valuable for record purposes, but does not offer authentic evidence that Thorpe was the designer of any of the buildings. The designs of Kirby Hall, Northants, Wollaton, Notts., and Longleat House, Wilts., have been attributed to him.

TITE, Sir William, CB, FSA, FRS, FRIBA,: 1798–1873

Born in the City of London, where his father, Arthur Tite, was a successful merchant: educated at day schools in Tower Street and at Hackney: articled to David Laing 1812: attended Sir John Soane's Royal Academy Lectures: by 1824 had set up in practice: travelled in Italy for a year *c.* 1851–2. Tite was a Director of two Banks: M.P. for Bath 1855–73: Royal Gold Medallist 1856: Master of the Spectacle Makers' Company 1862: President of the Cambridge Camden Society 1866: knighted 1869: a Governor of Dulwich College and of St Thomas's Hospital: member of the Metropolitan Board of Works: President of the Architectural Society: twice President of the RIBA: a Trustee of the Soane Museum: Hon. Secretary to the London Institution. In Parliament, he introduced and carried the Metropolis Local Management Act (1864) and promoted the Metropolis Improvements Bill (1867): he was a frequent contributor to professional journals, including the *Transactions of the RIBA*: was the author of *Descriptive Catalogue of Antiquities found in the Excavations of the New Royal Exchange*: delivered many lectures on architecture and archaeology. His architectural practice, both public and private, was very large, and he became successful, extremely well known, and had a distinguished career: he was closely associated with the railway companies of the day, and did much work for them, including the design of stations on the line between Paris and Le Havre: he was in partnership with E. N. Clifton, also a railway architect, for many years. His work included the Scottish Presbyterian Church, Regent Square, St Pancras, London (1824–7): Mill Hill School, Middx. (1825–7: additions since): Golden Cross Hotel, Strand, London (1832: dem. South Africa House now occupies the site): Chapels at the South Metropolitan Cemetery, West Norwood, London (1838): Nine Elms Railway Station, Battersea, London (1838): the Royal Exchange, Threadneedle Street, London (1841–4): Carlisle and Edinburgh Caledonian Railway Stations (1847): Perth Railway Station (1848): Brookwood Cemetery, Surrey (1854: with Sydney Smirke): St James, Gerrards Cross, Bucks. (1859: with E. Trotman).

TOWNSEND, Charles Harrison, FRIBA: 1850–1928
He practised chiefly in London and the southern counties of England: was Master of the Art Workers' Guild: designed textiles and wallpapers: contributed many articles to professional journals. At Hampstead Garden Suburb, Middx., largely laid out between 1907 and 1910, he designed Nos. 135–41 Hampstead Way: his other work included the Bishopsgate Institute, London (1894): St Martin, Blackheath, nr. Wonersh, Surrey (1895): Whitechapel Art Gallery, London (1897–8): Horniman Museum, Forest Hill, London (1902): St Mary the Virgin, Great Warley, Essex (1904): the School, Penn, Bucks. (1910).

TRESHAM, Sir Thomas: 1543–1605
A member of the Tresham family of Rushton Hall, Northants, he inherited the estates in 1558; was knighted 1575; became a Roman Catholic in 1580 and, as a result of this conversion, suffered imprisonment and fines. Though there is disagreement over the authorship of his designs, his work is generally believed to have included the Market House, Rothwell, Northants (c. 1577: assisted by William Grumbold, mason): the Triangular Lodge, Rushton, Northants (1593–5): Rushton Hall, Northants (1595).

TROLLOPE, Robert: d. 1686

A mason and architect of York, who began to practise in Newcastle-on-Tyne in the mid-seventeenth century, and became well known locally. His work in Northumberland included the Guildhall, Newcastle-on-Tyne (1658: much altered and remodelled since): Christ Church, North Shields (1658–68: rebuilt since): Capheaton Hall (1668).

THE TRUBSHAW FAMILY

The name of a Staffordshire family of masons, builders and architects. Richard (1689–1745) was a prosperous builder at Haywood, Staffs.: he is believed to have worked at Oxford in his youth. He carried out additions and alterations at many large houses, for the local gentry: built the wings and refronted the central block of Emral Hall, Flint. (1724–7: with Joseph Evans: dem.): Holy Trinity, Baswich, Staffs. (1739–40: with Richard Jackson): St Peter, Marchington, Staffs. (1724: altered since). His son, Charles Cope (1715–72), born at Haywood, Staffs., studied under Scheemakers in London, and became a sculptor and monumental mason. He also carried on his father's building and architectural practice: his work included the building of the Temple of the Winds at Shugborough Park, Staffs. (1764: to the designs of James Stuart). His son, James, the elder (1746–1808), continued the family business, and was County Surveyor of Staffordshire, but little is known of his work. His son, James, the younger (1777–1853), educated at Rugeley, learned the building and masons' trade from his father, and after some experience at Fonthill Abbey, Buckingham Palace and Windsor Castle set up his own business in Stone, Staffs., c. 1800. In 1808, he took over the family business at Haywood, and became a successful builder, architect and civil engineer. He was a member of the Society of Civil Engineers, and Engineer to the Trent and Mersey Canal Company: he was in partnership with Thomas Johnson of Lichfield. The work of James Trubshaw the younger included Ashcombe Hall, Staffs. (c. 1808–11): St Michael, Great Wolford, Warwicks. (1833–5). Thomas, FSA (1802–42), the son of James the younger, practised as an architect and landscape gardener in Staffs., and the neighbourhood, where he designed a number of churches, and Manley Hall, nr. Lichfield.

TRUBSHAW, Charles, FRIBA: 1841–1917
He was Architect to the Midland Railway Company for many years, before his retirement in 1905. He specialized in railway work – hotels, stations, depots, warehouses, offices – and practised in the Midlands and North. His work included the Queen's Hotel, Leeds, Yorks.: the Midland Hotel, Central Railway Station, Manchester (1897–1903): the South African War Memorial, Derby (1899–1902): Midland Railway Station, Sheffield, Yorks. (1905).

TRUEFITT, George, FRIBA: 1824–1902
A pupil of L. N. Cottingham: articled to Sancton Wood; became his assistant: and also worked as assistant to Harvey Eginton of Worcester: visited France and Germany. He established a large practice, mostly in church building, which included commissions at the Glen Tana Estate, Aberdeenshire, and in the south of France: he was Architect to the Tufnell Estate in London, and designed houses in Camden Road, Islington. His work included Royal Exchange Assurance offices, Chancery Lane, Manchester (built as Brooks's Bank): St George, Tufnell Park, London (1868): St George, Worthing, Sussex (1868): the rebuilding of St Leonard, Blakmere, Herefs. (1877): St John, Bromley, Kent (1880): St John, Farley Hill, Berks. (1890–2).

TUFNELL, Edward: 1678–1719
The son of John Tufnell, Master Mason to Westminster Abbey, which post Edward Tufnell held from 1696 to 1719. He became well known as a master builder, working on repairs to Westminster Abbey under Sir Christopher Wren: on contracts for some of the Fifty New Churches authorized in 1711: and on rebuilding at Langleys, Great Waltham, Essex (c. 1719). His son, Samuel (d. 1765), became Master Mason at Westminster Abbey in 1737, and practised as a builder and sculptor. He is believed to have assisted with the rebuilding of the tower of St Margaret, Westminster, London (1735–7): he built and possibly designed Nos. 11–14 Cavendish Square, London; and, with Andrews Jelfe, carried out the building of Westminster Bridge, London (1738–50: dem. and rebuilt since).

UNDERWOOD, George Allen: nineteenth century
He worked for Sir John Soane from 1807 to 1815, and then set up in independent practice at Cheltenham. He became County Surveyor of Dorset and Somerset, and practised in the west of England. His work included the Masonic Hall, Cheltenham, Glos. (1817–23): Holy Trinity, Cheltenham (1820–22): Frome Bridge, Som. (1821): the Royal Literary Institution, Bath, Som. (1823–5: dem.): St Mary, Timsbury, Som. (1826): Christ Church, Frome, Som. (1844: alterations since).

UNDERWOOD, Henry Jones: 1804–52
Studied under Sir Robert Smirke: and at the Royal Academy Schools in 1825. He built up his own practice at Oxford, with some success, and was in partnership with E. G. Bruton, who took over the practice when Underwood committed suicide. Underwood was the author of *Elevations, Sections and Details of Littlemore Church* (1845): and *Oxford Parish Burial Ground Chapels* (1849). His work included the porter's lodge, Library and Lecture Room at the Botanical Gardens, Oxford (1835): Ascension Church, Littleworth, Berks. (1839: chancel later): Holy Trinity, Lower Beeding, Sussex (1840: enlarged since): SS Mary and Nicholas, Littlemore, Oxon. (c. 1841): rebuilding of the Vicarage, Whaplode, Lincs. (1842): the Swedenborgian Church, Henry Street, Bath, Som. (1844): the Rectory, Didcot, Berks. (1852: completed by Bruton).

UNWIN, Sir Raymond, FRIBA: 1863–1940
Born in Yorkshire, the son of William Unwin of Balliol College, Oxford: educated Magdalen College School, Oxford. He was trained as an engineer, but became a distinguished town planner with an international reputation. He was in partnership with the architect, Barry Parker, and joint author with him of *The Art of Building a Home*. Together, they laid out the first garden city in England, at Letchworth, Herts., in 1903: this was followed by the garden village of New Earswick, nr. York, for the Joseph Rowntree Village Trust (1902 onwards: Unwin was Architect to the Trust from 1902–19: Barry Parker from 1919–46): Hampstead Garden Suburb, Middx. (1906 onwards): Pinehurst Estate, Swindon, Wilts. (1919): Barry Parker, in 1927–39, laid out the Shelthorpe Road

Estate, Loughborough, Leics. Unwin was Director of Housing to a Ministry of Munitions Department during the First World War: he then became Chief Technical Officer for Building and Town Planning at the Ministry of Health; served on government committees connected with housing and town planning; lectured at Birmingham University and abroad: among his published works was *Town Planning in Practice* (1906). He succeeded Sir Ebenezer Howard as President of the International Federation for Housing and Town Planning in 1928: was President of the Town Planning Institute: President of the RIBA 1931–3: knighted 1932. He designed and built St Andrew, Barrow Hill, nr. Staveley, Derbys. (1895). The architectural work of Barry Parker, who also practised privately, included Woodcote, Church Stretton, Salop (1895–1903): Kildare Lodge, Minehead, Som. (1903): Oakdene, Rotherfield, Sussex (1907): The Clock House, Cowfold, Sussex (1913–14).

VANBRUGH, Sir John: 1664–1726 (Portrait: see Plate II)
Born in London, the son of Giles Vanbrugh, a merchant of Flemish descent: his childhood was spent at Chester. He was a soldier from 1686 to 1702, serving at first in the Earl of Huntingdon's regiment of foot: he spent eighteen months in French prisons, including the Bastille: later he held the rank of captain in the marines, and rejoined the Earl of Huntingdon's regiment before he finally left the Army. Vanbrugh became a successful dramatist, his first play, *The Relapse*, being produced in 1696, and *The Provok'd Wife* in 1697. He was a member of the Kit-Kat Club: from 1704 to 1725 Claren-ceaux King of Arms; knighted in 1714. His architectural career began in 1699 with the designs he prepared for Castle Howard, Yorks., for his friend and patron the third Earl of Carlisle: he was appointed Comptroller of H.M. Works in 1702: became Surveyor of Gardens and Waterworks belonging to the Royal Palaces in 1714: and Surveyor to Greenwich Hospital in 1716: he was professionally associated with Nicholas Hawksmoor, who certainly contributed much to Vanbrugh's designs, and was also his personal friend. Vanbrugh's work included Castle Howard, Yorks. (1699–1726: assisted by Hawksmoor: west wing by Sir Thomas Robinson): the King William Block and completion of the Great Hall at Greenwich Hospital, London (c. 1703–28): Blenheim Palace, Oxon. (1705–20: Hawksmoor was his assistant and later took entire charge): King's Weston, Glos. (1711–14): the Town Hall, Morpeth, Northumb. (1714: burned since, but restored to original design): Vanbrugh Castle, Westcombe Park Road, Greenwich, London (1717–26): Robin Hood's Well, nr. Doncaster, Yorks. (c. 1720): Seaton Delaval, Northumb. (1720–28: much damaged by fire since).

VARDY, John: d. 1765
He was Clerk of the Works at Greenwich 1736–45: Hampton Court 1745–6: Whitehall and St James's 1746–54: Kensington 1754–61, and Chelsea Hospital 1756–65. For William Kent, he published *Some Designs of Mr Inigo Jones and Mr William Kent* (1744), and he was professionally associated with Kent, William Robinson, and Kenton Couse. He exhibited at the Society of Artists 1761–4. His son, John, is believed to have designed the exterior of Uxbridge House, Bur-lington Gardens, London, with Joseph Bonomi, in 1792. The work

of the elder Vardy included the building of the Horse Guards, White-hall, London (1750–60: with William Robinson and to the designs of William Kent): Spencer House, Green Park, London (1756–65: under the supervision of Colonel Gray of the Society of Dilettanti): a range of buildings to the west of Westminster Hall, London (1758–70: with Kenton Couse: destroyed by fire 1834).

VERITY, Thomas, FRIBA: 1837–91
He practised in partnership with G. H. Hunt, and in his later years with his son, F. T. Verity, and was well known as a designer of theatres: he was Consulting Architect to the Lord Chamberlain. His work included the Criterion Restaurant, Piccadilly Circus (1870–4): the Spa Buildings, Scarborough, Yorks. (1877–80: with Hunt): the Comedy Theatre, Panton Street, Haymarket, London (1881): Hill's Hygienic Bakery, Buckingham Gate, London (1887): the Guildhall, Nottingham (1888: with Hunt): Nos. 96–97 Piccadilly, London (1891: with F. T. Verity: built as the New Travellers' Club): the French Hospital, Shaftesbury Avenue, London (with F. T. Verity, who added an annexe).

VERITY, Francis Thomas, FRIBA: d. 1937
Born in London, the son of Thomas Verity: educated Cranleigh: articled to his father: was also a pupil of Phené Spiers: studied at the Royal College of Art, South Kensington; at University College; at the AA; and in Paris. He was in partnership with his father: succeeded him as Architect to the Lord Chamberlain's Department: and was European adviser to the Paramount Cinema Company. Verity specialized in the design of theatres and cinemas, chiefly in London, but also in Paris. In London, he built flats at No. 12 Bayswater Road, and Nos. 11a and 11b Portland Place. His work included the Pavilion, Lord's Cricket Ground, London (1890): St John's Hospital, off Leicester Square, London (1897): the Scala Theatre, Charlotte Street, London (1904): Sudan House, Cleveland Row, London (1905): the Pavilion, Shepherd's Bush, London (1923).

VERTUE, Robert: d. 1506, and William: d. 1527
The sons of Adam Vertue, a mason, with whom Robert worked as an apprentice at Westminster Abbey. The brothers were both King's Master Masons, Robert in 1506 and William in 1510. Together, they were the designers of Bath Abbey Church (1501

onwards). Robert designed Henry VII's Chapel at Westminster Abbey (*c.* 1503–12), and this was continued by William after his brother's death. William was the designer of the chancel vault of St George's Chapel, Windsor, Berks. (1506–11): Lupton's Tower at Eton College, Bucks. (1515: with Henry Redman): and probably of the Chapel of St Peter ad Vincula in the Tower of London (1520).

VOYSEY, Charles Francis Annesley: 1857–1941

Born at Hessle, nr. Kingston-upon-Hull, the son of the Rev. C. Voysey, Vicar of Healaugh, Yorks.: his grandfather, Annesley Voysey, had built lighthouses and bridges. Educated Dulwich College: articled to J. P. Seddon: worked for him, and later for Saxon Snell and George Devey: set up in independent practice in London in 1881. He became a leader of the Modern Movement: was Master of the Art Workers' Guild 1924: was one of the first Designers for Industry (later RDI) of the Royal Society of Arts: Royal Gold Medallist 1940. He designed many country houses, also textiles, wallpapers, carpets, bookplates, and furniture and fittings: was the author of *Individuality* and *Reason as a Basis of Art*, and of many professional papers and lectures. His work included 14 South Parade, Bedford Park, London (1889): Nos. 14–16 Hans Road, Kensington, London (1891): Lowicks, nr. Frensham, Surrey (1894): Annesley Lodge, Hampstead, London (1895): Greyfriars, Puttenham, Surrey (1896): Dixcote, North Drive, Tooting Bec, London (1897): New Place, Haslemere, Surrey (1897): Broadleys, Windermere, Westmorland (1898): Spade House, nr. Folkestone, Kent (1900): The Orchard, Chorleywood, Herts. (1900–1): Sanderson's factory, Barley Mow Passage, Turnham Green, London (1902: now Alliance Assurance): Holly Mount, Knotty Green, Bucks. (1906–7).

VULLIAMY, Lewis: 1791–1871

The son of Benjamin Vulliamy, the clockmaker: articled to Sir Robert Smirke: studied at the Royal Academy, winning Silver and Gold Medals: from 1818–22 travelled on the Continent. He then set up in private practice, became successful and well known, and built many churches. He published *The Bridge of the Sta. Trinita at Florence* (1822): and *Examples of Ornamental Sculpture in Architecture, from Greece, Asia Minor, and Italy* (1823). His work included Boothby Pagnell Hall, Lincs. (1824): St Barnabas, Addison Road, Kensington, London (1828): St Michael, Highgate, London (1830): the

Law Society, Chancery Lane, London (1831): the Congregational Church, Vineyard, Richmond, Surrey (1831): Christ Church, Woburn Square, London (1831–3): Hickey's Almshouses, Sheen Road, Richmond, Surrey (1834): Christ Church, Todmorden, Yorks. (1834): refronting of the Royal Institution, Albemarle Street, London (1838): St Mary's Rectory, Burston, Norfolk (1840): rebuilding of Westonbirt House, Tetbury, Glos. (c. 1850): Dorchester House, Park Lane, London (1851–71: dem. 1929): Shernfield Park, Frant, Sussex (1853).

VULLIAMY, George John: 1817–86
Born in London, the nephew of Lewis Vulliamy: educated Westminster School: articled to the engineering firm of Joseph Bramah & Sons: and to Sir Charles Barry from 1836 to 1841: travelled on the Continent and in Asia Minor and Egypt 1841–3. Vulliamy set up his own practice in London in 1843, also assisting his uncle: he was Superintending Architect to the Metropolitan Board of Works from 1861 to 1886, and for many years Secretary of the Royal Archaeological Institute of Gt Britain and Ireland. With Alfred Mott, he built many Fire Stations in the metropolitan area, and designed the pedestal and sphinxes for Cleopatra's Needle on the Victoria Embankment, in London. His work included the Swiss Protestant Church, Endell Street, London (1853): the Fire Station, Bishopsgate, London (1885).

WALLACE, William: d. 1631
A Scotsman, who was appointed King's Master Mason in Scotland
in 1617: he may have visited England and the Netherlands. He is
believed to have built part of Linlithgow Palace (1619 and 1620),
and his work included Wintoun House, Haddingtonshire (1620),
and Heriot's Hospital, Edinburgh (1628–31: continued after his
death by his assistant, William Aytoun, though financial setbacks
delayed its completion till after 1650).

WALTERS, Edward: 1808–72
Born at Fenchurch Buildings, in the City of London, the house
and office of his father, John Walters, an architect who was Surveyor to the London Hospital, and designed St Paul, Shadwell,
Stepney, London (1817–21). Edward Walters was educated at
Brighton: a pupil of Isaac Clarke: worked for Thomas Cubitt,
Lewis Vulliamy, and Sir John Rennie, for whom he superintended
the construction of arsenal buildings and a small-arms factory in
Constantinople in 1822–37: he returned to England in 1838,
visiting Italy *en route*. Walters set up in practice in Manchester
in 1839: in addition to many warehouses and commercial buildings
in the city, he designed several local railway stations for the Midland
Railway Company, and laid out the line between Ambersgate and
Manchester in collaboration with W. H. Barlow, in 1860. His
work in Manchester included a warehouse at 15 Mosley Street
(1839), and one at the corner of Aytoun/Portland Streets (later
Hickson, Lloyd & King): the Union Chapel (1841): warehouses
for James Brown, Son & Co., at 9 Portland Street (1851) and in
George Street: the Free Trade Hall, Peter Street (1853–6): Williams
Deacon's Bank, Mosley Street (1860: built as the Manchester and
Salford Bank).

WARDELL, William Wilkins: 1823–1900
Born in London: went to sea as a youth: on his return was employed
in the London offices of a surveyor, and of an architect. He worked
at first on railway surveying, but, becoming a friend of A. W. N.
Pugin, he turned to ecclesiastical work, and built many Roman
Catholic churches in England between 1846 and *c.* 1857, when he
emigrated to Australia. He set up in practice in Melbourne, where

he had a distinguished public career. He was Chief Architect to the government authorities in Melbourne: Inspector-General of Public Works and Buildings in Victoria 1869–78: superintended the construction of many public buildings in Melbourne, and was Architect to the English, Scottish & Australian Bank. His work included the Convent of the Holy Child Jesus, Hastings, Sussex (1846–8: additions since): St John the Baptist, Hackney, London (1847: severely war damaged): Our Lady of Victories, Clapham, London (1849–51: except Lady Chapel and north transept): Our Lady Star of the Sea, Croom's Hill, Greenwich, London (1851): St Joseph's Almshouses, Brook Green, London (1851): Virgo Fidelis Convent, Upper Norwood, Surrey (1857: additions since): St John's College, Sydney University, Australia (1852): Cathedral of St Mary, Sydney, Australia (1865): Cathedral of St Patrick, Melbourne, Australia (1865).

WARE, Isaac: d. 1766
Believed to have been a chimney sweeper's boy, but apart from his humble origins, nothing is known of his early life: he became the protégé of an influential nobleman, possibly Lord Burlington, who financed his education and a visit to Italy, and introduced him to other potential patrons. Ware held a number of official posts: Clerk of the Works at Windsor Castle 1729: Clerk of the Works at Greenwich 1733: Clerk Itinerant and Draughtsman to the Board of Works c. 1733: and Secretary to the Board of Works 1736. He published *Designs of Inigo Jones and Others* (1st edition possibly 1735, others in 1743 and 1756): *The Complete Body of Architecture* (1st edition possibly 1735: others, 1756, 1760, 1767): a translation of *Palladio* (1738): a translation of Sirrigatti's *Practice of Perspective* (1756): an edition of Brook Taylor's *Method of Perspective* (1766). He made the official drawings for Kent's design for the Horse Guards (1750–58): was Master of the Carpenters' Company in 1763. Much of his work has disappeared, but it included the conversion of Lanesborough House, Hyde Park Corner, London, into an infirmary, the Lock Hospital (1733: rebuilt as St George's Hospital by William Wilkins in 1828): Westbourne House, Paddington, London (1742: dem.: Porchester Hall occupies the site): Clifton Hill House, Clifton, Bristol (1746–50): Chesterfield House, South Audley Street, London (1748–9: dem. 1937): Wrotham Hall, Potters Bar, Middx. (1754). Foot's

Cray Place, Kent, has also been attributed to Ware (built *c.* 1754).

WARE, Samuel, FSA: 1781–1860

Studied at the Royal Academy 1800: exhibited there 1799–1814. He contributed papers to *Archaeologia*: was the author of *Remarks on Theatres, and on the propriety of vaulting them with brick and stone, with an Appendix on the construction of Gothic vaulting* (1809): *A Treatise of the Property of Arches* (1809): and *Tracts on Vaults and Bridges* (1822). His work included the Burlington Arcade, Piccadilly, London (1815–19): and the internal remodelling of Burlington House, Piccadilly, London (1816–18).

WASTELL, John: d. *c.* 1515

He probably learned his trade at Canterbury, where he became Master Mason to Cardinal Morton, and built the central tower of the Cathedral (1490–*c.* 1497). Wastell then moved to Bury St Edmunds, Suffolk, where he is believed to have contributed much to the building of the Cathedral (*c.* 1510–30). He was Master Mason for the work done at King's College Chapel, Cambridge, in 1508–15, which included the great vault of the chapel, and he is believed to have designed the retrochoir at Peterborough Cathedral, Northants (*c.* 1496–1508).

WATERHOUSE, Alfred, RA, FRIBA: 1830–1905

Born in Liverpool, the son of Alfred Waterhouse: educated Grove House School, Tottenham: articled to Richard Lane of Manchester: travelled and studied in France, Germany and Italy. He first practised in Manchester, then moved to London: he had a long and successful career, and an enormous practice, in which he was joined in partnership by his son, Paul, in 1891. Waterhouse was Architect to the Prudential Assurance Company for many years, and built offices for them in most large provincial towns: he was a member of the Organizing Committee for the Imperial Institute, and of the Westminster Abbey Commission: he won the Paris Exhibition Grand Prix for Architecture 1867: Royal Gold Medallist 1878: President of the RIBA 1888–91: President of the Society for Checking the Abuses of Public Advertising: and Lord of the Manor of Yattendon, Berks. His work (easily identified by the terracotta in which he delighted) included the Assize Courts, Manchester (1859–64: war damaged): Barcombe Cottage, Fallowfield,

Manchester (1861: later the Barcombe Hotel): Union Society, Cambridge (1866): West Memorial Institute, and Amersham Hall, Caversham, Reading (1865–6): Reading School, Berks. (1865–7): the Broad Street façade of Balliol College, Oxford (1866–8): the Town Hall, Manchester (1868): Tree Court, Caius College, Cambridge (1870): Municipal Buildings, Reading, Berks. (1872–5:) additions since): the Natural History Museum, South Kensington, London (1873–81): Girton College, Cambridge (1873: completed by Paul Waterhouse): the Seamen's Orphanage, Liverpool (1874): Baptist Free Church, Caversham, Reading, Berks. (1875–7): the Reading Room, Yattendon, Berks. (1878): Prudential Assurance Company's head office, Holborn, London (1879 and 1899–1906): St Paul's School, Hammersmith, London (1881–5): St Elizabeth, Reddish, Stockport, Cheshire (1883): the Town Hall, Hove, Sussex (1882): Buckhold House, Berks. (1884–5): the National Liberal Club, Whitehall Place, London (1885–7): Royal Infirmary, Liverpool (1887): Metropole Hotel, Brighton, Sussex (1888: many additions since): the School, Yattendon, Berks. (1891): Royal Institution of Chartered Surveyors, Gt George Street, London (1896–8: additions by Paul Waterhouse): University College Hospital, London (1897–1906: completed by Paul Waterhouse): Prudential Assurance Company's offices, North Street, Brighton, Sussex (1904).

WATERHOUSE, Paul, FRIBA: 1861–1924
The eldest son of Alfred Waterhouse: educated at Eton, and Balliol College, Oxford. In 1891 he went into partnership with his father, and continued the practice after his retirement in 1901, completing University College Hospital, London, designed by Alfred Waterhouse in 1897, and himself designing the Medical School and Nurses' Home, and making additions to other of his father's buildings. Paul Waterhouse was President of the RIBA 1921–3, and Chairman of the Board of Architectural Education. His work included the tower wing at Girton College, Cambridge (1887): No. 15 Buckingham Street, Adelphi, London (1906): the Schools of Chemistry, Oxford (1913).

WATSON, John Burges, FIBA: 1803–81
Studied under William Atkinson, and at the Royal Academy, where he exhibited 1824–38. He was a water-colour artist, and

246

amateur musician: set up in practice in 1825 as an architect and landscape gardener: was for many years Surveyor to the Pentonville Estate: a founder of the Architectural Society. His work included St Mary, Staines, Middx. (1828): the Vicarage at Norton, Herts. (1831): and the lodge for the Ornithological Society, on the lake in St James's Park, London (1840).

WEBB, Sir Aston, KCVO, CB, RA, FRIBA: 1849–1930
Born at Clapham, London, the son of Edward Webb, a well-known water-colour artist and engraver: educated at private schools in Brighton: articled to Banks and Barry: spent a year in continental travel. Webb set up in practice in London in 1873: he collaborated closely with E. Ingress Bell, FRIBA (1837–1914), with whom he was appointed Consulting Architect to the Crown Agents for the Colonies, in 1882. Webb was President of the AA 1884: President of the RIBA 1902–4: knighted 1904: Royal Gold Medallist 1905: awarded the Gold Medal of the American Institute of Architects 1907: President of the Royal Academy 1919–24: one of the earliest members of the Royal Fine Art Institution: a Trustee of the Soane Museum: Chairman of the Board of Architectural Education: received many national and professional honours. He was later assisted by his son, Maurice. Aston Webb's work included the Victoria Law Courts, Corporation Street, Birmingham (1887–91: with Ingress Bell): No. 23 Austin Friars, London (1888: with Ingress Bell): the restoration of St Bartholomew-the-Great, West Smithfield, London (1890s): Victoria and Albert Museum, London (1891: built 1899–1909): the French Protestant Church, Soho Square, London (1893): Royal United Service Institution, Whitehall, London (1893–5: with Ingress Bell): Christ's Hospital, Horsham, Sussex (1893–1902: with Ingress Bell): Mumford's Flour Mills, Greenwich, London (1897): the School, Ticehurst, Sussex (1899): planning of the Victoria Memorial, and rond-point outside Buckingham Palace, London (1900–1: sculpture by Sir Thomas Brock): Birmingham University, Edgbaston, Birmingham (1900–9: with Ingress Bell: considerable additions and replanning since): St Michael's Court, Caius College, Cambridge (1903): Royal School of Mines, South Kensington, London (1909–13): Admiralty Arch, London (1911): the refacing of Buckingham Palace, London (1913): Library and George V Gateway, Leys School, Cambridge (1913–14).

WEBB, JOHN

WEBB, John: 1611–72
Born in London, but his family came from Somerset: educated at Merchant Taylors' School, 1625–8, and then became a pupil of Inigo Jones, whose niece he married. Webb was assistant to Jones for many years, worked closely with him before and during the Civil War, when both were Royalists, and the reliable identification of the work of each is far from certain. In 1666, Webb became Assistant-Surveyor of the King's Works, his petition for the Surveyorship being passed over in favour of Sir John Denham, and again, in 1669, in favour of Sir Christopher Wren. In 1655, using material prepared by Inigo Jones, Webb published *The Most notable Antiquity of Great Britain, vulgarly called Stone-Heng. . . . Restored, by Inigo Jones Esq., Architect General to the King*, and in 1665 *Vindication of Stone-Heng Restored*, a reply to criticisms of the first book. His work included the south front of Wilton House, Wilts. (1649: Inigo Jones advised on the design): Lamport Hall, Northants (c. 1654–7): portico and interiors at The Vyne, Hants (c. 1655): Amesbury House, Amesbury, Wilts. (1661: since dem. and rebuilt to similar design by Thomas Hopper): alterations to the Queen's House, Greenwich, London, and addition of bridges on east and west fronts (1661–2): King Charles II Block, Royal Naval College, Greenwich, London (1665–8).

WEBB, Philip Speakman: 1831–1915
Born in Oxford, the son of a doctor: educated Aynho Grammar School, Northants: articled to John Billing of Reading: worked in the office of G. E. Street, in Oxford, where he met William Morris, and later became Street's chief assistant. Webb started independent practice in London in 1856, and joined the firm of Morris, Marshall, Faulkner & Co., which Morris founded in 1861, and for which Webb designed jewellery, embroidery, stained glass, furniture and decorative schemes. In 1877, he and Morris founded the Society for the Protection of Ancient Buildings. Webb's work included the Red House, Upton, nr. Bexleyheath, Kent (1859): Fairmile, nr. Cobham, Surrey (1860: later a school): No. 1 Palace Green, Kensington, London (1863): Nos. 91–101 Worship Street, Shoreditch, London (1863): No. 19 Lincoln's Inn Fields, London (1868): No. 35 Glebe Place, Chelsea, London (1869): Upwood Gorse, Caterham, Surrey (1873: and subsequent additions): Smeaton Manor, Gt Smeaton, Yorks. (1875–8): the School at East

248

Rounton, Yorks. (1876): Clouds, East Knoyle, Wilts. (1879: much altered since): offices of Dorman Long, Zetland Road, Middlesbrough, Yorks. (1883): Coneyhurst, Ewhurst, Surrey (1886): Standen, East Grinstead, Sussex (1891–4): Hurlands, Puttenham, Surrey (1898).

WEBSTER, George: nineteenth century
His family practised as architects and sculptors in Kendal, Westmorland: much of their monumental work is found in Lancashire, and other north-western and mid-western counties. George Webster designed the Assembly Rooms, Kendal (1825–7: later the Town Hall): Eshton Hall, Yorks. (1825–7): St Paul, Lindale, Lancs. (1828–9): the Town Hall, Settle, Yorks. (1832).

WHICHCORD, John, the elder: 1790–1860
Born at Devizes, Wilts., the son of a local surveyor: articled to C. Harcourt Masters of Bath, in 1806: worked under D. A. Alexander in London, and at Maidstone, where Whichcord later practised, and where he built the Corn Exchange and Kent Fire Office. He was County Surveyor of Kent, Surveyor to the Medway Navigation Company, and was assisted from 1845 by his son, John. His work included Holy Trinity, Maidstone, Kent (1826–8: alterations since): the Godstone Union Workhouse, Bletchingley, Surrey (c. 1840: later Orchard Croft): St John the Evangelist, Blindley Heath, Surrey (1842: with Walker): St Philip, Maidstone, Kent (1858): the Kent County Prison, Canterbury, Kent (c. 1858–9: with Blandford).

WHICHCORD, John, the younger, FSA, FRIBA: 1823–85
The son of John Whichcord of Maidstone: educated there, and at King's College, London: studied at the Royal Academy and in his father's office, where he did much railway surveying in Kent, and hydraulic work on the River Medway. From 1846 to 1850 he travelled widely on the Continent and in Asia Minor. He was in partnership for a time with Arthur Ashpitel, and with him published *Observations on Baths and Wash-houses*, and *Erection of Fireproof Houses in Flats*: Whichcord's own published work included *The History and Antiquities of the Christ Church, Maidstone*, and *The History and Antiquities of St Mary's, Aldermanbury*. He was District Surveyor of Deptford 1854: President of the RIBA 1879–81: President of the

Architects' Benevolent Society 1881: Consulting Architect for the Houses of Parliament in Cape Town: a Railway Surveyor at the Board of Trade. He designed office and commercial buildings in the City of London, and his work included St Mary, Shortlands, Kent, and the parsonage: Grand Hotel, Brighton, Sussex (1862–4): National Safe Deposit, Queen Victoria Street, London (1873).

WHITE, John: *c.* 1747–1813
Surveyor to the Duke of Portland, for whom he laid out the Portland Estate in London, from 1787 onwards; and in which White himself had a large speculative interest. He submitted a number of plans for the development of Marylebone Park and its neighbourhood, but the project was assigned to John Nash. White practised as an architect and builder in London. His work included houses on the west side of Harley Street, between New Cavendish Street and Weymouth Street: a workhouse and infirmary for St Marylebone, which he designed without fee (1775 and 1796–7): and Glevering Hall, nr. Easton, Suffolk (1792–4). His son, John (d. 1850), educated at Ray's Academy in London, assisted his father in the Portland Estate Surveyorship: succeeded to his practice; was District Surveyor for St Marylebone 1807–50: a Commissioner of the Property Tax: and a Commissioner of Sewers for Westminster. He published *On Cementitious Architecture as applicable to the construction of Bridges*: *An Essay on the Formation of Harbours of Refuge* (an account of a floating breakwater which he had patented): and *Some Account of the Proposed Improvements in the Western Part of London by the Formation of the Regent's Park, etc.*

WHITE, William, FSA, FRIBA: 1825–1900
The son of the Rev. Francis White, curate of Blakesley, Northants, and great-nephew of Gilbert White of Selborne: articled to D. G. Squirhill of Leamington: worked in the office of Sir George Gilbert Scott in London: set up in practice in Truro *c.* 1847. White did much church building and restoration in Cornwall: was a supporter of the Ecclesiological Society, and a contributor to professional journals: President of the AA 1868–9. His work included All Saints, Notting Hill, London (1852): the Church of St Hilary, at St Hilary, Cornwall (1854): St Lawrence's Rectory, Lurgashall, Sussex (1854): St Michael's Retreat House, Wantage, Berks. (1855: additions since): the rebuilding of St Petrock, Little Petherick,

Cornwall (1858): St Mark, Battersea Rise, London (1873):
Winscott, nr. St Giles in the Wood, Devonshire (1864): St Stephen,
Reading, Berks. (1864-6: enlarged since): St John, Felbridge,
Surrey (1865): the church and vicarage (later school), Merifield,
Cornwall (1865): Holy Trinity, Barnstaple, Devonshire (1867):
St Mary, Langdon Hills, Essex (1876): St Luke, Balham, London
(1883).

WIGHTWICK, George: 1802-72
Born near Mold, Flint., the son of a country gentleman: educated
at Wolverhampton Grammar School, and Lord's School, Tooting:
articled to Edward Lapidge: visited Italy 1825-6: then worked
for Sir John Soane as a kind of secretary-companion. He went to
Plymouth in 1829, where he practised as an architect in partnership
with John Foulston, and independently after Foulston's retirement,
till 1851. He was the author of many books, including *Select Views
of Roman Antiquities* (1827): *Remarks on Theatres* (1832): *The Palace
of Architecture* (1840): and *Hints to Young Architects* (1846). He also
lectured and contributed articles to such publications as Loudon's
Architectural Magazine, and Weale's *Quarterly Papers on Architecture*.
Apart from buildings in which he collaborated with John Foulston,
his work included the Guildhall, and the Grammar School, Helston,
Cornwall (1834): the Devon & Cornwall Female Orphanage,
Plymouth (1834): St Michael, Bude, Cornwall (1835): the Esplanade, Plymouth (1836): St John's Chapel, Pendarves House,
Treslothan, Cornwall (1841): St Mary, Portreath, Cornwall
(1841): St Luke, Tideford, Cornwall (1845): Holy Trinity, Plymouth (1845).

WILD, James William: 1814-92
The son of the artist Charles Wild: articled to George Basevi in
1830: was established in his own practice by 1840: between 1842
and 1848 he travelled on the Continent and in Asia Minor and
Egypt, making a study of Arab art and architecture, on which he
became an authority. Wild was appointed to supervise the architectural decorations at the Great Exhibition of 1851, and from
1853 worked as an expert on Arabian art at the South Kensington
Museum, where he remained for many years. He was Curator of
the Soane Museum from 1878 to 1892: and a contributor to

Loudon's *Encyclopaedia of Cottage, Farm and Villa Architecture* (1833). He designed the Consular buildings at Alexandria and Teheran: his work included Holy Trinity, Blackheath, London (1840): Christ Church, Streatham, London (1842): St Mark, Alexandria, Egypt (1848): St Martin's Northern District School, Endell Street, London (1849): the Dock Tower, Grimsby, Lincs. (1852): architectural courts at the South Kensington Museum (*c.* 1853): the Bethnal Green Museum, London (1875).

WILDS, Amon: *c.* 1762–1833
A Sussex builder, who worked first at Lewes, then, with his son, extending his practice to Brighton as well, and finally, *c.* 1820, he moved to Brighton and in 1822 went into partnership with C. A. Busby. The device of an ammonite on buildings, found at Lewes and Brighton, is believed to signify the work of Amon Wilds or his son. Wilds was Surveyor to the Brighton Town Commissioners 1825–8, and became a Commissioner in 1832: much of the work he built was designed by Busby or by his son, Amon Henry, and included a large part of Kemp Town, and Hove development. Amon Wilds was the architect of 166 Castle Place, Lewes, Sussex (1810): Nos. 4–6 Richmond Terrace, Brighton, Sussex (1818): the Elim Free Church, Union Street, Brighton, Sussex (1825).

WILDS, Amon Henry: b. *c.* 1790
The son of Amon Wilds. He practised as an architect and builder, first at Lewes with his father, then (1815–22) at Brighton with his father and C. A. Busby. With the latter, he probably contributed much to the architectural design side of the partnership, his father acting as builder. In 1822, the younger Wilds began to practise on his own account; a great deal of his work was in Brighton, where he was a Commissioner from 1845–8. He is believed to have designed Chestham Park, nr. Henfield, Sussex, and he laid out Park Crescent, Worthing, Sussex (1829). In Brighton, his work included Holy Trinity, Ship Street (1817: enlarged and altered since): Oriental Place (1825): No. 31 Cannon Place (*c.* 1825–33: formerly the Royal Newburgh Assembly Rooms): Western Terrace, including No. 9 Western Pavilion (*c.* 1827): Hanover Crescent (*c.* 1827): Silwood Place (1827): Christ Church, New Road (1830): a fountain on the Steine (1846).

WILKINS, William, the elder, FSA: 1751–1815

Born at Norwich, the son of William Wilkins, a local plasterer: worked at first with his father: later, the development of his talent for drawing enabled him to set up in architectural practice. From *c.* 1780 he lived in Cambridge, but continued to practise in Norwich as well: in 1800 he took over the lease of Norwich Theatre, in which his father had also had an interest, and carried out considerable alterations and improvements there. He was the author of various papers on antiquarian subjects. His work included The Cottage, Northrepps, Norfolk (*c.* 1792): Stanfield Hall, nr. Wymondham, Norfolk (1792): restoration and conversion into the County Gaol, of Norwich Castle (1792–3): Donington Hall, Castle Donington, Leics. (1793): at Caius College, Cambridge, enlargement of the Master's Lodge (1795).

WILKINS, William, the younger, RA: 1778–1839

Born in Norwich, the son of William Wilkins, who practised there as an architect: educated Norwich Grammar School and Caius College, Cambridge, of which he was later a Fellow: travelled in Italy, Greece and Asia Minor 1801–5: then set up in architectural practice in Cambridge. He was a member of the Society of Dilettanti: Surveyor to the East India Company from 1824: Professor of Architecture at the Royal Academy 1837. He continued his father's management of the Norwich theatre, and had interests in many others in East Anglia; built up a large and successful practice; and was an acknowledged leader of the Greek Revival in architectural design. His published works included *Antiquities of Magna Graecia* (1807): *The Civil Architecture of Vitruvius* (1812): *Atheniensia, or Remarks on the Topography and Buildings of Athens* (1816). His work included Downing College, Cambridge (1807–20): the Nelson Column, O'Connell Street, Dublin (1808: destroyed 1966): Haileybury College, Herts. (1809: additions since): the Nelson Column at Gt Yarmouth, Norfolk (1817): Friends' Meeting House, York Street, Bath, Som. (1817–19: built as the Freemasons' Hall): New Court, Trinity College, Cambridge (1821–3): University College, Gower Street, London (1827–9: with J. P. Gandy-Deering): St George's Hospital, Hyde Park Corner, London (1828–9: additions since): the National Gallery, Trafalgar Square, London (1832–8).

WILLIAM THE ENGLISHMAN: fl. 1174–84
Referred to by some writers as William Anglus, he appears to be the first Englishman to have carried out architectural work, recorded as such. He succeeded William of Sens in the work of repair and rebuilding at Canterbury Cathedral after the fire of 1174: this work included the completion of the Choir, and building of the Trinity Chapel and Corona.

WILLIAM OF WYKEHAM: 1324–1404
Born at Wickham, Hants, of yeoman stock: educated at the Grammar School of St Swithun's Priory in Winchester. Sir John Scures, Lord of the Manor of Wickham, became his early benefactor: Wykeham was his secretary from c. 1338–c. 1346, and then entered the King's service, becoming Clerk of the Works at Windsor 1356–61, and in 1359 Chief Warden and Surveyor of the Royal Castles of Windsor, Leeds, Dover and Hadleigh, and of all Royal Manors and Parks. At the same time, his ecclesiastical and political careers developed. He was a Clerk in Holy Orders in 1349: ordained Priest 1362: Archdeacon of Lincoln and Provost and Prebendary of Wells 1363: Keeper of the Privy Seal 1364: Bishop of Winchester 1367: Lord Chancellor 1367–71, and again 1389–91. It is probable that his architectural career was mainly administrative, and that his master mason, William Wynford, was responsible for the architectural design and details of much of his work. Wykeham supervised rebuilding at Windsor Castle, Berks. (1360–9): planned, administered and organized the building of New College, Oxford (1380–9): Winchester College, Hants (1388–94): and the repair of Winchester Cathedral (begun 1394).

WILLSON, Edward James, FSA: 1787–1854
Born at Lincoln, the son of a local builder and cabinet-maker: worked in his father's business, and acquired much architectural knowledge by his own local studies. He found patrons among the Cathedral clergy: set up architectural practice in Lincoln: was County Surveyor of Lincs. 1833: a City Magistrate 1834: Mayor of Lincoln 1852: a topographical enthusiast, and the literary collaborator of John Britton in *Architectural Antiquities* (1805–14): *Cathedral Antiquities* (1814–35): and *Picturesque Antiquities of English Cities* (1830): and of the Pugins in *Specimens of Gothic Architecture* (1821–3), and *Examples of Gothic Architecture* (1831–8). Willson did

much church building and restoration: his work included St Saviour, East Retford, Notts. (1829): St Mary, Grantham, Lincs. (1832): the Stables at Leadenham Hall, Lincs. (1833): St Michael, Buslingthorpe, Lincs. (1835): restoration at Lincoln Castle (1835–45): the Chapel in the grounds of Hainton Hall, Lincs. (1836): Pelham's Pillar, nr. Brocklesby Park, Caistor, Lincs. (1840–9): St Mary, Hainton, Lincs. (1848: except tower and spire).

WINDE, Captain William, FRS: d. 1722
Born in Holland, possibly at Bergen-op-Zoom, sometime in the early 1640s, the son of Lt.-Col. Henry Winde, a Royalist who had taken refuge abroad. William Winde went to England at the Restoration, and in 1667 was commissioned in the King's Troop of the Royal Regiment of Horse. His military career lasted until 1688: he fought at Sedgemoor, but, disappointed in hopes of promotion as an Engineer, he turned to architecture, in which he is believed to have received some training from Sir Balthasar Gerbier, whom he succeeded as the architect of Hamstead Marshall, Berks., in 1667. Winde's work included the completion of Hamstead Marshall Manor House, Berks. (begun by Sir Balthasar Gerbier *c*. 1660: destroyed by fire 1718): Newcastle House, Lincoln's Inn Fields, London (1685: rebuilt by Sir E. Lutyens): possibly Belton House, Lincs. (1685): Cliveden House, Bucks. (1665–80: dem. and rebuilt by Sir Charles Barry): Buckingham House, St James's Park, London (1705: incorporated into Buckingham Palace by John Nash).

THE WING FAMILY
A father and son of this name had a flourishing architectural practice in Leicester and the district. The elder Wing designed and built the Church of St Peter, Galby, Leics. (1741). The younger (d. *c*. 1794) was the architect of St John the Baptist, King's Norton, Leics. (1760–75), and St Peter, East Carlton, Northants (1788). John Wing, possibly of the third generation, practised at Bedford, where he built the County Gaol (1801), the Bridge, and the Lunatic Asylum.

WOOD, Edgar: 1860–1935
Born at Middleton, nr. Manchester, the son of a wealthy millowner: articled to James Murgatroyd of Manchester: set up

independent practice there 1885: he was in partnership with J. H. Sellers from 1900–22, when he retired to live in Italy and paint. Wood was President of the Manchester Society of Architects 1911–12: he inaugurated and was President of the Northern Artworkers' Guild: he designed furniture, cutlery and household equipment, and was an exponent of the Art Nouveau style. His work included a shelter and drinking fountain at Middleton, Lancs. (1887): Long Street Methodist Church and School, Middleton (1899: additions to Newbold Revel, Stretton-under-Fosse, Warwicks. (c. 1900: later St Paul's College): Banney Royd, Halifax Road, Huddersfield, Yorks. (1900–1: later Fire Service HQ.): the Clock Tower, Lindley, Huddersfield (1902): the First Church of Christ, Scientist, Victoria Park, Manchester (1903): St Saviour's Vicarage, Thurlstone, Yorks. (1906): Upmeads, Stafford (1908).

WOOD, John, the elder: 1704–54

Born in Bath, the son of George Wood, a local builder. John Wood's first patron was Lord Bingley, for whom he worked in Yorkshire, and who, it is believed, introduced him to London. By 1727 he had established himself in Marylebone, practising chiefly as a planner and speculative builder. About 1725 he became interested in the replanning of Bath: in 1727 he returned there, and concentrated upon this work until his death. A political crisis in the affairs of the project in 1727 was overcome by Wood making himself solely responsible for the planning and construction of Queen Square. His success at Bath increased his practice, and he became well known in fashionable circles. He published *The Origins of Building, or the Plagiarisms of the Heathens Detected* (1741): *An Essay towards a Description of Bath* (1742): *A Description of the Exchange of Bristol* (1743): *Choir Gaure, vulgarly called Stonehenge. . . . Described, Restored and Explained* (1747): and *Dissertation upon the Orders of Columns and their Appendages* (1750). His work in Bath included St John's Hospital and Chandos House (1727–30): Gay Street (1727 onwards: completed by his son, John): Queen Square (1729–36): Prior Park, Combe Down (1735–48: except the east wing: remodelled since): Royal Mineral Water Hospital (1737–42): North and South Parades (1740–3): The Circus (begun 1754: completed by his son, John). He also built Belcombe Court, nr. Bradford-on-Avon, Wilts. (1734): the Exchange and Market, Bristol (1740–3): Liverpool Town Hall (1747–54: rebuilt since).

XI

SIR GEORGE
GILBERT SCOTT
1811–78

[RIBA

GEORGE GODWIN
1815–88

RIBA]

XII

SIR MATTHEW DIGBY
WYATT
1820–77

[RIBA

SIR EDWIN LUTYENS
1869–1944

*National Portrait
Gallery, London*]

WOOD, John, the younger: 1728–81

The son of John Wood of Bath, with whom he worked, first as an assistant, and then as partner. On his father's death, he took over his work of planning in Bath, and became the leading architect in the city. He does not appear to have practised in London, but designed buildings in other parts of the country. He published *A Series of Plans, for Cottages or Habitations of the Labourer* (1781). His work in Bath included York House Hotel, George Street (1765–9): Royal Crescent (1767–74): Bennett Street, Russell Street, and Alfred Street (*c.* 1768–74): New Assembly Rooms (1769–71: severely war damaged): the Hot Baths (1776–8). He also built Buckland House, Berks. (1757): the wings at Standlynch House, Wilts. (1766: later Trafalgar House): St Nicholas, Hardenhuish, Wilts. (1779).

WOOD, John Turtle, FSA, HON.FRIBA: 1821–90

Born in London: educated under a tutor at Cambridge: visited Venice 1850. It is possible that he was articled to H. E. Kendall, and he was in practice in London in 1853, but in 1858 he was appointed Architect to the Smyrna and Aldin Railway, and settled in Asia Minor: he designed and built railway stations for this concern. Wood is famous for the excavations he carried out at Ephesus, where he began work *c.* 1863, and where he discovered the Temple of Diana and other important antiquities. His book, *Discoveries at Ephesus, including the Site and Remains of the Great Temple,* was published in 1877.

WOOD, Sancton, FRIBA: 1816–86

Articled to Sir Robert Smirke, and completed his training under Sydney Smirke. Wood was District Surveyor of Putney and Roehampton, and of St Luke's, Chelsea: a member of the Institute's Board of Examiners: a Fellow of the Institute of Architects of Ireland: Architect to the Rugby & Stamford Railway: the Syston & Peterborough Railway: the Limerick Junction line in Ireland: and to a number of building estates. His practice consisted mostly of railway work, and he built stations for the Eastern Counties Railway, and in Ireland for the Gt Southern & Western Railway. His work included Cambridge Railway Station (1845): Kingsbridge Station, Dublin (1845–61): Nos. 42–44 Gresham Street/King

R

Street, London (1850): blocks of houses facing Hyde Park, in Lancaster Gate, London (1857).

WOODS, Joseph, FSA: 1776–1864

Born at Stoke Newington, London, the son of Joseph Woods: educated at home and at a Quaker school in London: articled to D. A. Alexander: entered Royal Academy Schools 1798. He set up in practice in 1800, but did little actual building, apart from the Commercial Sale Rooms, Mincing Lane, London (1811–12: dem.), and Clissold House, Clissold Park, Stoke Newington, London (1820–30). He is better known as the editor of the 4th volume of Stuart's *Antiquities of Athens* (1816). Woods was the first President of the London Architectural Society, which he founded in 1806, and to whose *Essays* he contributed. He travelled widely on the Continent in 1816–19 and 1825–6: was an amateur botanist of considerable repute; a member of the Geological and Linnean Societies. He published *Letters of an Architect from France, Italy and Greece* (1828), and *Tourist's Flora: A Descriptive Catalogue of the Flowering Plants and Ferns of the British Islands, France, Germany, Switzerland, Italy and the Italian Islands* (1850).

WOODYER, Henry: 1816–96

A friend and pupil of William Butterfield: began to practise independently in 1846, and worked chiefly in Surrey and Berkshire, building schools, many churches, and carrying out church restorations. His work included the National Schools, Ripley, Surrey (1846: altered since): St Mark, Wyke, Ash, Surrey (1847): St Martha, Chilworth, Surrey (1848–50): Holy Innocents, Highnam, Glos. (1848–51): the Convent of St John the Baptist, Windsor, Berks. (1853–96: built as the House of Mercy): St Michael's College, Tenbury, Worcs. (1855): St Mary, Buckland, Surrey (1860): St Paul, Wokingham, Berks. (1862–4): Christ Church, Reading, Berks. (1862–74): rebuilding of east wing of Wotton House, Surrey, and Hill Cottage in the grounds (1864): St Peter, Hascombe, Surrey (1864): St Andrew, Grafham, Surrey (1864), and probably Grafham Grange, which was his home: Cranleigh, School, Surrey (1865: additions by Sir Edwin Cooper): St Paul, Langleybury, Herts. (1865): St Martin, Dorking, Surrey (1868–73).

WORNUM, George Grey, CBE, FRIBA: 1888–1957
Born in London, the son of Dr George Wornum, nephew of R. S. Wornum, and grandson of Ralph Nicholson Wornum, Keeper and Secretary of the National Gallery and a well-known art critic and writer. Grey Wornum was educated at Bradfield College, and the Slade School: studied at the AA, where he won the Travelling Studentship and Silver Medal 1909: articled to his uncle: worked in the office of Simpson and Ayrton: set up in practice 1910: served in the First World War. He was in partnership with P. D. Hepworth in 1919; later with Louis de Soissons; and in 1950 with Edward Playne. Wornum was President of the AA 1930–1: a member of the Institute's Council: Vice-President 1950–1: Royal Gold Medallist 1952: an Hon. Fellow of the American Institute of Architects. In 1936 he was one of the three architects appointed to organize the London decorations for the Coronation of King George VI: in the same year he took charge of the decoration of passenger accommodation in the *Queen Elizabeth*. He contributed to *Housing, a European Survey*, published by the Building Centre in London; and was joint author, with John Gloag, of *House Out of Factory* (1946). Wornum's work included the Earl Haig Memorial Homes at Meadow Head, Sheffield, Yorks. (1928–9): and at Morden, Surrey (1931 and later: both with L. de Soissons): the Royal Institute of British Architects, Portland Place, London (1932–4): the British Girls' College, Alexandria, Egypt (1935): flats at Ladbroke Grove, London (1936: in collaboration with a team of architects): the City of Westminster Central Cleansing and Transport Department, Ebury Bridge Road, London (1936–8): Hearts of Oak Benefit Society Convalescent Home, nr. Broadstairs, Kent (1937): the replanning of Parliament Square, Westminster, London (1952).

WORNUM, Ralph Selden, FRIBA: 1847–1910
The son of Ralph Nicholson Wornum, Keeper and Secretary of the National Gallery: articled to Professor Roger Smith 1865: awarded the Royal Academy Travelling Studentship 1872: served on the Council of the Institute and was an examiner in design. For ten years he was in partnership with Edward Salomons, FRIBA (1827–1906), an able draughtsman and water-colour artist, and the designer of the Synagogue, Harrow Road, London (1862–3: with N. S. Joseph): Caen Wood Towers, Highgate, London (1870–2:

with J. P. Jones): and the Crematorium, Manchester (1892: with A. Steinthal). Wornum's work included chambers at Broad Court, Bow Street, London; Agnew's Galleries, Old Bond Street, London (1877: with Salomons): large villas at Biarritz.

WORTHINGTON, Thomas, FRIBA: 1826–1909
Born in Salford, Manchester: articled to Bowman and Crowther, the authors of *Churches of the Middle Ages*, to which Worthington contributed many drawings. He was awarded the Society of Arts Gold Medal 1845 and the Institute Silver Medal 1847: worked for Sir William Tite: visited Italy 1847: after a further period with Tite, set up his own practice in Manchester: he was later in partnership with his son, Percy Scott, and with John Elgood. Worthington was a Vice-President of the Institute and served on the Council: a Fellow and President of the Manchester Society of Architects: the author of *The Dwellings of the Poor* (1893). In Manchester the work of his partnership included the Manchester Botanical Society Building (1854): Manchester and Salford Baths and Laundries (1857): Albert Memorial (1862) and Memorial Hall (1865) in Albert Square: Chorlton Union Hospital (1865: later part of Withington Hospital): the City Police and Sessions Court, Minshull Street (1868). Outside Manchester, they designed the Fountain at Bolton Hall, Bolton Abbey, Yorks. (1886): the Royal Bath Hospital, Harrogate, Yorks. (1888–9): Manchester College, Oxford (1891–3).

WOTTON, Sir Henry: 1568–1639 (Portrait: see Plate I)
Born at the Manor House of Boughton Malherbe in Kent: educated Winchester and Oxford. Though not a practising architect, his interest and understanding of architecture were profound. He was a gifted poet and diplomatist: travelled widely in Europe: was knighted in 1603: Ambassador to Venice 1604–19: Provost of Eton 1623: Ambassador to the Duke of Savoy 1624. He was the author of *The Elements of Architecture collected by Henry Wotton, Kt. from the Best Authors and Examples*, published 1624, a book that had a profound influence upon architectural taste in the seventeenth century.

WREN, Sir Christopher: 1632–1723 (Portrait: see Plate II)
Born at East Knoyle, Wilts., the son of the Rev. Christopher Wren, rector there: educated Westminster School, and Wadham College,

Oxford, where he met many of the scientists who later founded the Royal Society. He became interested in science, particularly in anatomy and astronomy, produced a number of scientific inventions, conducted experiments, constructed ingenious models and diagrams, and made drawings. He was an MA in 1653, and a Fellow of All Souls, Oxford, the same year: Professor of Astronomy at Gresham College, London 1657: Savilian Professor of Astronomy at Oxford, and DCL 1661. Wren's architectural career began in 1663 when he became a member of the Commission for repairing St Paul's Cathedral: he visited France in 1665: in 1666 he was appointed one of the King's Commissioners responsible for the rebuilding of London after the Great Fire; in this capacity he was directly responsible for the design and construction of fifty-two rebuilt City churches, much other rebuilding, and the design and supervision of the new St Paul's Cathedral. Wren was Surveyor-General of the King's Works 1669–1718: knighted in 1673: Comptroller at Windsor 1684–1716: the first Surveyor of Greenwich Palace 1696–1716: in charge of repairs to Westminster Abbey 1699–1723: President of the Royal Society 1681–3: a member of the Hudson's Bay Company Council: M.P. for Plympton 1685–7: and Weymouth 1701–2. His enormous output of work included Pembroke College Chapel, Cambridge (1663–5): the Sheldonian Theatre, Oxford (1664–9): St Bride, Fleet Street, London (1671–8): St Paul's Cathedral, London (1675–1710): the Royal Observatory, Greenwich, London (1675–6): the Library of Trinity College, Cambridge (1676–84): Tom Tower, Christ Church, Oxford (1681–2): St James, Piccadilly, London (1682–4: badly war damaged and rebuilt to Wren's design): the Royal Hospital, Chelsea, London (1682–91): the Royal Hospital for Seamen, Greenwich, London (1696–1702): Marlborough House, London (1709–11).

WRIGHT, Stephen: d. 1780

Assistant to William Kent: Clerk of the Works at Hampton Court in 1746: Master Mason of Works from 1758–80. His patron was the Duke of Newcastle. His work included Wimborne House, No. 22 Arlington Street, London (c. 1740–55): University Library, Cambridge (1754–8): Clumber House, Notts. (1767: dem.): wings at Milton House, Berks. (1776).

WYATT, Benjamin: 1745–1818

Born in London, the fifth son of Benjamin Wyatt (1709–1772) of Weeford, Staffs., a farmer who also practised locally as a builder. The younger Wyatt spent much of his life as Agent to Lord Penrhyn, who owned large slate quarries in Wales, and for whom he carried out much architectural and building work on the estate and at Port Penrhyn. He also designed the Caernarvon and Anglesey Dispensary (1809–10), practising from Lime Grove, nr. Bangor.

WYATT, Benjamin Dean: 1775–c. 1850

Born in London, the eldest son of James Wyatt: educated at Westminster School, and Christ Church, Oxford: from 1798–c. 1802 he was in India, in the service of the East India Company: in 1807, having returned to England, he became private secretary to Sir Arthur Wellesley. When this appointment ended in 1809, he began his career as an architect, studying under his father, whom he succeeded as Surveyor to Westminster Abbey 1813–27. He was assisted in much of his work by his younger brother Philip (d. 1836) who had worked in his father's office. B. D. Wyatt was involved in a professional dispute over the design of Drury Lane Theatre, and published *Observations on the Principles of the Design for the Theatre now building in Drury Lane* in 1811: re-issued in 1813 under the title of *Observations on the Design for the Theatre Royal, Drury Lane, as erected in 1812.* His work included Drury Lane Theatre, London (1811–12: porch and colonnade added later): the Market Cross, Devizes, Wilts. (1814): Crockford's Club, St James's Street, London (1827: with Philip Wyatt: internal alterations and refacing since: later the Devonshire Club): the Oriental Club, Hanover Square, London (1827–8: with Philip Wyatt: dem.): refacing, in Bath stone, of Apsley House, Hyde Park Corner, London, with the addition of the Corinthian portico, and a gallery on the west side (1828: with Philip Wyatt): the Duke of York's Column, Waterloo Place, London (1831–4).

WYATT, James, RA, FSA: 1746–1813

The sixth son of Benjamin Wyatt of Weeford, Staffs. From 1762–8 he was in Italy, where he studied architecture under Antonio Viscentini at Venice. On his return, his first commission, the Pantheon in Oxford Street, London (1770–2: destroyed 1792), brought him immediate fame: he was soon established in a successful and ever-growing practice: and had many fashionable, wealthy and influential clients. He was Surveyor to Westminster Abbey 1776: Surveyor-General and Comptroller of the Works 1796: a founder member of the Architects' Club 1791. He carried out many cathedral restorations: his work included Upper Grove House, Roehampton Lane, London (1777: later the Froebel Institute): No. 9 Conduit Street, London (1779): interior remodelling at Cobham Hall, Kent, and design of the Mausoleum in the park (*c.* 1783): interior of Heveningham Hall, Suffolk (1784): St Swithun, East Grinstead, Sussex (1789): Goodwood House, Sussex (*c.* 1790–1800: also in the grounds Valdoe and Kennels Lodges, the Orangery, and Dower House): Frogmore House, Windsor Great Park, Berks. (1792): Fonthill Abbey, Wilts. (1796–1807): the Royal Military Academy, Woolwich, London (1805): Ashridge House, Herts. (1808: completed by Sir Jeffry Wyatville: later Bonar Law College).

WYATT, Lewis William: c. 1778–1853
The son of Benjamin Wyatt of Lime Grove, nr. Bangor, Caernarvonshire: studied at the Royal Academy Schools: was a pupil of his uncle, Samuel Wyatt, and later assistant to his uncle, James Wyatt. Set up independent practice *c.* 1802: became Clerk of the Works at Whitehall 1818: published *Prospectus of a Design for Various Improvements in the Metropolis* (1816). His work included Stoke Hall, East Stoke, Notts. (1812): Willey Hall, Salop (1812–15): Nos. 12–17 Suffolk Street, London (1822–3).

WYATT, Sir Matthew Digby, FSA, FRIBA: 1820–77 (Portrait: see Plate XII)
Born at Rowde, nr. Devizes, the son of Matthew Wyatt, and younger brother of T. H. Wyatt, to whom he was articled: from 1844–6 he travelled on the Continent, completing the drawings for his book, *Specimens of Geometrical Mosaics of the Middle Ages*, published 1848. In 1849, Wyatt reported to the Society of Arts on an industrial exhibition held in Paris: in 1851 he was appointed Secretary to the Executive Committee for the Great Exhibition: in 1855, he became Surveyor to the East India Company: he was Hon. Secretary to the RIBA 1855–9: a Vice-President of the Institute: Royal Gold Medallist 1866: awarded the Telford Medal of the Institute of Civil Engineers, and foreign honours: the first Slade Professor of Fine Arts at Cambridge: President of the Graphic Society. His

many published works included *The Industrial Arts of the Nineteenth Century* (1851-3): *Specimens of Ornamental Art Workmanship in Gold, Silver, Iron, Brass and Bronze* (1852): *Illuminated Manuscripts as Illustrative of the Arts of Design* (1860): *The History of the Manufacture of Clocks* (1868): *An Architect's Notebook in Spain* (1872). Wyatt was an architect of great influence and importance; a designer of carpets, tiles and wallpapers; a national figure, with an extensive and prosperous practice. His work included the Byzantine, English Gothic, Italian, Pompeian and Renaissance Courts at the Crystal Palace, re-erected at Sydenham, London (1854): Paddington Station, London (1854-5: in association with I. K. Brunel and Owen Jones): Chapel at Warley Barracks, Little Warley, Essex (1857): Royal Engineers' Crimean War Memorial, Chatham, Kent (1861): Fernery in the gardens of Ashridge House, Herts. (1864): Addenbroke's Hospital, Cambridge (1864-5: additions since): Possingworth Manor, Sussex (1866): the Rothschild Mausoleum, Jewish Cemetery, West Ham, London (1867): the courtyard of the former India Office, Government Offices, Whitehall, London (1867): Oldlands, Herron's Ghyll, Sussex (1869).

WYATT, Samuel: 1737-1807
Born at Weeford, the third son of Benjamin Wyatt (d. 1772). Samuel worked on carpentry contracts at Greenwich Hospital Chapel (1779) and Somerset House (1782): and became Clerk of the Works at Chelsea Hospital in 1792. He established a successful architectural and building practice in London, and invented a hinge which caused simultaneous opening of the leaves of double doors: among his clients were the engineers Boulton and Watt. His work included Herstmonceux Place, Sussex (1777): Albion Place, and the Albion Mill, Blackfriars, London (1784-6: the Mill destroyed by fire 1791): Trinity House, London (1792-4: rebuilt to original design after war damage): Stornoway House, Cleveland Row, St James's, London (1794-6): the Market House, Marlow, Bucks. (1807: later the Crown Hotel).

WYATT, Thomas Henry, FRIBA: 1807-80
Born in Ireland, the son of a Police Magistrate, Matthew Wyatt, the first cousin of Samuel, Benjamin and James Wyatt. Thomas Wyatt was educated privately and in Brussels: he started in a commercial career, but abandoned this for architecture, and was articled to

Philip Hardwick. In 1838 he set up in practice, for a time in partnership with David Brandon. Wyatt was Honorary Architect to the Institution of Civil Engineers, the Athenaeum Club, the Middlesex Hospital, and the Governesses' Benevolent Society: Consulting Architect to the Commissioners in Lunacy, the Incorporated Church Building Society, the Salisbury Diocesan Church Building Society: President of the Architects' Benevolent Society: Vice-President of the Architectural Society: President of the RIBA 1870: Royal Gold Medallist 1873. His practice was very large: he did much church building and restoration, particularly in Wiltshire: his work included the Assize Court (1835) and Roundway Hospital (1851), both at Devizes, Wilts.: St Andrew, Bethnal Green, London (1841: with Brandon): SS Mary and Nicholas, Wilton, Wilts. (1843: with Brandon): St Mary's Rectory, Broughton Gifford, Wilts. (c. 1850): Orchardleigh Park, Som. (1855–8): Garrison Church of St George, Woolwich, London (1863): the Exchange Buildings, Liverpool (1865): Holy Trinity, Fonthill Gifford, Wilts. (1866): St Peter, Wimblington, Cambs. (1874): Holy Cross, Whorlton-in-Cleveland, Yorks. (1877): St Andrew, Bredenbury, Herefs. (1877): the Manor House, North Perrott, Som. (1878): Knightsbridge Barracks, London (1878–9): southern part of Brompton Hospital, Fulham Road, London (1879–82).

WYATVILLE, Sir Jeffry, RA, FSA, FRS: 1766–1840
Born at Burton-on-Trent, the son of Joseph Wyatt (b. 1739), who was the fourth son of Benjamin Wyatt of Weeford, Staffs.: Joseph Wyatt practised as an architect at Burton-on-Trent, but with little distinction. Jeffry Wyatt was trained by his uncles, Samuel and James, and set up in private practice in London, in 1799, in partnership with a builder, John Armstrong. He was very successful and became well known in fashionable circles: in 1824 he was commissioned to convert and reconstruct Windsor Castle to the needs of a nineteenth-century Royal residence, and at the same time was permitted to adopt the surname of Wyatville: he was knighted 1828. An account of his work at Windsor, *Illustrations of Windsor Castle by the late Sir Jeffry Wyatville, R.A.*, edited by Henry Ashton, was published in 1841. He carried out extensive alterations and additions at Longleat, Wilts. (1801), Wollaton Hall, Notts. (1804 and 1824), and Chatsworth, Derbys. (1820–40): his work included remodelling of Woolley Park, Brightwalton, Berks. (1799): Nonsuch House, Cheam, Surrey

(1802–6): Endsleigh Cottage, Endsleigh, Devonshire (1810): Bretby Park, Derbys. (1812–13): Stubton Hall, Lincs. (1813–14): Philipps House, nr. Dinton, Wilts. (1813–16): Combination Rooms, Gateway Tower, rebuilding of east front and other alterations, at Sidney Sussex College, Cambridge (1821–32): King William's Temple (the Pantheon), Kew Gardens, Surrey (1837): Buxton Lodge, Edensor, Derbys. (c. 1840).

WYNFORD, William: late fourteenth century

He may have been born at Winsford, in Somerset, and is first heard of in 1360, as Warden in charge of masons' work on the rebuilding of Windsor Castle, where William of Wykeham was Clerk of Works. Wynford acted as Wykeham's assistant, working closely with him for over forty years. In 1363 he was a Master Mason at Wells Cathedral, where, sometime after 1386, he built the south-west Tower: with Wykeham, he probably designed New College, Oxford (1380–89), and Winchester College (1388–94). In addition to his official work, he had, from c. 1372, a flourishing private practice: he was a colleague and contemporary of Henry Yevele, with whom he worked on rebuilding at Winchester Castle in 1390 and 1397.

YENN, John, RA: 1750-1821
Studied under Sir William Chambers, and at the Royal Academy Schools, where he won the Gold Medal in 1771. He was Clerk of the Works at Richmond New Park Lodge 1780: Clerk of the Works at Kensington Palace, Buckingham House, and the Royal Mews: Surveyor of Greenwich Hospital 1788: a member of the Architects' Club 1791: Treasurer of the Royal Academy 1796: for many years a close friend and associate of Sir William Chambers. His work included the west front of King Charles Block, Royal Naval College, Greenwich, London (1811-14): Trafalgar Quarters, Dreadnought Hospital, Greenwich, London (1813).

YEVELE, Henry: *c.* 1320-1400
Born probably at Yeaveley, Derbys., the son of Roger de Yevele, believed to have been a mason. Henry's brother, Robert, was Warden of the Masons at the Tower of London in 1362, and Henry also became a mason. Details of the early years of his career are unknown, but he undoubtedly acquired much experience; survived the Black Death; and may also have travelled widely, before he became well known as a mason in London. He was appointed King's Master Mason at Westminster in 1365 under Edward III, and continued to serve under Richard II and Henry IV. His interests in the Isle of Purbeck included the Wardship of Langton Manor, and there can be little doubt that he was easily able to obtain large quantities of valuable building stone. He became famous as a master mason-designer, and citizen of London, and acquired a considerable fortune. His work included Queenborough Castle, Kent (1361: dem. (1629): The Bloody Tower, Tower of London (1361): the nave of Canterbury Cathedral (1377 and 1391): the remodelling of Westminster Hall, London (1395-1402): a stone bridge over the river Medway at Rochester, Kent (1382-92: dem.).

YORKE, Francis Reginald Stevens, CBE, FRIBA: 1906-62
The son of an architect, F. W. B. Yorke: educated at Chipping Camden School, Glos., and trained at the School of Architecture, Birmingham University. A founder of the MARS Group (Modern Architectural Research), which flourished during the 1930s, and did much to encourage the growth of a contemporary style of

architecture in Gt. Britain: Yorke was a leader of this modern movement as it was then called. In 1933 he was for a time assistant editor of the *Architect's Journal*: editor of *Specification* from 1935 till his death: the author of *The Modern House* (1934): *The Modern Flat* (1937): *A Key to Modern Architecture* (1939: with Colin Penn): *The New Small House* (1953: with Penelope Whiting). His collaboration with Marcel Breuer, with whom he designed Sea Lane House, East Preston, Sussex (1937), was interrupted by the Second World War, after which he joined Eugene Rosenberg and Cyril Mardall, a partnership which was responsible for much housing and school building in the New Towns, notably at Harlow and Stevenage, and which was awarded the London Architecture Medal of the RIBA in 1962, for their new office premises at Greystoke Place, Chancery Lane, London. Other work of the partnership included West Park County Modern School, Leeds (1951–3): Central Colleges, Leeds (1953): extensions to Southlands College, Wimbledon, Surrey (1957 and 1959–62): Gatwick Airport, Surrey (1958): the Hospital, West Green Drive, Crawley, Sussex (1960–2): Keddie's Store, Southend-on-Sea, Essex (1961–3).

INDEX OF PERSONS

(other architects, partners, and collaborators)

Abbott, 95
Abraham, H. R., 20
Adams, H. Percy, 124
Alexander, Daniel, the younger, 24
Allason, Thomas, the younger, 24
Alley, P. B., 79
Anderson, J. Macvicar, 52
Armstrong, John, 265
Armstrong, R., 69
Ashbee, C. R., 124
Atkinson, John, 27
Atkinson, T. D., 92
Atkinson, William, the younger, 27
Aytoun, William, 243

Bailey, James, 160
Baird, John, elder and younger, 232
Baker, H. A., 100
Baker, Richard, 31
Banckes, Henry, 32
Banks, Robert Richardson, 32, 33
Barclay, Hugh, 213
Barlow, W. H., 243
Barry, J. Wolfe, 136
Basill, Simon, the younger, 34
Batterbury, Thomas, 144
Baud, Benjamin, 101, 102
Bayle, James, 188
Beazley, Charles, 35
Bell, Ingress, 247
Bentham, General Sir Samuel, 22
Billerey, F., 42
Blandford, 249
Blyth, John, 58
Bonomi, Ignatius, 44
Bonomi, Joseph, the younger, 44, 208
Bowen, James, 20
Brakspear, W. H., 229
Brandon, Joshua Arthur, 45
Brayley, Edward, 46
Breuer, Marcel, 268
Bridges, James, 177

Broadbent, F. G., 106
Brooks, James Martin, 47
Browne, Robert, 90
Browning, Bryan, 48
Brunel, I. K., 264
Bruton, E. G., 237
Buckler, Charles Alban, 50
Burn, Robert, 52
Burnet, John, 52
Bury, C. A., 118
Bywaters, James, 133

Carline, John, the younger, 58
Carline, Thomas, 58
Carpenter, Richard Herbert, 58, 59
Carter, John Coates, 212
Catt, Arthur, 69
Chatwin, P. B., 62
Child, 105
Clapham, F. D., 163
Clarke, Isaac, 243
Clarke, John, 217
Clayton, A. B., 28, 204
Cole, John, 211
Colling, William, 70
Collins, E. S., 145
Corfiato, H. O., 197
Corlette, H. C., 168
Corson, William, 72
Cory, 44
Cottingham, N. J., 72
Craig, C. A., 123
Crichton, Richard, 193
Cubitt, William, 74
Cundy, Joseph, 75
Cundy, Thomas (III), 76
Currey, Percivall, 76
Curtis, H. L., 106

Deane, Thomas Manly, 81
Deare, John, 174
de Grey, Earl, 67
Dickson, T., 229

Dixon, Joseph, 59
Donaldson, James, 84
Douglas, Campbell, 49, 213
Dunn, Archibald Mathias, 117
Dunnett, 94
Dymond, George, 98

Easton, John Murray, 200
Eastwood, J. H., 82
Edge, Charles, 232
Edmeston, James, 208
Elger, John, 89
Elgood, John, 260
Elmes, H. J., 89
Ensor, John, 60
Evans, Joseph, 235

Fawckner, 113
Fentiman, 40
Ferrey, Benjamin E., 93
Field, J., 202
Fletcher, Herbert P., 93
Flockton, William, 95
Foote, Robert, 232
Forrest, G. Topham, 41
Forshaw, J. H., 19
Foster, James, the younger, 96
Foster, John, the elder, 96
Foster, Thomas, 96
Fox, Sir Francis, 132
Fowler, John, 114
Fowler, Joseph, 99
Fulljames, 205

Gandy, Michael, 101
Gell, Sir W., 101
Gibbs, of Sheffield, 95
Gibson, George, 89
Gill, C. Lovett, 197
Gill, J. Elkington, 157
Gimson, Ernest, 42
Gloag, John, 259
Godwin, Henry, 104, 105
Good, J. H., 33
Goodridge, A. S., 107
Goodwin, 69
Gordon, 210
Grainger, Richard, 83

Graveley, Edmund, 139
Green, Benjamin, 108, 109
Griffith, John William, 64, 110
Grumbold, William, 234
Gruning, 163
Gutch, G., 105
Gwilt, George, the younger, 111
Gwilt, John Sebastian, 111

Habershon, Edward, 113
Habershon, William Gillbee, 113
Hadfield, Charles, 113, 114
Hakewill, James, 115
Halfpenny, John, 115
Hall, Edwin Stanley, 200
Hamp, Stanley, 69
Hansard, Octavius, 136
Hansom, Charles, 117
Hansom, Edward, 117
Hansom, Henry, 117
Harris, W., 26
Haycock, J. H., 231
Hayley, William, 228
Hays, W. B., 25
Hayward, William, 112
Hellicar, E., 197
Hepworth, P. D., 259
Hewitt, Samuel, 102
Hine, George Thomas, 122
Hiorne, David, 122, 123
Hiorne, Francis, 123
Hiorne, John, 123
Holford, Lord, 124
Holme, Arthur, 76
Honeyman, John, 156
Houfe, E. A. S., 197
Howard, Sir Ebenezer, 238
Howard, John, 39, 100
Hunt, G. H., 240
Hussey, R. C., 199
Hutchinson, Henry, 199

I'Anson, E. B., 129
Inglelow, Benjamin, 59
Inwood, Charles Frederick, 130
Inwood, William, 129, 130
Ireland, Joseph, 208
Isaacs, Lewis H., 96

Ivory, Thomas, the younger, 131
Ivory, William, of Saffron Walden, 131

Jackson, Richard, 235
Janyns, Robert, elder and younger, 134
Jearrad, C., 134
Jersey, Thomas, 173
Joass, J. J., 36, 37
Jobbins, 84
Johns, J., 113
Johnson, J., 64
Johnson, Thomas, 235
Johnston, Richard, 136
Jones, J. P., 260
Jones William, 167
Joseph, N. S., 259
Jupp, William, the elder, 138

Kay, William Pordon, 140
Keene, Theodosius, 141
Kemp, Thomas Read, 55
Kendall, H. E., the younger, 142
Kenyon, A. W., 82
Keppie, John, 156, 213

Langley, Thomas, 148
Lauder, Alexander, 150
Lebons, John, 193
Lee, Charles, 54
Lee, Thomas, the elder, 149
Leeson, E. W., 124
Legg, George, 231
Lindley, William, 128
Lisle, Bertram, 118
Little, 83
Lodge, T. A., 147
Lorne, Francis, 52
Lucas, 147
Lumby, Thomas, 154
Lynn, 148

Maddox, George, 53, 176, 208
Manley, Thomas, 114
Manwaring, Boulton, 223
Mardall, Cyril, 268
Maughan, Joseph, 98
Mawson, Richard, 152
Mawson, William, 152

May, W. C., 110
Medland, James, 188
Mewès, Charles, 79
Moffatt, William Bonython, 209
Moffatt, W. L., 128
Moore, Leslie, 161
Moore, Richard, 161
Morris, Robert, 161, 162
Morris, William, 248
Mott, Alfred, 242
Mouatt, Dr F. J., 222
Mountague, Frederick William, 162
Mountague, James, 162
Murgatroyd, James, 255
Murray, W. G., 85

Newall, Walter, 72
Newman, J., 129
Newton, W. G., 167
Nicholson, Michael Angelo, 169
Norman, Alfred, 122
Norman, J., 110

Odgers, 122
Okeley, William, 96
Oliver, Thomas, the younger, 172

Pain, George Richard, 173
Pain, James, the elder, 173
Pain, William, 173
Paine, James, the younger, 173
Paley, E. G., 214, 215
Papworth, George, 175
Parker, Barry, 237, 238
Parkinson, W., 45
Passmore, Herbert, 58
Peach, Stanley, 193
Pearson, F. L., 179
Pearson, Lionel, 124
Peck, Frederick, 69
Penn, Colin, 268
Peters, O. B., 122
Peto, Harold, 102
Philips, 116
Pick, Frank, 124
Pierce, S. Rowland, 133
Pilkington, Redmond William, 181
Pinch, John, the younger, 181
Pite, Alfred Robert, 181, 182

Platt, George, 182
Playne, Edward, 259
Pocock, William Wilmer, 184
Porter, George, 231
Potter, Joseph, 98
Powning, John, 98
Price, John, the younger, 187
Prichard, John, 62, 212, 213
Pritchard, of York, 80
Pritchett, James, the younger, 188
Prowse, Thomas, 207

Rawlinson, Sir Robert, 68, 89
Redman, Henry, 241
Repton, G. S., 165, 195, 196
Rhodes, Henry, 63
Rickards, E. A., 147
Rickman, Edwin, 199
Robinson, Stephen, 69
Rogers, Thomas, 60
Rosenberg, Eugene, 268
Roumieu, Charles, 107
Rushton, T. J., 168
Russell, S. B., 71

Salomons, Edward, 259, 260
Sandby, Paul, 206
Sands, William, the younger, 207
Saxon, 165
Scott, A. T., 30
Sens, William of, 254
Sharp, Samuel, 214
Sibbald, William, 193
Simpson, J., 124
Smeaton, John, 149
Smith, Professor Roger, 259
Smith, William, 218
Spiers, Phené, 240
Squirhill, D. G., 250
Stark, William, 183
Steinthal, A., 260
Stevens, 69
Stevenson, J. J., 203
Stewart, James, 147
Stokes, G. H., 178
Stokoe, John, 224
Stride, Lewis, 47
Swainson, Harold, 150

Tait, Thomas, 52
Talman, John, 228
Taylor, Sir John, 180
Teulon, William Mitford, 231
Thomson, George, 232
Thornely, Sir Arnold, 19, 145
Tilley, Herbert, G., 94
Tilley, John, 57
Trotman, E., 234
Tufnell, Samuel, 135, 236
Turner, Richard, 53
Turner, Thackeray, 31

Vardy, John, the younger, 239
Varley, John, 83
Vaughan, Thomas, 102
Vince, 210
Viollet-le-Duc, 166
Viscentini, Antonio, 262

Wadling, 205
Walker, 249
Wallen, John, 129, 136, 144
Walpole, Horace, 38, 60, 63, 91, 182
Walters, John, 243
Watson, William, 188
Weightman, John Grey, 113, 114
Welch, Edward, 116, 117
Westwood, P. J., 90
Whineray, B. B., 227
White, John, the younger, 250
Whiting, Penelope, 268
Whitworth, Robert, 194
Wigge, Gilbert, 227
Wilson, Henry, 212
Wilson, Sir William, 220
Windyer, R. C., 188
Wood, W. B., 132
Woodhead, 128
Woodward, Benjamin, 81
Woodzell, 69
Woolfe, John, 100
Worthington, Percy Scott, 260
Wyatt, George, 184
Wyatt, Joseph, 265
Wyatt, Philip, 262

Yeates, Alfred, 102
Yerbury, F. R., 133

INDEX OF PLACES

Aberford, Yorks
  Parlington Park, 151
Aberystwyth, Cards
  Assembly Rooms, 196
Abbey Dore, Herefs
  St Mary, 19
Abbotsford, Roxburghshire, 42
Abbotskerswell, Devon
  St Augustine's Priory and Nunnery, 117
Abbotsleigh, Som
  Leigh Court, 127
Aberdeen
  Assembly Rooms; Athenaeum; Girls' High School; Marischal College; North of Scotland Bank; Royal Infirmary, 217
Acton, Middx
  Goldsmiths' Almshouses, 35
Adcote, Salop, 216
Addington Palace, Surrey, 163
Addiscombe, Surrey
  St Mary Magdalene, 146
Addlestone, Surrey
  St Paul, 208
Adforton, Herefs
  St Andrew, 213
Aldbourne, Wilts
  School, 55
Alderbury, Wilts
  St Marie's Grange, 190
Aldermaston Court, Berks, 118
Alderton, Wilts
  St Giles and Vicarage, 232
Aldworth House, Sussex, 145
Alexandria, Egypt
  British Girls' College, 259. Consular buildings; St Mark, 252
Alloway, Ayrshire
  Burns Memorial, 116
Almer, Dorset, 35
Alnwick, Northumb
  Castle, 48, 205. Denwick and Lion Bridges, 20. Percy Tenantry Column, 223. St Mary, 109. St Paul, 205
Althorp Park, Northants, 125
Alton Towers, Staffs, 20, 24
Amcotts, Lincs
  Rectory, 99
Amesbury House, Wilts, 248
Annesley, Notts
  All Saints, 132
Anwick, Lincs
  Haverholme Priory, 142
Arbury Hall, Warwicks, 123
Ardeley, Herts
  St Lawrence; Village Hall, 87
Ardenrun Place, Sussex, 166
Ardingly School, Sussex, 218
Ardington, Berks
  Holy Trinity, 65
Ardrossan, Ayrshire, 169
Ardsley, Yorks
  Christ Church, 128
Arlington Court, Devon, 149
Arundel, Sussex
  Castle, 123. Castle Goring, 192. St Philip Neri, 117
Ascot, Berks
  All Saints, 179. Ascot Heath House, 144
Ascott, Bucks, 83
Asgill House, Surrey, 230
Ash, Surrey
  St Mark, 258
Ashburton, Devon
  Market House, 122
Ashcombe Hall, Staffs, 235
Ashdown House, Sussex, 149
Ashford, Middx
  Welsh Charity School, 66
Ashridge House, Herts, 263, 264
Aston Clinton, Bucks
  Rectory, 146
Atcham, Salop
  Severn Bridge, 112

S

273

Atherstone, Warwicks
  St Scholastica's Priory, 117
Attingham Hall, Salop, 112, 195, 223
Audley End, Essex, 21, 48
Aveley, Essex
  Belhus, 160
Avoncliff, Wilts
  Aqueduct, 194
Aylsham, Norfolk
  Workhouse, 85
Aynhoe Park, Northants, 26
Ayot St Lawrence, Herts
  St Lawrence, 197

Babbacombe, Devon
  All Saints, 55
Babraham Hall, Cambs, 117
Backworth Hall, Northumb, 167
Bagby, Yorks
  St Mary, 146
Bagshot Park, Surrey, 93
Bagthorpe, Norfolk
  St Mary, 85
Balcombe Place, Sussex, 66
Baldersley, Yorks
  Park; St James; School; Vicarage, 57
Baltimore, Maryland, U.S.A.
  Cathedral, 149
Banbury, Oxon
  St Mary, 68, 69
Bangor, Caernarvon
  University College, 119
Barnsley, Yorks
  St Peter, 161
Barnstaple, Devon
  Guildhall, 149. Holy Trinity, 251
Bartestree, Herefs
  Convent, 190
Barton, Cambs
  Vicarage; School, 92
Basildon Park, Berks, 59
Bassingbourn, Cambs
  Kneesworth Hall, 184
Baswich, Staffs
  Holy Trinity, 235

Bath, Som
  Abbey, 209, 240. Abbey Cemetery, 153, 157. Alfred St., 257. Avon St., 225. Avon-Kennet Canal, Bathampton, 194. Bathwick Hill, 160. Bennett St., 257. Beauford Sq., 225. Blue Coat School, 157. Camden Crescent, 91. Catholic Apostolic Church, 157. Cavendish Crescent and Place, 181. Chandos House, 256. Christ Church, 174. Circus, 256. Cleveland Bridge, 107. Congregational Churches, 107. Corridor, 107. Doric House, 101. Friends' Meeting House, 253. Gay St., 256. Grosvenor Place, 91. Grove St. Prison, 29. Guildhall, 29, 31. Holy Trinity, Combe Down, 107. Hot Baths, 257. Kensington Chapel, 174. Kingsmead Sq. and St., 225. Kingston Baths, 135. Lansdown Crescent, 174. Lansdowne Tower, 107. Masonic Hall, 135. Menstrie Museum, 158. Milsom St., 135. Monmouth St., 225. New Assembly Rooms, 257. New Quay, 225. New Sydney Place, 181. North Parade, 135, 256. Northumberland Bldgs., 31. Octagon Chapel, 152. Oxford Row, 29. Paragon Crescent, 29. Poor Law Institution, 142. Prior Park, 256. Pump Room, 31. Queen Sq., 181, 256. Royal Crescent, 257. Royal Literary Institution, 237. Royal Mineral Water Hospital, 256. Royal School, 113. Russell St., 257. St Catherine's Almshouses, 157. St James, 135, 174. St James's Sq., 174. St John's Hospital, 256. St Mary, Bathwick, 181. St Matthew, Widcombe, 157. St Michael, 157. St Paul, Prior Park, 208. St Swithin, Walcot, 174. Sion Hill Place, 180. Sion Row, 91.

Bath, Som—*continued*
Somerset Place, 91. Somerset-
shire Bldgs., 31. South Parade,
256. Swedenborgian Church,
237. Technical School, 181.
Theatre Royal, 174, 180. Wid-
combe Crescent, 158. York House
Hotel, 257
Batourin Palace, Russia, 57
Battle Abbey School, Sussex, 66
Bayham Abbey, Sussex, 45
Bayham Castle, Sussex, 146
Bayon's Manor, Lincs, 169
Beaconsfield, Bucks
Hall Barn, 57. St Michael, 189.
Wilton Park, 138, 228
Bear Wood, Berks, 30, 144
Beaumanor Park, Leics, 192
Beaumont-cum-Moze, Essex
St Leonard, 114
Beckenham, Kent
Christ Church, 40. St Barnabas
Vicarage, 166. Town Hall, 147
Beckham, Norfolk
St Helen, 113. Workhouse, 85
Beddington House, Surrey, 24
Bedford
Asylum; Bridge, Gaol, 255. Rose
Inn; Swan Inn, 125
Bedlington, Northumb
Hartford House, 224
Bedstone Court, Salop, 119
Beech Hill, Berks
St Mary and Parsonage, 55
Belcombe Court, Wilts, 256
Belfast, N. Ireland
County Court; Gaol; Northern
Bank, 148. Parliament House,
145. Queen's College; Ulster
Institute for the Deaf, 148
Bellingham Bridge, Northumb, 109
Belper, Derbys
St Peter, 113
Belton House, Lincs, 255
Benacre Hall, Suffolk, 46
Berkhamsted, Herts
Haresfoot House, 183
Bessborough House, Ireland, 106

Bestwood Lodge, Notts, 231
Betteshanger House, Kent, 83, 154
Beverley, Yorks
Court House; Gaol, 188. St
Mary, 211
Bexleyheath, Kent
Red House, 248
Bickley, Kent
St George, 166
Bilbrough, Yorks
Manor House, 161
Billericay, Essex
St Andrew's Hospital, 209
Bilston, Staffs
St Leonard and Parsonage, 107
Bingley, Yorks
Milner Field, 119
Birkenhead, Cheshire
Christ Church, 134. Park, 178
Birkenshaw, Yorks
St Paul, 28
Birmingham, Warwicks
All Saints, 199. Barclays Bank,
232. Bishop Latimer Church,
Handsworth, 39. Blue Coat
School, Harborne, 192. Botanical
Gardens, Edgbaston, 153. Cathe-
dral, 26. Cavalry Barracks, 192.
City Museum and Art Gallery;
City Temple; Congregational
Chapel, Edgbaston; Council
House, 232. Crescent, 192. Cur-
zon St. Goods Station, 117. Grand
Hotel; Greek Orthodox Church,
62. Holy Trinity, Bordesley, 107.
Jaffray Hospital, Erdington, 232.
Lloyds Bank, 62. Midland Bank,
199. Orion Insurance, 151.
Queen Elizabeth Hospital, 147.
St Agatha, Sparkbrook, 39. St
Alban, Bordesley, 179. St Barna-
bas, Erdington, 199. St Chad's
Cathedral, 190. St George, Edg-
baston, 208. St James, Edg-
baston, 231. St James, Hands-
worth, 87. St Martin, 62. SS.
Mary and Ambrose, Edgbaston,
63. St Oswald, Bordesley, 39.

Birmingham, Warwicks—*continued*
St Paul, Aston, 62. St Peter's College, Selly Oak, 93. St. Thomas, 199. Synagogue, 232. Town Hall, 117. University, Edgbaston; Victoria Law Courts, 247

Birstwith, Yorks
Swarcliffe Hall, 120

Bishop's Stortford, Herts
Colleges, 65

Bishopthorpe, Yorks
St Andrew, 98

Blackdown, Sussex
Aldworth House, 145

Blackdown Hill, Som
Wellington Memorial, 149

Blagdon, Northumb
Cale Cross, 223

Blakmere, Herefs
St Leonard, 236

Blandford, Dorset
Bryanston, 216. Coupar House; Greyhound Inn; National Provincial Bank; Red Lion Inn; SS Peter and Paul, 35

Blankney, Lincs, 169

Bledlow Ridge, Bucks
Chapel of Ease, 39. Holy Trinity, 112

Blenheim Palace, Oxon, 32, 121, 138, 239

Bletchingley, Surrey
Orchard Croft, 249. Sandhills, 156

Blickling Hall, Norfolk, 44, 131

Blindley Heath, Surrey
St John, 249

Bocking, Essex
St Francis, 38. St Peter, 159

Boconnoc House, Cornwall, 182

Bodmin, Cornwall
Mental Hospital; Workhouse, 97

Bognor, Sussex
St Wilfrid, 189

Bolsover Castle, Derbys, 221

Boltby, Yorks, 52

Bolton Abbey, Yorks
Hall, 260

Bolton, Lancs
All Martyrs, Lever Bridge, 215. All Saints, 226

Boothby Pagnall Hall, Lincs, 241

Boreham House, Essex, 216

Boscombe, Hants
St Clement, 212

Boston, Lincs
Barclays Bank, 152. Fydell House, 207

Botleys, Surrey, 73

Boughton Park, Northants, 52

Boulogne, France
War Cemetery, 124

Bourne, Lincs
Town House, 48

Bournemouth, Hants, 93
Bath Hotel, 93. St Alban, 189

Bovingdon, Herts
St Lawrence, 54

Bowden Hill, Wilts
Spye Park, 52

Bowood, Wilts, 21, 67, 141

Boyles Court, Essex, 151

Bracknell, Berks
Holy Trinity, 69

Bradfield College, Berks, 211

Bradford, Yorks
Bradford Club; Exchange, 152. Holy Trinity, 214. Manningham Mills, Lister Park; Markets; St George's Hall, 152. St John Bowling, 214. Titus Salt monument, Lister Park; Town Hall; Victoria Hotel; Yorkshire United Independent College, 152

Bradford-on-Avon, Wilts
Belcombe Court, 256

Bradwell-Juxta-Mare, Essex
Bradwell Lodge, 135

Braiseworth, Suffolk
St Mary, 147

Bray, Ireland
Town Hall, 81

Brearton, Yorks
St John, 188

Bredenbury, Herefs
St Andrew, 265
Brentwood, Essex
Church Schools, 208. Mental Hospital, 142
Bretby Park, Derbys, 266
Bretton Park, Yorks, 34
Bridgend, Glam
Southerndown Hotel, 213
Bridgnorth, Salop
St Mary Magdalene, 231
Brigg, Lincs
St John, 169
Brighton, Sussex
Alliance Building Society, 106. Brunswick Town, 55. Cannon Place (No. 31); Christ Church, 252. College, 209. Elim Free Church, 252. Embassy Court, 67. Gothic House, 55. Grand Hotel, 250. Hanover Crescent; Holy Trinity, 252. Kemp Town, 55, 75, 142, 252. Marine Parade (No. 70), 88. Marine Pavilion, 125. Metropole Hotel, 246. Montpelier Place, 74. Mrs Fitzherbert's house, 185. Oriental Place, 252. Pavilion Bldgs, 129. Portland Place, 55. Prudential Assurance Co. North St., 246. Queen's Park, 32. Railway Station, 161. Regent Cinema, 28. Richmond Terrace (Nos. 4–6), 252. Royal Pavilion, 165, 185. St George's Chapel, 28. St Martin, 65. St Mary's Hall, 34. St Paul, 58. St Peter, 32. St Wilfrid, 106. Silwood Place, 252. Stanmer House, 86. Steine, 252. Sussex County Hospital, 32. Western Terrace, 252
Brightwalton, Berks
Woolley Park, 265
Bristol, Som, 177
All Saints, Clifton, 226. Anderson's Rubber Co. Stokes Croft, 104. Assembly Rooms and Hotel, Clifton, 109, 140. Bank of England, 68. Baptist College, 24. Blaise Castle; Bridge, 177. Buckingham Baptist Chapel, Clifton; Brunel House, 184. Caledonia Place, Clifton, 96. Camp House, Clifton, 86. Christ Church, 177. Clifton College, 117, 168. Clifton Hill House, 177, 244. Commercial Rooms, 55. Coopers' Hall, 115. Drinking Fountain, Clifton Down, 105. Exchange, 256. Female Orphanage Asylum, 86. Guildhall, 184. Highbury Chapel, 55. Horsefair, 96. House of Charity, 212. Library, 177. Litfield House, Clifton, 86. Market, 256. Municipal Library, 124. New Mall, Clifton, 96. Old Council House, 219. Queen Charlotte St. (No. 59), 225. Redland Chapel, 115, 177. Redland Court, 225. Royal Infirmary, 114, 124. Portland Sq., 114. Prospect House, Clifton, 177. St. Andrew, Clifton, 96. St Mark, Easton, 86. St Mary-on-the-Quay, 184. St Mary, Tyndalls Park, 205. St Matthew, Kingsdown, 199. St Michael, 177. St Paul, 114. Theatre Royal, 177. Victoria Rooms, Clifton, 86. Westminster Bank; Wool Hall, 184
Broadstairs, Kent
Hearts of Oak Convalescent Home, 259
Brocket Hall, Herts, 174
Brockhampton-by-Ross, Herefs
All Saints, 151
Brockhampton Park, Herefs, 56
Bromley, Kent
St John, 236
Bromley Common, Kent
Holy Trinity, 127
Bromyard, Herefs
Brockhampton Park, 56
Brookwood Cemetery, Surrey, 219, 234

Broomfield Manor, Devon, 83
Broseley, Salop
  All Saints, 88
Broughton Gifford, Wilts
  Rectory, 265
Broxbourne, Herts
  St Augustine, 225
Brussels Exhibition (1935), 201
Buckhold, Sussex
  Holy Trinity, 142
Buckhold House, Berks, 246
Buckland, Surrey
  St Mary, 258
Buckland House, Berks, 257
Bude, Cornwall
  St Michael, 251
Bulstrode Park, Bucks, 93
Buntingsale House, Salop, 220
Burbage, Leics
  St Catherine, 113
Burgess Hill, Sussex
  St John, 54
Burn Hall, Co. Durham, 44
Burnham-on-Crouch, Essex
  Royal Corinthian Yacht Club, 90
Burnley, Lancs
  St Mary, 114
Burslem, Staffs
  Etruria Works, 180
Burston, Norfolk
  Rectory, 242
Burton Constable, Yorks, 152
Burwood, Surrey
  Mental Hospital, 65
Bury St Edmunds, Suffolk
  Athenaeum, 207. Cathedral, 245.
  Gaol, 56. Ickworth House, 207.
  St Mary, 72. St Peter, 115.
  Town Hall, 21
Busbridge, Surrey
  Hall, 74, 102. St John, 210
Buslingthorpe, Lincs
  St Michael, 255
Butleigh Court, Som, 50
Butterleigh, Devon
  Hillersdon House, 35
Buxton, Derbys, 27, 59, 178
  Congregational Church, 76.

Devonshire Royal Hospital, 76,
  77. Empire Hotel, 100. Holy
  Trinity, 77. Palace Hotel, 76

Caerhays Castle, Cornwall, 165
Caernarvon
  Assembly Rooms and Baths, 185.
  Dispensary, 262
Caistor, Lincs
  Pelham's Pillar, 255
Calcutta, India
  Birkmyre Hotel, 147
Caledon Castle, Ireland, 71
Calverhall, Salop
  Holy Trinity, 166
Cambo, Northumb
  Holy Trinity, 109
Cambridge, Cambs
  Addenbroke's Hospital, 264. All
  Saints, 43. Botanic Gardens, 92.
  Caius College, 53, 246, 247, 253.
  Cavendish High Tension Labora-
  tory, 124. Cavendish Laboratory,
  92. Cemetery, 146, 153. Chem-
  ical Laboratory, 244. Cheshunt
  College, 127. Christ Church, 186.
  Christ's College, 197, 209. Clare
  College, 53, 210. Clare Hall, 91.
  Downing College, 253. Emman-
  uel College, 53, 92, 171, 224,
  227. Fitzwilliam Museum, 34.
  Garret Hostel Bridge, 164. Girton
  College, 246. Henry Martyn
  Memorial Hall, 187. Hughes
  Hall, 92. King's College, 92, 103,
  245. Law School, 132. Leys
  School, 247. Museums of Arch-
  aeology and Geology, 132. Nat-
  ional Institute of Agricultural
  Botany, 127. New University
  Library, 210. Newnham College,
  62. Pembroke College, 210, 261.
  Perse School for Boys, 92. Peter-
  house, 53, 92, 209. Pitt Press, 42,
  92. Queen's College, 53, 92.
  Railway Station, 257. Royal
  Albert Almshouses, 69. St Andrew

Cambridge, Cambs—*continued*
the Great, 186. St Catherine's
Hall, 91. St John's College, 199,
209, 227. St Mary-the-Less, 23.
St Paul, 186. School of Medicine,
187. Scott Polar Research Insti-
tute, 30. Selwyn College, 62.
Senate House, 53, 103. Sidney
Sussex College, 227, 266. Trinity
College, 32, 91, 227, 253, 261.
Trinity Hall, 53, 197. Union
Society, 246. University Library,
261. Westminster College, 118,
119
Camerton Court, Som, 196
Canklow House, Yorks, 182
Cannes, France
Protestant Church, 221
Canterbury, Kent
Cathedral, 71, 87, 245, 254, 267.
Gaol, 56, 249. St Augustine's
College, 55, 126
Canons House, Middx, 32, 133, 187
Cape Town, S. Africa
Rhodes Memorial; St George's
Cathedral, 30
Capheaton Hall, Northumb, 235
Cardiff, Glam
Civic Centre, 147. St Mary, 97.
University College, 58
Carlisle, Cumberland
Courts of Justice, 169. Railway
Station, 234
Carlton Towers, Yorks, 38, 191
Carmarthen
Bishops's Palace, 96
Carshalton, Surrey
All Saints, 41. House, 138
Carton, Ireland, 60
Cashel Place, Ireland, 179
Cassiobury Park, Herts, 158
Castell Coch, Glam, 51
Castle Donington, Leics
Donington Hall, 253
Castle Eden, Co. Durham, 167
Castle Goring, Sussex, 192
Castle Howard, Yorks, 68, 121, 202,
228, 239

Castletown, Ireland, 179
Caterham, Surrey
Guards' Depot Chapel, 56. Up-
wood Gorse, 248
Caythorpe, Lincs
Vicarage, 99
Chailey, Sussex
Heritage School Chapel, 71. St
Mary, 211
Chalfont St Peter, Bucks
Chalfont House, 38, 64. St
Peter's Rectory, 206
Charlton Marshall, Dorset, 34
Charlton, Wilts
Park, 46. Trafalgar (Standlynch)
House, 161, 196, 257
Chart Park, Surrey, 27
Charterhouse School, Surrey, 118,
210
Chatham, Kent
Crimean War Memorial, 264.
Melville Hospital, 229
Chatsworth, Derbys, 26, 27, 53, 178,
228, 233, 265
Chatton, Northumb
Vicarage, 84
Cheadle, Staffs
St Giles, 190
Cheam, Surrey
Nonsuch House, 265
Chelmsford, Essex
Barclays Bank, 41. Cathedral,
168. Gaol, 127. Holy Trinity,
Springfield, 196. Moulsham
Bridge; St Mary's Cathedral,
135. St Michael and All Angels,
Galleywood Common, 205. Shire
Hall, 135
Cheltenham, Glos
Christ Church, 134. Holy Trinity,
237. Lansdowne Estate, 134.
Lansdowne Terrace (Nos. 15–17),
175. Literary Institution, 134.
Masonic Hall, 237. Montpelier
Estate and Pump Room, 175.
Queen's Hotel, 134. St John, 175.
St Peter, 80, 90

Chepstow, Mon
  Bridge, 194
Chertsey, Surrey
  Bridge, 174. St Peter, 63. Town
  Hall, 39
Cheshunt, Herts
  Theobalds Park, 167
Chester
  Castle; Grosvenor Bridge, 119
Chestham Park, Sussex, 252
Chichester, Sussex
  Council House, 161. St John, 89.
  St Peter, 58
Chiddingfold, Surrey
  Pickhurst, 49
Chiddingstone Causeway, Kent
  St Luke, 38
Chigwell Row, Essex
  All Saints, 213
Chilton Foliat, Berks
  Chilton Lodge, 181
Chilworth, Surrey
  St Martha, 258
Chippenham, Wilts
  Town Hall, 232
Chipperfield, Herts
  St Paul, 54
Chiswick House, Middx, 44, 143
Chobham, Surrey
  Gordon Boys' Home, 56
Chorleywood, Herts
  The Orchard, 241
Church Stretton, Salop
  Woodcote, 238
Clacton-on-Sea, Essex
  St James, 161
Clandon Park, Surrey, 130, 150
Clandown, Som
  Holy Trinity, 158
Clare House, Kent, 183, 212
Claremont House, Surrey, 48, 123
Claydon House, Bucks, 202
Cleatham Hall, Lincs, 99
Cleeve, Som
  Holy Trinity, 157
Clevedon, Som
  Christ Church, 199

Climping, Sussex
  St Mary's Parsonage, 184
Cliveden, Bucks, 66, 255
Clonskeagh, Ireland
  Masonic Boys' Schools, 86
Cloverley Hall, Salop, 166
Clumber House, Notts, 261
Coalbrookdale, Salop
  Bridge, 187
Coatham, Yorks
  Christ Church, 69
Cobham, Surrey
  Bridge, 111.   Fairmile,   248.
  Lodge, 175. Park, 33, 263
Cobham Hall, Kent, 195
Colburn, Yorks
  St Cuthbert, 197
Colchester, Essex
  Essex & Suffolk Equitable Insur-
  ance, 146. St James the Less,
  208. St John, 40. St. Mary-at-
  the-Walls, 187. Town Hall, 37.
  The Turrets, 154
Coleby Hall, Lincs, 61
Coleorton Hall, Leics, 79
Coleshill, Warwicks
  SS Peter and Paul, 218
Coleshill House, Berks, 186
Colwick Hall, Notts, 59
Combe Martin, Devon
  Arlington Court, 149
Compton Place, Sussex, 57
Congleton, Cheshire
  Town Hall, 104
Copt Oak, Leics
  St Peter, 192
Copthorne, Sussex
  Newlands, 221. St John, 113
Corbie, France
  War Cemetery, 124
Cork, Ireland
  Bank of Ireland, 81. Courthouse,
  81, 173. Prison, 173. St Finbar's
  Cathedral, 51. Savings Banks, 81
Cornbury House, Oxon, 158
Corsham, Wilts
  SS Philip and James, 115

Coventry, Warwicks
  Cemetery, Cheylesmore, 178.
  Drapers' Hall, 199. Holy Trinity,
  71. St Peter, 87
Cowfold, Sussex
  Clock House, 238
Cowley Manor, Oxon, 64
Coxwold Hall, Lincs, 70
Cranley School, Surrey, 258
Crawley, Sussex
  Hospital, 268. SS Francis and
  Anthony, 106, 107
Creeton, Lincs
  Rectory, 48
Cromer Hall, Norfolk, 85
Cromford, Derbys
  Willersley Castle, 232
Croome, Worcs
  Court, 21, 48. St Mary Mag-
  dalene, 48
Crowcombe Court, Som, 130
Crowell, Som
  Rectory, 192
Crowhurst, Sussex
  Ardenrun Place, 166
Croydon, Surrey
  Addington Palace, 163. Bedding-
  ton House, 24. Christ Church,
  231. College of Art, 28. Free-
  masons' Asylum, 80. St. Michael,
  179. Technical College, 28.
  Whitgift School, 40
Cuckfield, Sussex
  Danehurst, 128. Holmbush, 88
Cuddesdon, Oxon
  Theological College, 226
Cumberland Lodge, Bucks, 206

Dallington, Sussex
  Oldcastle, 167
Danehill, Sussex
  All Saints, 43
Darlington, Co. Durham
  Mechanics' Institute, 188
Dartford, Kent
  Gas Works; The Towers, 74

Dartington, Devon
  Broom Park and Huxham's Cross
  Estates, 82, 83
Daventry, Northants
  Holy Cross, 123
Dawley, Salop
  Holy Trinity, 88
Dawlish, Devon
  St Michael, 177
Debden, Essex
  Bank of England Printing Works,
  201. St Mary, 60
Deepdene House, Surrey, 29, 127
Denstone, Staffs
  All Saints, 226. College, 59, 218
Denton, Co. Durham
  St Mary, 188
Derby
  Arboretum, 153. Cathedral (All
  Saints), 103, 220. Christ Church,
  113. Gaol; St John, 107. St
  Mary's Cathedral, 190. South
  African War Memorial, 236.
  Town Hall, 113
Dethick, Derbys
  Lea Wood, 166
Devizes, Wilts
  Assize Court, 265. Castle, 107.
  Market Cross, 262. Roundhay
  Hospital, 265. Town Hall, 31
Dewsbury, Yorks
  St John, 230
Didcot, Berks
  Rectory, 237
Dillington House, Som, 180
Dinton, Wilts
  Philipps House, 266
Dittisham, Devon, 82
Ditton Park, Bucks, 29
Dobroyd Castle, Yorks, 104
Doddington, Lincs
  St Peter, 154
Doncaster, Yorks
  Christ Church, 128. Cusworth
  Hall; Mansion House, 173. Robin
  Hood's Well, 239. St Mary; St
  James, 36
Donnington Grove, Berks, 64

Donnington Hall, Leics, 253
Dorchester, Dorset
 Gaol, 40
Dorking, Surrey
 Chart Park, 27. Holmdale, Holmbury St Mary, 226. St Martin, 258. St Mary, Holmbury St Mary, 226
Douglas, I.O.M.
 St Matthew, 179. St Thomas, 63
Dover, Kent
 Gaol, 90. Lord Warden Hotel; Pilot House, 35
Dovercourt, Essex
 Alexandra House, 217
Downham Market, Norfolk
 Howdale Home, 85
Downside Abbey, Som, 100, 107
Doxford Hall, Northumb, 83, 84
Drayton House, Northants, 228
Drumcondra House, Ireland, 179
Dublin
 Blackhall Pl. and St., 131. Blue Coat School, 130, 131. Church of the Calced Carmelites, 175. Clontarf Casino, 61. Collins Barracks, 51. Commercial Union offices, 81. Custom House, 100. Daly's Club House, 135. Dr Steevens's Hospital, 51. Four Courts, 71, 100. General Post Office, 136. Graduates Memorial Bldg., 86. Green Street Courthouse, 136. Gresham Hotel, 28. Henrietta St. (Nos. 9, 10), 60. Hibernian Marine and Military Schools, 71. Kildare Club, 81. Kingsbridge, 175. Kingsbridge Railway Station, 257. King's Inns, 100. Leinster House, 60. Municipal Bldgs., 131. National Gallery, 97. National Library of Ireland, 81. Nelson Column, 136, 253. New Assembly Rooms, 136. Newgate Prison, 71. O'Connell Bridge, 100. Parliament House, 100, 136, 179. Printing House, 60. Richmond Bridge, 208. Rotunda Hospital, 60. Royal Exchange, 71. St George, 136. St Kevin; St Patrick's Cathedral, 86. St Stephen's Green (No. 80), 60. Science and Art Museum, 81. Swift's Hospital, 71. Trinity College, 51, 60, 81. Tyrone House, 60. Viceregal Lodge, 136
Dumbleton Hall, Worcs, 196
Dumfries
 Burns Mausoleum, 128
Dunlop House, Ayrshire, 116
Dunster School, Som, 205
Durham
 Gaol, 44. St Nicholas, 188
Dyrham Park, Glos, 228

Earsdon, Northumb
 St Alban, 109
East Carlton, Notts
 St Peter, 255
East Clandon, Surrey, 106
East Grinstead, Sussex
 St Swithun, 263. Standen, 249
East Knoyle, Wilts
 Clouds, 249
East Lavington, Sussex
 Lavington Park, 152
East Malling, Kent
 Clare House, 183, 212. Horticultural Research Station, 147
East Molesey, Surrey
 St Mary, 54
East Preston, Sussex
 Sea Lane House, 268
East Retford, Notts
 St Saviour, 255
East Rounton, Yorks
 School, 248, 249
East Stoke, Notts
 Stoke Hall, 263
Eastbourne, Sussex
 Cavendish Hotel, 145. College, 77. Compton Place, 57. St Peter, 77. St Saviour, 226
Eastnor Castle, Herefs, 219

Easton, Suffolk
Glevering Hall, 250
Easton Neston, Northants, 121
Eastwell Park, Kent, 44
Eaton Hall, Cheshire, 140, 185
Ebberston Hall, Yorks, 57
Edensor, Derbys, 178
Barbrook House, 178. Buxton Lodge, 266
Edgcote House, Northants, 220
Edinburgh
Academy, 52. Bank of Scotland, 193. British Linen Bank, 49. Broughton Place Church, 89. Burns Monument, 116. Caledonian Railway Station, 234. Calton Hill, 183. Deaf and Dumb Institution; Dr Jamieson's Chapel, 108. Dugald Stewart Monument, 183. George IV Bridge, 116. Gt. King St., 193. Heriot's Hospital, 243. Holyrood Palace, 49. Hopetoun House, 22, 49. International Exhibition (1886), 52. Johnson Terrace, 116. Medical Schools, 25. Montrose Memorial, 26. Moray Estate, 108. Museum of Antiquities, 26. Museum of Science and Art, 97. National Gallery, 183. National Portrait Gallery, 26. Observatory, 183. Parliament House, 193. Queen St., 21. Regent Bridge, 89. Register House, 193. Royal Bank of Scotland, 62. Royal High School, 116. Royal Infirmary, 22. Royal Scottish Academy, 183. St Cecilia's Hall, 163. St John's Chapel, 52. St Paul's Chapel, 89. St Stephen, 183. Scott Memorial, 141. Surgeons' Hall, 183. Tolbooth Church, 108. Tron Kirk, 163. Union Bank of Scotland, 49. University Bldgs., 183. Waterloo Place, 89
Edmonton, Middx
St Aldhelm; St Michael, 58

Elgin, Moray
St Giles, 218
Elham, Kent
St Mary, 87
Ellesmere College, Salop, 59
Eltham Palace, Kent, 139
Ely, Cambs
Cathedral, 23, 80, 91
Emral Hall, Flint, 235
Endsleigh Cottage, Devon, 195, 266
Englefield Green, Surrey
SS Simon and Jude, 146
Epping, Essex
St John, 43
Epsom, Surrey
Atmospheric Railway Station, 45.
College, 66. Durdans, 83, 167
Erlestoke Park, Wilts, 223
Escot House, Devon, 200
Esher Place, Surrey, 73
Eshton Hall, Yorks, 249
Eton College, Bucks, 32, 69, 132, 172, 215, 241
Ettington Park, Warwicks, 213
Evesham, Worcs
Dumbleton Hall, 196
Ewell, Surrey
St Mary, 66
Ewhurst, Surrey
Coneyhurst, 249. Hurtwood, 43.
SS Peter and Paul; Rectory, 87
Exeter, Devon
Gaol, 40. Higher Market, 98.
Holy Trinity, 143. Mamhead, 205. St David, 58. St James's Priory Estate, 82
Exmouth, Devon
The Barn, 187
Exning House, Suffolk, 135
Eydon Hall, Northants, 152
Eye, Northants
St Matthew, 34, 84
Eyeford Park, Glos, 80
Eyewell House, Som, 80

Fairwarp, Sussex
Christ Church, 120

Fakenham, Norfolk
  Corn Hall, 48
Falmouth, Cornwall
  All Saints, 212
Farley Hill, Berks
  St John, 236
Farnham, Bucks
  Park; St Mary, 166
Farnham, Essex
  Hassobury House, 118. St Mary the Virgin, 65
Farnham, Surrey
  Crooksbury Lodge, 155
Farrington Gurney, Som
  St John, 181
Faversham, Kent
  Our Lady of Charity, 78
Felbridge, Surrey
  St John and Vicarage, 251
Felbrigg Hall, Norfolk, 173, 174
Felsted School, Essex, 41, 135
Fetcham Park, Surrey, 228
Finborough Hall, Suffolk, 207
Finedon Hall, Northants, 195
Fishtoft, Lincs
  Rectory, 142
Flax Bourton, Som
  Cambridge House Hospital, 209
Flaxton-on-the-Moor, Yorks
  St Lawrence, 26
Folkestone, Kent
  Spade House, 241
Folkingham, Lincs
  House of Correction, 48
Fonthill Gifford, Wilts
  Abbey, 263. Holy Trinity, 265. House, 42
Foot's Cray Place, Kent, 244, 245
Forceville, France
  War Cemetery, 124
Ford Castle, Northumb, 49
Ford Manor, Surrey, 144
Foremark Hall, Derbys, 123
Forest Row, Sussex
  Ashdown House, 149. Hollyhill, Coleman's Hatch, 211. Shalesbrooke, 156. Village Hall, 49

Fosdyke, Lincs
  All Saints, 48
Fountains Abbey, Yorks, 211
Framlingham College, Suffolk, 69
Frant, Sussex
  Shernfield Park, 242
Frensham, Surrey
  Lowicks, 241
Friern Barnet, Middx
  Colney Hatch Asylum, 80
Frimley, Surrey
  Park, 149. St Peter, 177
Frogmore House, Bucks, 263
Frome, Som
  Bridge; Christ Church, 237. Holy Trinity, 107
Fulbourn, Cambs
  Asylum, 148
Fulmer, Bucks
  Fernacres, 202

Gainsborough, Lincs
  St John, 65, 159
Galby, Lincs
  St Peter, 255
Ganarew, Herefs
  Leys, 52
Garboldisham Manor, Norfolk, 210
Garendon Hall, Leics, 191
Gargrave, Yorks
  St Andrew, 120
Garnons, Herefs, 29
Garsdon, Wilts
  All Saints, 69
Gatton Park, Surrey, 72
Gatwick Airport, Surrey, 268
Gayton, Norfolk
  Workhouse, 85
Gerrards Cross, Bucks
  St James, 234
Gibside Chapel, Co. Durham, 174
Gillingham, Kent
  St Augustine, 161
Glasgow
  Bank of Scotland, 203. Bridge of Sighs; British Linen Bank, 116. Caledonia Rd. Free Church, 232.

Glasgow—*continued*
Carlton Place, 169. Central Station Hotel, 25. Cleveden Crescent; Clyde Trust Bldg.; Clydesdale Bank, 52. Cornhill House, 213. Custom House, 229. Davidson of Ruchill Monument, 203. Dumbarton Rd. (No. 56), 213. Egyptian Halls, 232. *Glasgow Herald* offices, 156. Govan Parish Church, 25. Gt. Western Terrace, 232. Greek Orthodox Church, 213. Grosvenor Terrace, 203. Holmwood House, Cathcart, 232. Hutcheson's Hospital, 116. Ingram St. (No. 211), 156. International Exhibition (1881), 213. John St. Church, 203. Kelvinside Academy, 213. Necropolis, 116. Park Church, 203. Pearce Institute, 25. Pollok House, 20. Queen's Cross Church, 156. Royal Exchange, 116. Royal Institute of Fine Arts, 52. St Andrew's Cathedral, 108. St Andrew's Hall, 213. St Cuthbert, 156. St David, 199. St Mary's Episcopal Cathedral, 209. Sauchiehall St. (No. 199); School of Art; Scotland St. School, 156. Stock Exchange, 52. Trades House, 21. University, 52. Walmer Crescent, 232. Western Club, 116

Glevering Hall, Suffolk, 250
Glossop, Derbys
Town Hall, 114
Gloucester
Gaol, 40
Glynde, Sussex
St Mary, 202
Godalming, Surrey
Bridge, 111. Tuesley Court, 80
Godstone, Surrey
Ouborough, 215
Goldings House, Herts, 83
Goodwood House, Sussex, 61, 161, 263

Goole, Yorks
St John, 128
Grace Dieu Manor, Leics, 192
Grafham, Surrey
Grange; St Andrew, 258
Grantham, Lincs
St Mary, 255
Gravesend, Kent
Henleys' factory, 145. St James, 80
Gt. Amwell, Herts
Myddleton Monument, Mylne Mausoleum, 164
Gt. Bookham, Surrey
Millfield, 202
Gt. Dixter, Northiam, Sussex, 155
Gt. Finborough, Suffolk
Finborough Hall, 207
Gt. Houghton, Northants
St Mary, 123
Gt. Packington, Warwicks
St James, 44
Gt. Smeaton, Yorks
Smeaton Manor, 248
Gt. Stainton, Co. Durham
All Saints, 188
Gt. Warley, Essex
Boyles Court, 151. St Mary, 234
Gt. Wolford, Warwicks
St Michael, 235
Gt. Yarmouth, Norfolk
Nelson Column, 253. Northgate Hospital, 48. St George, 187. St James, 213. St Nicholas Hospital, 181. St Peter, 208
Greenford, Middx
Holy Cross, 197
Greystead, Northumb
St Luke and Parsonage, 214
Grimsby, Lincs
Dock Tower, 252. Royal Hotel, 114
Grimsthorpe Castle, Lincs, 48
Grimston Park, Yorks, 54
Grinshill, Salop
All Saints, 58
Grittleton House, Wilts, 232
Groombridge, Kent
Leys Wood, 216

Hackness Hall, Yorks, 27
Hackthorn Hall, Lincs, 152
Hadlow, Kent
Castle, 229. Grange, 189
Haileybury College, Herts, 253
Hainton, Lincs
Hall, 27, 48, 255. St Mary, 255
Hale House, Hants, 26
Halnaker House, Sussex, 155
Halstead, Essex
Cottage Hospital, 217
Ham Common, Surrey
St Andrew, 148
Ham House, Surrey, 195
Hamilton Palace, Scotland, 116
Hammerwood, Sussex
House, 149. St Stephen, 47, 113
Hampton, Middx
Hampton Court Bridge, 155. St
Mary, 148
Hampton Lucy, Warwicks
St Peter, 199
Hamptworth Lodge, Wilts, 80
Hamstead Marshall, Berks, 103, 255
Hanwell, Middx
St Mary, 209
Happisburgh Manor, Norfolk, 42
Hardwick Hall, Derbys, 221
Hardenhuish, Wilts
St Nicholas, 257
Hare Hall, Essex, 174
Haresfoot House, Herts, 183
Harewood, Yorks, 59
House, 27, 59
Harlaxton Manor, Lincs, 52, 205
Harpenden, Herts
St John, 87. St Nicholas, 218
Harrogate, Yorks
Methodist Church, 153. Royal
Bath Hospital, 260. St Wilfrid,
161
Harrow, Middx
Public Hall, 121. School, 30, 62,
67, 121, 187
Harrow Weald, Middx
Grimsdyke, 216
Hartford, Conn., U.S.A.
Trinity College, 51

Hartford House, Northumb, 224
Harting, Sussex
Uppark House, 141, 228
Harwich, Essex
Lighthouse, 24. Town Hall, 25
Hascombe, Surrey
St Peter, 258
Haslemere, Surrey
Lythe Hill House, 68. New
Place, 241. Red Court, 166
Hassobury House, Essex, 118
Hastings, Sussex
Convent of the Holy Child, 244.
Holy Trinity, 231. Pelham Cres-
cent, 140. St Andrew, 47, 113.
St Mary-in-the-Castle, 140. St
Mary Magdalen, 158. St Peter,
47. St Thomas, 50
Hatfield House, Herts, 34
Hatfield New Town, Herts
Secondary Modern School; Tech-
nical College, 201
Haugham, Lincs
All Saints, 169
Haverholme Priory, Lincs, 142
Havering-atte-Bower, Essex
Bower House, 95
Haywards Heath, Sussex
Railway Viaduct, 161. St Francis
Hospital, 142. St Wilfrid, 43
Heath House, Yorks, 173
Helmsley Lodge, Yorks, 32
Helston, Cornwall
Grammar School; Guildhall, 251
Henfield, Sussex
Chestham Park, 252
Henley-on-Thames, Oxon
Bridge, 112. Park Place, 182
Hereford
Cathedral, 72, 73. Nelson
Column, 118
Herstmonceux, Sussex
Place, 264. Windmill Hill Place,
196
Hertford
Christ's Hospital, 171. County
Hall, 133. Hospital, 221. Shire
Hall, 20

Heveningham Hall, Suffolk, 230, 263
Hewarth, Co. Durham
St. Mary, 224
High Wycombe, Bucks
Guildhall, 141. Market Hall, 21. St Francis, 210. Wycombe Abbey School, 58
Highnam, Glos
Holy Innocents, 258
Hildenborough, Kent
St John, 63
Hildersham Hall, Cambs, 148
Hillersdon House, Devon, 35
Hitchen, Herts
Holy Saviour, 55
Hoarwithy, Herefs
St Catherine, 213
Hoddesdon, Herts
Clock Tower, 221
Holdernesse, Yorks
Grimston Garth, 59
Holkham, Norfolk
Hall, 45, 46, 143. St Withberga, 70
Holmwood, Surrey
St John, 120
Holt, Norfolk
Home Place, 187
Holywell, Northants
St James, 142
Honiton, Devon
St Paul, 98. Widworthy Court, 196
Hooton, Cheshire
St Paul, 70
Horbury, Yorks
St John, 159. SS Peter and Leonard, 59
Horncliffe, Northumb
Long Ridge Tower, 50
Horseheath Hall, Cambs, 186
Horsforth, Yorks
Newlaithes Hall, 154
Horsham, Sussex
Christ's Hospital, 247. Coolhurst, 202. Primary School, 220
Horstead Place, Sussex, 80

Horwood House, Bucks, 42
Houghton Hall, Norfolk, 57, 199
Hove, Sussex
St Patrick, 142. Town Hall, 246
Hovingham, Yorks
All Saints, 120
Howgill, Yorks
Holy Trinity, 215
Howick Hall, Northumb, 30, 167
Huddersfield, Yorks
Banney Royd; Clock Tower, Lindley, 256. College, 188. Holy Trinity, 230. Lion Bldg.; Railway Station; St Peter, 188
Hughenden Manor, Bucks, 146
Hull, Yorks
Docks, 120. Guildhall, 71. Railway Station, 26. Royal Institution, 47
Humshaugh, Northumb
St Peter and Parsonage, 214
Hungerford, Berks
Park, 167. St Lawrence, 181
Hunstanworth, Co. Durham, 231
Huntly, Aberdeen
Duchess of Gordon's Schools, 218
Hurstpierpoint, Sussex
Holy Trinity, 32. St John's College, 58
Hutton Buscel, Yorks
School, 55
Hylands, Essex, 29

Ickworth House, Suffolk, 207
Ilford, Essex
Church Schools, 208. St Andrew, 30. St Mary, 208. St Peter, 27
Ilkley, Yorks
College of Housecraft, 47. Heathcote, 155
Ilminster, Som
Dillington House, 180
Ingatestone, Essex
The Tiles, 217
Inkpen, Bucks
School, 226

Inverary Castle, Argyllshire, 161, 162
Ipswich, Suffolk
  Gaol, 40. St Andrew, Rushmere, 114
Iver Heath, Bucks
  Warren House, 88

Jacobstowe, Devon
  Broomfield Manor, 83
Jerusalem
  St James's Cathedral, 113. War Cemetery, 52
Jodhpur, India
  Maharajah's Palace, 147
Johannesburg Exhibition (1936), 201

Kedleston Hall, Derbys, 174
Keighley, Yorks
  Mechanics' Institute, 153
Kelham Hall, Northants, 209
Kelmarsh, Northants
  Hall, 103. St Dionysius, 70
Kendal, Westmorland
  Town Hall, 249
Kenwick Hall, Lincs, 161
Kew, Surrey
  Bridge, 174. Gardens, 53, 61, 166, 266. St Anne, 144
Kilcarty House, Ireland, 131
Kildare, Ireland
  Castletown, 179
Kilkenny, Ireland
  Bessborough House, 106
Killarney, Ireland
  Asylum, 81
Killingworth, Northumb
  St John, 140
Kilndown, Kent
  Christ Church, 126
Kimberworth, Yorks
  St Thomas, 113
Kingsbury, Middx
  St Andrew, 80
King's Lynn, Norfolk
  Customs House; Duke's Head Inn, 37. General Hospital, 26. King Edward VII Grammar School, 62. Market Cross, 37
King's Norton, Leics
  St John, 255
King's Weston, Glos, 239
Kingston Bagpuize, Berks
  Rectory, 64
Kingston Lacy House, Dorset, 186
Kingston, Som
  Tetton House, 106
Kingston-upon-Hull, see Hull
Kingston-upon-Thames, Surrey
  Bridge, 148. Dr Barnado's Home, 221. St Raphael, 176
Kingswood, Glos
  Holy Trinity, 96
Kington, Herefs
  Lady Margaret Hawkins Grammar School, 19
Kinlet Hall, Salop, 220
Kinmel Park, Denbighs, 166
Kinnerley, Salop
  St Mary, 188
Kinross House, Kinross-shire, 49
Kirby Hall, Northants, 233
Kirby Hall, Yorks, 59
Kirby Muxloe Castle, Leics, 73
Kirtlington Park, Oxon, 220
Kitley House, Devon, 196
Kneesworth Hall, Cambs, 184
Kneller Hall, Middx, 157
Knepp Castle, Sussex, 165
Knotty Green, Bucks
  Holly Mount, 241
Knutsford, Lancs
  Library, 79
Kronstadt, Russia
  Naval Hospital and Barracks, 57

Lacock Abbey, Wilts, 160
Lake, I.O.W.
  Church of the Good Shepherd, 161
Lamberhurst, Kent
  Scotney Castle, 205

Lambourn, Berks
Almshouses, 54
Lambton Hall, Co. Durham, 44
Lampeter, Cards
St David's College, 67
Lamport, Northants
All Saints, 220. Hall, 248
Lancaster
Gaol, 119. Lune Aqueduct, 194.
Public Bath, 101
Lancing College, Sussex, 58, 59
Landford, Wilts
Hamptworth Lodge, 80
Langdon Hills, Essex
St Mary, 251
Langley, Bucks
Actors' Orphanage, 145. Hall,
149. St Mary, 91
Langley Park, Norfolk, 46
Langleybury, Herts
St Paul, 258
Lathom Hall, Lancs, 150
Launceston, Cornwall
Town Hall, 122
Lavington Park, Sussex, 152
Laxton Hall, Northants, 196
Leadenham Hall, Lincs, 255
Leamington, Warwicks
Christ Church, 202. St Mark, 210
Leatherhead, Surrey
Bridge, 111
Leeds, Yorks
Armley Cemetery, 188. Bank of
England, 118. Central Colleges,
268. City Baths; Congregational
Church, Headingley Lane 47.
Grammar School, 33. Grand
Theatre, 72. Holy Trinity, 115.
Holy Trinity, Meanwood, 192.
Institute of Science, 47. Marshall
Mills, 44. Municipal Bldgs., 72.
Queen's Hotel, 236. St Anne's
School, 105. St Chad, Far
Headingley, 36. St Hilda, Cross
Green Lane, 159. St John,
Roundhay, 230. St Wilfrid, 161.
Spenfield, Otley Rd.; Sun Fire
offices, 72. The Towers, Park-

lands Estate, 191. Town Hall,
47. University, 147. Victoria
Chambers, 152. West Park
Modern School, 268
Leek, Staffs
All Saints, 216
Leicester
County Rooms; Southgate St.,
135
Leigh Court, Som, 127
Leigh Delamere, Wilts
Almshouses; St Margaret and
Parsonage, 232
Leigh-on-Sea, Essex
St Mary, 168
Leiston, Suffolk
St Margaret, 146
Lennox Castle, Scotland, 116
Leominster, Herefs
Old Town Hall, 19
Letchworth, Herts, 237
Lewes, Sussex
Bridge, 86. Castle Place (No.
166), 252
Leyton, Essex
Master Bakers' Benevolent Insti-
tution, 144
Lichfield, Staffs
Manley Hall, 235
Lilburn Tower, Northumb, 84
Lilystone Hall, Essex, 50
Limerick, Ireland
Prison, 173
Limpley Stoke, Wilts
Dundas Aqueduct, 194
Lincoln
All Saints, 98. Bishop's Hostel,
154, 161. Castle, 255. Cathedral,
91, 98. Cathedral School, 52.
Corn Exchange, 169. County
Record Office, 154. Gaol, 59, 69.
Library, 41. St Nicholas, 209.
School of Art, 154
Lindale, Lancs
St. Paul, 249
Linden House, Northumb, 83
Lindisfarne Castle, Northumb, 155

Lingfield, Surrey
Ford Manor, 144
Linley Hall, Salop, 138
Linlithgow Palace, Scotland, 243
Liskeard, Cornwall
Workhouse, 97
Little Horstead, Sussex
Horstead Place, 80
Little Horwood, Bucks
Horwood House, 42
Little Petherick, Cornwall
St Petrock, 250, 251
Little Warley, Essex
Warley Barracks, 264
Littlemore, Oxon
SS Mary and Nicholas, 237
Littleworth, Berks
Ascension Church, 237
Liverpool, Lancs
Albany Bldg, 70. Bank of England, 68. County Asylum, Rainhill, 89. Customs House, 97. Docks, 120. Exchange Bldgs, 265. Gambier Terrace; Huskisson Memorial; Infirmary; Lime St. Railway Station, 97. Liverpool, London & Globe offices, 68. Lyceum Club, 119. Metropolitan Cathedral, 155. Philharmonic Hall, 76. Royal Exchange Assurance Bldgs, 110. Royal Infirmary, 246. Sailors' Home, 76. St Andrew, 96. St Anne, Aigburth, 76. St Clare, Sefton Park, 224. St George, Everton, 199. St George's Hall, 68, 89. St John, 152. St Luke, 96. St Michael-the-Hamlet, 199. St Paul, 152. Seamen's Orphanage, 246. Students' Union, 194. Town Hall, 256. Wellington Assembly Rooms, 22. White Star Line offices, 216
Liverpool, Australia
St. Luke, 109
Liversedge, Yorks
Christ Church, 230

London
Abney Park Cemetery, 128. Adelaide House, 53. Adelaide Rd., Hampstead, 215. Adelphi, 21. Admiralty, 21, 199. Admiralty Arch, 247. Admiralty House, 68. Agnew's Galleries, Old Bond St., 260. Agricultural Hall, Islington, 69. Albany, 125. Albert Gate, Knightsbridge, 75. Albert Hall, 97, 211. Albert Hall Mansions, 216. Albert Memorial, 209. Albion Mills, Southwark, 194, 264. Alfred Place, 78. All Hallows, London Wall, 78. All Hallows, Southwark, 210. All Saints, Blackheath, 93. All Saints, Camden Town, 130. All Saints, Fulham, 41. All Saints, Lambeth, 188, 189. All Saints, Margaret St., 55. All Saints, Notting Hill, 250. All Saints, Tooting, 161. All Souls, Langham Place, 107, 165. All Souls School, 182. Alliance Assurance offices, Pall Mall and St James's St., 216. Alliance Assurance, Turnham Green, 241. Alliance Fire Co. offices, 24. Amen Court (Nos. 4–9), 63. Annesley Lodge, Hampstead, 241. Apsley House, 262. Archway Hospital, Islington, 222. Argyll House, 150. Arlington St. (No. 16), 103; (No. 22), 143, 261. Armourers' Hall, 106. Ascension, Church of the, Lavender Hill, 47. Assumption, Church of the, Kensington, 105. Athenaeum Club, 53. Atlas Fire Assurance offices, Cheapside, 127. Austin Friars (No. 23), 247; (No. 28), 194. Australia & New Zealand Bank, Threadneedle St., 118

Bank of Australasia, Lothbury, 64. Bank of Ceylon, Ludgate Hill, 183. Bank of England, 30, 41, 222, 230. Bankside Power

London—*continued*

Station, 210. Banqueting House, 137. Battersea Park, 180. Battersea Polytechnic, 163. Battersea Power Station, 210. Battersea Town Hall, 163. Battlebridge, St Pancras, 102. Bayswater, 68. Bayswater Rd. (No. 12), 240; (No. 140), 224. Bedford College, 62. Bedford Park, 216. Bedford Place, 54. Bedford Sq., 151. Belgrave Mansions, 75. Belgrave Sq., 34; (No. 12 Portuguese Embassy), 219; (No. 24 Spanish Embassy), 142; (No. 37 Seaford House), 117. Belgravia, 74, 75. Belmont House, Lewisham, 229. Berkeley House, 158. Berkeley Sq. (No. 44), 143. Bethlehem Hospital (Moorfields), 126; (Southwark), 152. Bethnal Green Museum, 252. Billingsgate Market, 136. Birkbeck Schools, Hackney, 145. Bishopsgate (No. 136), 197; (fire station), 242; (Institute), 234. Blackfriars Bridge, 71, 163. Blackwall Tunnel, 40. Bloomsbury, 54, 74, 75. Bloomsbury Sq., 195. Bloomsbury Central Baptist Church, 104. Boodles' Club, 74. Booth Training College, Denmark Hill, 210. Borough Polytechnic, 202. Bovril Ltd., Finsbury, 147. Bracken House, 197. Bricklayers' Arms Station, 74. Britannic House, 155. British & Foreign Bible Society, 129. British Medical Association, 155. British Museum, 52, 219. Broad Court, Bow St., 260. Broadcasting House, 67. Broadway (No. 55), 124. Brockwell Hall and Park, Lambeth, 203. Brockwell Estate, Lambeth, 175. Brompton Cemetery, 101, 102. Brompton Hospital, 265. Brompton Oratory, 110, 208, 224. Brook St. (Nos. 59–61), 88. Brooks's Club,

125. Brunswick Sq., 68. Bryanston Sq., 177. Buckingham Gate (No. 20), 41. Buckingham Palace, 42, 75, 165, 180, 247, 255. Buckingham St. (No. 15), 246. Burlington Arcade, 182, 245. Burlington Gdns (No. 7), 44, 150, 239; (Nos. 10, 12), 125. Burlington House, 33, 44, 57, 82, 219, 245. Burlington School for Girls, Hammersmith, 53

Caen Wood Towers, Highgate, 259. Caledonian Market, 51. Camden Rd., Islington, 236. Canada House, 219. Cannon St., 51. Carey St. (No. 51), 217. Carlton Club, 127. Carlton House, 160. Carlton House Terrace, 165. Carmelite St. (fire station), 40. Carpenters' Hall, 138, 184. Cartwright Gdns, 54. Catholic Apostolic Church (Gordon Sq.), 45; (Paddington), 179. Cavendish Sq. (Nos. 17, 18), 141. Cecil House, 34. Cedar Terrace, Clapham Common, 145. Cenotaph, 155. Central Hall, 147. Chandos House, 21. Charing Cross Hospital, 54, 232. Charing Cross Station, 98; hotel, 33. Chelsea Embankment (No. 3), 43; (No. 13), 129. Chelsea Physic Garden, 171. Chelsea Polytechnic, 49. Chelsea Town Hall, 49. Chester Place, 229. Chesterfield House, 244. Child's Bank, Fleet St., 104. Chiswick Park Underground Station, 124. Christ Church, Bermondsey, 25. Christ Church, Chiswick, 209. Christ Church, Hampstead, 80. Christ Church, Marylebone, 117. Christ Church, St Pancras, 180. Christ Church, Southwark, 187. Christ Church, Stepney, 215. Christ Church, Streatham, 252. Christ Church, Victoria St., 186; and Vicarage,

London—*continued*
213. Christ Church, Woburn Sq., 242. Christ's Hospital, 126, 171, 215. Church House, 30. City Temple, 152. Civil Service Stores, 153. Clapham Park, 75. Clarence House, 165. Clarendon House, 186. Claridge's Hotel, 102. Clerkenwell, 164. Cleopatra's Needle, 242. Clissold House, Stoke Newington, 258. Coal Exchange, 51. Cockfosters Underground Station, 124. Coleherne Court, Redcliffe Gdns, 58. College of Heralds, 20. College of Nursing, 72. Collingham Gdns, 102. Colonnade House, Blackheath, 212. Comedy Theatre, 240. Commercial Sale Rooms, Mincing Lane, 258. Connaught Hotel, 96. Conduit St. (No. 9), 263. Conservative Club, 34, 219. Constitution Arch, 53. Constitutional Club, 88. Corn Exchange, 129. *Country Life* offices, 155. County Fire office, Regent St., 20, 167. County Hall, 145. Covent Garden Floral Market, 33. Coventry House, Piccadilly, 75. Crescent Lane Flats, Clapham, 133. Criterion Restaurant, 240. Crockford's Club, 262. Crown Life offices, Bridge St., 81. Crystal Palace, 44, 137, 264. Cunard House, 80. Custom House, 146, 219

Dean's Yard, 209. Deptford Town Hall, 147. Devonshire Club, 262. Devonshire House, 143, 194. Dibden House, Maida Vale, 58. Dr Johnson's Bldgs, 219. Dr Williams's Library, 85. Dorchester House, 242. Dover House, 174. Dover St. (No. 37), 230. Downing St. (Nos. 10–12), 73. Drapers' Hall, 132, 134. Dreadnought Hospital, Green-wich, 226, 267. Drury Lane Theatre, 35, 223, 262. Duke of York's Column, 262. Duke of York's HQ, Chelsea, 206. Duke St., 63. Dulwich Art Gallery, 223. Dulwich College, 33. Dyers' Hall, 86

East India House, 138. Eaton Sq., 74. Egyptian Hall, 202. Electra House, 30. Eltham Lodge, Woolwich, 158. English Electric Co. offices, Strand, 124. Eton Rise, Hampstead, 215. Euston Station, 117, 118

Farringdon Market, 162. Finsbury Sq., 78. Fishmongers' Almshouses, Wood Green, 159. Fishmongers' Hall, 200. Fitzjohn's Ave, Hampstead (No. 1), 224. Fitzroy Sq., 21. Fleet St. (No. 10), 88. Foreign Office, 209. Founders' Hall, 23. Frascati's Restaurant, 70. French Hospital, 240. French Protestant Church, 247. Froebel Institute, 262. Frognal, Hampstead (No. 39), 216. Frognal Grove, Hampstead (No. 105), 95. Fulham Public Library, 119

Garden Court Bldg, 205. Garrick Club, 158. Garrick St. (No. 14), 40. German Hospital, 85. Gifford House, Roehampton, 189. Glebe Place (No. 35), 248. Gloucester Gate, 208. Gloucester Rd. Underground Station, 217. Gloucester Sq., 229. Gloucester Terrace, 208. Golden Cross Hotel, Strand, 234. Golden Sq. (Nos. 34–6), 224. Golders Green Crematorium, 102. Goldhawk Rd. (Oakburn), 45. Goldsmith Bldg, 205. Goldsmith's College, Deptford, 215. Goldsmiths' Hall, 23, 117. Gosletts', Charing Cross Rd., 94. Gray's Inn, 141. Gt.

London—*continued*

Burlington St. (General Wade's house), 44. Gt. Central Rly. Hotel, 88. Gt. Exhibition (1851), 137, 200, 251. Gt. Western Rly. Hotel, Paddington, 118. Gt. Winchester St. (No. 23), 79, 80. Greenwich (schools), 203. Gresham St. (Nos. 42–4), 257, 258. Greystoke Place, Chancery Lane, 268. Grosvenor Gdns, 75; (No. 28), 31. Grosvenor Hotel, 145. Grosvenor Place, 75. Grosvenor Sq., 216; (No. 41), 83. Grosvenor St. (No. 16), 137. Grove Chapel, Camberwell, 203. Guildhall, 78. Guildhall Library and Museum, 136. Guildhall School of Music, 136. Guinness Brewery, Willesden, 210. Guinness Trust Flats, Lambeth, 156. Guy's Hospital, 120

Hampstead Garden Suburb, 80, 127, 155, 234, 237. Hans Rd. (Nos. 14–16), 241. Hare Court (Nos. 2–3), 132. Harecourt Congregational Church, Islington, 113. Harley St., 250; (Nos. 26, 46), 94. Harrington Gdns, 102. Harwood Rd. School, Eel Brook Common, 62. Hasilwood House, 80. Haymarket Theatre, 165. Hay's Wharf offices, Southwark, 106. Her Majesty's Theatre, 180. High Holborn (No. 94), 119; (Nos. 127–9), 124. Highbury Park Presbyterian Church, Islington, 113. Highgate Cemetery, 102. Highgate School, 68. Hill's Bakery, Buckingham Gate, 240. Hoare's Bank, Fleet St., 176. Holborn (Model Dwellings), 200. Holborn Viaduct Hotel and Railway Station, 96. Holloway Prison, 51. Holy Ghost, Church of the, Wandsworth, 224. Holy Redeemer, Church of the, Chelsea,

105. Holy Redeemer, Church of the, Clerkenwell, 212. Holy Saviour, Herne Hill, 108. Holy Trinity, Bermondsey, 142. Holy Trinity, Blackheath, 252. Holy Trinity, Brompton Rd., 85. Holy Trinity, Clapham, 73. Holy Trinity, Kingsway, 37. Holy Trinity, Lambeth, 33. Holy Trinity, Latimer Rd., 216. Holy Trinity, Marylebone Rd., 223. Holy Trinity, Paddington, 76. Holy Trinity, Prince Consort Rd., 43. Holy Trinity, Roehampton, 189. Holy Trinity, Shoreditch, 192. Holy Trinity, Sloane Sq., 212. Holy Trinity, Southwark, 36. Home Office, 209. Horniman Museum, Forest Hill, 234. Horse Guards, 143, 240. Horticultural Hall, 201. Hospital for Sick Children, 33. Houses of Parliament, 32, 33, 210. Hungerford Market, 98. Hyde Park (lodges), 53. Hyde Park Sq., 229

Immaculate Conception, Church of the, Farm St., 66, 208. Immaculate Heart of Mary, Church of the, Hackney, 50. Imperial College of Science, 211. Imperial Gaslight Co. offices, Hoxton, 88. Imperial Institute, 70. Imperial War Museum, 152, 219. Incorporated Accountants' Hall, 179. India House, 30. Ingram House, 119. Inveresk House, 79. Institute of Chartered Accountants. 37. Institute of Journalists, 96, International Exhibition (1862), 97. Islington Public Library, 156

Jermyn St. (Turkish baths), 64. Junior Carlton Club, 45

Kennington Oval, 83. Kennington Park, 180, 200. Kennington Park Place, Southwark (No. 5), 216. Kensington Court (No. 1),

London—*continued*

132. Kensington High St. Underground Station, 217. Kensington Palace, 121. Kensington Palace Gdns, 180; (No. 8a), 137; (No. 13), 198; (Nos. 18–19), 45. King George VI Monument, 83. King's Bench Walk (gatehouse), 61. King's Cross Station, 74. Knightsbridge Barracks, 265. Kodak House, 52

Ladbroke Grove, 25, 259. Lamb's Chapel and Almshouses, 26. Lambeth Bridge, 41. Lancaster Gate, 258. Lancaster Rd., Paddington (No. 235), 38. Law Society, 242. Lawn Road Flats, Hampstead, 67. Leadenhall Market, 136. Leighton House, 23. Lincoln's Inn, 36, 117. Lincoln's Inn Fields (No. 13), 222; (No. 19), 248; (Nos. 57–8), 138; (No. 65), 151. Lindsey House, 137. Literary Institute, Islington, 108. Lloyd's Shipping Register, Fenchurch St., 70. Lloyd's, Leadenhall St., 72. London Bridge, 194. London Bridge Railway Station, 35, 200. London, Edinburgh & Glasgow Assurance offices, Euston Rd., 182. London Fever Hospital, 98. London Hospital, 223. London Tavern, 138. Lonsdale Sq., Islington, 58. Lord's Cricket Ground, 25, 30, 240. Lower Chapman St., Stepney, 90. Lowndes Sq., 74. Ludgate Hill, 70. Luxborough Lodge, Marylebone, 222. Lyric Theatre, 180

Mallord House, Chelsea, 145. Mann Crossman Brewery, 66. Manresa House, 61. Mansion House, 78, 162. Mansion House Underground Station, 124. Mark Lane (Nos. 59–61), 23. Marlborough House, 32, 261. Marshall & Snelgrove, 136. Mecklenburgh Sq., 68, 140. Melbourne House, 62. Melbury Rd., Kensington (No. 9), 51. Mercers' Hall, 134, 171. Merchant Taylors' Almshouses, Lewisham, 139. Merchant Taylors' School, 129. Metropolitan Water Board, Finsbury, 201. Middle Temple Clock Tower, 208. Middle Temple Gateway, 170. Middlesex Hospital, 174, 227. Middlesex Sessions House, Clerkenwell Green, 60. Midland Bank, Piccadilly, 155. Milner Sq., Islington, 108. Moreton House, Hampstead, 100.

Mount St. (No. 5), 102; (Nos. 87–102), 43; (Nos. 105–6 and 110–13), 102. Montague St., 54. Montague Sq., 177. Monument, 125. Moorgate Underground Station, 217. Mumford's Flour Mills, Greenwich, 247. Museum of Economic Geology, 180

National Gallery, 253. National Liberal Club, 246. National Portrait Gallery, 63. National Provident Institution, Gracechurch St., 144. National Provincial Bank, Bishopsgate, 104. National Safe Deposit, Queen Victoria St., 250. National Scottish Church, 31. Natural History Museum, 246. Naval & Military Club, 46. Nelson Column, 192. Nelson St., Greenwich, 140. New Bond St. (Nos. 49–50), 137; (Nos. 144–6), 147; (No. 148), 104. New Bridge St. (No. 14), 152. New River Co. offices, 163. New Scotland Yard, 216. Newcastle House, 255. Newgate Prison, 78. Nichols Sq., Shoreditch, 229. Nile St., Shoreditch, 184. Nine Elms Railway Station, 234. Noel Park Estate, Wood Green, 184. North Drive, Tooting Bec, 241. Northampton In-

London—*continued*

stitute, 163. Northern Assurance office, Moorgate, 163. Northumberland House, 95. Nunhead Cemetery, 51, 102

Old Bailey, 163. Old Bond St. (No. 11), 147; (No. 25), 68; (No. 32), 182. Old Broad St. (No. 19), 117. Old County Hall, 158. Olympia, 90. Opera House, Covent Garden, 33. Ordnance Office, 28. Oriental Club, 262. Our Lady, Lisson Grove, 208. Our Lady of Victories, Clapham, 244. Our Lady Star of the Sea, Greenwich, 244. Oxford & Cambridge Club, 219. Oxford St. (Nos. 363–7), 90

P. & O. offices (Cockspur St.), 43; (Leadenhall St.), 76. Paddington Station, 264. Palace Gate (No. 10), 67. Palace Green (No. 1), 248. Palace St. (No. 43), 38. Palace Theatre, 70. Pantheon, 262. Paper Bldgs, 219. Paragon, Blackheath, 212. Park Lane (No. 100), 29. Parliament Sq., 259. Passmore Edwards Library, Southwark, 180. Pavilion, Shepherd's Bush, 240. Peckham Cemetery, 102. Pelham Crescent, 34. Pelham Place, 34. Pembroke College Mission Church, Southwark, 187. People's Palace, 203. Peter Jones, 194. Phoenix Assurance, Fleet St., 215. Piccadilly (Nos. 96–7), 240; (Nos. 100, 101), 88. Piccadilly Circus, 41. Piccadilly Circus Underground Station, 124. Piccadilly Hotel, 216. Pimlico Literary Institute, Ebury St., 101. Pitzhanger Manor, Ealing, 223. Playhouse, 42. Plowden Bldgs, 208. Pontings, 217. Poplar (LCC School), 203. Porchester Hall, 244. Port of London Authority Bldg, 72. Portland Place, 21; (Nos. 11a, 11b), 240. Portman House, 226. Portuguese Embassy, 219. Powell Almshouses, Fulham, 213. Provost Rd., Hampstead, 215. Prudential Assurance Co., Holborn, 246. Public Record Office, 180

Quadrant, Regent St., 41. Queen Anne Mansions, 203. Queen Anne's Gate (Nos. 6–12), 89; (No. 34), 42. Queen Mary's Hostel, Kensington, 124. Queen's Chapel, Marlborough Gate, 137. Queen's Gate (No. 167), 156; (Nos. 170, 185), 216. Queen's Hall, 145. Queen's House, Greenwich, 137, 248. Queen's Park Estate, Paddington, 184

Ranelagh Gdns, 138. Regent's Park, 53, 165, 179. Regent St., 20, 54, 165. Reuters, 155. Richmond Terrace, Whitehall, 63. Ritz Hotel, 79. Roan School, Blackheath, 94. Roehampton House, 26. Rothschild Mausoleum, West Ham, 264. Royal Academy, 180. Royal Academy of Music, 102. Royal Automobile Club, 79. Royal College of Music, 41. Royal College of Physicians, 126, 219. Royal College of Surgeons, 79. Royal Courts of Justice, 226. Royal Empire Society, 30. Royal Exchange, 134, 234. Royal Exchange Bldgs, Cornhill, 102. Royal Geographical Society, 216. Royal Hospital, Chelsea, 121, 222, 261. Royal Hospital for Incurables, Wandsworth, 110. Royal Hospital for Seamen, Greenwich, 167, 214, 226, 239, 261. Royal Institute of British Architects, 259. Royal Institute of Chemistry, 52. Royal Institute of Painters in Water Colours, 203.

London—*continued*

Royal Institution, 223, 242. Royal Institution of Chartered Surveyors, 246. Royal Masonic Hospital, 53. Royal Military Academy, Woolwich, 263. Royal National Orthopaedic Hospital, 183. Royal Naval College, Greenwich, 248, 267. Royal Observatory, Greenwich, 261. Royal Opera Arcade, 165. Royal School of Mines, 247. Royal Scottish Corporation offices, Fleet St., 85. Royal Society of Arts, 21. Royal Society of Medicine, 37. Royal United Service Institution, 247. Royal Victoria Patriotic School, Wandsworth, 120. Russell Sq., 54, 195

Sacred Heart Convent, Hammersmith, 38. St Agnes, Kennington, 210. St Alphege, Greenwich, 121. SS Andrew and Michael, Greenwich, 62. St Andrew, Bethnal Green, 265. St Andrew, Garratt Lane, 163. St Andrew, St Pancras, 121. St Andrew, Wandsworth, 102. St Ann's Vestry Hall, Carter Lane, 94. St Anne, Islington, 108. St Anne, Soho, 69. St Anne, Wandsworth, 219. St Anne's House, Lambeth, 101. St Anne's Court, Wardour St., 51. St Augustine, Clapham Common, 145. St Augustine, Kilburn, 179. St Augustine, Queen's Gate, 55. St Barnabas, Addison Rd., 241. St Barnabas, Hackney, 194. St Barnabas, Homerton, 27. St Barnabas, Pimlico, 76. St Bartholomew, East Ham, 159. St Bartholomew-the-Great, Smithfield, 247. St Bartholomew's Hospital, 103, 129. St Botolph, Aldgate, 78. St Bride, Fleet St., 261. St Bride's Vicarage, 62. St Chad, Shoreditch, 47. St Charles

Hospital, Paddington, 222. St Clement, Paddington, 205. St Columba, Shoreditch, 47. St Cuthbert, Philbeach Gdns, 108. St Cyprian, Clarence Gate, 71. St Dominic, St Pancras, 50. St Dunstan-in-the-East, 146. St Dunstan-in-the-West, 215. St Edward's House, Gt. Smith St., 58. St Ethelburga, Bishopsgate, 110. St Gabriel, Warwick Sq., 76. St George, Battersea, 42. St George, Bloomsbury, 121. St George, Camberwell, 36. St George, Campden Hill, 140. St George, Hanover Sq., 133. St George, Tufnell Park, 236. St George, Woolwich, 265. St George's Circus, 78. St George's Hospital, 159, 244, 253. St Giles-in-the-Fields, Holborn, 95. St Hugh, Bermondsey, 59. St James, Bermondsey, 208. St James, Islington, 66. St James, Piccadilly, 197, 261. St James, Spanish Place, 105. St James, Stepney, 148. St James, Sussex Gdns, 105. St James-the-Less, Vauxhall Bridge Rd., 226. St James's Club, 75. St James's Park, 247. St James's Sq. (No. 4), 150; (No. 5), 46; (Nos. 9, 10), 95; (No. 15), 226; (No. 32), 69. St James's St. (No. 10), 180. St James's Theatre, 35. St John, Bethnal Green, 223. St John, Blackheath, 27. St John, Deptford, 118. St John, Hackney, 223. St John the Baptist, Hackney, 244. St John, Hoxton, 88. St John, Islington, 32. St John the Evangelist, Islington, 208. St John, Kennington, 107, 226. St John, Kensal Green, 142. St John, Lewisham, 168. St John, Red Lion Sq., 179. St John, St John's Wood, 118. St John, Smith Sq., 26. St John, Walham

London—*continued*

Green, 229. St John's Hospital, 240. St John's National Schools, Islington, 32. St John's Priory, Clerkenwell, 211. St Joseph's Almshouses, Brook Green, 244. St Jude, Kensington, 105. St Katharine's Dock, 231. St Katharine's Hospital, 186. St Leonard, Shoreditch, 78. St Leonard, Streatham, 177. St Luke, Balham, 251. St Luke, Chelsea, 208. St Luke, Eltham, 161. St Luke and Vicarage, Kentish Town, 62. St Luke, Redcliffe Sq., 105. St Luke's Hospital, 78. St Margaret, Lewisham, 48, 111. St Margaret, Wesminster, 134, 193, 225. St Mark, Battersea Rise, 251. St Mark, Finsbury, 164. St Mark, Hamilton Terrace, 76. St Mark, Islington, 108. St Mark, Kennington, 204. St Mark, North Audley St., 101. St Mark, Paddington, 140. St Mark, Silvertown, 231. St Mark, Wood Green, 184. St Martin, Gospel Oak, 146. St Martin-in-the-Fields, 103. St Martin's Almshouses, Camden Town, 214. St Martin's School, Endell St., 252. St Martin's Schools, Adelaide St., 229. St Mary-at-Hill, 111; (Nos. 6, 7), 102. St Mary Boltons, Kensington, 105. St Mary, Ealing, 231. St Mary, Fulham Rd., 117. St Mary-le-Strand, 103. St Mary, Marylebone Rd., 118. St Mary Magdalene, Munster Sq., 58. St Mary, Paddington Green, 183. St Mary, Shoreditch, 217. St Mary, Somers Town, 130. St Mary-the-Less, Lambeth, 36. St Mary, Woolnoth, 121. St Mary, Wyndham Place, 219. St Mary's Hospital, 72, 127. St Mary's Rectory, Woolwich, 175. St Marylebone, Power Station, 194. St Marylebone, Public Library; Town Hall, 71. St Marylebone, Workhouse, 250. St Matthew, Bethnal Green, 78. St Matthew, Brixton, 185. St Michael, Blackheath Park, 220. St Michael, Chester Sq., 75. St Michael, Highgate, 241. St Nicholas, Tooting, 28. St Olave's School, Bermondsey, 163. St Pancras, Euston Rd., 130, 184, 185. St Pancras Station Hotel, 209. St Paul, Baker St., 149. St Paul, Battersea, 69. St Paul, Chiswick, 77. St Paul, Covent Garden, 118, 137. St Paul, Deptford, 26. St Paul, East Smithfield, 200. St Paul, Hammersmith, 108, 213. St Paul, Millwall, 145. St Paul, Putney, 65, 159. St Paul, Shoreditch, 40. St Paul, Stepney, 243. St Paul, Upper Norwood, 140. St Paul, Wilton Place, 76. St Paul's Cathedral, 65, 67, 121, 261. St Paul's School, 246. St Peter ad Vincula, Tower, 241. St Peter, Deptford, 158. St Peter, Ealing, 212. St Peter, Eaton Sq., 115. St Peter, Gt. Windmill St., 45. St Peter, Hammersmith, 148. St Peter, Paddington, 25. St Peter, Regent Sq., 130. St Peter, Vere St., 103. St Saviour, Chelsea, 34. St Saviour, Hampstead, 33. St Sophia, Bayswater, 211. St Stephen, Dulwich, 33. St Stephen, Hammersmith, 205. St Stephen, Rochester Row, 93. St Stephen, Rosslyn Hill, 231. St Swithin's House, Walbrook, 227. St Swithun, Hither Green, 166. St Thomas, Fulham, 190. St Thomas, Greenwich, 111. St Thomas, Stepney, 220. St Thomas's Hospital, 76, 202. Savoy Court, 69. Savoy Hotel, 69. Savoy Theatre, 180. Scala

London—*continued*
Theatre, 240. School of Hygiene
& Tropical Medicine, 127. Scottish Presbyterian Church, St
Pancras, 234. Seaford House,
117. Second Church of Christ,
Scientist, 52, 53. Sekforde St.
Finsbury (Savings Bank), 34.
Severndroog Castle, Woolwich,
138. Shaftesbury Ave (Nos. 58,
60), 119. Shell Centre, 201.
Shepherd's Market, 216. Shoreditch Technical College, 204.
Shot Tower, Lambeth, 204.
Simpson's, Piccadilly, 90. Sion
College, 41. Skinners' Hall, 139,
171. Sloane Place, 125. Smithfield
Market, 136, 162. Soane Museum, 222. Somerset House, 62,
180, 219. South Africa House,
30, 234. South Audley St. (Nos.
1, 2), 68; (No. 71), 216. South
Bank Exhibition (1951), 67. South
Kensington Museum, 252. South
Kensington Underground Station,
217. South Parade, Bedford
Park (No. 14), 241. Southwark,
25. Southwark Bridge, 102,
194. Southwark Cathedral, 111.
Southwark St. (Nos. 91–3), 88.
Spanish Embassy, 142. SPCK,
Northumberland Ave, 104. Spencer House, 240. Stafford Cripps
Estate, Finsbury, 90. Stationers'
Hall, 163. Stock Exchange, 24.
Stoke Newington Waterworks,
164. Stone Bldgs, 230. Stornoway House, 264. Stratton St.
(No. 8), 102. Sudan House, 240.
Suffolk St. (No. 5), 229; (No. 6),
74; (Nos. 12–17), 263. Sun Life
offices, Threadneedle St., 67.
Surrey Institution, 177. Surrey
Sq., Southwark, 212. Swan Walk,
Chelsea (No. 35), 104. Swiss
Cottage, 202. Swiss Protestant
Church, Endell St., 242. Synagogue, Harrow Rd., 259

Tavistock Sq., 54. Temple Bar
Memorial, 136. Temple Gardens
Bldg, 33. Thackeray Hotel, 121.
Third Church of Christ, Scientist,
147. Thornton Terrace, Clapham Common, 145. Thurloe
Place, 34. Tite St. (No. 31), 88;
(No. 33), 104. Tollington Park,
Islington, 108. Tower Bridge,
136. Tower of London, 111, 205,
267. Travellers' Club, 32. Treasury Bldgs, 32, 143. Trinity House,
264. Tylers' and Bricklayers'
Almshouses, Islington 110

Union Club, 145. United Service
Club, 165. Universal House,
Southwark Bridge Rd., 90. University College, 85, 101, 151, 197,
253. University College Hospital,
246. University of London, 124.
Upper Grosvenor St. (Nos. 1, 21),
145. Uxbridge House, 44, 150,
239

Vanbrugh Castle, Greenwich,
239. Vaudeville Theatre, 180.
Vauxhall Bridge, 194. Victoria
& Albert Museum, 247. Victoria
Hospital, Chelsea, 222. Victoria
Memorial, 247. Victoria Park,
180. Victoria Underground Station, 217. Vintners' Hall, 134

Wapping (Docks), 24. Wardour
St. (No. 45), 119; (Nos. 103–9),
42. Waterloo Bridge, 194, 210.
Waterloo Place, 54. Watermen's
Hall, 39. Watling House, 201.
Wembley (British Empire Exhibition), 43. West Drive, Streatham (No. 2), 224. West Norwood Cemetery, 234. Westbourne House, 244. Westbourne
Terrace, 229. Westminster (housing estates), 155. Westminster
Abbey, 71, 121, 241. Westminster
Bank, Southampton Bldgs, 145.
Westminster Bridge, 135. West-

London—*continued*
minster Cathedral, 38. Westminster Cleansing Dept., Ebury Bridge Rd., 259. Westminster Hall, 71, 267. Westminster Hospital, 130. Wesminster Palace, 32. Westminster School, 44. Westminster Technical Institute, 40. Westwood Hill, Sydenham, 179. Whitbread's Stores, Gray's Inn Rd., 177. Whitechapel Art Gallery, 234. Whitehall (government offices), 49, 50, 264. White House, 28. Whiteley's 37. Whittington's Almshouses, Highgate, 220. Wigmore St. (Nos. 38, 40), 69. Willett & Co., Sloane Sq., 163. Wilton Crescent, 31. Wimborne House, 143, 261. Wimpole St. (No. 30), 94. Worship St. (Nos. 91–101), 248

YMCA, Gt. Russell St., 184. YWCA, Gt. Russell St., 155. York Water Gate, 103

Zoological Gardens, 53, 205

London Colney, Herts
All Saints Convent, 224. St Peter, 220
Long Eaton, Derbys
Trent College, 69
Long Horsley, Northumb
Linden House, 83
Long Ridge Tower, Northumb, 50
Longdon, Salop
Aqueduct, 231
Longford Hall, Salop, 44
Longhirst, Northumb, 84
Longleat House, Wilts, 195, 221, 233, 265
Longner Hall, Salop, 165
Longworth House, Herefs, 140
Lough Castle, Ireland, 173
Lough, Lincs
Kenwick Hall, 161. St James, 211
Loughborough, Leics
Emmanuel Church, 199. Shel-

thorpe Rd. Estate, 237, 238. Town Hall, 218
Loughton, Essex
Hall, 166. St John, 219
Louvencourt, France
War Cemetery, 124
Low Marple, Cheshire
St Martin, 212
Lower Beeding, Sussex
Holy Trinity, 237
Lowestoft, Suffolk
St Luke's Hospital, 96. St Peter, 48
Lowfield Heath, Sussex
St Michael, 51
Lowther Castle, Westmorland, 219
Loxwood, Sussex
St John, 184
Lucknow, India
Post Office, 147
Ludlow, Salop
Butter Cross, 31
Lugwardine, Herefs
Longworth House, 140. New Court, 214
Lurgashall, Sussex
Rectory, 250
Luton Hoo, Beds, 21
Lydbury North, Salop
Walcot, 61, 62
Lyme Hall, Cheshire, 150
Lynford, Norfolk
Hall, 52. Our Lady of Consolation, 66

Macclesfield, Cheshire
Assembly Rooms and Town Hall, 107
Madeley, Salop
St Michael, 231
Maidenhead, Berks
All Saints, 226. Bridge, 230. SS Andrew and Mary Magdalene, 55. Town Hall, 141
Maidstone, Kent
Corn Exchange, 249. County Prison, 24. Holy Trinity; Kent

Maidstone, Kent—*continued*
   Fire Office, 249. St Philip, 249.
   The Mote, 24
Maldon, Essex
   Hospital, 69
Mamhead, Devon, 205
Manchester, Lancs
   Albert Memorial, 260. Art Gallery Annexe, 32. Assize Courts, 245. Athenaeum, 32. Bank of England, 68. Barbour & Ashton warehouse, 109. Barcombe Hotel, Fallowfield, 245, 246. Baths and Laundries; Botanical Society Bldg, 260. Brown, Son & Co. warehouses, 243. Church of the Holy Name, 117. City Art Gallery, 32. College of Commerce, 109. Comedy Theatre, 79. Corn Exchange, 147. Corpus Christi Schools, Miles Platting, 224. Crematorium, 260. Deaf, Dumb & Blind Asylum; Dispensary, Chorlton, 147. First Church of Christ, Scientist, 256. Free Trade Hall, 243. Friends' Meeting House, 147. Hicksons' warehouse, 243. Holy Trinity, 215. Manchester & Salford Bank, 229. Memorial Hall, 260. Midland Hotel, 236. Moral and Industrial Training Schools, Swinton, 229. Mosley St. (No. 15), 243. Police & Sessions Court, 260. Portico Library, 119. Prince's Theatre, 79. Richmond Chapel, 147. Royal Exchange Assurance offices, 236. Royal Institution of Fine Arts, 32. Rylands Library, 62. St Barnabas, 229. St Cross, 55. St Francis, Gorton, 191. St George, 107. St George, Chorley, 199. St Luke, Cheetham, 28. St Wilfrid, Hulme, 190. Town Hall, 107, 246. Town Hall, Chorlton, 147. Union Chapel, 243. Water St., 79. Williams Deacon's Bank (St Ann St.), 109; (Mosley St.),

243. Withington Hospital, Chorlton, 260
Manley Hall, Staffs, 235
Mansfield, Notts
   St Mark, 161
Manton, Lincs
   Cleatham Hall, 99
Mappleborough Green, Warwicks
   Holy Ascension, 63
Marazion, Cornwall
   All Saints; St Michael's Mount, 205
Marchington, Staffs
   St Peter, 235
Mark Cross, Sussex
   Mayfield and St Joseph's Colleges, 191
Market Drayton, Salop
   Buntingsale House, 220
Market Lavington, Wilts
   Manor House, 63
Market Weston, Suffolk
   St Mary, 73
Marlborough College, Wilts, 43, 100
Marlow, Bucks
   All Saints, 130. Crown Hotel, 264. St Peter, 190
Marsden, Yorks
   St Bartholomew, 98
Marske-by-the-Sea, Yorks
   St Mark, 68
Matfen Hall, Northumb, 199
Melbourne, Australia
   St Patrick's Cathedral, 244
Meldon Park, Northumb, 84
Melksham, Wilts
   St George's Hospital, Semington, 142
Melsetter House, Orkney, 151
Meltham Mills, Yorks
   St James, 188
Mentmore House, Bucks, 178
Mereworth Castle, Kent, 57
Merifield, Cornwall, 251
Mertoun, Berwicks, 49
Michelstown Castle, Ireland, 173
Mickleham, Surrey
   Norbury Park, 206

Mid Lavant, Sussex
Small House, 187
Middle Claydon, Bucks
Claydon House, 202
Middlesbrough, Yorks
Dorman Long offices, 249. St
Barnabas, 98
Middleton, Lancs
Methodist Church, 256. Schools,
213
Midhurst, Sussex
King Edward VII Sanatorium,
124. Wispers, 216
Midsomer Norton, Som
St John, 181
Mildenhall, Wilts
School, 20
Mill Hill School, Middx, 70, 234
Milner Field, Yorks, 119
Milton House, Berks, 261
Milton House, Northants, 95
Minehead, Som
Kildare Lodge, 238. Periton
Mead, 127
Misterton, Som
St. Leonard, 142
Moccas Court, Herefs, 140
Montgomery
Market Hall, 31
Montreal, Canada
Mansion House, 184
Moor Park, Herts, 150, 233
Morden, Surrey
Earl Haig Homes, 82, 259
Moreton-in-the-Marsh, Glos
St David, 80. Sezincote House,
69
Morpeth, Northumb
Grammar School, 93. Longhirst,
84. St James, 93. Town Hall, 239
Mote, The, Kent, 24
Moulton Chapel, Lincs
St James, 207
Much Birch, Herefs
SS Mary and Thomas, 96
Munstead, Surrey
House, 224. Munstead Wood;
Orchards, 155

Murston, Kent
All Saints, 51
Murthley House, Perthshire, 108

Naples, Italy
Protestant Church, 221
New Court, Herefs, 214
New Delhi, India
Government Bldgs, 30, 155
New York World Fair (1939), 201
Newark, Notts
Town Hall, 59
Newborough, Staffs
All Saints, 211
Newbury, Berks
St George, Wash Common, 87.
St Nicholas School, 55
Newcastle-under-Lyme, Staffs
Bank House; Etruria Hall, 180
Newcastle-upon-Tyne, Northumb
All Saints, 223. All Saints
Cemetery, 109. Assembly Rooms,
167. Blackett St., 171. Central
Railway Station, 84. Eldon Sq.,
83. Elswick Hall, 224. General
Cemetery, 84. Guildhall, 235.
High Level Bridge; Jesmond
Parish Church, 84. Leazes Cres-
cent and Terrace, 171. Literary
and Philosophical Society, 108,
109. Moot Hall, 224. Northern
Academy of Art; Royal Arcade,
84. Royal Grammar School, 71.
St Ann, 167. St Mary's Cathedral,
190. Theatre, 109
Newhaven, Sussex
Christ Church, 47, 113
Newlaithes Hall, Yorks, 154
Newmarket, Suffolk
Jockey Club, 197
Newport, Essex
Grammar School, 166
Newport, Salop
Longford Hall, 44. SS Peter and
Paul, 185

Nice, France
English Hotel; Protestant Church, 221
Nonsuch House, Surrey, 265
Norbury Park, Surrey, 206
Normanton, Rutland
Park, 75, 138. St Matthew, 75
North Mimms Park, Herts, 27
North Perrott, Som
Manor House, 265
North Runcton, Norfolk
All Saints, 37
North Shields, Northumb
Christ Church, 235. New Quay, 223. Scotch Church, 83. Town Hall, 84
Northampton
All Saints, 37. Theatre, 180. Town Hall, 104
Northfleet, Kent
Notre Dame, 210
Northiam, Sussex
Gt. Dixter, 155. Turner Mausoleum, 219
Northrepps, Norfolk
The Cottage, 253
Northwood House, I.O.W., 157
Norton, Herts
Vicarage, 247
Norwich, Norfolk
Artillery Barracks; Assembly Rooms, 131. Blackfriars Bridge, 222. Castle, 225, 253. Cathedral, 48, 225. City Hall, 133. Corn Exchange, 33. Cow St. (Nos. 15-17), 45. Fye Bridge, 225. Guildhall, 33. Hospital, 131. Jarrolds' Works, 48. Methodist Meeting House; Octagon Chapel, 131. St Andrew's Hospital, Thorpe, 225. Shirehouse, 45. Surrey St. (No. 11), 45; (Nos. 25-35), 131. Theatre, 131, 253
Nostell Priory, Yorks, 173
Nottingham
Castle, 122. Guildhall, 240. Highfields Park, 127. Nottingham Park Estate, 122. St Stephen, 58.

Shire Hall, 100, 181. Theatre, 180. University, 127. Victoria Railway Station, 122
Nunnery, The, I.O.M., 181
Nunnykirk Hall, Northumb, 84
Nutfield Priory, Surrey, 104

Oakley Park, Salop, 67
Ogston Hall, Derbys, 122
Old Hall Green, Herts
St Edmund's College, 190
Oldham, Lancs
Dronsfields' offices, 213. St Mary, 147
Ombersley, Worcs
St Andrew, 199
Orchardleigh Park, Som, 265
Ormsby Hall, Lincs, 154
Osborne House, I.O.W., 75
Osterly, Middx
Gillette factory, 94
Otterburn, Northumb
St John, 84
Ottershaw, Surrey
Botleys, 73
Ottery St Mary, Devon
Escot House, 200
Over Stowey, Som
Quantock Lodge, 66
Overstone Park, Northants, 80, 231
Oxford
All Saints, 23. All Souls College, 64, 121. Anthropological Museum, 81. Ashmolean Museum, 67, 68. Balliol College, 141, 246. Bodleian Library, 210. Botanical Gardens, 237. Brasenose College, 132. Campion Hall, 155. Christ Church College, 64, 141, 193, 261. Clarendon Bldg, 121, 138. Divinity School, 172. Examination Schools, 132. Exeter College, 209. Hertford College; High Schools, 132. Indian Institute, 62. Jesus College, 50. Keble College, 55, 56. Magdalen Bridge, 112. Magdalen College, 50, 72,

Oxford—*continued*
172. Manchester College, 260.
Mansfield College, 62. Martyrs'
Memorial, 209. Meadow Bldg,
81. Merton College, 134. New
College, 254, 266. Peckwater
Quadrangle, 23. Physiological
Laboratory, 81. Queen's College,
121. Radcliffe Camera, 103, 121.
Radcliffe Infirmary, 149, 206.
Radcliffe Observatory, 141. St
John's College, 172. Schools
of Chemistry, 246. Sheldonian
Theatre, 261. Taylorian Insti-
tute, 67, 68. Town Hall, 118.
Trinity College, 132. University
College, 43. University Museum,
81. Worcester College, 64, 121,
141

Painshill Park, Surrey, 138, 148
Pangbourne, Berks
  Church Cottage, 224. Tower, 37.
  Shooter's Hill House; Whit-
  church Rd., 224
Panshanger House, Herts, 29, 195
Papworth House, Cambs, 56
Par, Cornwall
  St Mary, 226
Paris Exhibition (1925), 201
Parlington Park, Yorks, 151
Pavolvsk, Russia
  Great Palace, 57
Peasmarsh House, Sussex, 85
Peckforton Castle, Cheshire, 205
Pendlebury, Lancs
  Lodge; Rectory; St Augustine;
  School, 43
Pendleton, Lancs
  St Thomas, 107, 147. Town Hall,
  79
Penistone, Yorks
  Cubley Garden Estate, 30
Penn, Bucks
  School, 234
Penn Street, Bucks
  Holy Trinity, 93

Penrhyn Castle, Caernarvon, 127
Penzance, Cornwall
  Trellissick House, 202
Peper Harow House, Surrey, 61
Perlethorpe, Notts
  St John, 206
Perth, Scotland
  Railway Station, 234
Peterborough, Northants
  Cathedral, 245
Petersham, Surrey
  House, 32. Sudbrooke House,
  103
Petworth, Sussex
  Holy Trinity Chapel, Ebernoe,
  113. House, 48
Philadelphia, Penn, U.S.A.
  Bank of Pennsylvania, 149
Pitsford, Northants
  Village Hall, 127
Plas Newydd, Anglesey, 185
Plymouth, Devon
  All Saints, 122; and Vicarage,
  212. Armada Monument; Arti-
  sans' Dwellings, 110. Athenaeum,
  97. Bank of England, 67. Break-
  water, 194. Civil & Military
  Library, Devonport, 97. Female
  Orphanage, 251. Guildhall, 91,
  104, 122. Holy Trinity, 251.
  Ker St., Devonport, 97. Library
  and Museum, Devonport, 122.
  Market, Devonport, 205. Naval
  Column, Devonport, 97. New
  Custom House, 146. Raglan
  Barracks, Devonport, 97. Royal
  William Victualling Yard, Ston-
  house, 195. St Catherine, 97.
  St Mathias, 122. SS Mary and
  Boniface Cathedral, 117. St
  Peter, 188. Town Hall, Devon-
  port; Union St. Stonhouse; Wind-
  sor Villas; Wyndham Sq., Ston-
  house, 97
Polesden Lacey House, Surrey, 75
Polstead Hall, Suffolk, 181
Pont Blean, Cards, 31
Port Eliot House, Cornwall, 195

Portreath, Cornwall
St Mary, 251
Portsmouth, Hants
Cathedral, 168
Possingworth Manor, Sussex, 264
Potters Bar, Middx
Wrotham Hall, 244
Powderham Castle, Devon, 98
Powerscourt, Ireland, 60
Prestwood, Bucks
Holy Trinity, 146
Pretoria, South Africa
Union Bldgs, 30
Princetown, Devon
Dartmoor Prison, 24. Duchy
Hotel, 197. St Michael, 24. Tor
Royal, 197
Priorslee, Salop
St Peter, 87
Pudsey, Yorks
St Lawrence, 230
Puttenham, Surrey
Greyfrairs, 241. Hurlands, 249
Pyrford, Surrey
St Nicholas, 132

Queen Camel, Som
Eyewell House, 80
Queenborough Castle, Kent, 267

Racton Tower, Sussex, 41
Radway Grange, Warwicks, 160
Radwinter, Essex
St Mary, 166
Ragley Hall, Warwicks, 103, 126
Raithby, Lincs
St Peter, 169
Ramsgate, Kent
Grange, 190. Harbour, 215. St
Agustine, 190. St George, 142
Ranmore Common, Surrey
Denbies, 75
Rawcliffe, Yorks
St James, 128
Rawmarsh, Yorks
St Mary, 188
Raynham Hall, Norfolk, 143

Reading, Berks
Albion Place, 39. All Saints,
205. Amersham Hall, Caver-
sham; Baptist Church, Caver-
sham, 246. Christ Church, 258.
Eldon Sq., 39. Gaol, 209. Holy
Trinity, 39. Municipal Blgs,
246. St Mary, 39. St Stephen,
251. School, 246. Seven Bridges
House, 222. Simeon Monument,
223. Southampton Place, 39.
Telephone Exchange, 224. Uni-
versity, 200. West Memorial
Institute, Caversham, 246
Red House, The, Kent, 248
Redhill, Surrey
Earlswood Asylum, 209
Remenham, Berks
St Nicholas, 183, 184
Richmond, Surrey
Asgill House, 230. Bridge, 73,
174. Congregational Church;
Hickey's Almshouses, 242. Holy
Trinity, 45. Our Lady of Peace,
106. Royal Model Laundry, 75.
St Mathias, 209. Star and Garter
Home, 72. Star and Garter
Hotel, 33. The Wick, 163.
White Lodge, 122, 161. Wick
House, 62
Richmond, Yorks
Railway Station; School, 26
Ripley, Surrey
Schools, 258
Ripon, Yorks
Cathedral, 211. Holy Trinity,
230
Rivenhall Place, Essex, 195
Roche Court, Wilts, 228
Rochester, Kent
Bridge, 267. Castle, 111. Cath-
edral, 72, 98, 111. Foord's Alms-
houses, 80
Roecliffe, Yorks
St Mary, 214
Rokeby, Yorks, 202
Roker, Co. Durham
St Andrew, 187

Romford, Essex
  Hare Hall, 174. Workhouse, 88
Rose Ash, Devon
  St Peter, 205
Roseneath, Dumbartonshire, 44
Rotherfield, Sussex
  Oakdene, 238
Rotherham, Yorks
  Crofts, 182. Ferham Estate, 95.
  Moorgate Hall, 182. St Bede,
  114. Wortley Hall, 182
Rothwell, Northants
  Market House, 234
Rougham Hall, Norfolk, 170
Rousdon, Devon
  House; St Pancras, 102
Rugby School, Warwicks, 114, 132,
  168
Rushton, Northants
  Hall; Triangular Lodge, 234
Russborough, Ireland, 60
Rye, Sussex
  Saltcote Place, 41. Town Hall,
  135
Ryston Hall, Norfolk, 186

Saffron Walden, Herts
  Barclays Bank, 166
St Agnes, Cornwall
  St Agnes, 205
St Albans, Herts
  Abbey, 36. Christ Church, 176.
  St Peter's St. (No. 103); Town
  Hall, 220
St Clement, Cornwall
  Pencalenick, 205
St Giles in the Wood, Devon
  Winscott, 251
St Hilary, Cornwall
  St Hilary, 250
St Leonards, Bucks
  Hen Grove, 127
St Leonards-on-Sea, Sussex
  Christ Church, 40. Convent, 191
St Marie's Grange, Wilts, 190

Salford, Lancs
  St Ignatius, 79. St John's Cath-
  edral, 114. St Philip, 219
Salisbury, Wilts
  Cathedral, 66, 82. Guildhall, 181
Saltcote Place, Sussex, 41
Saltaire, Yorks
  Congregational Church, 153.
  Housing Estate, 152, 153
Sandbeck Hall, Yorks, 174
Sandhurst, Berks
  Royal Military Academy, 206.
  Wellington College, 215
Sandringham, Norfolk
  House; York Cottage, 88
Saxby, Leics
  St Peter, 198
Saxlingham, Norfolk
  St Mary's Parsonage, 222
Scarborough, Yorks
  Baptist Church, 153. Christ
  Church, 28. Grand Hotel, 47.
  Holy Trinity, 63. Museum 214.
  Railway Station, 26. St Peter,
  105. St Saviour, 159. Spa Bldgs,
  214, 240
Scole, Norfolk
  St Andrew, 70
Scotney Castle, Kent, 205
Scrawton, Yorks
  St Mary, 98
Scrivelsby Court, Lincs, 195
Seaford, Sussex
  St Leonard, 39. Surrey Con-
  valescent Home, 63
Seagry, Wilts
  St Mary, 115
Seaham Harbour, Co. Durham
  Londonderry Institute, 171
Seale, Surrey
  Hampton Lodge, 185
Seaton Delaval, Northumb, 239
Seghill, Northumb
  Holy Trinity, 109
Send, Surrey
  Sendholme, 83
Sennicotts, Sussex
  Oakwood House, 89

U

Sessay, Yorks
St Cuthbert, 55
Settle, Yorks
Holy Ascension, 199. Town Hall, 249
Sevenoaks, Kent
Almshouses, 44. St Julien's, 175. School, 44
Sevington, Wilts
School, 232
Sezincote House, Glos, 69
Shardeloes, Bucks, 149
Sharlston, Yorks
St Luke, 159
Sheffield, Yorks
Christ Church, Fulwood, 185. Corn Exchange, 114. Cutlers' Hall, 95. Earl Haig Homes, 82, 259. Firth College; King Edward VII School; Mappin Art Gallery, 95. Midland Railway Station, 236. Nether Edge Hospital; New Chapel (Cemetery), 95. Royal Infirmary, 183, 192. St George, 128. St John, 95. St Mary, Bramall Lane; Savings Bank, 185. The Mount, 95. Town Hall, 163. Victoria Hotel, 114. Williams Deacon's Bank, 95
Sheffield Park, Sussex, 195
Shelley, Essex
St Peter, 113
Shenfield Place, Essex, 126
Shenley, Herts
Rectory, 27
Shenstone, Staffs
St John, 104
Shepton Mallet, Som
Market Cross, 158
Sheringham Hall, Norfolk, 195, 196
Shernfield Park, Sussex, 242
Shoreham, Sussex
Buckingham House, 192. Town Hall, 219
Shortlands, Kent
St Mary, and Parsonage, 250
Shotesham Park, Norfolk, 222

Shrewsbury, Salop
Castle, 231. Claremont Bldgs, 57. English Bridge, 112. Gaol, 231. Infirmary, 31. Lord Hill's Column, 119. Our Lady of Help Cathedral, 190. St Alkmund, 57. St Chad, 223. St Julian, 187, 188. St Michael, 58. Welsh Bridge, 57
Shrubland Park, Suffolk, 174
Shugborough Park, Staffs, 226, 235
Sidcup, Kent
St John, 189
Sidmouth, Devon
All Saints, 230
Silvermere, Surrey, 29
Skegness, Lincs
St Matthew, 99
Skirbeck, Lincs
Old Rectory, 148
Sleaford, Lincs
Carre's Almshouses; Sessions House; Sleaview, 142
Slinfold, Sussex
St Peter, 93
Slough, Bucks
Town Hall, 133
Smeaton Manor, Yorks, 248
Snelston Hall, Derbys, 72
Solihull, Warwicks
Grammar School, 63
South Benfleet, Essex
Parish Hall; St Mary, 168
South Elkington Hall, Lincs, 169
South Stoke, Lincs, 52
Stoke Rochford Hall, 52
South Weald, Essex
Almshouses; School, 231
Southampton, Hants
All Saints, 196
Southchurch, Essex
Holy Trinity, 71
Southend-on-Sea, Essex
All Saints, 47. Keddie's Store, 268. Kursaal, 217. Library; Technical College, 119
Southill, Beds, 125
Southwell, Notts
Bishop's Palace, 58

Spade House, Kent, 241
Spalding, Lincs
  High St. (No. 12); Holland House; Westbourne Lodge, 207
Spilsby, Lincs
  Sessions House, 142
Spinkhill, Derbys
  St Mary's College, 66
Spye Park, Wilts, 52
Stafford
  Upmeads, 256
Staines, Middx
  St Mary, 247
Stalybridge, Cheshire
  St Paul, 229
Stamford, Lincs
  Bridge, 48. Fryer's Callis, 34. Girls' High School, 48. Hospital, 101. Institution; Toll House, 48. Truesdale's Hospital, 34
Standlynch House, Wilts, see Trafalgar House
Stanfield Hall, Norfolk, 253
Stanford Hall, Leics, 220
Stanmer House, Sussex, 86
Stanmore, Middx
  Canons House, 32, 133, 187
Stapleford, Leics
  St Mary Magdalene, 198
Staveley, Derbys
  St Andrew, Barrow Hill, 238
Stert, Wilts
  St James, 115
Stevenage, Herts
  St Nicholas Rectory, 167
Stirling
  Wallace Monument, 203
Stisted Hall, Essex, 115
Stock, Essex
  Lilystone Hall, 50
Stockfield Park, Yorks, 174
Stockport, Cheshire
  Grammar School, 117. Infirmary, 147. St Elizabeth, Reddish, 246
Stockton-on-Tees, Co. Durham
  St James, 188
Stockton, Warwicks
  St Michael, 218

Stoke d'Abernon, Surrey
  Woodlands Park, 183
Stoke Hall, Notts, 263
Stoke Rochford Hall, Lincs, 52
Stokesay, Salop
  Court, 119. Onny Bridge, 231
Stone, Staffs
  St Michael, 31
Stoneleigh Abbey, Warwicks, 220
Stony Stratford, Bucks
  St Giles, 123
Stourbridge, Worcs
  St Mary, 87
Stourhead, Wilts, 57, 95
Stourport, Worcs
  Bridge, 187
Stowe, Bucks, 21, 103, 182
Stowell Court, Som, 80
Stratford-upon-Avon, Warwicks
  Holy Trinity, 123. St Gregory, 191. Welcombe House, 66, 157
Stratton-on-the-Fosse, Som
  Christ Church, 181
Strawberry Hill, Middx, 38, 63, 64, 91
Stretton-on-Dunsmore, Warwicks
  All Saints, 199
Stretton-under-Fosse, Warwicks
  St Paul's College, 256
Stroud, Glos
  Holy Trinity; St Paul, 96
Stubton Hall, Lincs, 266
Studley, Warwicks
  Castle, 35. St Mary, 117
Studley Royal, Yorks
  St Mary, 51
Stuttgart, Germany
  Protestant Church, 221
Sudbrooke House, Surrey, 103
Sugley, Northumb
  Holy Saviour, 109
Sulhamstead Park, Berks, 24
Sunderland, Co. Durham
  Exchange, 224
Surbiton, Surrey
  Southborough House, 165
Sutton Scarsdale, Derbys
  Sutton Hall, 220

Swallowfield Park, Berks, 228
Swarcliffe Hall, Yorks, 120
Swindon, Wilts
    Pinehurst Estate, 237
Swinton Park, Yorks, 154
Sydney, Australia
    Court House; Macquarie Tower;
    St James, 109. St John's College;
    St Mary's Cathedral, 244

Tattershall, Lincs
    Holy Trinity, 73
Taverham Hall, Norfolk, 45
Tavistock, Devon
    St Mary Magdalene, 66
Tealby, Lincs
    Bayon's Manor, 169
Teddington, Middx
    National Physical Laboratory, 58
Teheran, Persia
    Consular Bldgs, 252
Teigh, Rutland
    Holy Trinity, 198
Teignmouth, Devon
    Assembly Rooms; Den Crescent;
    St Michael, 177
Tenbury, Worcs
    St Michael's College, 258
Tenby, Pem
    Royal Hotel, 232
Terling Place, Essex, 135
Tetbury, Glos
    Westonbirt House, 242
Tetton House, Som, 106
Thakeham, Sussex
    Little Thakeham, 155
Theale, Berks
    Holy Trinity, 50
Theobalds Park, Herts, 167
Thorpe Acre, Leics
    All Saints, 192
Thorpe Hesley, Yorks
    Holy Trinity, 188
Thoresby House, Notts, 205, 206,
    228
Thorneyburn, Northumb
    St Aidan's Parsonage, 214

Thurlstone, Yorks
    Vicarage, 256
Thurston, Suffolk
    St Peter, 114
Ticehurst, Sussex
    Furze House, 142. School, 247
Tickencote, Rutland
    St Peter, 68
Tideford, Cornwall
    St Luke 251
Tilbury, Essex
    Baggage Hall; Docks, 72
Tilmouth, Northumb
    Tilmouth Park Hotel, 33
Timsbury, Som
    St Mary, 237
Titsey Place, Surrey, 83
Todmorden, Yorks
    Christ Church, 242. Dobroyd
    Castle; Town Hall; Unitarian
    Church, 104
Torquay, Devon
    Imperial Hotel, 66. St Mary
    Magdalene, 205
Tortworth Court, Glos, 231
Totnes, Devon
    Bridge, 98. Follaton House, 196
Tottenham House, Wilts, 75
Tottenham, Middx
    Holy Trinity, 208
Totteridge, Herts
    The Croft, 70
Trafalgar House, Wilts, 161, 196,
    257
Treslothan, Cornwall
    Pendarves House Chapel, 251
Tring, Herts
    Railway Station, 22
Trowse Newton, Norfolk
    Crown Point Hall, 69
Truro, Cornwall
    Cathedral, 179
Tsarskoe Seloe, Russia, 57
Tuesley Court, Surrey, 80
Tunbridge Wells, Kent
    Calverley Estate; Holy Trinity,
    53. St John and Parsonage, 108

Tutbury, Staffs
St Mary, Stretton, 65, 159
Twerton, Som
Gaol, 158
Twickenham, Middx
Carpenters' Almshouses, 184.
Holy Trinity, 34, 84. Marble
Hill, 122, 161. St Mary, 133.
St Stephen, 153. Strawberry
Hill, 38, 63, 64, 91. Whitton
Park, 161
Tynemouth, Northumb
Collingwood Monument, 84.
Holy Saviour; Tyne Master Mari-
ners' Asylum, 109

Uckfield, Sussex
Highview House, 142. The Rocks,
219
Ugthorpe, Yorks
Christ Church, 69
Ullenhall, Warwicks
St Mary, 213
Ulverscroft, Leics
Lea and Stoneywell Cottages, 42
Upminster Court, Essex, 194
Uppark House, Sussex, 141, 228
Upper Dicker, Sussex
Holy Trinity, 85
Upper Norwood, Surrey
All Saints, 208. Virgo Fidelis
Convent, 244
Upper Weston, Som
All Saints, 181
Uppingham School, Rutland, 167
Utterby, Lincs
Rectory, 99

Virginia Water, Surrey
Christ Church, 184
Vowchurch, Herefs
Poston Lodge, 62. St Bartholo-
mew, 19
Vyne, The, Hants, 64, 248

Wadhurst, Sussex
Bayham Abbey, 45. Castle, 146.
Lorien, 39

Wainfleet, Lincs
All Saints, 214
Wakefield, Yorks
Boys' Grammar School, 147.
Town Hall, 69
Walberton House, Sussex, 218
Wallingford, Berks
St Mary, 45
Wallington, Surrey
Holy Trinity, 113
Walthamstow, Essex
County School for Girls, 167. St
Barnabas, 58. St Saviour, 84
Walton-on-Thames, Surrey
Mount Felix, 32
Walton-on-the-Hill, Surrey
St Peter, 24
Wanstead, Essex
Holy Trinity, 99. Hospital, 64.
House, 57. Infant Orphan Asy-
lum, 230. Royal School, 209.
St Mary, 118
Wantage, Berks
St Michael's Retreat House, 250.
Town Hall, 142
Wardour Castle, Wilts, 174, 221
Wareside, Herts
Holy Trinity, 221
Wargrave, Berks
Convent, 37
Wark-on-Tyne, Northumb
St Michael and Parsonage, 214
Warminster, Wilts
Town Hall, 42
Warter, Yorks
St James, 113
Warwick
Judge's Lodging, 114, 115. St
Mary, 220. St Mary the Im-
maculate, 190. St Peter's Chapel,
123. Shire Hall, 123, 160
Washington, D.C., U.S.A.
British Embassy, 155. Capitol,
149. Cathedral, 43
Waterford, Ireland
Court House and Gaol, 100.
House of Correction, 89

Watton, Norfolk
Wayland Hall, 146
Watton-at-Stone, Herts
Woodhall House, 151
Welbeck Abbey, Notts, 221
Welcombe House, Warwicks, 66, 157
Welford, Berks
St Gregory, 54
Wellingborough, Northants
St Mary, 71
Wellington, Salop
All Saints, 223
Wells, Som
Bishop's Palace, 93. Cathedral, 93, 266
Welwyn Garden City, Herts, 82
Wendover, Bucks
House in the Fields, 197
Wentworth Castle, Yorks, 38
Wentworth Woodhouse, Yorks, 95
West Deeping, Lincs
Old Rectory, 47, 113
West Grinstead, Sussex
Knepp Castle; Park, 165
West Hartlepool, Co. Durham
Christ Church, 146. St Paul, 98
West Hoathly, Sussex
Chiddinglye, 105
West Hyde, Herts
St Thomas, 221
West Lavington, Sussex
St Mary Magdalen and Rectory, 55
West Malling, Kent
St Leonard's Tower, 110
West Wycombe, Bucks
Dashwood Mausoleum, 35. Park, 195, 196, 197
Westcliff-on-Sea, Essex
St Alban, 168
Westhope Manor, Salop, 80
Westmeston, Sussex
Middleton Manor, 196
Weston, Lincs
School, 39
Westonbirt House, Glos, 242

Weybridge, Surrey
St James, 179
Whaplode, Lincs
Vicarage, 237
Whitby, Yorks
Railway Station, 26
Whitchurch, Middx
St Lawrence, 133
Whitchurch, Salop
St Alkmund, 220
Whiteley Village, Surrey, 41, 156, 167
Whitton, Middx
Kneller Hall, 157
Whitton Park, Middx, 161
Whitwood, Yorks
St Philip, 65
Whorlton-in-Cleveland, Yorks
Holy Cross, 265
Wicken, Northants
St John, 207
Wickwar, Glos
Parsonage, 83
Widford, Essex
St Mary, 205
Widford, Herts
Blakesware, 83
Widworthy Court, Devon, 196
Wilbury House, Wilts, 37
Wilcot, Wilts
Ladies' Bridge, 194
Willen, Bucks
St Mary Magdalene, 126
Willersley Castle, Derbys, 232
Willey Hall, Salop, 263
Wilsford, Wilts
Lake House, 42
Wilton, Wilts
House, 122, 137, 161, 248. SS
Mary and Nicholas, 265
Wimbledon, Surrey
All Saints, 159. King's College
School, 94. Ridgeway (No. 54), 132. St John, 132. Southlands
College, 268
Wimblington, Cambs
St Peter, 265

War Cemetery, 124

Wimpole, Cambs
Hall, 160. St Andrew, 95

Wincanton, Som
Balsam, Ireson, Rodber Houses; 'The Dogs'; White Horse Hotel, 130

Winchester, Hants
Castle, 266. Cathedral, 132, 254. College, 254, 266. Palace, 82. St Peter's Chapel, 60

Windermere, Westmorland
Belle Isle, 183. Broadleys, 241

Windsor, Bucks
Bateman's Villa, 38. Beaumont College, 91. Castle, 42, 193, 254, 265, 266. Cumberland Lodge, 206. Frogmore House, 263. Great Park, 206. St George's Chapel, 90, 91, 134, 241. St John's Convent, 258. St John's School, 38. St Leonard's Hill, 206

Windsor, Australia
St Matthew, 109

Winkfield, Berks
New Lodge, 54

Winsley, Wilts
Conkwell Grange, 80. St Nicholas, 184

Winslow Hall, Bucks, 32

Winterborne Stickland, Dorset, 35

Winterbourne, Berks
Bussock Wood, 156

Winterslow, Wilts
Roche Court, 228

Winterton, Lincs
Dent Cottage, 152. West St. (No. 35), 99

Wintoun House, Haddingtonshire, 243

Wisbech, Cambs
Castle; Crescent, 159. Museum, 50

Wissington, Suffolk
Wiston Hall, 222, 223

Witham, Essex
All Saints, 48

Wivenhoe Hall, Essex, 127

Woburn, Beds
Abbey, 95, 125. St Mary, 66

Wokingham, Surrey
Glebelands, 166. St Paul, 258

Wollaton Hall, Notts, 221, 233, 265

Wolterton Hall, Norfolk, 199

Wolverhampton, Staffs
Library, 119. St John, 31. St Mary, 192. Town Hall, 159

Wolverton, Bucks
Holy Trinity, 115

Wonersh, Surrey
St Martin, Blackheath, 234

Woodbridge, Suffolk
Seckford Hospital, 67

Woodcote Hall, Salop, 68

Woodford, Essex
Bancroft's School, 41. Gwynne House, 175

Woodford, Wilts
Heale House, 42

Woodhouse Moor, Yorks
St Mark, 214

Woodlands Park, Surrey, 183

Woolhampton, Berks
Kennet Orleigh; The Court, 156

Woolley Park, Berks, 265

Woolverstone Hall, Suffolk, 135

Worcester
Beveré Hall; Infirmary, 140. Perdiswell House, 56. St Martin, 140

Worfield, Salop
Davenport House, 220

Worlingham Hall, Suffolk, 207

Wormley, Herts
Wormleybury, 163

Wormley, Surrey
King Edward's Schools, 219

Worplesdon, Surrey
Merrist Wood, 216

Worth, Sussex
Paddockhurst, 206

Worthing, Sussex
Beach House, 192. Casino, 105. Holy Trinity, 69. Park Crescent, 252. Pevensey Garden Estate,

311

Worthing, Sussex—*continued*
  133. St George, 236. St Paul,
  192
Wortley Hall, Yorks, 182
Wothorpe, Lincs
  Clare Lodge, 48
Wotton House, Surrey, 88, 258
Wrawby, Lincs
  Rectory, 169
Wraysbury, Bucks
  Hall, 70. St Andrew, 45
Wrenthorpe, Yorks
  St Anne, 159
Wrest Park, Beds, 148, 150
Wrotham Hall, Middx, 244
Wroxton Abbey, Oxon, 170
Wye, Kent
  Eastwell Park, 44
Wykeham, Yorks
  Parsonage and School, 55

Wymondham, Norfolk
  Stanfield Hall, 253

Yarmouth, *see* Gt. Yarmouth
Yarmouth, I.O.W., 24
Yattendon, Berks
  Reading Room; School, 246
Yaxham, Norfolk
  Rectory, 154
York
  Assize Courts, 59. Concert Room,
  214. Deanery; Friends' Meeting
  House, 188. Gaol, 26, 27. House
  of Correction, 28. Knavesmire
  Racecourse, 59. Library, 28.
  New Earswick, 237. Savings
  Bank; School of Art, 188
Ypres, Belgium
  Menin Gate, 41